The Presence of the Past
in a Spanish Village

The Presence of the Past in a Spanish Village

SANTA MARÍA DEL MONTE

✦

by Ruth Behar

PRINCETON UNIVERSITY PRESS

Copyright © 1986 by Princeton University Press
Published by Princeton University Press, 41 William Street,
Princeton, New Jersey 08540
In the United Kingdom: Princeton University Press, Oxford

Library of Congress Cataloging-in-Publication Data

Behar, Ruth, 1956-
[Santa María del Monte]
The presence of the past in a Spanish village : Santa María del Monte /
by Ruth Behar.—1st Princeton paperback printing.
p.   cm.
Originally published under title: Santa María del Monte.
Includes bibliographical references and index.
ISBN 0-691-09419-5
1. Santa María del Monte del Condado (Spain)—
Rural conditions.
2. Peasantry—Spain—Santa María del Monte del Condado.
3. Villages—Spain—Case studies. I. Title.
HN590.S383B44   1991
307.72'0972'52—dc20   91-27791

ISBN 0-691-02866-4 (pbk.)

Publication of this book has been aided by a grant from the Paul Mellon Fund of
Princeton University Press and the Program for Cultural Cooperation between
Spain's Ministry of Culture and North American Universities

This book was originally published in 1986 under the title *Santa María del Monte*;
first Princeton Paperback printing, under the present title, 1991

9 8 7 6 5 4 3 2

DESIGNED BY LAURY A. EGAN

Printed in the United States of America

Frontispiece Spread: View of Santa María from the west, with the Cantabrian
Mountains in the background

Contents

✣

List of Illustrations

PHOTOGRAPHS
(All photographs by Ruth Behar, taken in 1984)

Frontispiece. View of Santa María from the west, with the Cantabrian Mountains in the background

(BETWEEN PAGES 204 AND 205)

1. Balbino and Hilaria with a cart of oats
2. Nieves and Germiniano winnowing chick peas
3. Sixto and Inés finishing off the milking of the cows
4. An evening meal in the kitchen
5. Members of the village religious confraternity of San Roque in the *casa de concejo*
6. Sixto demonstrating how a wheatsheaf was gathered between thumb and forefinger when grains were harvested with a sickle
7. Inés with *ceranda* (sieve)
8. Láutico and Julita with their youngest grandchild
9. Hermelinda with newborn piglets

The motifs from the medieval agrarian calendar introducing the various parts of the book are based on the frescoes decorating the Pantheon of the Kings in the Monastery of Saint Isidore in León, as reproduced in Manuel Viñayo González, *Pintura Románica: Panteon Real de San Isidoro-León* (León: Real Colegiata de San Isidoro, 1971).

MAPS
(All maps by David Frye)

DIAGRAMS
(All diagrams by David Frye)

GRAPHS
(All graphs by David Frye)

List of Tables

✝

Acknowledgments

I FIRST went to live in Santa María del Monte, the Leonese village on which this study is based, in the summer of 1978 at the suggestion of James W. Fernandez, who kindly made arrangements for me to work there. My deepest thanks go to him for the continual support and encouragement he has given me from the first period of research to the last and during every stage of the writing, which he has commented upon and criticized virtually page by page.

For many inspiring conversations covering the gamut of anthropology and her support of my work, I warmly thank Hildred Geertz, from whom I have learned so much of what I know about the discipline. I would like to thank Teofilo Ruiz, Jane Schneider, Natalie Zemon Davis, and Luis Fernández-Cifuentes, all of whom provided very helpful comments and suggestions on various parts of the text and encouraged my historical endeavors. The critical reading given my work by William Christian and an anonymous reviewer for Princeton University Press have helped me to improve this book, and I am grateful to them. I owe special thanks to Gail Ullman, editor at Princeton University Press, for taking on the project and for her sustained interest and enthusiasm. I am grateful to Marilyn Campbell for her careful and sensitive editing of this book, and to Laury Egan for its design. For her conscientious typing of the doctoral thesis on which this book is based, I sincerely thank Pauline Caulk.

Here I would not like to forget two of my early teachers, who first awakened my interest in anthropology: the late Juan Roura-Parella, a man of the old world of Spanish letters, who gave me the idea of studying anthropology during a summer spent with him and his wife, Teresa, in Cataluña, and Johannes Fabian, my first teacher of anthropology, who gave me hope after I had lost it.

This research began as part of a cooperative project on regionalism in northern Spain directed by James W. Fernandez and Carmelo Lisón Tolosana. I thank them both and the United States-Spanish Joint Committee for Cultural and Educational Cooperation for the support given me during my first three summers of research in León in 1978, 1979, and 1980. Support for a year's field research in Santa María and archival research in local, provincial, and national archives, from 1980 to 1981, was provided by a Fulbright/Spanish government grant. I warmly thank Ramón Bela and Patricia Zahniser of the Fulbright Commission in Madrid for the cordial assistance they gave me throughout my stay. It is with much gratitude, too, that I acknowledge a dissertation fellowship from the American Association of University Women Educational Foundation, which provided aid for writing up my study. Finally, I would like to thank the United States-Spanish Joint Committee for a travel grant that enabled me to return to Spain in the summer of 1984, and the Rollei division of Berkey Marketing Company for a loan of photographic equipment for that visit.

In Spain I accumulated many debts, and I fear that a few lines here will not do justice to the many people who gave of their time and knowledge so freely and openly. On our visits to Madrid, Carmelo Lisón Tolosana displayed great hospitality toward my husband and me, and I thank him for many wonderful conversations and his warm encouragement.

I wish to thank the staffs of the various archives where I worked, in particular the Archivo Histórico Provincial de León, the Archivo Histórico Diocesano de León, the Archivo Histórico Municipal del Ayuntamiento de León, the Archivo Histórico Nacional, the Archivo General de Simancas, and the Museo Nacional de Etnología. I am grateful to the Instituto de Reforma y Desarrollo Agrario (IRYDA) of León for providing maps and information on land consolidation in Santa María and nearby villages. Above all, I would like to thank Don José María Fernández Catón, director of the Archivo Histórico Diocesano de León, and a fine medieval scholar, for his aid in my historical research and his kindness in allowing me to consult various uncatalogued documents.

Let me also express my gratitude to Don Efigenio Martínez, parish priest of Santa María during my stay, for giving me full access to the records of the parish, and in general for his kindness to us; to Moisés Jalón, *alcalde municipal* of Vegas del Condado, for allowing us to consult the records of the municipality; to Gregorio Boixo for helpful conversations about the recent history of the local rural economy; and to Fray Orencio Llamazares for aid in understanding the history of Santa María and neighboring villages. I would also like to thank the *presidentes* of

Villamayor, Barrio de Nuestra Señora, Ambasaguas, Santovenia del Monte, and Valdefresno for providing access to the council records of these villages.

To the people of Santa María del Monte I owe my greatest debt. Though Santa María is located next to a national highway, it is far enough from the tourist routes for us to have been the first Americans to visit the village. At first our presence was a mystery to people: Were we spies, or had we somehow been sent by the government to learn ways of raising their taxes? After it became clear that we were merely there to study the village, people came to judge us on our own character and behavior—as everyone is judged in Santa María—and we were soon taken in with an affection and warmth that made me feel totally at home, in a way I rarely have anywhere else. They opened their houses to me; welcomed me, though a woman, to the male arena of the *concejo*; and invited me to participate in every aspect of their lives, from family feasts to chatting by the woodstove to the gathering of the harvest.

I can honestly say that everyone in Santa María assisted me in one way or another. But I especially want to thank the following people: Balbino Llamazares and Hilaria Carral, Leonardo Mirantes, Sixto Mirantes, Julita Llamazares and Láutico Robles, Manuel Robles, Jerónima Mirantes and Felicísimo Llamazares, María Ribero and Virgilio Llamazares, Apolonia Robles, Maximina Sánchez, Justa Llamazares, Saturnina Llamazares, Isolina de la Puente and Venerable Prieto, Nieves Mirantes and Germiniano Carral.

I leave to the end my thanks to David Frye, beloved husband, friend, and fellow anthropologist, who worked with me in the villages and in the archives, followed from start to finish the progress of my writing, enduring patiently my many low moments, and who unselfishly gave of his time and energy in so many ways. Not least I owe to him all the illustrations that grace this work.

Princeton, 1981–Mexquitic, 1985

The Presence of the Past
in a Spanish Village

Introduction

LIKE all ethnographies, this book is a product of a particular historical moment. I carried out my fieldwork in a small village in the foothills of the Cantabrian Mountains of northern Spain at a time when its people were coming to terms with the fact that the way of life they and their ancestors had known was slipping from the present and becoming part of an all too well-defined past. The search for an understanding of the dialectic of past and present had taken on a certain urgency, for suddenly there was a historical paradox to solve: how could the past have been a presence for so long, and yet, in just a few years, become hopelessly out of date? There was an awakening of self-consciousness about the past as past, though this was combined with an acute sense that the past was still present, and visible in everything from the layout of the fields to the structure of the houses. Thus the reader will find that I have not separated the history from the ethnography in this book. Rather than providing a history of the village from its origins and following it with a description of the village in the present day, I have attempted to weave together throughout the text historical and ethnographic materials, just as the past and the present are woven together in the life and thought of the people.

The idea for this book took form gradually in the course of several visits to Santa María del Monte, the Leonese village on which this study is based, from 1978 to 1981. In Santa María I had my first real encounter with rural life, and with peasants. I had a background in Spanish literature and in the great tradition of Spanish thought. But I had no idea, when I set foot in the village for the first time, that there had been anything like a peasant written tradition in Spain. Then, just before I left Santa María at the end of my first summer of fieldwork, I gained access to some of the village's community records, which pass from one *presidente* to another.

I learned of a lengthy suit from 1701 over grazing rights, where the village acted as a corporate body to defend its communal pastures against

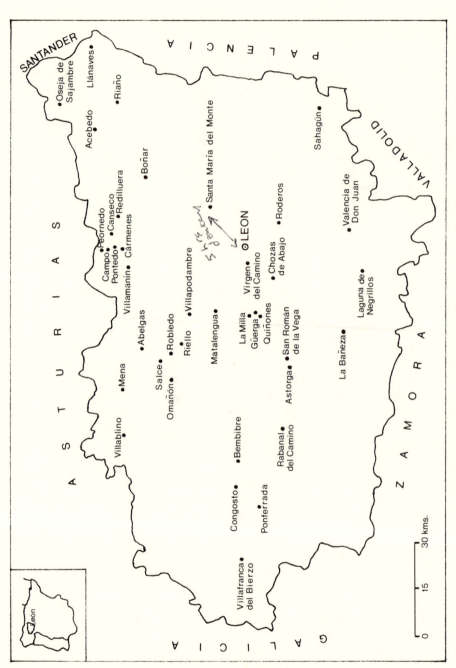

Map 1. The province of León, showing villages mentioned in the text

the usurpations of a wealthy cattle-owner; this case evoked for me the spirit of Lope de Vega's *Fuenteovejuna*, in which the *pueblo* as a whole takes the blame for the killing of a tryant. I discovered a manuscript bound in parchment that turned out to be a set of village customary laws, "ordinances," as they were called, from 1776, which dealt with aspects of communal life ranging from proper behavior at council meetings to the organization of herding in common; and I just barely had a glance at another manuscript, one of the books of council records from the end of the nineteenth century, where the great transformations of a difficult historical moment now lay quiescent.

This whetted my appetite for local documents, and on a subsequent yearlong visit to Santa María I was able to go through the entire collection of village records at my leisure, since they had by then passed to the house of a family with whom we had lived during our first stay and who therefore knew us well. As we became accepted into the village I began asking people if they had any family inheritance documents in their houses, and before I knew it I had before me a pile of old papers worthy of a historian.

What impressed me most about the records was that they made up a corpus of texts largely conceived, and by the end of the nineteenth century largely written, by several generations of peasants. They seemed to me to form part of a local tradition that had long flowed, at its own pace and rhythm, alongside a "great tradition"—not the "great tradition" of literature, however, but that of legal thought about how a republic was best governed. Of course there was hardly anything unique about the batch of documents I uncovered in Santa María; many similar records, especially of ordinances, had been collected and analyzed by Joaquín Costa and other liberal jurists of turn-of-the-century Spain, who made a strong case for the tradition of "agrarian communalism" in the northern and central provinces. I found this fact not daunting but encouraging, for my findings could therefore be seen in the larger context of a peasant discovery of writing as a means of preserving the communications of the ancestors, and of fixing the contracts of the present for whatever use they might have in the future.

As I studied the documents that came my way and considered the pattern of life and thought that was reflected in them, I asked several of the older people in the village to read the texts of their ancestors with me. Our discussions about the records, and the way of life they bear witness to, was the genesis of the present book. It was my informants,

thoughtful and sharp historians, who drew parallels between the past
recorded in the documents and the very recent past of their experience;
it was they who helped me to see the "presence of the past" in their
society and culture, and to interpret the shape and meaning of a present
increasingly losing touch with the world inscribed in the old records.
Thus my affair with history took form and grew in a milieu that was
through and through anthropological, that is, rooted in dialogue with
contemporaries.

This book is a product of a particular historical moment in yet another
sense. It is part of the rethinking taking place in the way anthropologists
construe their subject matter, especially the relationship between, to
borrow the title of a recent book by Johannes Fabian, "time and the
other."[1] Just as historians have discovered anthropology in recent years,
in the process creating a new ethnographic history, so anthropologists
have discovered history, and the infusion of a deeper level of historicity
into ethnography has created a new genre of historical ethnography.[2]
To retrieve the history of the people who were once thought to be without
history is one of the aims of this new historical anthropology: the image
of the "timeless primitive," like that of the peasant who lives outside of
history, have been shown to be illusions by anthropologists whose research is informed by a historical consciousness—and an awareness of
their subjects as their contemporaries.[3] At the same time, the retrieval
of such forgotten histories brings us back, in a new way, to the study
of pattern in culture, whether approached from the point of view of
political economy, religion, the transformation of history into myth and
of myth into history, or from a combination of perspectives.[4]
    My efforts at working within this new genre of ethnography grows
out of my research into local documents largely written and preserved
by several generations of peasants. Here it is the image of the "literate
peasant" that emerges, as I reconstruct patterns of house and family,
community and commons through a combination of analysis of village
records and of ethnographic examples. The approach is at once anthropological and historical, for I study the present in the perspective of the
long past, and the past in the perspective of the present.
    The analysis departs from three classes of local documents: "kitchen
documents," or family papers, which are unofficial records of the division
of a family's inheritance; records of village customary laws, known as
"ordinances" (ordenanzas), which document the patterns and ideals of

community life; and records of the acts of the village council (actas de concejo), which begin to appear in the middle of the nineteenth century at a time of unprecedented social and economic change, when most villagers have become literate and fully conscious of themselves as the makers of their own history. These are records one can find in many villages in Spain, and they attest to the long involvement of localities in the written tradition, and larger history, of the nation. I use the records as a starting point for probing deeper into cultural notions of the house, kinship, marriage, community, reciprocity, money, and the land, to dig, in a sense, beneath the surface of that which is visible in the present.

Thus I undertake an "archaeology" of a house, uncovering a process of inheritance that begins with the house partitioned into three parts and ends a half century later with the house pieced together again into its current form. To do so the analysis moves from materials in family papers to the reconstruction of events as informants remembered them from their different perspectives as actors in the division.

Later in the book, I document a period of change at the end of the nineteenth century that prepared the way for the rural exodus of the last two decades. In that analysis three simultaneous historical events are considered: the unprecedented population expansion which created a precarious situation of land hunger; the clearing of the communal woods to meet the need for land; and the emergence of a bureaucratic state intent on redefining the old categories of property through disentailment reform, which made such clearings on the commons illegal. All these events are recorded in village documents as well as in the testimony of the descendents of the villagers who lived through the events, and I use both to offer a fresh, local point of view on the changes in rural life that were taking place throughout Spain at the end of the last century.

Santa María del Monte is a small village, surrounded by other small villages, in the northern Spanish province of León, lying twenty kilometers to the northeast of the provincial capital. Its population has returned today to the level at which it maintained itself fairly steadily for centuries before the end of the nineteenth century—120 permanent residents, compared to 330 in the years before the rural exodus of the 1960s and 1970s. In the past, the village was somewhat secluded, being surrounded on all four sides by woods; yet it could never have been called isolated. It is less than an hour's walk to the nearest villages. A road to Asturias once passed through the woods of Santa María from the city of León, five hours away on donkey-back. Today a highway passes within three hundred meters of the village houses, traversed twice daily by a bus which leaves one in the city in forty minutes.

The village is located on the northern border of the area of the Sobarriba, so named because it is located "above the riverbanks" (*super ripam*) of the Porma to the east, and of the Torío to the west. Administratively it formed part of the Hermandad de la Sobarriba during most of its history, and thus the village was directly under the rule of the city of León. Mention is made of Santa María as early as 1179 in a donation of properties from various villages in the Sobarriba to the monastery of San Isidoro in León.[5] We can assume that the village was founded some time during the era of the early resettlement of Spain, a fact attested to by local legend, which places its origin in a distant, but vivid, medieval past.

With the municipal reforms of the 1830s, the centuries-old Hermandad de la Sobarriba was dismantled: twelve villages of the lower Sobarriba became the new municipality of Villaturiel, twenty villages of the upper Sobarriba formed the municipality of Valdefresno, and yet another five villages, Santa María among them, were shifted to the former Jurisdiction of Vegas del Condado to form the municipality of the same name (see Map 2). Yet the Sobarriba, as a local geographic term, continues to exist and is now generally viewed as coinciding with the municipality of Valdefresno, whose miniature, arid villages are contrasted by the people with the Ribera, the area of somewhat larger and well-irrigated villages stretching alongside the narrow rivers which descend from the mountains to the north. Santa María is viewed as being outside both areas: intermediate in size, lying far above the riverbanks, yet amply watered by springs; if you asked someone whether it is Sobarriba or Ribera you would probably be told it is neither, but rather *del Monte*, of the woods, as its name implies.[6]

What sets Santa María apart from the villages of the Sobarriba is precisely the abundance of woodland and woodland products that it enjoys, not only firewood but honey, large flocks of sheep, and fresh spring water, which gives it a greater independence, to the degree that the village is freed from the almost exclusive monoculture of wheat or rye characterizing much of the lowlands. What sets it apart from the villages of the Ribera is not the absence of a nearby river, since Santa María does have its own irrigation system, but the village's greater conservatism or traditionalism, and its greater sense of solidarity, which

5 hrs donkey to Leon
now = 40 min on bus

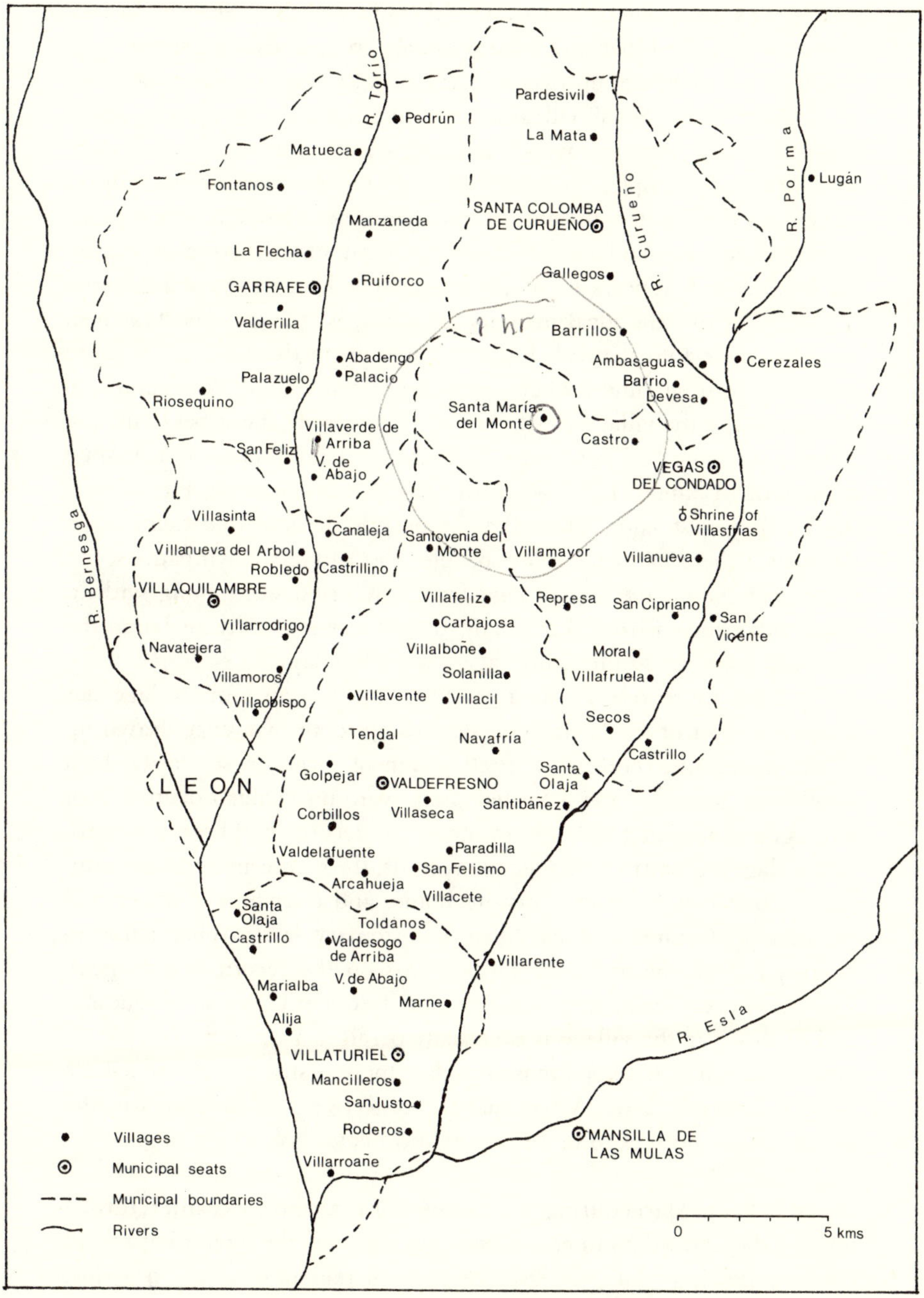

Map 2. Seven municipalities of central León

Villages
Municipal seats
Municipal boundaries
Rivers

0   5 kms

LEÓN

R. Torío
R. Curueño
R. Porma
R. Bernesga
R. Esla

Pardesivil
Pedrún
La Mata
Matueca
Fontanos
Manzaneda
SANTA COLOMBA DE CURUEÑO
Lugán
La Flecha
GARRAFE
Ruiforco
Gallegos
Valderilla
1 hr
Barrillos
Abadengo
Ambasaguas
Cerezales
Palazuelo
Palacio
Barrio
Riosequino
Santa Marías del Monte
Devesa
Villaverde de Arriba
Castro
San Feliz
V. de Abajo
VEGAS DEL CONDADO
Villasinta
Canaleja
Santovenia del Monte
Shrine of Villasfrías
Villanueva del Arbol
Villamayor
Villanueva
Robledo
Castrillino
VILLAQUILAMBRE
Villafeliz
Represa
San Cipriano
Villarrodrigo
Carbajosa
San Vicente
Navatejera
Villalboñe
Moral
Villamoros
Solanilla
Villafruela
Villaobispo
Villavente
Villacil
Secos
Tendal
Navafría
Castrillo
Golpejar
Santa Olaja
Corbillos
VALDEFRESNO
Villaseca
Santibáñez
Valdelafuente
Paradilla
Arcahueja
San Felismo
Villacete
Santa Olaja
Toldanos
Castrillo
Valdesogo de Arriba
Villarente
Marialba
V. de Abajo
Alija
Marne
VILLATURIEL
Mancilleros
San Justo
Roderos
MANSILLA DE LAS MULAS
Villarroañe

people say forms a contrast with the Ribera villages, for centuries in easy contact with each other and with outsiders from north and south.

Of course, in Spain, no two villages are alike, and Santa María is not representative of Spanish villages, nor even of Leonese villages. Its abundant spare land, most of it woods, has long affected the tone of communal life; thus, for example, the availability of land to clear for planting at the end of the nineteenth century cushioned the divisive effects of population expansion, and made for solidarity rather than social atomism. Although there appears to be greater factionalism in the village now than in the past, the ideal of unity, of *unión*, is still an important one, even if people find it much harder to live up to these days. We were told a number of times, when the subject of the Civil War came up, that no one in the village was killed, as they were in the Ribera villages, because someone had denounced them to the Civil Guards out of spite or hatred. In Santa María, when the guards came looking for "Reds," the village priest said, "Here I'm the only Red," and told them to go on; in fact there had been a few people who had leftist sympathies, but given that the village kept a solid front, the priest went along with it. Even today such a front is maintained, and it is especially visible in the virtually unanimous attendance at mass on Sundays.

Or, even more relevant to this study, the fact that the village has preserved most of its documents—according to an inventory drawn up in the nineteenth century—is itself a sign of a certain solidarity. In a number of nearby places I visited there were no village documents of any significance left at all, and in others the records had been scattered. One village's Catastro de Ensenada records, the eighteenth-century land survey, had ended up in a private home, and elsewhere a house had acquired a document of its village's customary laws. What tends to happen is that one *presidente* fails to pass on the records to the next, sometimes because of negligence, but more frequently because of feuding, and in this way the village is eventually bereft of its history. In spite of factionalism and increased tension today, there is still enough of a sense of community in Santa María that the collective past enshrined in the old records continues to be respected and kept whole.

I lived in Santa María during the summers of 1978 and 1979, and returned toward the end of summer in 1980, staying until the beginning of fall of the following year. My last visit was in the summer of 1984, just before this book was completed. I have given my impressions free rein in a report on that visit that forms the Epilogue. But the bulk of the book is based on the twenty months of research I carried out from 1978 to 1981, though the "ethnographic present" is a long one, and sometimes extends over hundreds of years.

During my three years' acquaintance with the village I observed many changes. In 1978 the oldest couple in the village, both just turned ninety, though ailing, were still very much a presence there. When I knew them, the wife sat on a bench in her daughter's kitchen, cloaked in black, hardly speaking but following every cadence of the conversation, while her husband I encountered shelling chickpeas in the courtyard. When I returned in 1979 she had died, and by the following year so had he. With their passing, the village lost its last living links to a previous century.

In other ways the village was indeed becoming very much a part of the twentieth century. On my first two visits to Santa María there was still no sewage system, but by my last it had already been installed, and many families had in the meantime put in freshly tiled bathrooms. Across the highway from the village an entrepreneur had bought, before my first arrival, a number of small parcels of abandoned rye fields and had cleared the scrub forest that was already growing on them. By the end of my final stay, he had turned this land into an *urbanización*, a summer resort in the countryside, and managed to resell many of the plots to people from León and Asturias looking for a quiet place to spend vacations. Almost overnight, it seemed, thirty, forty, and fifty houses had sprung up, their mishmash of styles standing in contrast to the solid mud walls of the conjoining village houses which had taken form over many years.

The village itself has become something of a resort for those who emigrated to the cities in the previous decades and who now return with their urbanized children to spend weekends and holidays in their natal homes. By 1982 the streets of the village had been paved and more running water had been brought to the village system from springs in the woods to meet the new pressures on natural resources that the proliferation of bathrooms and washing machines had created.

A major change which had been on the verge of occurring during my three years' acquaintance with the village was the government-sponsored consolidation of the scattered parcels that make up each family's landholdings. The plan seeks to transform the dozens of tiny fields belonging to a household into three or four larger, more regular plots, as well as build roads in order to make them accessible by cow team or, increasingly now, by tractor. The village had requested this service shortly before my first arrival, and during my various visits I was able to watch as people scrutinized the series of maps which the engineers brought to the village meeting house at every stage of the process. On each visit it seemed the plan would go into effect by the following year, yet with all the dissatisfactions people had with the plots given them by the engineers it never did. Then, finally, in the new year of 1984 the government's bulldozers finished major work on the roads and the people were given the computer printouts listing the numbers of the fields that the engineers had devised for them.

I might have left the description of Santa María at this level of observation. But such an account, it seemed to me, would have obscured much of the history and culture of the village and its people. I would have been giving too much weight to changes that, in the end, were extremely recent, beneath which lay the more solid substratum of a deeper, enduring pattern of life.

Thus I might have written in more detail of the rural migration, or the transformations that have been wrought in the traditional patterns of agricultural life and work during the last two decades, or the turn toward conceiving of the village as a holiday resort for the urban emigré. Without wishing to deny the importance of these recent changes, I saw a need for a more retrospective account, one that would document the pattern of life in the years and centuries previous to the contemporary changes set in motion since the Spanish Civil War.

For the most part, anthropological accounts of rural life in Spain have been studies of contemporary social change rather than studies of long-term cultural continuity. When historical materials are used, they tend to be presented in an introductory chapter which is loosely connected to the rest of the work, and rarely integrated into the body of the text. This is a familiar criticism, one that has been made not only of Iberian but of Mediterranean studies.[7]

But I feel I should not be too quick to criticize the work of my predecessors in the anthropological study of Spanish rural life. It is only because there already existed very detailed studies of the recent transformations in the social and economic world of Spanish communities that I felt I could embark on a project that highlights cultural continuity in the long term.[8] Every ethnography must be viewed in the context of its time, and an anthropologist who lived in Spain during the 1960s and

1970s would certainly have been more inclined toward the study of social change than cultural continuity. If I had lived in Santa María ten or fifteen years earlier it is likely I would have followed the same route. For in those years I would have witnessed the great waves of migration out of the village, felt the quakes in the old social-religious order, seen lands worked yesterday abandoned today while the first tractor plowed up new earth, and, like Heraclitus, been impressed by how all is flux. In contrast, the changes I observed at the end of the 1970s and the beginning of the 1980s were but the last flutterings of this process of demographic, social, and economic transformation. Arriving later, during the calm following the storm, a different picture came into view.

One could say that a critical distance had been reached: things had changed to a point where one could take a longer perspective on village life, see where the changes of the last few decades had led and reflect on what things had been like in times past. It was not the effects of sudden, recent change that was foremost in people's thoughts; what called for explanation, meditation, was the sense that things had for so long hardly changed at all. I found I could not take continuity for granted, or assume I knew of what the "traditional" past had consisted. Thus I set myself the task of seeking out those aspects of the old rural culture that had endured, that had not been lost in the midst of change, or that had disappeared only recently, leaving their mark on the memory of the people. It seems clear now that only an understanding of past patterns could have given me a perspective on the significance that the present-day changes hold for the people of Santa María, who, like so many other people of modern Spain, have stood witness to the passing of an age.

Although this work is primarily a historical ethnography of a Leonese village, it is also a study of an area, that of central León, and to some degree of a region, that of León and Castile. In a yet broader sense it describes a form of economy and culture that was widespread throughout rural Europe until the eighteenth and nineteenth centuries. This form of life associated with a household economy and the culture of the common fields, which elsewhere had already fallen away or undergone profound transformation by the turn of the century, in León survived the pressures of demographic change, disentailment reform, and the growth of bureaucratic state structures, persisting virtually to the present day.

Was such long-term persistence merely the result of the inertia and inability to adapt to new forms which is proverbially associated with the "peasant way of life?" Not in the least. The history I trace in these pages of a tenacious pattern of economy and culture, though continuous, though animated by certain recurrent themes and conflicts, is by no means an "immobile" one. On the contrary, the people of Santa María continually recast the forms of the past in the idiom of their historical moment, and it was through those very forms that they forged an adaptation to the profound social, economic, and political changes that are so often assumed to have destroyed the old agrarian regime.

Though certain forms of family and village organization were especially long-lived in Santa María, similar patterns of persistence can be found elsewhere in northern Spain and Europe.[9] As Marc Bloch had written, "if we seek to explain the physiognomy of modern rural France, we shall find that the antecedents of nearly every feature recede into the mists of time."[10] Or more generally, referring to the daily routines of material life in Europe until the beginning of the nineteenth century, Fernand Braudel introduced the notion of *longue durée*, time that is "slow-moving, sometimes practically static."[11] Nor is it just the pattern of rural life in Europe that has been especially persistent. In a recent study of political and social institutions in late nineteenth- and early twentieth-century Europe, Arno Mayer emphasizes "the forces of inertia and resistance that slowed the waning of the old order," which persisted past the time when Europe is generally thought to have "crossed the threshold of modernity."[12] It is becoming increasingly clear that schemes of inevitable evolutionary progress, including modernization theory, cannot be imposed easily on our ethnographic and historical data—not even for Europe. As Natalie Zemon Davis remarks in an essay on anthropology and history, "Markets do not always drive out gifts, centers do not always eliminate particular localities, and history does not always replace myth."[13]

Yet it is still true that the nature of persistence, what it was that persisted, varied from place to place and from country to country. In Spain, as Antonio Domínguez Ortiz has written, "there was nothing . . . that could be compared to the profound agricultural revolution which took place in England in the eighteenth century."[14] The agricultural revolution, what Marc Bloch had referred to as "that disruption of agrarian techniques and customs,"[15] was, indeed, slow in reaching most of León and Castile, and only in the last few decades has it really made much headway. Such practices as the alternation of cropping and fallowing, the opening up of the harvested fields to all the cattle of the community for grazing, the imposition of servitudes on various private properties which made them subject to communal use, and the very existence of common lands—in short, the whole communal organization of agriculture—persisted in villages like Santa María virtually to the present day. And the enclosure movement, which was at the heart of the agricultural revolution in England, simply did not "take off" in this Spanish region of small landholders living in the miniature settlements bequeathed to them by their medieval forebears. In central León, the enclosure of the scattered, tiny parcels that make up family holdings began in earnest in the 1970s, and in Santa María this reform was just completed in 1984. There it is the long tradition of strong corporate village organization—centering largely on the defense of the common lands from outside encroachments—that has played a major part in the resistance to the agricultural revolution and the persistence into our time of a regime, in many ways medieval, in places like Santa María.

For those readers who come to this book with a background in Mediterranean ethnography, it is this regime, its strength and its persistence, that will most clearly be seen as setting León (and much of central and northwestern Spain) apart. Spain is generally conceived of as a Mediterranean country; yet if we consider the ecological criteria that are most often cited as defining "the Mediterranean," we will find that much of Spain, including León, most of Old Castile, and the entire Atlantic coast is excluded.[16] Demographically, León is characterized by a settlement pattern of small, rural villages—1,500 of them, the majority with less than 250 inhabitants—as opposed to the pattern of large, urban-oriented agrotowns that is typical of the European Mediterranean. Socially, there is a marked absence of stratification in the central Leonese village, so that the class concept—so important to an understanding of the larger towns of Andalusia or Aragon—has less relevance here. Economically, resources and land are distributed, if not equally, at least equitably enough, so that no one is without "four parcels of land" and a "little pair" of cows; property is circulated through an equal inheritance system, and rights to communal goods are guaranteed to all households of the community. Although economic differences do exist, the landless proletariat is not a regular feature of villages in central León, and the large landowner, so frequent in the Mediterranean, is a rarity.[17]

The honor and shame complex, which has been found to be so prominent in the Mediterranean, is not part of Leonese gender relations.

Rather, men and women, both property-owners, and yoked into a team by marriage, are to be found working side by side in the fields and in the marketplace, planning and making decisions together. Virtually the only exclusively "male" arena is the village council, though this again forms a contrast to the situation in the Mediterranean, where, politically, the mass of rural people have no voice in local political decision-making. Finally, the peasant ethos one finds in León is based in a sense that it is honorable to work the land and that such labor in some way dignifies.[18] Thus by most criteria the tenor of life in Santa María and other Leonese communities is closer to that of a Castilian hamlet or a Swiss Alpine village than to an Aragonese or Andalusian agrotown.[19] Other comparisons could be made, but these will suffice to point out the different nuances in the tenor of life in "European" Spain and "Mediterranean" Spain.[20]

Obviously these are not rigid distinctions, for the line separating the two Spains is an elusive one, in the end, and neither form homogenous "culture areas."[21] Still, I feel there is a need to draw these comparisons to set the stage for the discussion to follow. The processes of cultural persistence and change that I describe here in relation to Santa María and central León occurred in response, often, to movements affecting all of Spain and much of Europe as well: population growth, the rationalization of the old agrarian regime, disentailment, the reform of local government by the national state. But in Santa María and surrounding villages these changes were faced in ways consistent with the long run of cultural, social, and economic life: land from the commons was cleared, disentailed properties were collectively bought back from the state, and things continued more or less as they always had. A class system did not take form, rural revolt did not occur. The old agrarian regime simply persisted in the midst of a much-changed world, to die unsung.

In the five parts of this book I explore different aspects of the "presence of the past" in Santa María and the surrounding area. The period covered is roughly that from the beginning of the eighteenth century to the 1960s and 1970s, the years of the rural exodus; yet materials from the medieval and early modern periods are also included, while it is the present that serves as the point of departure for my exploration of the past.

I begin in Part One with an essay on the rural landscape of León. In the landscape, the past, especially the medieval past, has left its most palpable imprint. There is historical depth too in the pattern of economic life, with its absence of commerce and its strongly agrarian character, and in the pattern of social organization, where most are farmers of middling rank.

Parts Two, Three, and Four form the heart of the book. There I take a fresh look at the topics that have always been central to European ethnography: family and community.

Part Two deals with the Leonese house in the very broad sense in which it is thought of locally. The discussion moves from questions of architectonics to the complexities of the equal inheritance system, the relationship between parents and children, the conception of marriage, and the position of women. Weaving together examples from the past and the present, I try to give a sense of the historical continuity that characterizes these aspects of Leonese society and culture, showing how people have been dividing, building up, and redividing their houses for three centuries; showing how profound is the ambivalence that has long underlain rural family relations, at once permeated with the spirit of the gift and the contract; and showing how women, as property-owners, were ever on a par with their husbands, in marriage and in the essential labor of producing property to leave to their descendents.

Parts Three and Four move to the domain of the community and village social organization. The focus first is on the the village council or assembly, the *concejo abierto*, the primary form of local government in the small villages of rural León since early medieval times. The institution of meeting in *concejos* disappeared in the larger towns of León and Castile by the fourteenth century, but it persisted in many villages of northern Spain to the present day. There are resonances between the *concejo* of the past and the present in the definition of the *concejo* as a republic of village households, in which every paterfamilias has a voice and a vote; in the rowdiness, feasting, and garrulousness that made the *concejo* meetings look like the epitome of misrule to bishops on their pastoral visits to the villages; in the ambivalence that the problem of authority regularly called forth among a people who conceive of their body politic as ideally democratic and leaderless; and in the enforcement of customary forms of social and religious behavior with fines, penalties, and sanctions, for community solidarity was never wholly spontaneous, nor was it ever accepted as a given by villagers themselves. The question of persistence is of particular interest here, considering that after the municipal reforms of the 1830s, the *concejo* was shorn of all legal authority. Yet despite this and further efforts to undo the pattern of local autonomy represented by the *concejo*, even through the Franco dictatorship, the *concejo* continued to meet, impose fines for failure to comply with traditional forms of social solidarity, and govern itself, to the extent that it still could, by the customary laws of the locale.

I introduce the notion of a "web of use-rights" in Part Four to speak of the various communal properties, obligations, and reciprocities that persisted in much of rural Spain and Europe until the end of the last century, and in Santa María virtually to the present day. These include the "servitudes" that weighed down private property in the old communal organization of agriculture; the system of communal herding by turn, in which all the cattle-owning households were obligated to take part; the present-day cow company with its mutual assistance for losses of cattle; and the use-rights given to citizens of the community over common lands and woods, without which most people would not have survived the subsistence crisis of the late nineteenth and early twentieth centuries. In this part of León the way of life associated with the common herds and fields was very long-lived, and again in spite of legal reforms that might have led to its destruction. Its persistence was not, however, automatic or passive, but involved a constant adaptation to changing demographic, political, and ideological conditions. Thus when faced with disentailment in the nineteenth century, the people of Santa María organized themselves to prevent the loss of their common lands, either by buying them back or by obtaining legal exemptions from sale. Through the discussion of the local effects of disentailment—so unlike what has often been assumed to have been its effects in Spain as a whole—I point out how different were the views toward the commons held by the centralizing state and village communities.

The writing and keeping of documents plays an important role in Spanish society and culture, even on the local level, as I try to show. In Part Five I turn to this theme, undertaking an interpretive analysis of how the written word, history, and the past are conceived and understood by the people of Santa María and other Leonese villages. The Epilogue brings the account up to date, and gives a portrait of the village in 1984.

Part One

Chapter 1

✛

A Portrait of a Landscape
and of a People

IT WAS late June and I was riding in a cart with a village man, his team of cows pulling us slowly along the rocky, winding path. We were on our way to a meadow in that part of Santa María's landscape known as San Pelayo, where his brother and sister-in-law, having left earlier by donkey, were haymaking. As the cart jolted us up and down, my companion spoke to me of how his world had started to change forty years ago, "when petroleum came." Reflecting on the longevity of certain features of the local economy, he went on: "How must the world have been in the past; it seems it was standing still, the way they went on using the Roman plow." I asked him why things had remained static for so long. And he replied: "It must have been a punishment, I don't know, but it was only forty years ago that the world started to evolve, at least in Spain where we are a few years behind the times. They say we are on the road to development."[1]

Indeed, to read Marc Bloch's account of medieval French rural life or George Homan's of medieval England is to read a description of the agrarian regime in León during the first half of this century, even that of the present in many aspects. The presence of the medieval past has been displaced only recently in Santa María, as my informant tells us; nor is he alone in thinking that the modern world has caught up with the village and with Spain in the last forty years, in other words, since the Civil War, and that before all was a still time, the *longue durée* that Fernand Braudel has made famous.

Older villagers have told me that they, their fathers, and their grandfathers were still harvesting wheat and rye with the sickle until the end of the 1920s, and oats until 1945. They remember the great resistance of the elders to adopting the scythe as a tool for harvesting the grain for their daily bread. It seemed to them that the scythe wasted too much of the harvest. When cut by the swinging motion of the scythe, the stalks dropped to the ground, the grain falling from them, and more grain was lost when the stalks were later gathered up into sheaves. With the sickle one lost none of the grain, for bunches of the stalk were grasped with the hand, cut and bound in a single process. In an area of poor rocky soils, where wheat will hardly grow, and the rye that was gathered was just enough for subsistence, their conservatism was not unfounded. But, as elsewhere in Europe (though there the new technology had already been adopted by the eighteenth and nineteenth centuries), the scythe eventually won the day and by 1938, as a village man could recall, it was in use to harvest all the grains except for oats.[2]

The rural landscape

It is not just the longevity of traditional harvesting methods that gives people their sense of the presence of the past. The rural landscape itself, in its general features, bears the marks of its archaic origins. The lack of enclosures, the predominance of the open fields, the small scattered parcels forming a vast mosaic over the cultivated terrain, these features still characterized the land tenure system of the village and the surrounding area until 1983. Now that the consolidation of parcels plan has been carried out, all this has changed—but the way of life associated with the old system of land tenure has yet to be forgotten.

Perhaps even more than in the layout of the landscape—where the subtle changes that have taken place through the centuries in the size and shape of the fields are not so open to view—it is in the names given to the hills, paths, ridges, valleys, springs, and fields that so much of the past is embodied. These topographic names, as William Christian observed, are part of a uniquely local lexicon.[3] They are also part of a uniquely local history, writ on the land, passed down from generation to generation, and bearing testimony to a very human landscape, as human as the women and men who have lived and worked within it through the centuries. I have counted as many as two hundred such place names in Santa María, and many of them already turn up in

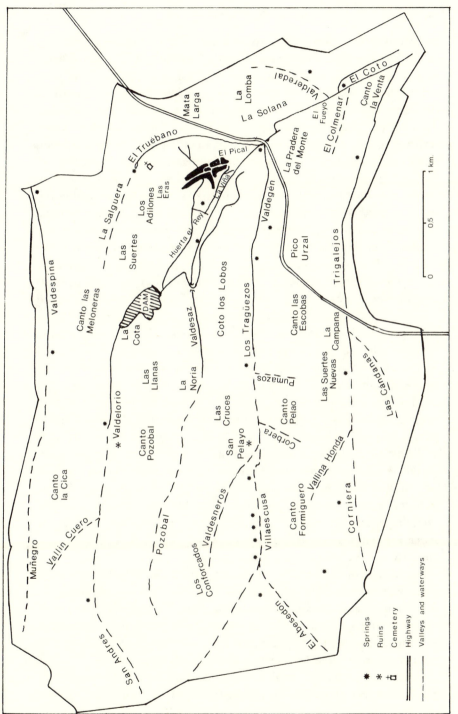

Map 3. Local place names within the boundaries of Santa María del Monte

Springs
Ruins
Cemetery
Highway
Valleys and waterways

1 km.

0.5

0

Muñegro
Vallin Cuero
Canto la Cica
Valdespina
Canto las Meloneras
La Salguera
El Truebano
Mata Larga
La Lomba
La Solana
Valderedal
El Coto
Canto la Venta
El Colmenar
El Fueyo
La Pradera del Monte
El Pical
La Viña
Las Eras
Los Adilones
Las Suertes
Huerta el Rey
Valdegen
Pico Urzal
Trigalejos
Canto las Escobas
Las Campana
Suertes Nuevas
Las Campanas
La Cota
DAM
Valdesaz
Coto los Lobos
Los Tragüezos
Pumazos
Canto Pelao
Corbera
Valdelorio
Canto Pozobal
Las Llanas
La Noria
Las Cruces
San Pelayo
Corniera
Vallina Honda
Canto Formiguero
Valdesneros
Villaescusa
Los Contorcados
Pozobal
San Andres
El Abesedon

sixteenth- and eighteenth-century sources. Nor should we forget their highly practical import—practical not so much in the sense of being utilitarian but of being lodged in practice—for it is these manifold place names that have always helped villagers to keep track of their many scattered parcels in the open field system. They are the reference points of a mental map that makes possible a very exact situating in space, expressing once again that distinctly human predilection for giving meaning to the small world into which destiny has cast one.

Having spoken of the medieval past, let us look briefly at the formation of this rural landscape in the period of the early Reconquest and settlement of northwestern Spain (eighth to tenth centuries). During this era, active repopulation and colonization of the deserted areas in the northern part of the peninsula was supported by the expansion southward of the Christian frontier into areas long under Moorish domination; at the same time, the continual formation of new settlements made this politico-religious expansion possible. The early Spanish kings, who understood very well the strategic value of human numbers, allowed relatively free occupation and settlement of the land by individuals and family groups. Of generally poor means, they came on their own, or under the auspices of monastic or secular lords, and in time took possession by the rights of *pressura* and *scalio* of those unoccupied lands that they could clear and cultivate.[4]

As a result of this pattern of settlement, small peasant proprietorship found ideal soil in which to develop, in León as in the whole northwest of Spain. An estate or manor system never took root, as it did in parts of the south, settled centuries later and no longer so freely in the final period of the long crusade to reconquer Spain for Christianity.[5] In conjunction with the system of individual or family proprietorship arose the complementary system of communal tenure over what were often quite extensive tracts of wooded areas and wastes. Formed at a time when there were vast uninhabited spaces, *territorios yermos y desiertos*, lying open for settlement, the older communities of the north had a population density that remained always quite low, and dramatically so in proportion to the formidable unworked spaces that formed a thick border around the tiny parcels of cultivated land. Santa María is an exemplary case of this medieval settlement pattern, encircled as it is by a ring of cultivated lands that are encircled, in turn, by a wider fringe of woods.

The legacy of the medieval system of land tenure is still evidenced in the preponderance of small landholders in central León. Most Leonese *labradores* have traditionally owned holdings of less than three hectares composed of many minute and fragmented parcels, which vary in size from a tenth to a fourth of a hectare and are scattered about a single village territory.[6] The significant social consequence of this is that the land is fairly well distributed: in the past, as in the present, it is rare to find villagers who do not own some property, however meager, for basic subsistence needs. Differences in wealth between individual villagers have never been sharp enough to produce a class of landless rural workers.[7]

The proportion of communal land in this part of León is very high: in most villages more than 50 percent of the terrain is communal, and in many, Santa María among them, it makes up more than 70 percent of the total.[8] Of these lands, the major part is made up of woodland (*monte*). The rest generally consists of wastes (*baldíos*) and grazing land (*pastos*), with the few productive natural meadows usually serving, in the recent past, as restricted pastures (*cotos boyales*) for beasts of burden. In its extensiveness, if not in its social structural features, this vast common land held by the village community as a social body forms a latifundio of sorts, which is in stark contrast to the pattern of minifundio and privatization that characterizes cultivated land.

Such a pattern of land tenure neatly fitted the demography of the area. The earliest reliable population figures, which date from the late sixteenth century, show that the median size of villages in central León was twenty-five households, and a third of them had fewer than twenty households. This demographic pattern is still found in the eighteenth century and into the first half of the nineteenth, though by this time there were already indications of the dramatic population growth that was to become general in the entire area by the end of the century. Looking at the area as a whole, it is the stability in the size of settlements in central León throughout the old regime that is most striking. The largest villages in the area, Vegas del Condado, Barrillos, Villaquilambre, and Cerezales, had populations ranging from forty to sixty households from 1738 to 1798, while León, the provincial capital, in the same period had a total population of around six thousand.

Of course we can only speak of stability in a general sense, for if we look more closely at the year-by-year shifts in population in any single village we discover the drastic fluctuations that always lay beneath the apparent stability of the old agrarian regime.[9] Some of these population shifts were particular to a village, others affected a wider area, even an

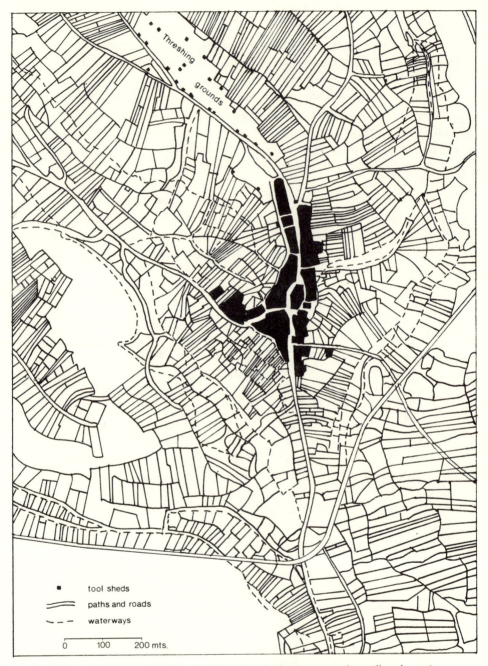

Threshing grounds

● tool sheds
══ paths and roads
‑ ‑ ‑ waterways

0   100   200 mts.

Map 4. Fragmentation of landholdings (detail of area surrounding village houses)

entire region. Such, for instance, was the crisis of 1803-1804, which began
with a tertian fever epidemic in all of León and Castile and was intensified
by disastrous harvests and inflated prices for the little grain that was to
be had. Thirty-six people died in Santa María in these two years—a
quarter of its population—while in nearby Barrillos the grain harvest
fell to a fraction of what it had been ten years earlier and the number
of tithe contributors declined sharply.[10] These demographic crises led on
occasion to the actual disappearance of villages, but overall the basic
settlement pattern, the constellation of small villages nestled near one
another, continued unchanged.[11]

Beginning in the middle of the nineteenth century, population growth
makes steady advances. Though demographic crises still occur, as in 1883
when an outbreak of smallpox takes the lives of twenty-five children in
Santa María or in 1918 when the influenza epidemic causes the deaths
of another twenty-five people in the village, these no longer halt the
march of population growth. Causes of this growth can be sought on
the local level. In Santa María a lower age at marriage, a longer span
of childbearing years, and a slightly shorter interval between births all
contributed to the increase in family size that marked the period from
1850 to 1927.[12] After 1927 it is a lower mortality rate rather than a high
birth rate that sustains demographic growth, which continues until the
mid-1950s. Yet the rise in population which affected Santa María and
the surrounding area in this era was not a purely local phenomenon but
part of a Spanish and even European trend.

We can see in miniature how the population was escalating in the
period by glancing at the figures for Santa María, which went from 135
inhabitants in 1797 to 201 in 1854 and 270 by 1885, reaching a peak of
315 by 1955. A similar pattern can be seen in the figures for the area as
a whole.[13] Given the long-established pattern of small villages, rather
like those of the early medieval settlement, this sudden overpopulation
represented an unprecedented change, which villagers responded to by
clearing common woodlands to bring more land under cultivation, and
by virtually becoming woodspeople, the younger couples especially. This
era of expansion, of bustling activity in fields and woods, is the one
which villagers remember vividly and invoke when recollecting what
village life was like in times past, though as we have seen such expansion
was uncharacteristic of the long run of village history. "The houses were
full," as one of my informants recalled, "and between the 80 youths of

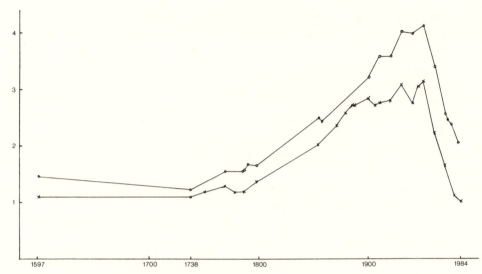

Graph 1. Total population, Santa María del Monte (x) in hundreds and Vegas del Condado (●) in thousands, 1597-1984

SOURCES: González, "Reconquista," pp. 256-264; AHDL, Fondo general, mss. 37, 68, 73, 79, 83, Arreglo parroquial (1854), and Uncatalogued (1797); AGS, DGR, 1ª Remesa, Respuestas Generales to the Catastro de Ensenada; AHN, Hacienda, libro 7457; RAH, Censo de Aranda and Censo de Floridablanca; Vicente de Cadenas y Vicent, *Padrones de hidalgos de los arrabales de León*; Archivo de la Real Chancillería de Valladolid, Protocolos, leg. 146, expte. 7; Ferreras Chasco, *El Norte*, tables 25, 27, and 31; *Censo de la pablación de España* (1863); Actas de Concejo, Santa María del Monte, 1871-1906; parish registers; personal observation (1978 and 1984).

Santa María and those of the other pueblos there were maybe 200 men in the *monte*, clearing land."[14]

Although villagers resourcefully confronted the crisis of numbers on their own, as they expanded into more and more marginal land it eventually became clear that the solution did not lie in the local landscape. With the support being given to industry in the later part of the Franco regime, the younger people who could no longer make ends meet had an outlet, which they turned to in increasing numbers during the 1960s and 1970s. Most went to Madrid and Bilbao, a handful left for Switzerland and France, later returning to settle in urban Spain. But it was not just a call to industry that drew people away from the village; it was a call to urban life. Thus, many of the people who left the village went no further than to non-industrial León, twenty kilometers away, a city that in this century has grown from 15,000 to 150,000, absorbing much of the rural population of the province.[15]

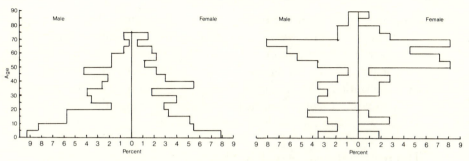

Graph 2. Population pyramids, Santa María del Monte, 1920 (left) and 1978 (right)

People recognize the sad necessity of the emigration—sad because of the eerie stillness of the present in comparison with the activity of the remembered past. Today the population of the village has returned to the level at which it maintained itself fairly steadily before the middle of the nineteenth century. But if we look at the composition of the population we find a drastic change: the population pyramid has become inverted, as the number of young couples and children decline and the elderly residents live to an increasingly old age. While half the population in 1920 was under twenty-two years of age, in the present half are over sixty, an age few attained in the past.[16] A symbol of the aging of the population is the school, attended in 1981 by eight children and a few years later by a mere five.

There is also a sadness in the perception of the older villagers that they will not be replaced when they are gone, that they are the last link in a human chain stretching back to the foundation of the village. Yet, they do see that there was no other way out of the crisis that an increase in their numbers had caused. One man, remembering the eighty-three *vecinos* in the village during the 1940s when he was starting to raise his family, made a keen remark: "If those people hadn't left today we would be dying of hunger" (*Ahora mismo si esa gente no se marcha pues hoy nos moriríamos de hambre*).

"Considering the poverty of the land"

When I first came to Santa María, people would often ask me why I had chosen so poor a place to visit—a place so *misere*, as they said. Of course in part they were simply trying to understand why a foreigner— a rare sight—had chosen to come to a small and obscure village rather than go to León or Madrid, cities with discothèques and movie theaters. And, one supposes, they were displaying a habitual guardedness toward the stranger. Yet there is more to this self-perception of the village as a very poor place than a characteristic politeness or reserve. It also stems from a realization that the village lands are generally poor, that it is difficult to wrest a living from them, and that the village therefore can hold little attraction for one who was not born there and raised on its soil.

This sense of the poorness of the place and its people finds expression in the testimony of an earlier generation of villagers, as we see in a sixteenth-century response to a questionnaire sent out by Phillip II on how the *alcabalas* (taxes on sales) were being collected, and on the general state of commerce and the economy in the villages of León and Castile. Of the twenty-three *vecinos* of Santa María in 1597, all but four were described as *pobre*, "poor," while those select few who escaped this description were still no more than *medianamente conforme a la pobreza de la tierra*, "middling well, considering the poverty of the land." As to commerce, it was limited to bringing "cattle and other things," to sell in León "because in said place there is no other trade or commerce . . . nor does anyone come there to sell anything because what they need they bring from [León] and other parts and because said place is small and its *vecinos* poor . . . there is no bakery nor butcher shop nor any sort of store." The tavern that they did have, apparently at the behest of León, was run by a *vecino* paid by the village for this service and excused from paying the *alcabala* on the sale of wine. Again, the respondents note that "since said place is poor and its *vecinos* few . . . not more than 50 *cántaras* of wine is spent there every year," about 30 liters a year per *vecino*.[17] The responses for all other villages in central León follow the same lines. To cite one more distinctive response, from nearby Santa Colomba de Curueño we hear that "there are no traders in said place nor is bread sold because they do not gather enough to sustain themselves nor to get through the year and because theirs is a mountainous and poor land." There was no regular tavernkeeper in Santa Colomba, and the obligation to service the tavern was circulated by turn, *a la corrida*, among all the *vecinos*.[18]

It is true that we must suspect the villagers of exaggerating somewhat the impoverished state of their economy in reporting to the tax collector; but even so their words are testimony to a widespread lack of commerce. And indeed so it has been almost to the present day. Formed perhaps in the medieval period when the members of these small communities "either worked together or died separately,"[19] this age-old economic pattern has become a kind of ethic, almost an ideal, in villagers' dealings with one another. As Susan Tax Freeman noted, referring to Soria, traditional community life, with its forms of mutual assistance, labor exchange, and redistribution of goods and services, expresses "a deeply rooted feeling against commercial trading."[20] Similarly, when William Christian writes of village life in Santander he speaks of "a kind of shame in the pure market transaction."[21] This ethic, of course, has always had the official support of the Catholic Church, with its disdain for relations of a bare commercial sort, a point that Max Weber made long ago.[22]

It is an ethic closely tied to the relative lack of economic stratification in central León where, in spite of the poorness of the terrain, there are no extremes of poverty nor of wealth among villagers such as one might find in other parts of Spain. For the forms of mutuality that are so prevalent here, as we shall see, in some sense are only practicable among social equals or near-equals. I often asked people in Santa María if they remembered having known anyone who made his living solely from working for others and earning a wage. As one man answered, "No, there was no one like that in the pueblo that I have seen, no, here in Santa María I haven't seen even one. Everyone had something, something. Everyone had his little pair [of cows], and on with it. Four parcels of land—that, yes."

He did admit, on the other hand, that in the *ribera*, the villages lining the more fertile riverbanks, there had been more economic differentiation, though it never reached the point of forming a true class system. And even in Santa María, where the land "was more equally distributed, always had been here," in the recent past there were still "four guys around who were more select, who weren't rich, rich, rich but, well, who managed better than the others."[23] As another man explained, the crux of the difference between the "four rich ones" and the other villagers was not the moneyed wealth of the former, who "had five *duros*, little money," but the fact that they at least did not owe money, as virtually everyone else did in the bleak period following the Civil War.[24] An older man voiced yet another view of the difference: the "rich" were those who grew their own wheat; the rest had to buy theirs, growing only rye. Subtle, then, was the differentiation that existed.

Beyond the recollection of present-day villagers, we know from eighteenth-century sources of a well-to-do villager from neighboring Villafeliz who owned eighty head of cattle, an enormous number by the standards of the area, and whose widow was to engage in lengthy litigation with the *vecinos* of Santa María over her rights to graze those cattle on the village's commons. In Santa María itself, we know of one particular family, that of Domingo de Salas and Paula de Celis, who at least for a time attained enough prosperity to endow a chaplaincy to be occupied by their descendents in the male line who entered the priesthood.[25] Just as there were some who were better off, so had there been some who were poorer. When she died in 1691, Catalina Suárez was not administered extreme unction, reported the parish priest, "for there were many days when she was mad and so was incapable of drawing up a testament, and she was a poor person [*pobre de solemnidad*] who went around begging, nor did she have land nor meadow nor house."[26] These cases exemplify the extremes of the economic range of the village in the old regime, but evidence from the same period, such as that found in the Catastro de Ensenada survey of 1751-1753, shows that the overwhelming majority fell within the middling ranks.

Though we cannot speak of economic stratification, then, there have long been, in Santa María and elsewhere in central León, economic differences that villagers never failed to recognize and take into account. This is clearly seen in the system of *repartimiento*, "assessment," by which money is raised according to certain criteria: in the sixteenth century, to raise the *alcabala*, by taxing each family according to what it has sold of its harvests or cattle, and even in recent years, to raise funds for paving village streets, by charging each house according to the size of its façade.

Thus in a council act from 1869 we find the *vecinos* meeting in their assembly or *concejo* to see how they were going to pay the annual leasehold over their common woods of San Pelayo, consisting of eight *cargas* of rye (about forty-eight bushels), which they owed to the Duke of Frías. They choose a commission of four *vecinos* to decide, along with the headman and his two assistants, how to distribute these eight *cargas* among the households, and they come up with the following assessment:

> First, that each untamed cow will enter into the contribution with twelve *reales*.
> Item, for each Mare idem, twelve *reales*.
> Item, for each work-animal six *reales*.
> Item, for each Donkey five *reales*.
> Item, for each offspring of a Mare five *reales*.
> Item, for each offspring of a Donkey two and a half *reales*.
> Item, for each sheep or goat two *reales*.

Item, for the use of the wood which each *vecino* acquires through his *suerte* [lot], fifty *céntimos*.

Item, for each cart of heather and heather trunks that each *vecino* brings from the woods ... four *reales*.

Finally, that each beehive that is on *concejo* lands will pay one *real*.[27]

This assessment, which is approved by all the *vecinos*, expresses a certain notion of economic justice widely held by Leonese *labradores*: that one should pay not only for what one owns, but for the use one makes of a particular resource, in this case the woods of San Pelayo. Hence the untamed cows, though worth less in monetary terms than a work cow or ox, are assessed for twice as much because they are taken to graze in the woods, while the beasts of burden graze in reserved meadows lying near the village. In fact, the entire assessment centers on the differential use of the woods, whether for grazing, cutting wood, or producing honey, and the question of ownership is only relevant insofar as it touches upon this use.

Similarly, when in the same year the *vecinos* wished to come up with an accord to organize the grazing of the untamed cows in the woods and of the work-animals in the reserved meadows, they name another commission of four men, two who own one pair of work-animals and two who own two pairs.[28] Or again, in 1899, the *vecinos* united in their assembly choose a commission of twelve men, both major and minor taxpayers, to agree on "the manner in which the *pueblo* is to govern itself in good order and manner to create a fund to bear the expenses the *pueblo* has every year."[29] The criteria they set down are very much like those which the previous generation of *vecinos* had agreed upon thirty years earlier to spread the burden of paying the leasehold to the Duke of Frías equitably around the village. What we see in all these cases of *repartimiento* is the emphasis given to achieving equity both in making decisions and in distributing economic burdens. Though differences in economic standing are recognized, an effort is always made to keep them from interfering with the ideal of economic justice.

To return to the comment made by my informant, though there were (and still are) economic differences, everyone had some property, a "little pair" of cows and "four parcels of land." This is what makes one a *labrador*, a property-owning, self-sustaining, independent farmer. People often spoke to me of the importance of having the status of *labrador* and of passing on this status to all of one's children, especially in the past when virtually everyone's prospects were rooted in the soil. They frequently expressed to me their preference for equal inheritance, which they, like their ancestors, practice, often contrasting it with the system of impartible inheritance that prevails in the neighboring region of Galicia, which they look upon with distaste. In their view it was imperative to assure each child a means of subsistence and livelihood, and even today when most of the offspring do not live from the land they are still sure to receive their piece of "the house," in the broad sense of the physical structure that houses the family, and the lands and the goods. For without property, particularly in the old rural economy, one fell down into the lowly ranks of wageworker or *jornalero*, one who works for others, who is not his own master.

Yet such ownership rights as *labradores* were able to transmit to their children could hardly have served, in the majority of cases, as a sufficient guarantee of economic survival and social status for generation upon generation of heirs. For what each heir received was but a fragment of a whole—rights in a piece of the house, a piece of the landed property, a piece of the family's goods. The entire edifice of private property would surely have crumbled and total impoverishment been the lot of every heir if there had not existed the means by which to build up a whole from the fragments; if, as is commonly thought, the fragmentation of property through partible inheritance were as unceasing and relentless as the unfolding of time and the generations.

In fact, Leonese *labradores* could rest secure in the knowledge that they gave their children rights not only to a piece of the house but also to a strong communal web of use-rights over village properties of meadow, woodland, and waste. Leonese *labradores*, like the English yeomen E. P. Thompson has written of, "could risk the practice of partible inheritance without condemning [their] children to poverty" in those villages where "the grid of communal inheritance was strong"[30]— where the communal inheritance complemented the family inheritance. Thus the curious contradiction: the possession of property, which the *labrador* considered to be so crucial a legacy to pass on to each child, actually depended upon the use in common of property that by virtue of belonging to all belonged to no one.

The agrarian economy, past and present

Today, as one climbs the highway from León to Santa María in summer, one's field of vision is filled gradually with the hues of the landscape:

the pale olive tones of brush and woods, dotted with the lilac and yellow of flowering heather, thyme, and broom; the rich gold expanse of rye billowing gently in the wind; and as one rounds a curve, a sudden patch of green meadows clustered near the houses of the village which have now come into view. A traveler in past times would probably have found a very similar range of tones in the landscape, though their composition has changed over the centuries. In the eighteenth century and before, it would have been the olive tones of brush and woods that would have permeated the canvas; at the turn of this century and after it would have been the rye that would have increasingly come to fill the traveler's field of vision; and at both times the patch of meadow would have been little more than a speck of green set between the dominant tones of fields and woods.

The changing canvas of the landscape that we picture here in our imagination is the most visible testimony to the changing life-way that has sustained the people who have inhabited it. Looking, for example, at the eighteenth-century rural economy of the village and the area we find, first of all, an overwhelming predominance of grain, most of it rye rather than wheat in the villages of poor soil such as Santa María; an occasional crop of barley was sown to rest the land.[31] This agrarian regime, like that which existed in most of Europe since medieval times, was based on an agro-pastoral economy.[32] The production of grain was complemented by the raising of animals, particularly cows and oxen, used above all as work-animals, and sheep and goats, which gave milk, meat, and wool. Virtually all these animals were sustained on common pastures, as natural meadows were few and far between, especially in the villages lying far from the rivers. To the south of Santa María donkeys could also be found working the land, while in the area of Santa María and further north mares were kept, not to work the land but to produce mules which were "usually sold at the fair of All Saints or Saint Martin" in León, from there probably passing on to the cereal plains of southern León and Castile.[33]

The agricultural production was rounded out by a small, but in terms of the local diet no doubt important, quantity of chick peas (both *titos cantudos* and *garbanzos*) and beans (*fréjoles*), and in yet fewer numbers, garden vegetables such as turnips and cabbage, garlic and onions, and even an occasional head of lettuce. Among the barnyard animals we find chickens and turkeys, ducks and geese, and above all the family pig— though the latter was not in the eighteenth century a barnyard animal in the strict sense. The village pigs were, like the sheep and goats, grazed in a common herd in the woods and upland pastures.[34] And in villages such as Vegas del Condado situated along the riverbanks, the diet was supplemented by the famous trout of the Leonese mountain streams. For saying mass on the day of Corpus Christi, the parish priest of Vegas was given "a *cántara* of wine, a cart of wood, and four pounds of trout"; this was a customary gift, "not something they owed him."[35]

Finally, there were the cash crops, such as they were, and the cottage industries, limited mainly to the growing of flax for linseed and thread which, like the sheepswool, was both used locally and sold in León. The minor industry of spinning white thread for sale flourished particularly in the villages of the Torío river valley. And, of course, there was wood throughout the northern part of central León, with Santa María, Villafeliz, and Santovenia forming the southern boundary of the wooded area. Wood was sold both in León and in the deforested villages lying further south.

This agrarian regime formed the basis of most people's livelihood. Compared to 1,748 *labradores* in 79 villages of central León, including Santa María, in the middle of the eighteenth century we find 25 carpenters, 21 blacksmiths, 27 weavers, 15 tailors, 2 tilemakers, and 2 *jornaleros*.[36] The majority of the artisans were also *labradores* who carried out their professions part-time as their services were required. There were also 62 parish priests, who made up the second largest economic group after the *labradores*. León, in contrast, presents a much more varied and basically urban picture. Living in the city were 140 *labradores*, 200 *jornaleros*, 147 resident poor or *pobres de solemnidad*, and 746 artisans, ranging from cabinetmakers to shoemakers and including one wigmaker and a dyer. Another large stratum was composed of the religious: 138 priests, 135 monks, 103 nuns, and 53 seminary students; in addition we can mention 37 soldiers and 25 prisoners in the royal jail.[37]

There were few changes in the agrarian regime through most of the following century. The potato was introduced, apparently at the beginning of the 1800s; mule breeding declined sharply in importance, while the use of the donkey as a work-animal spread, and as the population grew there was an increase in the number of sheep and goats grazing in the woods. Flax was still sown, being sold now to Asturias rather than to Leon.[38] Certainly the major change was the physical expansion of the area under cultivation at the expense of the woods as the years passed and the number and size of families grew. And as the twentieth century drew near, the woods were becoming even more depleted as the clearances continued and much wood was felled to supplement the live-lihood of the great numbers of people that now weighed upon the land.

The beginning of this century and especially the period after the Civil War were times of hunger. Two very evocative symbols for me of these times came up in conversations I had with a village woman in her seventies and another in her fifties. The older woman spoke to me of the *pan de picos*, "barb bread," the poorer people used to make in her native Barrillos in her mother's time. This was bread made from the seeds of burdock (*cadillo*), a plant that sprang up after the wheat was harvested. They would go with their wool blankets to the fields to glean the burdock flowers which, having barbs, would stick to the wool. After milling the burdock seeds they would use the flour to make bread, though some barbs inevitably found their way into the dough, thus the name "barb bread." She could remember overhearing a child telling his mother once "that he didn't want any more of that *pan de picos*."[39] The younger woman, remembering the period after the Civil War, told me of how she used to mix a few potatoes into the dough when making bread, so it would stretch a little further. Both the "barb bread" and the potato bread were of lower quality than the black rye bread that was the daily fare of most villagers at this time.

After the bleak decades of the 1930s and 1940s, the 1950s was a time of gradual improvement of the villagers' lot. Gradual, because the im-provements were at first greeted with great skepticism by the majority of the people. The Franco regime began to give visible expression to its autocratic statecraft by financing monumental irrigation works in various parts of Spain. In León two major dams were built in the northern mountains, one in the west in Barrios de Luna and the other directly north of Santa María, known as the dam of Vegamián after the largest of the twenty villages that were inundated by the new lake. At the same time a new canal was built along the Porma River, doubling the irrigated area of the villages along its banks.

Following in the spirit of the times, the people of Santa María financed and built their own miniature dam in one of the communal vales. This was a plan put forward by a few of the more progressive villagers, not without resistance from many of their neighbors, who were dubious about a project that was certainly going to be costly and whose benefits seemed much less certain. The opposition grew after the dam, completed in 1955, broke and flooded many of the village lands, not having been built sufficiently large or strong. But in spite of criticism it was expanded in 1957, and the lands watered by it soon became the most productive and highly valued ones of the village—this is the green patch one sees from the highway today.

The most important change in the agrarian regime of the village and the surrounding area in this century—perhaps in the last millennium—was the shift in emphasis from an agro-pastoral economy in which cows and oxen were raised mainly to be "motors of blood" for growing grain, to one in which grain is grown not to feed the family but the cows, now raised for milk and calves. In the past, since the cows were always working—and those which did not work were fed badly on the distant pastures of the common woods—they gave milk only every two years, when they were calving. I frequently heard that, before the 1950s, one had to go to Vegas or another village of the *ribera* for even a glass of milk when, say, the doctor ordered it be given to a sick child. This began to change in 1955 with the introduction in central León of one of the first artificial insemination programs in Spain. In conversations with the veterinarian who brought the new technology to the villages of the area, he often impressed upon me the skepticism of villagers that such a thing was possible, and it was only after he succeeded in artificially impregnating several cows thought to be infertile that the method won acceptance. But it was not until the 1960s and 1970s that the object of this program—the transformation of the old indigenous longhorn breed of work cow into a Swiss Alpine type of milk cow—was realized. Simultaneously a milk industry was growing in León to take in the milk that was now being produced in the villages.[40] And with the growth of cities came a growing demand for meat, particularly veal.

This shift in the local economy took place in tandem with both the increasing demand and growth of markets coming from the outside and with the flight of large numbers of people from the overpopulated villages. Though the improvements began to reach the village on the eve of the great wave of emigration, in truth they would not have been enough to change things radically had the village not been emptied of its excess population. Once this had taken place, those who stayed behind were able to concentrate their labors on the more productive lands of the village, renting them from those who had left and abandoning the least productive lands which had been worked in the long years of hunger. The sight of these lands reverting to heather and brush adds to the sense of sadness many feel at the current contraction of the village after the expansiveness of the preceding period, in spite of their recognition that they are all better off now that they are not forced to work such marginal lands to make their daily bread. There is a sense that the woods are again closing in on the village.

One result of this contraction is that much of the newly expanded irrigated area of the village, where beans and potatoes used to be grown to sustain the human population, has been converted to cultivated meadows and to the growing of fodder crops such as clover and barley to sustain the new, select cattle population. And, in the present, the rye and wheat produced no longer goes into the bread of village families, but to fatten the cows on which their livelihood now depends. Yet, though so many of the village lands are now dedicated to producing feed for the milk cows, half of the fodder (*pienso*) that they need must still be purchased. The same woman who spoke to me about "barb bread" also remarked that, before, "the cows used to be scrawny—today they have the cows more spoiled than the women, they give them flour and everything to eat."[41]

Though raising cattle has brought a new-won prosperity to the people, it has drawn them into the vicious circle of capitalism. For one thing, as people often told me, most of the money they make from selling milk has to be recycled back into the market because of the large amounts of fodder they must buy in order to feed the cows that give them the milk they sell. Just as contradictory is the fact that, in order to be less dependent on purchased fodder, they continue to work their rye lands with the very cows that they have raised, not as work cows, but as milk cows. And of course the harder they work their cows, the less milk they give. This is the situation in which virtually all the middle-aged couples have found themselves in the last few years, except for six households that own tractors to free their cattle from work.

The money that the villagers are paid for the milk they sell comes to them like a monthly wage, almost as if they were *jornaleros*. Thus for the first time in the village's history the old work ethic of the *labrador* is being worn away. There is more commerce in the village, as vendors with truckloads of goods, from bread, meat, fish, and fruit to mattresses and pots and pans, arrive almost daily to do business. One day as I was standing with a group of women waiting their turn to buy from the *fresquero*, called that because he brings fresh things, one of the women made a most telling comment: that today they buy their chickens from the truck vendors and sell the ones they raise themselves in León.

Yet it must be said that village people still attempt to maintain the old subsistence-based household economy of the *labrador*, raising a little of everything that they consume—a few lettuces, tomatoes, peppers, garlic, onions, and cabbages, potatoes, beans, and chick peas, besides raising rabbits, chickens, a Christmas turkey or duck, and again the family pigs. At the same time, they maintain the kind of thriftiness and inconspicuous consumption proverbial to the peasant. Here we return to the guise of *pobreza*, the poorness of the place and the people that had greeted me upon my first arrival in the village.

Thus even the retired people of the village, though they receive more money in the form of monthly pension checks than many of their younger neighbors make after all their hard work—25,000-30,000 *pesetas* a month per person—continue to keep a chicken and rabbit or two and to farm their kitchen gardens. Because they receive money so easily, most of which goes into the bank, and even manage to earn a bit more by selling a chicken now and then, they are looked upon with envy by the middle-aged couples working hard to make ends meet and, on top of that, paying their social security tax (*cupones*) monthly. Yet there can be no doubt that the prosperity of the retired is shared by the other villagers. Compared to past times, everyone has prospered since the 1970s, a fact that people readily recognize.

It is a prosperity that has come upon village people very quickly. Not surprisingly, then, many of them conceive of the past as locked in a still time, and of their world as only having evolved, as my informant told me in the haycart, in the last forty years. And it was this man's father who portrayed this contradictory prosperity to me once as resulting from the propagation of money, showing his understanding of the metaphysics of capital:

> With all this talk about there being a crisis, about there being unemployment, about there being what you will in Spain, from the Civil War to today there must be now, what can I tell you, a thousand times more money than there was before. A thousand times more, I don't know how much to tell you, speaking of thousands and thousands. Not only in Spain, but in general. You'd have to come up with a statistic and say, in Spain, how many millions the Bank of Spain could have. . . . Today, thousands and thousands and thousands of times more millions that the Bank of Spain has now than before, even with the crisis there is and the unemployment there is.[42]

Part Two

Chapter 2

The Village House

TRAVELING through central León at the close of the eighteenth century, Joseph Townsend described the adobe houses of its towns and villages as being "equally of mud wall, and mouldering away."[1] He was clearly not impressed. The contemporary view is more appreciative, tending to celebrate the remarkable fluidity of mud-wall houses. For example, Carlos Flores, the scholar of popular house forms, remarks that architectural "structures made of mud, with their bulges, deformations, tiny cracks and wrinkles, seem to attain an intermediate state between inert matter and living organic being, a quality which is lacking in other building materials often considered more noble and important."[2] In either case, the impression is of a house structure molded by the hand of time, by wear and corrosion, of a house structure in flux, indeed of walls mouldering away. Mud-wall houses, with their wrinkles, bulges, and deformations, literally age, and for this reason produce in the observer a strong sensation of mortality.

Mud walls and wood beams

It is in areas such as central León, where the climate fluctuates between cold, cruel winters and dry, hot summers, that mud or clay (the Spanish term *barro* means both) serves as a very desirable housebuilding material. During the winter the mud walls absorb the precious solar rays and keep inside the warmth of the fire which burns day and night in the kitchen; while in the summer they block out the heat, so that for the men and women who come back from the fields parched and worn the house is a haven from the intense midday sun. These qualities are readily apparent to the people who inhabit the houses and often extolled.³ However, it has become a thing of the past to build from scratch a house of mud wall; the techniques for doing so are not being passed on and in a generation or two will probably have been forgotten.

There are two kinds of traditional mud-wall houses: the older variety, of *tapial*, in which the wall is built up gradually from very large molds (*puertas de tapiar*) and the more recent variety made of adobe (from the Arabic for "sun-dried brick") in which the wall is built up in very much the same fashion as with industrially fashioned bricks. In general, the main difference between the two types of wall is that the material for *tapial* is made from a combination of earth and gravel, while that for adobe is made from a combination of earth and chaff or hay. In both the foundation is composed of various layers of rock and the rooftops of ovenbaked curve tiles; in both the sun is the major agent. The making of the material to build the walls takes much time and labor, since the earth must be turned and worked over and over before it can be used, mixed with just enough water so that it becomes malleable but not muddy. The wall is then built up of layers of the large molds in the case of *tapial*, or of the adobe bricks, using the same basic material in its wet state as mortar. After the walls are completed they receive a final coating made of earth and chaff (*trullado*) to provide a protective finish.

Since rain is infrequent, the walls do not melt all at once, as they would in most of the humid north of Spain. Instead they gradually wear down and only topple to the ground in dry León if they are not padded with fresh coats of the earth and chaff mixture (or today with cement) every few years. Mud-wall houses require continual maintenance. They lack the hardness and durability of stone.

The mud walls are like the flesh and blood of the house. But the house also has its skeleton to support the walls, its wood beams (*vigas*), which are almost always made of whole tree trunks. From the outside the beams are not so open to view. Although one may notice the tips of the three or four beams over the doors jutting out beyond the wall, it is primarily the massive, thick mud walls that dominate the façade. But once inside the house one discovers the deep structure, as it were, that holds it up.

The thickest trunks are used for the columns. These rest on a flattened stone base over which are positioned triangular wood supports that hold up the long horizontal pieces which in turn hold up the various beams that cut across the whole length of the house. The beams are in plain

Diagram 1. Village house façades, showing two styles of doors

sight within the house. One feels their strong presence: in the kitchen, even when they have been painted or covered with wallpaper, and in the bedroom, when staring up at the ceiling from one's bed. In those renovated village houses that imitate urban dwellings most closely, a false ceiling is constructed to hide the beams; for it is the beams in particular that give the house too rustic a look.

Aside from the columns and beams that bear the weight of the house, there are two other important features made of wood in the Leonese rural house. One is the *corredor*, a kind of open balcony with balustrades that runs almost completely around the upper level of the house or at least halfway around it, and whose railings are often finely carved. Then there are the doors that open onto the house, of which there is always a large set, known as the *puertonas*, and often a smaller door as well which is either cut into the larger one or set alongside it; this door is known as the *postigo* (diagram 1). The *puertonas* are needed to allow the cart, whether filled with hay, grain, wood, or manure, to be brought in and out of the house, for in León everything, from beasts to harvests, has its place in the house, *todo se mete en casa*, as people say.

From casa to chalet

Today we tend to think of the house as a human dwelling. But the rural Leonese house of old reflects a very different conception, one of the human dwelling as all but eclipsed by the quarters for the animals and the fruits of the harvest—the product of the combined labor of man and beast—which take up virtually all of the house space.

The eclipse of the human dwelling emerges clearly in the eighteenth century *respuestas particulares* of the Catastro de Ensenada, in which each and every house in a particular village is described in detail. The typical house had a kitchen, a portal, a *corral*, a stable, and a hayloft, and frequently a cellar as well. Sometimes there is an *ante-cocina* (an ante-chamber before the kitchen, known locally as the *prece-casa*), and now and then there are *soportales* (a portico or porch just outside the house, in front or in back). It is, however, very rare to find special sleeping or living quarters mentioned. When they come up, they are simply described as a *cuarto bajo* (low room) or a *cuarto alto* (high room), the first probably situated beside the kitchen and the second over the stable. Thus the human dwelling was generally pared down to the absolute minimum of a kitchen—the hearth—around which the family ate and slept.

In time the human dwelling began to occupy a slightly larger area within the economy of house space. In late nineteenth-century inventories of household property regular mention is made of a *cuarto, sala*, or *habitación* (all words denoting room or living quarters), of which there are usually two, sometimes three in a house. The kitchen too seems to expand to include the *ante-cocina* or *prece-casa*, the *cocina de horno* (kitchen with oven for baking), and the *cocina* itself. Mention is now made of special rooms to store grain, such as a *cuarto de pan* or *panera* (granary). These are all signs that the population is growing and the house is stretching to accommodate more members, while at the same time a new "urban" conception of the house is beginning to make itself felt in the village setting.

But these early encroachments of overall house space are of relatively minor importance. For the house continues to be primarily a storage place for the fruits of the harvest and a resting place for the beasts of burden and other animals. Only secondarily is it a human dwelling. It is not until this century, particularly in the last decade or two, that a much expanded human dwelling is finally brought to the forefront in a reversal of the old relationship between human and animal spaces.

In the older form of the human dwelling, as we can infer from the Catastro de Ensenada, the houses were quite low; most had a height of three *varas* (approximately 2.5 meters or 8 feet). When I inquired once about how people decided on the height of their houses in the past, I received an answer of charming accuracy from a village man. He said what you did was stand up straight and go like this—and he touched his head with the point of his thumb and spread his fingers apart—"y hala," that's where you put the ceiling. Indeed, the houses of the past are just a few inches higher than a village person's head (most people barely reach five feet), so that even a not very tall person like myself is something of a giant for these houses.

The location of the human dwelling in the past is also significant. It was tucked away in a far corner of the house and to reach it you had to cross the whole length of the *portal*, or entranceway, and pass through the *corral*, or interior courtyard, around which are set all the buildings of the house. It had one very small window, which looked out not onto the street, but onto the *corral*. The very center of family life, in other words, was at the greatest possible distance from the street and village life, for which there was a very good reason, of course: to prevent eavesdropping. As we know from the abundant anthropological literature on the subjects of secrecy and gossip, envy and lying in village communities, there exists a complex network of revelation and subterfuge in these communities, with people attempting to penetrate into the private comings and goings of other houses while seeking to maintain those of their own houses in a deeply veiled impenetrability. The location of the human dwelling in the older Leonese house form symbolically acknowledges this dynamic relationship between the various houses of a village. As villagers have explained it, their habit is to talk very loud (indeed during my first stay in the village I often used to think people were arguing with each other when they were just talking), and so anybody passing by can hear everything. In the past one especially had to watch out for the roving bands of *mozos* (young unmarried men) who were always out for a good joke based on people's private affairs, which they publicized in evening serenades.

The contemporary village house reverses two major features of the older house form. Beginning around the 1920s and later on in the generation setting up house immediately after the Civil War, there was a turn toward extremely high ceilings. The house was transformed practically overnight from its old dollhouselike dimensions to modern palacelike heights. One can see in some houses the very division between old and new heights in the walls, which up to one level are often made of *tapial*, and up to the next are made of adobe or even commercial brick. Together with the turn toward high ceilings came another revolution in house structure, the transformation of what had in many cases been a stable into a kitchen, which was now placed in the front of the house, with its large windows looking out onto the street.

Both styles are actually juxtaposed in several contemporary village houses, since what many people did was build their new kitchen up front and stack bedrooms over it, leaving the miniature old house in back intact. Going into these houses one has the impression that the past and the present, given shape in architectonic form, coexist in time and space.

The Civil War generation raised the ceilings and brought the human dwelling up front.[4] It is their offspring, the generation of people now in their thirties and forties, who are completing the "urbanization" of the house. And who better than they? For this is the generation that, in the last two decades, has left the village behind for the urban landscapes of León, Madrid, and Bilbao. In the years following the migration, so I was told, many village houses lay abandoned and dilapidated. But the emigrants have prospered, and now they bring their urban tastes and money back home to the their natal village, where they return to spend vacations and holidays.

One of the most important symbols of modernity is, of course, the bathroom. Thanks to the influence of urbanized sons and daughters, and in general an improved standard of living, the bathroom has come to take its place in the old Leonese village house. It appeared gradually, piece by piece, beginning around 1975 in Santa María (running water was brought to the houses in 1970). The symbolic importance of the bathroom was such that it was installed in many houses—which usually meant walling in a part of the *corral* and literally tacking it on to the rest of the house—even before the sewage system was completed in 1980. Thus for several years only the shower could be used. The toilet truly stood as a symbol, for in the houses that had one it was still necessary to relieve oneself as before in the stable or by the midden heap in the *corral*. I remember my amazement at being told upon my first arrival in Santa María in 1978 that there was a toilet in the house where I was to live, but that I was not to use it for more than my *aguas menores*, "little waters," since it drained right into the *corral*. For most elder villagers the toilet remains a symbol, since it is not they who use it, but their urbanized children and grandchildren.

A number of houses have gained extra rooms in recent years, as rooms that used to serve as storage places for harvested produce have increasingly become superfluous. Once a widow who no longer lives in the village but returns for holiday visits was showing me around her house. She pointed to one of the rooms, which now serves as a playroom for her grandchildren, and said that it used to be a granary. She could remember, as a child, that the room was so full of grain you could hardly open the door. Old sheepfolds have been made into dining rooms, parts of haylofts have become bedrooms. The house slowly loses most of its old agrarian functions, as the human dwelling is accented and expanded beyond the eighteenth-century possibility of a kitchen and rarely found sleeping quarters.

For the returning emigrants their house in the village becomes a quiet place in the country, a *"chalet"* in current Spanish usage, a home away from home designed for vacationing. The emphasis in the *chalet* is on comfort and festivity, and the areas of the house on which the emigrants lavish their energies are the living room, the bedrooms, the bath, the garden. But the houses of those who continue to farm and raise animals have managed to retain the personality of the old Leonese rural house. These houses, as in past times, shelter humans, animals, and harvests under a single roof. They still express a basic view of the house as consisting both of a human and an animal dwelling, existing side by side, together within the house. It is into the same house, whether through the *puertonas* or the *postigo*, that humans and animals enter. They cross the same threshold of the portal, a dark, almost tunnellike space, and pass together through the interior open space of the *corral*.

In these houses the *corral* is still the mediating ground between indoors and outdoors, humans and animals, nature and culture. It is in this central open space that the cows are yoked to the cart, the manure piled up, the firewood chopped, and the family pig annually slaughtered. The portal is still the general threshold of the house, though no longer is it the threshold for life-cycle passages. It was on a bench in this dark space, which is in the house but not *inside* the house, where in past times young men courted women. It was where, if the relationship crystallized in marriage, a young couple would kneel and receive their blessing from the mother and father of the bride.[5]

Of course, the remaining old-style houses cannot last much longer. In ten, twenty years the few couples left that farm will have retired and their houses will have become the *chalets* of their children. But one cannot turn back the hands of time.

An architect who married into a local family that no longer lives in the village made every effort to preserve his wife's parental house, to keep it looking just as it had in the past. Every rusty nail that was dug into the walls was left in its place, the old miniature windows were not enlarged, the layout of the rooms was left unaltered, even the kitchen was left in back. But he could not find a village man who would take seriously his request to have the façade coated with the earth and chaff mixture that gives the adobe house its unique tone and texture.

In the present, when women no longer make bread at home, one cannot find a man willing to make houses by kneading earth and chaff. Everyone praises the homemade bread of old, which had less air in it than that which the bakers make, just as they praise the superior adaptive properties of adobe over brick and cement. But just the same they buy their bread and when they build they do so with brick and cement.

In the end, the architect had to settle for the aesthetic effect of adobe. He convinced two carpenters to smother the façade liberally with cement, making bulges and ridges with it, and later had them paint it a saffron yellow, which approximates the color of the clay of the region. The effect is a studied rusticity, which is unique in the village and in the area. Although one or two houses have been left with their unadorned adobe façades, which allows one to see the rather thick layers of rock that serve as the foundation, not to mention their mud walls mouldering away, most have been covered with cement and painted white. The adobe façade is less neat-looking, people say; and it is true, a whitewashed house hides the wear of time better.

A tour of a village house

Let us now take a closer look at a particular house, one for which I have a special affection since I lived in it during my first period of fieldwork in Santa María. Turning to the diagram of the house (diagram 2), we see the large and small door beside each other, both opening onto the portal. From the portal we enter through another door into the human dwelling. To our left is the dining room, with its fancy table and chests, which is used only on such important ritual occasions as baptisms and funerals and on the days of the village fiesta, when the family dines together with its guests in unusual elegance on a fine linen tablecloth. The dining room is the refined version of the kitchen, where daily life unfolds by the woodstove and around a plain wooden table which has a drawer for bread and the perennial plate of sausage (*chorizo*) and

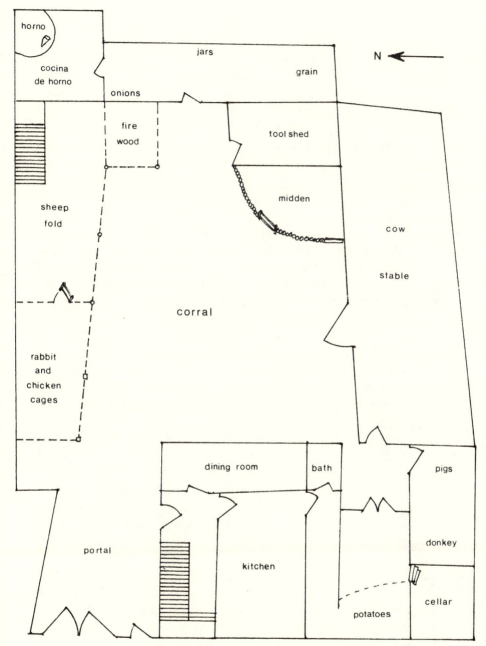

horno

cocina
de horno

jars

grain

N ←

onions

fire
wood

tool shed

sheep
fold

midden

cow

stable

corral

rabbit
and
chicken
cages

dining room

bath

pigs

donkey

portal

kitchen

cellar

potatoes

Diagram 2. A contemporary village house (Santa María del Monte, 1979) fatback (*tocino*) left over from an earlier meal. One sits on a bench called an *escañil* or *escaño*, of which there are sometimes two set around in a perpendicular, that with their long pillows serve as excellent cots for taking the siesta or resting on when one is ill. The kitchen in the winter is the only warm room in the house; the woodstove burns all day and during the long nights some women still weave a little and darn socks and patch up tattered clothing, following together with their husbands whatever happens to be showing on television.[6]

There is a door from the kitchen that leads to a hallway, where to one side there is a bathroom and to the other a pantry. In the pantry a large *arca* (wooden chest) holds the round loaves of bread (*hogazas*), and against the wall potatoes are piled up in a high mound. The dining room and bathroom were once parts of the *corral*, which were incorporated into the human dwelling within the last ten years. One must go outside again to the *corral* to enter the stables for the pigs and donkey, at the far end of which is the wine cellar, now used only for storage of bought wine. Above this whole ground floor of the house we find the four bedrooms on the second floor (not shown in the diagram). I slept in a room that I was told had been a hayloft and which with wallpaper, bed, and chests had been converted into a bedroom. The smell arising in the morning from the pigsty just under my room was an earthy reminder that the human and animal dwellings still coexist even in a modernized village house.

Now let us go to the far end of the *corral* at an exact diagonal to the present human dwelling. We find ourselves in the left-hand corner of the house and in the *cocina de horno*, which is where, I am told, in times past the center of family life was situated. All of these old kitchens have a hole in the middle of the roof, which served as the chimney when the fire for cooking was made on the floor. I know of one particular family that started out its life quite poor, in which all the children were brought up around just such a fire. But in the majority of cases by the turn of the century this room had already been transformed from a *cocina* to a *cocina de horno*, that is, into a room to bake bread in big mud ovens, and the kitchen with a woodstove (known as *cocina de trébede*) and chimney had moved either next door or, a little later, to the front of the house. In the house we are now examining, the old kitchen is now used to smoke sausages and ham, and this is the use it now has in most village houses. We see to the right a storage room for grains which are piled up in a mound by the wall, and there are onions hung up, most of which find their way into the blood sausages that are made around Saint Martin's Day in late November, and jars of preserves on the shelves. As we come out again, we find to our left a room where tools are kept and to our right the pile of firewood.

In the courtyard again, facing the portal, we have to our left the dung heap, which is periodically piled into the cart and taken out to dry for later use as fertilizer. The large stable on that side of the portal is for the cows, and it is where, until the completion of the sewage system two years ago, one would go and take some fresh hay from the pile and relieve oneself. Directly across from the stable is the sheepfold, which is fenced in with a wall made of twigs and branches like the ones that are used to enclose fields, and next to it are the rabbit and chicken cages. Over the rooms where tools are kept, and stretching in an ell shape across the sheepfold, is the *corredor*, where garlics and hot peppers are dried and fodder is stored. Over the stable is the hayloft (*pajar*), which runs across the whole length of it and extends over part of the pigsty, the stable for the donkey, and the cellar and joins up with the street through a hole (*bocarón*). The hay is fed into the *bocarón* from the street by someone standing in the cart, while another person in the hayloft arranges it inside.

So much, then, for a description of the components of a village house and their uses. Were we to rest content with this atemporal view of the house we would fail to realize that its present form and structure are a product of a historical process, a process of inheritance. If we look beyond the functional surface we find a rather different house, one that we barely recognize. This is what we uncover when we undertake an "archaeology" of the house.

Chapter 3

✝

An Archaeology of the House

IN CENTRAL LEÓN one finds that it is not the house which gives its name to the family, as is true in Galicia and Cataluña where the house of stone outlives the generations of families that pass through it.[1] In the Leonese context, the relationship between house and family is reversed: it is the generations of families—the lineage and all its ramifications—that outlive the house, which is constantly passing through various hands, in the process changing its shape and dimensions. Through equal inheritance what constitutes the house in each generation is an altogether different thing. The house in León is forever changing its name and its face.

Every piece of property that makes up *la casa*, including, as we will see, the very physical structure of the living quarters, is amenable to equal division.[2] Nothing is left out. From the linen to the clothing to the tools and the pots, every last item of material life is considered an essential part of the house, no less than the animals, the fruits of the harvest, the lard and sausages confected from the family pig, and the manure in the house and out in the family's fields. All form part, together with the landed property, of a single conception of *la casa*, "the house." Just as a plot of irrigated land may be divided up among all the offspring, male and female alike, for each to have some place to grow "four onions and four cabbages," as people like to say, so the physical house too, if there is only one, must in theory be divided up among all. In some cases I have studied this may involve as many as eight, ten, or twelve heirs.

In the inheritance systems of Galicia and Cataluña the house is given whole and passed on whole, while in the Leonese system the house is broken up and a new whole, reconstructed from the fragments is what is passed on. The Leonese system thus leaves it to the offspring to negotiate, not to say haggle, over the terms on which the house will stand or fall; unlike the Galician and Catalan systems, it does not impose a parental decision, or at least not so often. The results are varied. In the case of the physical house they generally follow one of two patterns: the house is split peaceably between two or more offspring, with each then forming a whole out of his/her allotted portion; or the house is divided between the siblings and is eventually reunited as the one sibling who remains in the house gradually buys back the other shares and reconquers the ground lost by the dissipating forces of equal inheritance.

A house reunited

Let us examine first the latter case—a house that is divided and in time reunited. In 1950 the house which we earlier described holistically belonged to several owners (diagram 3). The part of the house consisting mainly of the kitchen and stable belonged to the mother of the man, let us call him Basilio, who is now head of the household. Basilio's mother had inherited that piece of the house from her husband at his death in 1935. He had left her the entire property, both that which he himself inherited from his parents and the property, mainly consisting of land, which they had earned during their marriage (gananciales). Thus when his father died, Basilio and his siblings could have proceeded, once of age, to split the lands and moveable property, as well as the actual physical house, down the middle. In the customary way half of the inheritance would have gone to the surviving spouse, their mother, and the other half would have been split up among themselves, the offspring. There were four brothers involved in the inheritance, of whom only two were still alive in 1950. The other two brothers had died young and were being represented by their wives, standing in for the offspring of their dead husbands, the continuation of the line. The heirs decided to leave the house and all the furniture and goods in it, including a hog, a cow, and eleven sheep, to the mother, who in turn renounced her rights over some of the landed property, which could then be freely split among them.[3] By making such a pact the mother retained the ownership of that piece of the house until her death.

Now with the mother in her house lived Basilio, the present house owner, with his wife and their young daughters. One of Basilio's brothers had married into a village in the mountains and settled there, dying

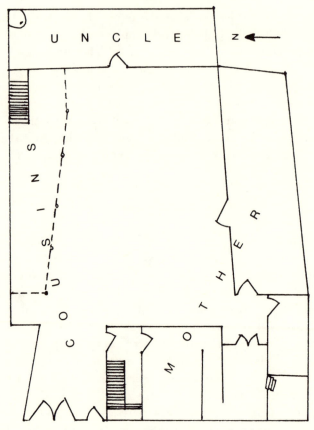

Diagram 3. Co-ownership of a village house (Santa María del Monte, around 1950)

young. Another brother had married a woman in the village and also died young. His young widow, with two infants from this marriage, then remarried another of Basilio's brothers, that is, her own brother-in-law and a paternal uncle of her children. This woman had been an only child whose mother had died young, and she lived with her father in the house which was to be left to her in its entirety. Now she was to have a stake in half of the other house, since the shares of not one, but two, husbands accrued to her. Strong-willed in temperament and fiercely self-righteous, she was to play a major role in the inheritance process, one that her mild-mannered husband himself was incapable of playing. But let us set aside this drama momentarily and finish with the matter of the ownership of the house.

Genealogical chart showing kinship relations among co-owners and others with claims on the house later reunited by Basilio.

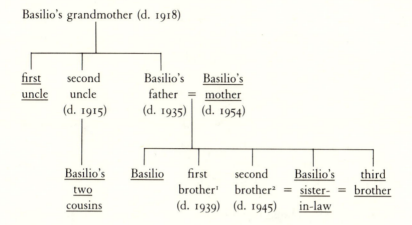

Basilio's grandmother (d. 1918)

| first uncle | second uncle (d. 1915) | Basilio's father (d. 1935) | = | Basilio's mother (d. 1954) | | | | |

| Basilio's two cousins | Basilio | first brother[1] (d. 1939) | second brother[2] (d. 1945) | = | Basilio's sister-in-law | = | third brother |

[1] Represented by his *widow*, who lives in a mountain village.

[2] Represented by his *widow*, who is now remarried to Basilio's third brother. Co-owners and persons with claims on the house around 1950 are indicated by underlining.

The part of the house that is now the sheepfold, the portal, and the bedroom above the portal belonged until 1951 to two of Basilio's paternal cousins. Basilio's cousins had inherited their share from their father, who died when the boys were young, and whose mother later remarried. Their mother had not wanted to let go of their piece of the house until her sons had come of age and could decide for themselves what to do. When the two brothers came of age, they married sisters and set up a combined household. The piece of the house they had inherited from their father they now used as a sheepfold (one of the brothers was a shepherd). In the room above the portal—now a bedroom—they kept a store of grain belonging to the veterinarian, who was then still paid in kind for his services, and for giving him the use of the room the brothers were freed from having to pay the yearly fee. The portal, in terms of strict ownership, was theirs and they could certainly have refused entrance to their aunt, Basilio's mother, or to Basilio himself had they wished to. But they were on good terms and tacitly gave their aunt and cousin use-rights over the portal, so that the matter of ownership—of the entrance and portal, at least—was in daily life quite forgotten.

The far left-hand corner of the house, that part encompassing the *cocina de horno*, the storage room, and the tool shed, belonged until 1960 to a paternal uncle of Basilio's, in other words, to his father's brother. Basilio's uncle used that part of the house mainly for storage, since he had another house in the village, where he lived with his family. This piece of house bordered on another house situated around the corner.

The house we have been examining thus had three owners (technically, four, but we can count the two cousins as a single owner since their property was undivided) whose three pieces faced a common *corral* over which all had use-rights. This situation was the outcome of yet an earlier division that had occurred in 1918 at the death of Basilio's grandmother, who had left this house to three of her children. These were Basilio's father, the only one of the three who lived in the house; Basilio's uncle who in 1951 still owned the part in back; and another of Basilio's uncles, who had died young and whose share in the partition went to his sons, Basilio's cousins. Though only Basilio's father and his family lived in the house, Basilio's uncle and cousins held on to their portions of it even after the death of Basilio's father and the passing of the house to Basilio's mother.

Certainly Basilio's cousins, who owned, after all, the very entrance to the house, felt the house was no less theirs than did Basilio's uncle who had to come into the house to get to his storage space; and neither felt any less the owner of the house than did its inhabitants, whose sheep bedded down at dusk in the courtyard for lack of a sheepfold, and whose own dwelling was cramped by stores of hay and grain for which there was no room elsewhere. A system of mixed ownership thus prevailed.

It was a system that is in keeping with the interlocking pattern of private property one finds in the old land tenure system. Boundary markers, sometimes just orally agreed on, sometimes materially embodied in a sign of a cross, separated the various parts of the house from each other in very much the same way as round stones set at each corner of a plot mark the ownership of land in the open field system. In such a system one feels a firm sense of ownership over one's portion, whether it be a piece of a house or a plot of land. Yet, at the same time, one's portion does not exist in a vacuum but within a vast mosaic composed of many other such pieces held by various owners. One is constantly being forced to let go of one's portion, to make it less one's own, within a system of use-rights. In a society where a house may be held by several owners at one time and any piece of land is cast in a sea of plots, there will be constant crossing over from one person's property to another's. The boundaries may be strict but one cannot help violating them.

Unlike the land tenure system, in the case of a house the system of use-rights is usually one stage in a family's inheritance process and one that tends to give way to a final settlement and strict private ownership. The house we have been examining, for example, was indeed rejoined in time, though it cost the present owner many pains and engendered a family feud whose embers have taken years to cool. The present owner, Basilio, was living with his wife and children in his mother's house. Basilio felt certain the house would one day be his; after all, it was he and his wife who took care of his mother, but also he could envision no counterclaims to the house on the part of the other heirs. Basilio's brother who had settled in the mountains was dead and his sister-in-law had no desire to come down to live in her husband's village. Basilio's brother who had married the widow of his other brother also posed no problem, since he was a man of peaceful ways and was quite settled in his wife's house. The real threat was to come from this sister-in-law of Basilio's, who had taken two of his brothers away from the fold.

In 1951 Basilio bought the share that belonged to his cousins. He would have bought their share sooner, but they refused to sell before then. The two were still living in a combined household and needed the sheepfold for their flock. Once they had built another house and cast lots to see who would get the old house and who the new, they were ready to sell and did so. As is customary when transactions of this kind take place between relatives, the cousins signed one deed attesting to the actual price of their share of the house and agreed to sign another deed that put the value of the share at less than a tenth of its real worth, "*para pasarlo por hacienda*," as they say, that is, to present it to the tax collector. It is very difficult for the Leonese *labrador* to part with money in general and much less so for taxes, so people consider it quite natural to help one another in such situations.

In buying the share belonging to his cousins, Basilio made an investment in the house before the question of dividing his mother's portion had come up. This action demonstrated his assurance that the house would eventually be his, a right his sister-in-law was to challenge. The same year that Basilio bought the portion belonging to his cousins he began to push for an agreement about his mother's portion of the house. Basilio felt the most logical arrangement was for him to buy out the shares of his sister-in-law in the mountains, his sister-in-law in the village, and his brother. Since his mother's portion was so small there really was, in Basilio's opinion, no sensible way to divide it.

But his sister-in-law in the village saw matters differently. She felt she had to fight for the rights of her two young children by her first husband. "Couldn't you just leave me their portion *en una orilla*," she said, "in a corner somewhere, until they grow up?" Basilio was infuriated by this request, remarking, "Of course, you carry away half the house." Responding sarcastically to her wish to maintain a little piece of the house for her fatherless offspring, he added: "If I leave you the hayloft where will I store my hay, if I leave you the doors, how will I enter the house?" But she persisted: "The house must be split and it must be split."

Both of them, of course, had a point. From the point of view of Basilio and his wife, it was unreasonable of their sister-in-law to demand that they split the house. She had a house all to herself, why then did she need another one? From their point of view she was being capricious and insensitive. She, on the other hand, and in this her father defended her, truly believed that her children should not be denied their share of the paternal house, for which money alone was no substitute. Recall in this context how Basilio's cousins had inherited as young children the piece of the house from their father which they found so useful when they were starting out in life.

The argument over the inheritance dragged on for three years until the death of Basilio's mother in 1954. The difficult sister-in-law finally gave in. Still there were disagreements as to the value of the house, and when that was decided upon at last, and the papers had been signed, there arose the question of the costs of the funeral. Basilio, smiling vengefully (in the rendition provided by his sister-in-law), declared that all the heirs would have to share the costs. She had expected that Basilio would pay for a larger fraction of the costs since he had gotten the house. But no, and to show that he had not forgiven his sister-in-law for the trouble she had caused Basilio would not let her take out the wine she had in his cellar. At one point during this protracted argument Basilio even threatened her father and her "with the shotgun in the kitchen." If she talks to Basilio now, she told me, it is only because he is a brother-in-law. But she too soon found her opportunity to exact vengeance. When Basilio came around with a paper for her to sign stating that the house had cost only half of what they had agreed on, so he would not have to pay so much in taxes, she promptly refused to sign, this time smiling back vengefully at him. As I mentioned earlier, there is an implicit agreement between people to help each other in dodging tax payment and such statements are signed as a matter of course. The sister-in-law's refusal to do so within such a system of thought was a willful affront; she made Basilio go to the trouble of bringing witnesses to attest to the true value of the house before she would agree to sign the false document.

After the heat of these events it was years before they talked; each side would pretend to ignore the other if they met on the street. Relations are now cordial but distant. The kinship link is virtually obscured, as was made clear to me on one particular occasion. I was on good terms with both families and had been invited to the house of the sister-in-law for the celebration of her husband's seventieth birthday. I had been to dinner at Basilio's house that day and afterwards we all prepared to go together for desert to the house of the sister-in-law. Suddenly Basilio's youngest son, then fifteen, asked his father why we were going there. He had to be reminded that those people were his aunt and uncle.

By 1960 the house was reunited (diagram 4). From his uncle Basilio bought the piece way in the back of the house. Since this piece bordered on another house, it was split up so that both houses incorporated a share of it. Basilio used his link of kinship to convince his uncle to split the lot somewhat less than equally so he would get the oven, which had a definite value at a time when women were still baking bread at home. Since the other house already had an oven anyway, this did not become a matter for grievance. The process of reuniting the pieces thus took almost ten years, though if we consider that the house was first split up in 1918 it really took much longer, almost half a century, or a full cyclical passage of the generations.

We turn now to an examination of the opposite case of house division, where a house is split and each part becomes a house unto itself. This case can be described more briefly than the previous one involving fragmentation and reunification since it is far simpler. I found an excellent example of this type of subdivision in the nearby village of Villamayor. Prior to 1940 this house was the typical Leonese house with its buildings forming a frame around the central open space of the *corral* (diagram 5). When it came time to divide the inheritance in 1940, the two brothers involved measured off equal shares of the house and built an adobe wall along the whole length of the *corral* to separate the two pieces. They were on good terms and the dividing wall they built only

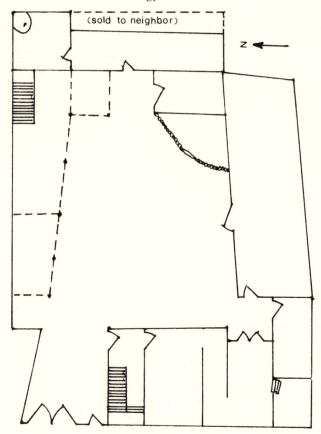

Diagram 4. The house reunited by a single owner (around 1960)

reached to the level of the *corredor*, acknowleding that the parts had once been part of a whole. The parental house was large and it easily yielded two houses for each of the sons (diagram 6). The brother who had gotten the share without the kitchen had to knock down a wall to open an entrance to his house, but then again the brother who had gotten the share with the kitchen did not get the hayloft and winepress. Since each was at once privileged and deprived by the share he had received, things were equal between them. The division was made peaceably, without cause for anger and resentment, and the family members on either side of the wall remain close-knit and united.

I have seen many houses in the villages of central León that have been sliced down the middle in the fashion described above. Many examples

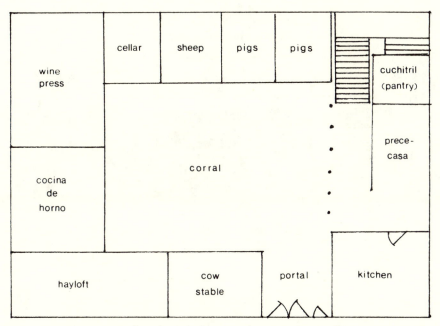

Diagram 5. A village house before partition (Villamayor, around 1940)

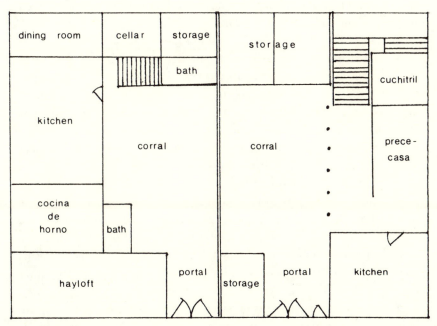

Diagram 6. The house split between two brothers (as it appeared in 1980). Note the contrast between the modernized house on the left and the more traditional house on the right.

Diagram 7. A view from the dividing wall of the same house

could be given. But it may be more interesting to mention, instead, the
manner in which the traditional practice of house division is carried on
in the present day.

In Santa María I observed two cases of contemporary house division.
Now that it has become fashionable among the middle classes to own,
besides a *piso* (an urban apartment) and a car, a *"chalet"* in the countryside,
the offspring who have migrated to the city are quite happy to inherit
a village house. If they have the means, they are more than willing to
invest money in their share in order to give it the proper air of leisure
and relaxation befitting a country villa. The two houses that in recent
years have been split in half were divided in a mode deeply influenced
by urbanized conceptions of the house. Rather than cutting the house
in half along the length of the *corral*, the recent trend has been to divide
it in half along the division into top and bottom floor, very much in the
form of a two-level duplex, each level going to one of the offspring. The
upstairs portion in both cases was taken by the sibling whose means
were better, since it involved building another kitchen and bathroom on
the upper floor. Yet the "poorer" sibling in each case was no less pleased
to receive the downstairs portion since he or she thereby got a complete
house. I often marveled at the ingenuity of this arrangement, which
takes an old practice and gives it such a curious modern twist.

The "piece of the house" in history

If we consider now a few examples of house division gleaned from historical sources, we can see that virtually the same principles of inheritance were at work in the past as in the present. This is one of the areas of Leonese culture that has maintained its historical depth despite the many important changes—demographic, economic, and political—that have taken place in the last two centuries.

In a case documented in 1704, Juan Díez of Navafría, Ramiro Díez, and Pedro Rodríguez as husband of Josepha Díez of Santibáñez de Porma, sell to their brother, Miguel Díez of Santibáñez, the rights they have to a house and its *corral* and *ferreñal* (an attached plot for growing forage), which were left at the death of Antonio Díez, their father. The scribe clearly states that the portions they have "in the house, its *corral* and *ferreñal* are three, in addition to one more which makes four that belongs to Miguel Díez our brother the buyer."[4] The details of this transaction imply, first, that the offspring had equal shares in the house, and, second, that the house never actually came to be divided. As the document states, it is the rights over the house rather than the actual portions that were being sold. The house, in this case, was thus not physically dismembered.

One might be led to argue, as a result, that the house is received whole and kept whole, in a way not unlike the Galician and Catalan systems we spoke of earlier. But the cultural reality of León is very different. Even if the ultimate effect of preventing fragmentation is achieved, it is acknowledged in the Leonese system that all the offspring have their "portions" in and their "rights" over the house.

Those offspring who sell their portion often do so to buy a portion in another house in which they have a greater stake. There is a kind of network of trading in houses. Thus we find in a case from 1784 that Tomas Gómez Torices and his wife, Lorenza Alonso, of Santa María del Monte, sell to Domingo González, resident of Barrillos, "a piece of a house in said village [of Barrillos] composed of two beams."[5] On the same day Manuel de Otero, of Santa María, sells to Lorenza Alonso, mentioned above, "two beams of a house, where the above-mentioned live."[6] In effect, two beams of a house are traded for two beams of a house, though in monetary terms it is not quite an equal trade, since the first purchase is worth 350 *reales de vellón* and the second just 220 *reales de vellón*. It is interesting that in these deeds of sale a piece of a house is measured, really conceived of, in terms of the roof beams of the house, as if the beams themselves constituted the portions. In another case from the same year, "three beams of a house" are sold in addition to "another piece of a house and a little bit of *corral*."[7]

In a case from 1786 concerning inhabitants of the village of Cerezales, Antonio González sells to his brother, Miguel González, and Florentina Díez, his wife, "a piece of a house . . . composed of a hayloft, stable, and portal which borders on all sides with the house of the buyers."[8] The house in this instance seems to have been physically divided by the brothers at one time, as we can infer from the fact that specific components of the house are being sold and not just the rights over the house or a theoretically held portion of it. The rooms mentioned border on all sides with the house of the buyers, which probably indicates that they were once part of a single house.

To turn now to an example from a later period, I will mention one particularly interesting case I found in a family or "kitchen" document that an informant kindly lent me. A family document is one composed by a local *fiel de fechos* (village community scribe) or simply by "*una persona curiosa*," a talented person, in this case one who not only can write but is conversant with the legalistic idiom of inventories and inheritance records. Since these documents were made up in the house, in fact in the kitchen, they were sometimes referred to as "*un papel de cocina*," or a "kitchen document."[9]

In these documents one is sometimes able to get more of a sense of the local idiom of house division. We find, in a case from 1860, Simón Díez and Isidora Mirantes of Santa Colomba selling to Toribio Mirantes (a brother of Isidora) and Nicolasa Ferreras of Santa María, "*un cacho de casa*." The term "*cacho*" is the more colloquial form of saying a piece of something, and its sense is closest to a "lump," "wedge," or "chunk" of something. It is often used to speak of a chunk of bread, as in the oft-heard expression, "*un cacho pan*" and more relevant in this context there is the expression "*hacer un cacho de papel*," meaning literally "to make a piece of paper," in other words, make a document.[10]

This "*cacho de casa*" is composed of a "*cocinona* . . . and another *cacho* in the *portalón* . . . and these two *suertes* [shares or lots] each has its *cacho de corral*."[11] Note the widespread linguistic device of adding a suffix to a word to denote large size, so that the kitchen, *cocina*, becomes *cocinona*, and the portal, *portalón*. Both the kitchen and the portal have their *cacho de corral*, their piece of *corral*. Toribio Mirantes not only buys the share pertaining to his sister, Isidora, but by 1863 he is ready to buy the share of his brother, Alejo Mirantes, of Villamayor, "which is composed of a *cacho* in the *portalón* ... with its *cacho de corral*."[12] Having bought the chunk of the *portalón* with its chunk of *corral*, he ends up with a complete house.

This case bears a strong resemblance to the ethnographic example we treated at length of a house reunited through the efforts of the one heir who stays on in the house and gradually pieces it together again. Toribio owed his success to the fact that his brother and sister married outside the village (in Villamayor and Santa Colomba, respectively) and founded houses elsewhere. Similarly, in the ethnographic example, one brother married out and two brothers successively married a woman who, as an only child, was to be the uncontested heir of an entire house.

Interestingly, the components of the house that Toribio Mirantes rejoins are referred to as two *suertes* (literally, "luck," in actual usage, "shares or lots won by luck"). The use of the term *suerte* to denote the pieces being sold is significant, since this is the same term used to speak of a lot or share of communal land. It points to a fundamental analogy between the ordering principles found in house and village organization, to a common underlying conception of property as something that is, in part, *only in part*, a gift won in the lottery of life. The other part, as we will later see, is won through a combination of hard work, economic sacrifice, and a spirit of reverent saving during a couple's married life.

Chapter 4

✛

The Idiom of Equal Inheritance

At WHATEVER POINT in the family life cycle the inheritance was divided, one main principle prevailed: each offspring ought to receive a share in every category of property the parents possessed. With respect to land, therefore, it was expected that each child should get a couple of dry cereal lands, at least one meadow, and if the parents were lucky enough to have it, a portion, however miniscule, of the all-too-scarce irrigated terrain. Household property, such as the yoke, the cart, or cooking utensils and, if there were many offspring, even the few cows, sheep, and goats in the house, were not often amenable to division in the same manner described above for land. In the majority of cases it became necessary to carefully weigh the value of items in one category of property against those in another until the scales held steady, a balancing trick that took a lot of maneuvering and patience, and sometimes a little manipulating of numbers. The portions were then, as today, distributed by the drawing of lots or through mutual agreement.

In reality utter equality is impossible to achieve. What the offspring must settle for, in the end, is an equitable division. When the ideal of equality is taken to extremes, there can result a futile and bitter battle between siblings for the same item of property, as we see from the following two illustrations. From his field research in his native village, Lisón Tolosana cites the case of the Aragonese brothers who fought for a yoke which had been rendered unnecessary to both by mechanization, but which each still wanted, until "one of the heirs to the yoke hacked it in half so that each could inherit 'his' part."[1] Levy takes us back to the classical world, and provides an illustration from the work of Aeschylus in which two brothers are depicted as ending the duel for their patrimony on all-too-equal terms: "each receives enough of the paternal lands to furnish him with a grave."[2] In this manner we find interwoven in the ancient drama of inheritance division elements of the comic and the tragic.

When we turn our attention to the question of just how an equality of inheritance is achieved when all goes smoothly, we are inevitably confronted with what could variously be called a peasant economic logic, or *mentalité*, or mode of thinking, one that has its own peculiar rationality. One is able to see this logic at work in the "kitchen documents," particularly in the inventories of household property, and in the *hijuelas*, from the root *hijo* or *hija* (child), meaning the inheritance portion of a particular son or daughter. Since these records are for personal rather than official use, they are couched in the local idiom. This is not to say that because these records are personal they are not binding upon the individuals involved. On the contrary, they are treated as evidence of a mutual agreement, upon which all have inscribed their signatures, and have the force of a legal document.

The oldest of such records I was able to find in Santa María goes back only as far as 1824, since most villagers throw away records that involve people whom they no longer remember. As they say, "What do we need so many old papers around the house for?" The records are mainly of interest if they have some bearing on the present. Once they go back three, four, or more generations they simply become "old papers" concerning agreements already buried and past and no longer binding. They lose their contextual meaning, and having lost this they lose their power over the individuals involved and thus their purpose for existing.[3]

The house of two sisters

Since we have discussed house division at length, let us now turn to the subject of how an equitable division is attained. We will take as our case study the division of a house between two sisters, Nicolasa and Felipa Ferreras of Santa María, in the year 1886.

The parental house is longer than it is wide. So the sisters decide to divide it into a front and back part, instead of across the *corral*, as did the brothers from Villamayor. The boundaries are then strictly defined according to certain natural landmarks of the house. A *señal* or marker is designated "by the path [which borders the house on the north side] next to a wooden roof support which is between two girders of the central cellar." One follows the imaginary line originating in the first marker going through the *corral* "to a boundary marker that is at a distance of one *vara* from the drainage hole and juncture of *tapiales,*" and situated, one assumes, more or less directly at the south side of the house. The wall, it is stated, should divide the two parts in half from "boundary marker to boundary marker." To this definition of boundaries they add two clauses: "no one will be allowed to build this wall higher than ten feet" and "there will be no pouring out of waters to the other part and the waters shall drain along the edge of the wall of this house and join up with the drainage hole."[4]

Once the location of the wall is decided, certain provisions are made for the back part. "Marked out for this part of the house is an oak which is in the land at the top of Las Cruces, the best one, which has been there four years." And the front part of the house is placed under an obligation to the back part. "The part of the house that borders on the main road will pay out 75 *pesetas* to the back part in three installments, the first installment in the year 1887 on the 11th of November, the second installment on the same day in the year 1888, and the third installment on the same day in the year 1889."[5]

How are we to interpret these curious prescriptions? They seem to be concerned, first of all, with the creation and maintenance of boundaries. We see that the boundary markers spotted at either end of the house are particular and local architectural features: first, a wooden roof support, then a juncture of *tapiales.* These become the two points between which the wall is to be constructed. They are perceived as the dividing line between the two parts of the house.

A crucial reference point is the drainage hole, the hole at the foot of a wall of the house through which the dirty waters of the stables and the *corral* drain into the street. We are told that the juncture of *tapiales* is at a distance of one *vara* (83.6 centimeters or 33 inches) from the drainage hole, which would seem to be located in the front part of the house since the dirty waters are said to join up there.

Why can't the back part simply have its own drainage hole? Why also the injunction against building the dividing wall higher than ten feet? Perhaps in a symbolic manner the sense that the two pieces remain part of a whole, despite the division, is therein given expression. Or there may be other more practical reasons. But what is most significant is the scrutiny given to the making of boundaries and, not only that, to the peaceful neighborly, or shall we say sisterly, maintenance of them. This calls for an agreement about the problem of drainage and the possibility that the dividing wall, if it grows too high, will become a barrier to communication and cooperation.

The second major concern is to make the two parts, or lots, equal in value. It is significant that these arrangements for house division come up in the inventory of household and landed property left at the death of Mateo Ferreras, the father of Nicolasa and Felipa. It is not clear at this point just who will get which part. That question will be left, as Levy puts it, "to the inexorable operation of chance," in other words to the casting of lots. Precisely because neither knows which part will be hers, the value of each part is scrupulously calculated and weighed against the other, and an effort is made to make the parts "as nearly equal in value as possible, and ... equally desirable."[6] Since it is clear that the front part is the more desirable portion, a sturdy oak and 75 *pesetas* are placed on the side of the back part to give it weight, to enhance, in other words, its value and desirability. We must remember that the front part will have access to *la calle real* (the main road), while the back part will only have access to a *calleja* (path). Thus some recompenses need to be made to the back part for this reason alone.

As we learn from the *hijuela* of Nicolasa Ferreras, she is the one who draws the lot for the front part. It is noted down that her part of the house must pay out the 75 *pesetas* to the other part, "because it has that much more frame and this is noted down here so that when the time comes it will be payed out."[7] We learn here that the value of the house has been calculated by a measurement of the frame. Since Nicolasa's part has incorporated more of the frame than Felipa's part, she must give her sister back "that much more frame" which she has gotten to make the shares equal in value. She must do so by giving her a money substitute, and by allowing Felipa to get the best oak they have in Las Cruces. The terms of the agreement are noted down in Nicolasa's *hijuela* so she will stick to it.

It is worth remarking that Nicolasa and her husband, Toribio Mirantes, do not end up living in the part of the house Nicolasa inherits in 1886. This is not surprising since by this time she is already forty-seven years old and he fifty-five. At this late stage in their lives they are long settled in the house Toribio had inherited from his parents in 1860, the same year he married Nicolasa. Of this house he had originally inherited only an eighth part. He bought out in 1860 and 1863 the shares

pertaining to two other siblings, as we saw earlier, and it is likely that
he bought out other shares as well, though I have no documentation for
any other purchases. What is, however, an interesting turn of events is
that some of the other shares corresponding to his siblings clearly did
not get sold to him but to another villager, Pablo Rodríguez. And these
shares, in fact, are in the front part of the house. So at the time Nicolasa
cast the lot for a front portion, she and Toribio were themselves living
in a back portion.

This we learn from the inventory drawn up at the death of Toribio
himself. "This house has its main entrance and the right of way to the
main road of the village through the *corral* and house of the heirs of
Pablo Rodríguez, without impediments of any kind, one of the main
doors of the portal opening onto the street being the property of this
house."[8] Clearly when the house, which must once have comprised the
part belonging to Pablo Rodríguez and to Toribio, was divided all the
heirs retained the right to enter the house through the main doors. The
front part was probably sold to another villager rather than to Toribio
because he either could not afford to buy out more shares, or simply
had enough with his portion. Some of the old houses are indeed very
large and could accommodate two or more families easily.

Toribio and Nicolasa, however, wisely retained ownership over one
of the doors to be sure that, come what may, the right of entrance to
the house would never be denied them. Recall how in our ethnographic
example three co-owners of the house had equal access to their respective
portions through the one set of main doors, though technically these
belonged to only one of the owners. The house of Toribio and Nicolasa
must have been set up in a similar way, except that rather than just
having use-rights over the entrance they had the more unquestionable
right of ownership. The logic seems to have been that if they owned
one of the main doors they had the right to go through it. For in the
fluid world of partible inheritance one could own a door without having
to own the house it opened onto; just as, in the opposite case, one could
own the house and not own the doors through which to enter it.

Now in the inventories of household and landed property, as has been
customary in Europe at least since medieval times, every item is not only
enumerated and described, but given a value in monetary terms. The
peasantry has never been a total stranger to the money economy of the
region and the nation. But what is more important in terms of this
argument is the extraordinary importance of money in the operation of

partible inheritance. As we shall see in the following pages, it is the translation of family property into conventional money values that makes its division into equal portions possible.

We noted in passing that Nicolasa was under an oligation to pay out 75 *pesetas* to her sister, Felipa, because she got the part of the house with "that much more frame." In other words, the measurement of the frame had been translated into money, so that the frame could metaphorically— that is, vis-à-vis money—be distributed equally. But besides money Felipa gets an oak. Why? We find the answer in an intriguing record of how the house's value was assessed:[9]

Frame of the house 45 feet at five *pesetas* a foot		225
Frame that goes around to where the roof slopes 47 feet measured from the *corral* at five *pesetas* a foot comes to		235
Roof slope of another 30 feet at 3 *pesetas* a foot at		90
Street doors at		50
Postigo (small door) at		6
Door of the small room at		6
Door of the hayloft		3
Door of the stable at one *peseta*		1
Door of the cellar at two *pesetas*		2
Door of the interior cellar		2 50
Door of the *prece-casa* at three *pesetas* and fifty *céntimos*		3 50
Door of the kitchen at same		3 50
Back door at		1
Door of the pigsty at 75 *céntimos*		75
Corral of this house at 50 *pesetas*		50
		679 25

Except for the *corral*, what is perceived to have value are the frame and the doors, in other words, those parts of the house that are made of wood. As we noted before, the houses are of mud wall; their natural condition is to moulder away and to return eventually to the dust from which they are made. The wooden frame and the beams support the weight of the house; they form the structure and skeleton. Mud and rocks for the foundations of the house are to be found in the landscape, to be had for the taking, but in the deforested lands of León and Castile wood has long been a commodity.[10] Our *labradores*, however, live in an area of extensive scrub forest, as the toponym of their village, of the "*monte*" or the woodlands, makes clear, where the sale of wood has long been an important source of supplementary income. So it is not surprising that it is wood—finely worked and finished of course, particularly the big main doors—that is perceived as having monetary value. It is the wood structure that symbolically represents the house.

But the enumeration of the doors, including even the low-priced door to the pigsty, is curious. Why are they all enumerated? Again in this instance I think it is necessary to look at the notions of property represented in such actions. As we saw earlier, Toribio and Nicolasa lived in a back portion of the house to which they had access through the house and *corral* of the people living in the front portion; they did so because they owned one of the main doors of the house. Owning the door, in true metonymic fashion, meant you had a right to go in and out of the house it opened onto. Similarly, in the assessment of the house, it is as if the doors stood metonymically in place of the rooms they open onto. The doors are the rooms.

Now it is clear just how it is that the house got divided into "equal" portions between Nicolasa and Felipa. They knew the front portion had "that much more frame" because they had measured the frame and calculated its value through a rate of worth per foot. You cannot literally give back "that much more frame," but you can give back a money equivalent of it. And since it is wood that is serving as the criterion of value, and Felipa's portion has less of the wood frame, it is not surprising that Felipa should thus also be given the best oak the family had in Las Cruces; an exchange of wood for wood.

In short, a recompense in money and kind brings the back portion into a balance with the front portion in the following way. The house is valued at 679.25 *pesetas*. Each portion would have to be for 339.6 *pesetas* for them to be equal. Nicolasa's portion of the house is valued at 439.75 *pesetas*. But she gives Felipa 75 *pesetas* in three installments, which leaves her with 364.75 *pesetas*. A good oak is worth about 50 *pesetas* and when this too is added to Felipa's portion it comes out equal to her sister's.

As a contrasting example of house assessment, we have the following case from the year 1888, which concerns the house of León Villapadierna, a fairly well-off *labrador* of the nearby village of Castro. His house was assessed as follows:[11]

The stable on the eastern side 24 feet at 5 *pesetas*	120
Cocina de horno and portal up to the *corredor* 24 feet at 6 *pesetas* a foot	144

The main kitchen, upper and lower levels, with the part of the *corredor* facing it 15 feet at 11 *pesetas* a foot	165
Ante-cocina, upper and lower levels, with the part of the *corredor* facing it 14 feet at 10 *pesetas* a foot	140
Stable for the oxen with its hayloft above, row of mangers and four chains 17 feet at 8 *pesetas* a foot	136
The hayloft next to said stable 18 feet at 9 *pesetas* a foot	162
The large main room with its wooden planks that are on top of the girders and the *corredor* with its planks and a window and picture frames in the main room 20 feet at 14 *pesetas* a foot	280
Interior large room and its door 14 feet at 12 *pesetas* a foot	168
The portal of the main doors including said doors	140
The *corral* assessed at	55 39

(Note: Total should be 1,535.75. This only adds up to 1,510.39. A page is probably missing.)

Here it is the rooms themselves of the house that are perceived to be its valuable features. Each room is measured and given a price in accordance with a hierarchy of values. It is difficult to tell exactly what the measurements refer to, but most likely the length of the room is serving as the basis for the calculations. The hierarchy of value per foot takes the following form:

1) At 14 *pesetas* a foot—the large main room (20 feet)
2) At 12 *pesetas* a foot—the interior large room (14 feet)
3) At 11 *pesetas* a foot—the main kitchen (15 feet)
4) At 10 *pesetas* a foot—the *ante-cocina* and the portal of the main doors (14 feet)
5) At 9 *pesetas* a foot—the hayloft (18 feet)
6) At 8 *pesetas* a foot—the stable for the oxen (17 feet)
7) At 6 *pesetas* a foot—the *cocina de horno* (24 feet)
8) At 5 *pesetas* a foot—the eastern stable (24 feet)

It is the human dwelling that is on top and the storage rooms and stables that are on the bottom, both literally and metaphorically. The two upper rooms are given more value per foot than the kitchen; their floors are of wood, and besides such rooms in this period are still some-

thing of a luxury in the house of a *labrador*. Again the big street doors
are given a high value, since these are elaborate structures made of thick
oak slabs, which require welding and an ironwork latch. The hayloft
comes next and it is accorded more value than the stables because it too
is on an upper floor; the stables and *cocina de horno* are on the bottom
floor and have a plain dirt ground and are rooms that require the least
amount of care in building and upkeep. In general the rooms on the
upper floor are on top, while those on the lower floor are on the bottom
of the hierarchy of values set up here.

How is the hierarchy set up? As we see, it is by a translation into
money. Here, as in the previous example, money is presupposed as an
objective correlative of value, whether it is the frame and doors of the
house or each room individually that are perceived to be of value. Certainly in this period the value of a house is more difficult to assess than
that of, say, a plot of land, which has a definite money value based on
its productivity. This is why we find a certain amount of variation, and
even confusion, in the way in which *labradores* assess the value of the
house.

On the other hand, land, like any other item in the house, or for that
matter the house itself, cannot really be said to be true commodities to
the *labrador* of this era. They are not objects of speculation sought out
with an eye toward profit-making, but those things that are needed for
subsistence and the continuance of life. In the accounting which the
transmission of the inheritance calls for, money serves as a purely symbolic mode of representation, by means of which the manifold categories
of property can be phrased in a common idiom, and thereby be rationally
and justly divided into equal portions. In the process of daily life and
work a translation into money was not usual or necessary; however, in
the key moments of property distribution it became essential.

The division of goods

Since we have already seen how the sisters, Nicolasa and Felipa Ferreras,
divided up the actual physical house of their parents, let us take a look
at how they split up some other items of property. We find, for instance,
in the inventory drawn up at the death of their father, this interesting
balance of payments:[12]

Nicolasa		Felipa	
The big jaunty cow	154	The chestnut cow	115
		A pig at	22 50
The stone trough	6	A cart with its wheel	22 50
	160		160 00

Although the sisters are not receiving exactly the same things, the portions are equal, as we see, in money terms—each side adds up to 160 *pesetas*. Money conventionally represents the equality that has been achieved by a careful balance of the weight of one side against the other. Nicolasa gets a better cow than Felipa, but she doesn't get the pig and the cart; but Nicolasa's portion would be a little less than Felipa's if she were to receive the cow alone, so she also gets the stone trough. In this way the scales are balanced. The two sisters divided up almost the whole of the parental inheritance in this manner.

Yet there are some categories of property of which they receive exactly equal portions, in kind and in money, as shown in the following example:[13]

Nicolasa		Felipa	
17 pounds of lard	12 50	17 pounds of lard	12 50
4½ *arrobas* of rye flour	9	4½ *arrobas* of rye flour	9
2 *arrobas* and 18 pounds of wheat flour	8 25	2 *arrobas* and 18 pounds of wheat flour	8 25
5 pounds of spun wool	7 50	5 pounds of spun wool	7 50
3 pounds of spun linen	2 25	3 pounds of spun linen	2 25
1 pound of spun burlap	35	1 pound of spun burlap	35
2 pounds to be spun at	50	2 pounds to be spun at	50
10 *arrobas* of potatoes	6 25	10 *arrobas* of potatoes	6 25
	68 22		68 22

The distribution of goods exemplified above virtually precludes a translation into money. Since the portions are exactly equal in kind there is no need really to translate them into an "objective" idiom of value. The translation into money here is not essential, it is routine.

Ideally the system calls for just this type of one-to-one correspondence between portions, with all the offspring receiving exactly equal shares of everything. The ideal can only be realized to an extent, of course,

and only with measurable items whose value and use is not adversely
affected by their division into a number of portions. Thus, food and
textiles, as in the above example, are divided into exactly equal portions
to go around for however many heirs there may be. Other items which
are conceived of as belonging to the same category as food and textiles
are the harvest of the family lands, the manure in the house and out in
the fields, and the family's trees and wood—all these things will always
be divided equally, even when many heirs are involved. Let us consider
for a moment the division of goods from this realm where an exact
equality reigns.

The harvest of the family lands, whether it has already been brought
into the house or is still out in the fields unreaped, is always included
as part of the *hijuela,* or inheritance portion, of each heir. In cases where
there is a surviving spouse, the widow or widower will usually be allotted
half of the product of the harvest, and the other half will be divided
among the offspring equally; where just the offspring are involved, the
whole is split between them.

For instance, we have the case of Nicolasa's husband, Toribio Mirantes,
whose father's property was split and distributed on 20 December, just
a month after his death in 1854. Not only is the produce of the previous
harvest distributed among the heirs, but a clause is added stating that
"mention has not been made of the cultivated fields that are sown and
have yet to be harvested, the part of which corresponds to this heir, once
the cost it entails has been verified and deducted, will be noted down
in this *hijuela.*" Come 2 September of the following year, the produce
of the sown land is computed, and from it is deducted the cost of labor,
the annual anniversary offering, and the various debts that have surfaced
in the course of the year, each heir receiving as his or her due share 7½
heminas of wheat and 13 *heminas* of rye.[14]

Similarly, when the inventory of property belonging to León Villapadierna of Castro is drawn up in March of 1888, the yield of the harvest
was not yet known. But again a few months later, once the harvest is
gathered, the share each heir receives "of the sown land that was pending"
is noted down at the end of his or her *hijuela.* The widow, María Gómez
Torices, received more or less half of the crop and the five offspring
received one-fifth each of the other half, or a tenth of the entire yield.
Thus, María Gómez Torices got 49 *heminas* of rye, 49 *heminas* of wheat,
and 6 *heminas* of oats, while each offspring received 9 *heminas* and a
celemín of rye, 10 *heminas* of wheat and 1 *hemina* of oats. From these

amounts they had already deducted "the cost of gathering it in barley and half of the oats."[15] All the barley that was gathered, which couldn't have been very much, and half of the oats thus went to those heirs who sowed and harvested the family lands as compensation, however meager, for their labor.

To the harvest all the heirs have a right, as we see, regardless of whether they have anything to do with bringing it home. In one inheritance record this notion of the harvest as something toward which the heirs have a "natural right" is nicely put in the phrase *"corresponde yjuelar a cada eredero de toda clase de pan."* To understand the meaning of these words, one should note first that the authors have coined a verb, *hijuelar*, to denote "to give an *hijuela*," and second that *pan* in this context does not just mean bread but all the harvested grains, in other words, the potential breadstuffs. To translate, then, roughly, "an inheritance portion is to be given to each inheritor of every class of bread." This includes for the three heirs a share of rye, wheat, another lower-grade wheat, barley, and oats. In the same list, interestingly enough, are included as corresponding to each heir, 4 carts of hay, 13 pounds of lard, a preserve jar, 2½ *cuartillos* of honey, 5½ *reales* worth of earthen pans and plates, 5 pounds of wool, and 3 carts of manure.[16]

In the division of the harvest among the heirs a few principles seem to be at work. One is that the harvest of the lands is still the property of the parent or parents at the time of death and thus should be counted in as part of the total family goods over which all the heirs have a right. Another is that the harvest is separable from the lands that produce it, and thus while each individual plot will not be split up equally among all the heirs, the total harvest should be. And last, there seems to be a certain symbolism in the idea that all have a right to the harvest of the family lands or, to put it in local terms, "to every class of bread." It takes the form of a "metaphorical extension" of the idea that no inheritor, no family member, should ever be denied his or her daily bread and sustenance.[17] In the old family-based subsistence economy of central León, where the harvested grains and crops and the produce of the pig raised at home were the basis of the diet, to have distributed such basic foodstuffs less than equally would have been tantamount to starving out a family member. For the harvest is at once the product of family land and labor and the means by which the family perpetuates itself.

This customary practice of dividing up the harvest continued well into this century in the villages of central León. It was an idea deeply rooted in the thinking of the *labrador*, as I have suggested, and one that was not easily done away with. One can readily understand how those offspring who sowed and harvested the land, usually just in return for their own sustenance, would resent an equal division of the entire yield for which they had sweated and worked, as we learn from the following story. A man from Villamayor married into Santa María and took up residence with his wife in the house of her father. His wife's other siblings had married out or were living in other houses in the village, so she was the only offspring left in the house of her father. Since this man and his wife were in her father's house, attending to him, they also worked all of his lands, the produce of which the husband, anyway, expected to keep. But his father-in-law, who had been married twice and had offspring from both marriages, died suddenly and the harvest had to be divided up equally. The husband was in a rage, but to no avail, that was the custom. This took place in 1941.

That the custom was still being followed ten years later is evidenced in a unique document that was drawn up by the household head, Basilio, of whom we spoke earlier, who reunited the house that his father originally inherited only a fraction of. In 1951 Basilio was living in his mother's house with his wife and daughters, as we have seen, and he was working all of his mother's lands, which were not to be divided until her death. He was well aware, of course, of the custom of dividing up the harvest. Knowing full well what could happen, he wrote out a document, which his mother appears to have dictated or at least approved of, to the effect that the harvest on the lands at the time of her death should remain his property and not be split up between all the siblings. This statement was signed by all the siblings or representatives thereof. As Basilio also knew, this piece of paper could have all the force of a legal document were disagreements later to arise.

The text in excerpted form reads as follows:

> First of all, for the work my son ... has been carrying out in the lands of my holding, without receiving a salary of any kind and only disinterestedly for his keep, it is my will to reward him, in that for the year after my death he should be enriched with what has been sown and harvested at that date and been gathered in my house ... and for that same period of one year ... all the *gananciales*, animals, and utensils of the house shall be the exclusive property of the son that has been working the lands.

After the formal closing of the document, stating the date, the place, and that all sign to express their agreement, an interesting afterthought is added: "also the hay from March onwards is counted in with the harvest and the sown fields."[18] The hay too was usually divided up between the siblings as part of the harvest and so that things would stand absolutely clear the addendum was wisely put in. Here we see, in short, the undoing of an old custom, which was clearly still so strong at the time that it could not have been undone without a formal written statement to sanction it.

As we noted earlier in the case of Nicolasa and Felipa, woolen and linen products were divided equally too, as these are also in a broad sense part of the yield of the family harvest. So too is the produce of the family pig and the meat of any other animal slaughtered at home. We find that at the death of León Villapadierna, for example, there was left in the house 3 *arrobas* of lard, 20 pounds of ham and shoulder pieces, 39 pounds of meat and bones of a he-goat and a pig, 16 pounds of sausages, and 100 *arrobas* (over a ton!) of white potatoes. The widow again received half of each of these food items and the five offspring a fifth each of the other half.[19] Even when such a distribution of food left each of the heirs with very small portions, it was still divided up. Thus when the mother of Toribio died in 1860 he received, as one of eight heirs, "the eighth part of the meat from the pig-slaughter, chickens, lard, and honey."[20]

Similarly, the manure in the house and out in the fields, an important by-product of the family animals and the source of nourishment of the land, was always distributed equally. There were, for example, twelve carts of manure altogether in and outside the house of León Villapadierna at his death, and of these his widow received six and the five offspring the other half. We have already seen how in a list of goods to be given to each inheritor, hay, lard, honey, wool, and three carts of manure were put in the same category of property that corresponded in kind to all.

In an area where wood was not only the basic energy source and crucial building material but an important source of supplementary income, it is not surprising to find that trees and wood are likewise given out in equal portions in kind and money. The pieces of cut wood lying about the house were easily split up among the heirs into equal portions, but the adjudication of the trees was usually a trickier matter, since they were often situated on plots of land belonging to other relatives.

For instance, in 1895 Saturnino Rodríguez of Santa María inherited from his mother twenty-four poplars "situated in the meadow of his uncle Tomás in Castro . . . which poplars he must split up without deceit with his three brothers and sister, Millán, Quintín, and Amancia." The four heirs inherited as well another nineteen poplars "situated in the meadow of their uncle Yldefonso in Castro," with the same stipulation to "*partir sin engaño*"—split up without deceit—a rhetorical incantation often sounded in these old records.[21] As these arrangements make clear, one could own the trees on a plot of land without owning the land on which they were planted and vice versa. This is a situation not unlike the one we saw earlier, where Toribio and Nicolasa owned one of the doors to the house but not the house through which they had to pass to reach their own.

In an earlier case from 1826, we find clearly expressed the separation that people made between the ownership of the trees on a plot of land and the ownership of the land itself. To Magdalena de Castro of Santa María were assigned the trees in the land that "went to her brother, Clemente, under the precise condition that they should be and remain in said land for all the time that their owner should deem necessary, as also occurs with others that Magdalena has in properties of said Clemente, which both are to conserve, the benefit of the pruning and felling of the wood going to the one to whom they have been adjudicated."[22]

In another case, which raises again the question of how money is used in the distribution of the inheritance, Toribio Mirantes receives his due share of an eighth part of the wood situated in the family fields. He is to receive "an eighth part of the wood in the family lands, thick and thin, of oak, poplar, and willow." But his share has been calculated in money terms. He is to receive this share of wood "under the condition that if the amount of 74 *reales* which corresponds to him exists in the fields he is inheriting then they shall be payed to him right there, and if they turn out not to have said amount, then in those of others, with the admonition that the wood that corresponds to one or another heir in the lands of another is to remain uncut until six years have passed."[23]

Toribio's 74 *reales* worth of wood, to which he had the same right whether on his or another sibling's land, brings us back full circle to the balance of payments we saw earlier involving the sisters, Nicolasa and Felipa. The first drew the lot for the better cow and stone trough, while the other ended up with the worse cow but also got a pig and a cart. In this distribution a translation into money terms gave the portions the semblance of equality. Most of the inheritance must, in fact, be distributed in this manner, for the majority of the goods, from tools, clothes, and cookware to livestock and land, if split up into exactly equal portions, like the harvest and foodstuffs, would be rendered useless and absurd. The degree of absurdity that can be reached is exemplified in the case cited by Lisón Tolosana in which a yoke was hacked in half so that each brother might inherit "his" part.

The example of how Nicolasa and Felipa distributed the two family cows can serve as the paradigm for the way moveable goods are distributed when there are not enough to go around equally in kind for all the heirs. In this category of property, as in all others, the ancient method of drawing lots is used to insure a just and fair division. Lots of equal worth must be devised, among which each heir chooses his or her "luck" (suerte). Although the ultimate decision as to who gets what is placed beyond the human realm, the making of equivalent—rather than equal—lots remains always the crucial human imperative.

The division of the land

When land is divided there is a weighing up of portions similar to that which took place with the jaunty cow, on the one hand, and the chestnut cow, on the other. But with the division of land the patterns are not as clearly discernible as they are with the division of the house or the harvest. There is great flexibility in the way the land is divided; no two families will follow exactly the same pattern. Where some will distribute the various types of land among the heirs without dividing too many of the plots themselves into pieces, others will choose to cut up a high proportion of the already tiny plots into yet smaller fragments to go around for all. Excluding the demographic factor, a number of internal factors influence the outcome, from the quality of the family's lands, to the nature of the relationships between family members, and even the temperament and personality of the participants often plays an important part in the degree of egoísmo, as people say, that is manifested in the division of the land.

However, in spite of the variations, two principles seem always to be present in the division of the land in all the cases, both past and present, which I have seen. The heirs divide up the land in such a way that each gets a few plots of every type of land, that is, some rye and wheat lands, some meadowlands and, if there are any, some irrigated and private

Chart 1

Type of land	No. of plots split in half	No. of whole plots to Nicolasa	No. of whole plots to Felipa
Woodlands	6	—	—
Wheatlands	4	3	2
Rye lands	8	9	12
Irrigated plot	1	—	—
Meadowlands	5	2	3
Totals	24	14	17

woodland. Each heir is always allotted roughly the same amount of every type of land. The underlying idea is that everybody should have a place to grow grain for their daily bread, a place to mow grass for cows, a place to plant four cabbages and four onions for the stew, and a place to cut firewood for the hearth.

Second, when the lands are split, it is always into exactly equal parts. For example, a land the size of 2 *heminas* will be split into portions of 1 *hemina* when there are two heirs, and into half-*hemina* plots when there are four heirs. When there are as many as, say, eight heirs, lands will be split between sets of two, three, or four siblings and again each of the parts will be of equal size.

For the sake of simplicity, and since we know so much already about how Nicolasa and Felipa split the house, the cows, the lard, and the wool, let us examine the division of the land between these sisters. The two women had fifty-five lands in total to work with from the parental inheritance. Of these there were six woodlands, nine wheatlands, twenty-nine rye lands, one irrigated plot, and ten meadowlands.[24] They split the lands as shown in the acompanying chart. All the plots of woodland, as chart 1 shows, were split in half between the two sisters. Earlier we noted that wood belongs in the same category as the harvests and food-stuffs, which were always distributed in exactly equal portions, the idea being that no heir should be denied so basic an energy source. Of course the yield of half a woodland is less than that of the original whole, but since it is land that is not worked, even a smaller plot provides a person with sufficient trees for firewood, building, trading, and selling.

With the wheatlands—which are accorded high value in this area of poor and rocky terrain where even wheat has trouble growing—the sisters seem to have made a compromise. They split four plots and the other five they distributed between themselves, Nicolasa getting three and Felipa two whole wheatlands. Thus in total Nicolasa received seven wheatlands and Felipa received six. The less valuable rye lands, of which there were so many, were not so subject to division: eight were cut in half, and Nicolasa got nine and Felipa twelve whole plots. This time Nicolasa's total of rye lands adds up only to seventeen while Felipa's adds up to twenty.

They split in half the only irrigated plot the family had, which was located in the highly valued area of La Viña that is composed of clusters of little kitchen gardens lying close to the nucleated settlement. The plot is miniscule to begin with—a mere quarter of an *hemina*—but the value of this little jewel, set at 75 *pesetas*, made it worth many times more than a quarter of an *hemina* of an average rye land, which they valued at 4 or 5 *pesetas*. Since it was the only irrigated plot the family had, it dutifully gets split into two portions, each an eighth of an *hemina* in size. The exaggerated fragmentation of La Viña, which is still clear today, attests to many similar divisions enacted in the past, and it is a cultural expression writ in land of the notion that each heir ought to receive a share of every category of landed property the family possesses.

With the meadowlands, which are also scarce in this area, the sisters compromised, as they did with the wheatlands, and divided half and distributed half undivided. In total Nicolasa got seven meadows and Felipa got eight. The meadowlands they do split in half are the best ones their parents possessed. They include two enclosed meadows, which in an area where open fields predominate are rare enough to merit special mention in the records. The other three meadows which were split were of high value and among them was a meadow situated in the nearby village of Castro, which at a 100 *pesetas* was the most valuable of all their meadows. Clearly neither sister could bear to give an inch where the best of their parents' property was concerned.

In short, we find in this case that with the more valuable lands a higher proportion are split, while the less valuable lands tend to be distributed between them. Nicolasa ends up with thirty-eight lands, valued at a total of 830 *pesetas*, and Felipa with forty-one lands, valued at 895 *pesetas*. These are not exactly "equal" portions, though they come close. We must keep in mind that Nicolasa had gotten the front portion of the house and the better cow, acquisitions that were brought into the accounting of the land. At stake we must always remember is the division of the house in the full sense of the term, which embodies the physical house and the goods within it, as well as the lands. Items from one category of property are weighed against those in another, so that in addition to using the idiom of money, it is the translation back and forth between various use-values that makes a system of "equal" inheritance possible.

The arrangements for the distribution of land between Nicolasa and Felipa represents an extreme of fragmentation which exists as one possibility within the equal inheritance system of León. For the sisters divide up a rather high proportion of the lands. They start with fifty-five parcels and end up with seventy-nine parcels, an increase of 44 percent in the total number of parcels. This is not at all an average rate of increase even for the year 1885, a period when the growth of population was putting unprecedented pressures on the land. We find in a case from 1895, involving the distribution of about the same number of parcels among four offspring, Saturnino, Quintín, Amancia, and Millán, whom we earlier encountered dividing up the family poplars, that there is just a 28 percent increase in the number of parcels.[25] Clearly the demographic pattern is not alone responsible for land fragmentation or the lack of it.

If the case of Nicolasa and Felipa, then, represents a propensity toward land fragmentation, that involving the division of land among the five offspring of Martín Mirantes in 1909 represents the other extreme of avoidance of fragmentation.[26] Admittedly the five offspring, Escolástica, Angel, Cosme, Teodora, and Luis, start out with more lands, a total of seventy-seven. Even so, they hardly split them up at all, as we see in chart 2.

Chart 2

| | No. of whole plots to: | | | | | No. of plots split: | | |
	E.	A.	C.	T.	L.	in half	in thirds	in fourths
Wheatlands	3	4	2	3	4	—	—	—
Rye lands	12	12	13	11	14	4	2	1
Meadowlands	2	2	1	3	1	—	—	—
Totals	17	18	16	17	19			
House-shares	1	1	1	1	1			
Moveable goods	—	—	all	—	—			
Livestock	1/3	1/3	1/3	—	—			

The five offspring do not split up the wheatlands or the meadowlands at all, but distribute them as whole plots among themselves. The wheatlands are given out more or less equally. Cosme only gets two, but Escolástica and Teodora get three each, while Angel and Luis get four each. With the meadows, there is a similar pattern of allotment. This time Luis, like Cosme, only gets one, while Escolástica and Angel each get two and Teodora gets three. Of rye lands, again, they get more or less the same amounts, this time Teodora gets the least, with eleven, while Escolástica and Angel each get twelve, Cosme thirteen, and Luis fourteen.

The rye lands, curiously, are the only lands they choose to split, four of which they split in half, two in thirds, and only one in fourths. The lands they split in half and in thirds were among the largest and most valuable, ranging in size from 1½ to 4 *heminas*, a good size in this area, and in value from 30 to as much as 180 *pesetas*, which is what their best rye land that was split in half was worth. The one land split into four parts, 2 *heminas* in size and priced at 20 *pesetas*, was not especially large or valuable, so it is hard to say why that land in particular was singled out for such severe division. What is, however, clear is that in this case the five offspring settled for a distribution of land that may not have produced altogether equal portions, but kept the family property more or less intact. It is significant that even those lands that were split were not pulverized into fifths, for example, to go around for all exactly equally, but split into halves or thirds. Although here they start with more land and there are five heirs involved, there was only a 14 percent increase in the total number of parcels.

In the distribution of the land it is Cosme who has gotten least of all. He only receives a total of sixteen plots, while Teodora and Escolástica get seventeen each, Angel gets eighteen, and Luis nineteen. But once again it is the house in the full sense of the term that must be considered in order to understand fully the equal inheritance process, and we find that it is Cosme who, on the other hand, is allotted all of the moveable goods, along with one-third of the livestock. Escolástica and Angel also get a third each of the livestock, while Teodora and Luis do not get any. We might have expected Teodora to get the livestock rather than Angel, but certainly not Luis, who has gotten the most lands, and thus does not need to be compensated with the moveable goods or the livestock. With respect to the inheritance, then, Luis is at the opposite end of the continuum from Cosme, and between them unfold the intermediate arrangements of their siblings. Again, a kind of balance is achieved between the portions and, as we see, though all the heirs do not receive a share of the moveable goods and livestock, none is left without a share of the house and some land in each of the three categories their parents possessed.

For an exactly equal distribution, each of their portions in money terms should have amounted to 587 *pesetas*, since the total value of the family property was set at 2,935 *pesetas*. In fact, the portions are equal within a range of ten *pesetas* more or less of the average, that is, not exactly equal, but certainly close to being so. Equivalences rather than exact equality was what this set of offspring sought and they achieved it in a manner that took money-values and use-values into account, and did not ravage the family property.

Chapter 5

✚

Parents and Children

WE HAVE been concerned up to now with the mechanics of partible inheritance in León, that is, with the related questions of what is inherited and how an equality of inheritance is achieved. It is time now to consider the broader social and cultural implications of the equal inheritance system and the problems and contradictions posed by it. For the inheritance system is profoundly affected by and in turn has profound effects upon the relationship between parents and children, on family structure and residence patterns, on the social structure, and on cultural conceptions of what kinship ought ideally to be like.

A tale of discord between the generations

To set the stage for a discussion of these topics I would like to begin with a story. It concerns a widow from Santa María del Monte who has grown too weak and old to take care of herself and is now the charge of her children. The story developed and took form in a conversation I had with two women from Santa María one autumn day as we sat in the kitchen warming ourselves by the woodstove.

They began by talking about how this widow, let us call her Filomena, had the bad fortune of not getting along with her daughter. When she became ill and could no longer fend for herself, the natural thing, the two women explained, would have been for her daughter to have taken her in and all would have been well. Filomena has three married sons also, but being with a daughter-in-law is not as good as being with one's own daughter, they told me. One of the women, let us call her Marina, citing a proverb, remarked, "mother and daughter can wear the same shirt but the daughter-in-law doesn't quite fit" (*madre e hija caben en una misma camisa y la nuera un poco más afuera*).

But in this case, mother and daughter did not fit either. When Filomena's daughter moved in with her temporarily some years ago, in itself an unusual turn of events, the daughter refused to do anything for her mother. She would wash her family's clothes in the washing machine she and her husband had installed, while her mother, who has rheumatism, had to go wash her own clothes by hand in the outdoor public washingplace (*caño*). Marina used to say to Filomena that she would wash her clothes for her, but how could she, what would people say, with her own daughter in the house (*teniendo la hija en casa, que diría la gente*). And Marina said that rumor had it that when Filomena's daughter swept the kitchen floor she only swept half of it, and left the other half for her mother to sweep.

I asked how this situation had developed. Marina said that Filomena and her daughter had an argument once about how much detergent to use to wash the clothes. Both Filomena's and her daughter's clothes were in the machine to be washed and Filomena said to her daugther that if she were washing she would only be using half as much detergent; with all the detergent her daughter was wasting she could wash twice as many things. Her daughter's temper flared and she told her mother that from now on she could wash her clothes herself, for she was not going to do it for her anymore. The separation of the activities of mother and daughter reached such a pitch that Filomena did not even use her daughter's gas stove, but heated water for herself in a little pot on the woodstove.

But surely such a turn of events was an overreaction, I said, to what was really no more than a normal mother's nagging. And Marina had to add that, well, relations had never been good in that family, and that the three brothers were no better than their sister. And the other woman, Josefa, joined in with the remark: "they're all a bunch of egotists." As soon as it became clear that Filomena could no longer fend for herself, her four children proceeded to strip her village house and distribute the booty among themselves. Marina and Josefa said that they had heard that one of Filomena's sons had removed the faucets and taken them with him to Bilbao, where he now resides with his wife and daughter. All the clothing and furniture were taken out of the house. Even the wiring was taken down so they wouldn't have to pay the modest fee to keep up the electricity.

When Filomena was in the hospital and the one son she has living in Switzerland came to see her—he was her last hope, since he is better off than his siblings—she asked that he stay overnight at the hospital with her. He said, no, he wouldn't, that he was on vacation, that his sister could stay with her if she wanted to. That was that; and he hasn't done anything for her since. Even so, Filomena says she would never deny him his share of the family inheritance, for he is a son all the same.

Both Marina and Josefa agreed that the only reason the other offspring have bothered to take Filomena in is because they get her entire pension check while she is in their houses. So the three offspring have devised a system whereby they circulate their mother and she spends four months with each one. In this way they take turns caring for her, since none wants the full responsibility of caring for her permanently. As Marina and Josefa said, and other people have noted as well, Filomena goes from house to house *a corrida*. The same term is used in communal contexts to speak of such things as the circulation of water rights in irrigation, or the passing from one house to another of an image of the virgin that was donated to the village, for all to have her in their houses for a time. To pass rights and goods around in an interhouse or social network is a legitimate form of achieving social order widely used in this society. But to go so far as to pass around a mother in this way is viewed as a pathetic sign of discord between the generations. When Filomena returned in the summer with the son living in Bilbao, who keeps a house in the village for holiday visits, Josefa asked her whether her children didn't at least give her a little pocket money. After all, what if she wants to give a *propina* (a tip or gift) to her grandchildren, or simply have some money of her own. Filomena's eyes welled up with tears as she said, "I don't see a cent."

I asked Marina and Josefa whether Filomena had been such a bad mother; had she somehow deserved such terrible treatment from her children? The answer came almost at once. About Filomena's character, they said that she was always very independent, very set in her ways, always wanting things done her way. And, they had to admit, Filomena herself had not been very good to her own parents or to her in-laws. It was especially her failure as a daughter-in-law which my storytellers underlined, and wove into a tale about inheritance—not the inheritance of property or material goods, however, but the inheritance of a festering sickness at the root of the family.

The pattern of discord between parents and children displayed in the treatment of Filomena by her offspring had a precedent in the treatment

of Filomena's father-in-law by his children. He had given his children
his lands to work, because he was old and could no longer work them
himself. He had expected to receive in return a fixed share of the harvest
for his own support, as was customary. But his children refused to give
him anything. He then took them to court in the hope of settling the
matter. But his children claimed they had made only a verbal agreement
to work their father's lands and it was their right to refuse to work
them any longer. So the dispute ended, with the poor man in the same
position as before, and with court fees to pay.

Later on, Filomena and her husband lived with her old parents-in-
law in their house. The old man was sick in bed by this time, though
no one knew exactly what ailed him. After the dispute with his children,
Josefa and her husband, Lorenzo, worked the old man's lands and paid
him a proper rent. Taking pity on the old man, Lorenzo used to bring
him firewood and visit him often. One day the old man confided in
Lorenzo and showed him his sickness. He had cancer, as Josefa put it,
in his parts (*en sus partes*). There was no remedy for it, as Lorenzo had
found out from the doctor, who said that nothing remained to be done
but to keep the man clean and comfortable.

And this Filomena did not do. Her horrible neglect announced itself
to the entire village when her father-in-law finally passed away. Shortly
before his death Josefa had visited the old man. He was in bed and she
tried to cheer him up by asking whether he would be up and about
soon. Before she could blink an eye he had lifted up the blankets. It was
all eaten away (*estaba comido todo*), blackened and worn like the bottom
of this pan, Josefa recollected, as she set it out to dry. When village
women came to shroud the body they found, in the words of Marina,
"fly shit, maggots, in his penis" (*cagada de mosca, cocos, en el pico*). His
sore was breeding maggots, that's how filthy he was, Marina reiterated,
summing it up thus: good goes far, evil farther (*el bien vuela, el mal
trasvuela*). There is a cruel but poetic justice in the mistreatment of
Filomena by her children; as our storytellers put it, "this already comes
from before" (*eso ya viena de antes*).

This remarkable tale has all the elements of a mythical social charter.
It is not, to be sure, an account of ordinary relations between parents
and children. On the contrary, it is a symbolic rendering of an extreme
version of those relations. Though it occurs but rarely, it is nonetheless
a possibility in this society when its cultural conceptions of what kinship
ought ideally to be like are turned upside down. As the story shows,

once this extreme is reached it is self-perpetuating: the cancerous nature of parent-child relations is passed down through the generations, inherited along with the house, the goods, the lands. People will often speak of a family in which parents and children alike are mean and selfish as being *de mala raza*, literally of a bad race or caste. In other words, family character is itself viewed as an inherited trait.

The tale revolves around the question: what do children owe to their parents, and by extension, to their parents-in-law? In the story told here, it is clear that the offspring feel they owe nothing, there is no debt to be repaid as far as they are concerned; this was no less true, as we saw, of Filomena than of her own children. In the view of the women telling the story, it is precisely the lack of a sense of moral indebtedness that is at the root of the sickness in that family. Filomena's egotism and neglect of her father-in-law is repaid in like coin by her children when she herself reaches old age—what she gave is exactly what she receives.

This is the gist too of the medieval tale of *Handlyng Synne*, which Homans cites in his work on thirteenth-century English rural life. The tale tells of a father who retires and passes his land on to his son. The son subsequently takes a wife and brings her home, beseeching her to treat his father well. Time passes and the son, himself now a father, falls behind in the care of his father, who has become a burden to him. In a symbolic gesture, the young grandson foreshadows what sort of "inheritance" awaits his father:

> At last, when his father was shivering with cold he bade his young son cover him with nothing more than a sack. The boy cut the sack in two, covered his grandfather with half of it, and showed his father the other half, to signify that just as his father had mistreated his grandfather, so the boy himself when his turn came would mistreat his father in his old age and cover him when he was cold with only half a sack.[1]

In the view of Homans, this tale could not have been an account of actual relations between fathers and sons. Fathers as a rule willingly passed their lands on to their sons when they reached old age, and surely they would not have done so if such rough treatment was always what awaited them in return. Even so, this is a cautionary tale of what can happen when, as in the early transmission of inheritance, the natural order of things is "reversed . . . by making fathers subject to their children."[2] This tale, like the one I heard in Santa María, is a meditation on an extreme which is atypical, and yet somehow indwelling, in the structure of rural family relations. The extremes which find expression in the two tales call our attention to the ambivalence that, across the centuries, is seen as inherent in these relations.

The sustenance owed to parents

This ambivalence in rural León is founded in a sense that relations between parents and children ought ideally to be unforced and disinterested when in fact they are often contractual and tainted with self-interest. Mauss had noted in the first paragraph of his famous essay on the nature of gift exchange that: "in theory such gifts are voluntary but in fact they are given and repaid under obligation."[3] In his conclusion he returned again to this idea of ambivalence in the gift as "a notion neither of purely free and gratuitous prestations, nor of purely interested and utilitarian production and exchange; it is a kind of hybrid."[4] Relations between parents and children in rural León, and perhaps in most old agrarian societies, are marked by just this kind of complex ambivalence: they are at once giftlike and contractual, a hybrid of the two.

In León, the hybrid character of these relations is clearly seen in the traditional custom whereby children provided a yearly "gift" of rye and wheat to their elderly retired parents for their support in exchange for being allowed to work their lands. The conventional amount of grain given consisted of twelve *cargas* for both parents, six for one parent, regardless of the quality and number of lands the parents possessed. In my various conversations on the subject with villagers of the area, who had themselves once provided this customary allotment to their parents, I discovered that this support is, indeed, conceived of as a gift freely given. I would ask: but wasn't this really a kind of rent you paid your parents in exchange for being allowed to work their lands? The answer was always that it was not rent, that it was not like paying rent to your parents. And I would persist: if it was not rent, then what was it? It was something you gave your parents for their support since you were now working their lands; this was how one woman put it. Or, in the words of one of my best informants, it was an *obsequio*—a gift.

Though viewed as a gift, it was one that was fixed in value and expected from the offspring as a matter of obligation, like the fulfillment of a contract. Thus when Filomena's father-in-law did not receive from his children the share of the harvest from his lands which, according to custom, they were under obligation to pay him, he felt he was in the right in taking them to court. But when the matter was taken to court the old man learned that his children were under no obligation to him—for how could the law enforce the payment of what is supposed to be a gift? Legally the arrangement was not a contract binding on the offspring. Where the law was concerned they owed their father nothing.

Custom, of course, decreed otherwise. And in most cases it was not challenged. But on this occasion, when it was, we discover that the customary support owed to parents by their children was not always freely given. In fact the terms of the support were sometimes stipulated in a written contract. Yet there is a great unwillingness to admit contractual types of relations into the domain of the family. Thus it seems inappropriate, even contradictory, to speak of the traditional support as a kind of rent. Trust, cooperation, and help freely given with no thought of interest or recompense ought to reign in the household, not the contractual sale, rental, and purchase of the marketplace. As Freeman observed in her work with villagers of the Old Castilian province of Soria, "families do not like to discuss contracts between members of the household. They consider such arrangements necessary, but somehow not ideal characteristics of parent-child relations."[5]

In the Leonese village, unlike the English champion village of the thirteenth century or the Galician village of the present day, the family inheritance was rarely passed on before the death of one or both parents. Once the parents reached old age and were too infirm to support themselves, they often lent out their lands and other property to their children. What the children gained in exchange for the customary parental tribute was thus the usufruct—or use-rights—over certain of the family lands, never the absolute right of ownership, which the surviving parent or parents retained.

A written contract from 1889 involving the widow, María Rodríguez of Santa María, and her only daughter, Leonor Sánchez, states that the widow is to keep fifteen lands, the threshing ground, and a large tract of private woodland which belonged to her husband, Angel Sánchez. "Said properties," the document reads, "are subject to the payment of an appropriate rent to the widow María Rodríguez in the capacity of *sufruto*." The neologism, *sufruto*, is a local reinterpretation of the Spanish term *usufructo*, from the Latin *usufructus*. "*Usufructo*" here becomes "*sufruto*" or "*su fruto*," in this case "its fruits," that is, the fruits or produce of the land, which are seen as owing to the widow. To earn their part of the usufruct, Leonor Sánchez and her husband, Pedro Ribero, agree to pay the widow on the 30th of September of every year "as long as said María lives, in the capacity of rent for the *sufruto* of the properties . . . six *heminas* of mixed grain wheat and rye, and one *hemina* of *titos* [a kind of chick pea], and 25 *pesetas* in coin."[6]

In a more recent document, from 1953, a prosperous widow from Santa María distributes the greater part of the family lands to her four offspring for them to hold in usufruct during her lifetime. In exchange the offspring promise in a notarized document to provide their mother with the following every year: "340 kilos of wheat . . . at 85 kilos per child; 336 kilos of rye at 84 kilos . . . per child; 132 kilos of barley each year and each child at 33 kilos; 108 kilos of oats at 27 kilos per child and each year . . . ; 16 kilos of red beans . . . at 4 kilos per child and each year; 12 kilos of chick peas at 3 kilos a child . . . and 4,400 *pesetas* in cash . . . at 1,100 *pesetas* each child and each year."[7]

The grains and the beans, which altogether add up to the conventional rate of six *cargas* per parent, were to be clean, dry, and ready for storing and consumption. It was also written into the contract that if the widow found these amounts insufficient or if she needed more aid from her children in case of illness, the offspring would pay whatever other costs arose. Only if they complied with their end of the bargain would the lands and goods which the widow gave to her children in usufruct become their property after her death. The widow retained the right to disinherit any of the offspring who failed to fulfill his or her promise to support her. Not that any of them failed to do so, or would have done so, as the youngest daughter of the widow, herself a widow now, said when she showed me this document. But, she explained, her mother was in the vulnerable position and could have lost everything; the written contract was her security.

It was to avoid an outcome such as befell Filomena's father-in-law that the customary parental tribute was sometimes inscribed in a contract. Villagers understood very well the legal power of the written word. But it would be misleading to say that a written contract was always felt to be necessary in these transactions. Filomena's father-in-law, to his regret certainly, made no written arrangement with his children, and this was true of a good many parents. For ideally, just as parents had supported their children and brought them up in the world, it was incumbent upon children to do the same for their parents once they were old and helpless.

Significantly, the "gift" or customary tribute that children gave their parents for the usufruct of their lands consisted always of a large component of basic foodstuffs, mainly grains and, as we saw above, a bit of money perhaps as well. Rents involving nonkin were normally paid wholly in money by the close of the nineteenth century, and certainly by the middle of the twentieth money rents were well established in the rural economy of León. But between parents and children—the closest of kin—it was still the rule until very recently to avoid pure money rents at all costs. As late as 1953, the obligation still consisted in providing for the parent's subsistence, in passing wealth over to them which was primarily for consumption, not for exchange.

A share of the actual fruits of the land—*su fruto*—was what pertained to parents, just as it was this which the children obtained from the land. The custom was thus one of sharing in the usufruct. In a sense, then, the foodstuffs that children gave to their parents was indeed a "gift." For the children put in the labor and made the expenditures which were necessary in order for the land to bear fruit, and their parents received a share of those fruits, as it were, for free. This was a tribute in the style of the old medieval feudal dues or "first fruits" owed to the church.

In the tale of Filomena, there are two interesting ironic reversals of this traditional pattern. Filomena's husband and his siblings rebel against the idea of providing a customary support for their parents. They give them nothing. Where Filomena and her own children are concerned, it is she who must give her pension check over to her children in order to pay for her keep. In the urban setting in which her children live they could not be expected to provide a gift of food to her, but they do not even give her a penny of her own pension check. The relationships in this family are based on blatant self-interest; there is no mediation whatsoever of kinship ideals, not even a pretense of using the idiom of the gift. Business is business, the children of both generations are not ashamed to say, in the family domain too.

Equal inheritance and the care of the aged

The case of this family is an extreme one. But it points to the fundamental problem, which was of particular importance in the old rural society, of how the parent or parents were to be cared for in their old age. As I noted earlier, the way in which Filomena is passed around from one offspring to another is condemned by villagers, who look in horror at the implantation within the family realm of a social ordering principle of circulating goods and rights. A parent should ideally be settled in one house, with one child, and not be forced to roam about from house to house like an itinerant beggar.

This preference as regards the residence pattern considered most suitable for an elderly parent in a sense puts into question the whole system of equal inheritance. For it is sometimes the case that the child who cares for his or her parents, or aids them most in tending to the fields, is rewarded with a greater share of the inheritance than the other offspring. This is "only fair," as people readily recognize, but the other offspring are always bitter when they learn of how their sister or brother has been favored.

The provision of a customary tribute to the elderly parents, in which all the children shared equally, militated against the possibility of favoritism. Looked at from this perspective, the way in which Filomena is passed around among her children is a similar mechanism for insuring exact equality. But it is a flawed mechanism. The son in Switzerland, who is not participating in the rotation of his mother, will also get his "equal" share of the inheritance, since Filomena refuses to favor any of her children. People say that if Filomena were to make a bequest of an extra plot of land to her daughter or promise to leave her the house, she would surely take her in on a permanent basis. But Filomena remains stubbornly attached to the idea of equality. So instead, as people say, she is treated equally badly by all her children.

There is a tradition in León of giving to that child who provides assistance to an elderly parent the village house, or at least a larger portion of it than to his or her siblings. For example, in 1749 Pedro Díaz of Santa María made this bequest to his son, Tomás: "for the great affection he had for him and for having assisted him in his old age" he gave him "four beams of the house starting from the oven in the house's lower part, and two *cargas* of rye, a cart, an ox, and a shaggy cape."[8] Pedro Díaz also made less elaborate bequests to his granddaughters, Antonia and María, and to his daughter-in-law, Lucía Juárez, the children and wife, respectively, of his other son, Alonso, who was left as heir of the rest of the family property with his brother, Tomás. But clearly Tomás, who gave of his time and labor to his father, was favored with an extra share of the inheritance.

To this day, the child who takes on the responsibility of caring for the elderly parent or parents is usually rewarded with the house. In a case which I observed, an old widow passed on to her youngest daughter, in whose charge she had been for many years, the family's spacious village house with its adjoining garden. This widow also left behind two other daughters and two sons. She had asked to be buried in Santa María and so was brought back on her deathbed from Gernika, where she had been residing with her daughter and son-in-law for the last fifteen years. She died at the close of 1980. Just five days later I chanced to hear one of her daughters-in-law discussing the unequal distribution of the inheritance.

"Everything is for Gabriela, the house, the portal, the garden, everything for Gabriela."

"Really," her two companions responded, "we always thought it would be *a mitades*" [split in half].

"No, no, and they all knew it too, except Jorge [her husband] and Petra [another daughter]."

"And she doesn't have any children," one of her companions noted regarding the favored sibling. "She should just have the house for her days and then it should return to all of you and to your children."

The attachment to the idea of an egalitarian distribution is so strong that a compromise is usually made in these cases: the child who provides assistance to the elderly parent gets half of the house, usually the living quarters, and the other siblings a share in the other half, which usually consists of the stables. In this case the daughter got the whole house, not just half, in what her sister-in-law considered to be a conspiratorial move. So it seemed to her as if everything was to be for this daughter, although in fact the goods and the lands are to be split equally among all the siblings. The fact that the favored daughter has no children makes the distribution seem especially unfair: why does she need such a large house just for her husband and herself? Since she has no heirs of her womb, a provision should have been made for the house to return to the family trunk after her death, so it would not be lost forever to the fruitful lines of descendents.

The "gift" that a parent gives to the child who provides assistance in old age need not necessarily be a house, however, though it is increasingly becoming so among a population that is losing its old rural orientation. In the past it was also common for a mother to leave a daughter who had assisted her the whole of her wardrobe of better clothes and a bed with its linen, pillows, and spread. She might also leave her an irrigated kitchen garden, so often associated with the feminine domain, to work with the hoe, as Froylana Díez did at the turn of the century. She left to her daughter, Valentina, all these things *"por sus asistencias"* (for her assistance).[9]

Yet more common still in the past was to give the whole of the usufruct of the lands over to that child who took in the elderly parents. This may well have been an earlier form of the practice of distributing the usufruct among the offspring, in which all contribute equally to the support of their parents. In an example from 1725 of this perhaps more archaic pattern, we find Joseph Martínez, widower from the lowland village of San Justo de las Regueras, giving the usufruct of all his goods and lands to one of his sons, Matheo, to have and hold during his lifetime, on condition that he look after Joseph's health and sustenance. Or, in the terms of the notarized agreement:

> ... being old, nearsighted, and suffering from frequent lapses which prevent him from working and maintaining himself by farming as he has done until now ... and seeing that he has much affection for Matheo Martínez his son ... agrees to pass on to him the benefit and use of all his property ... for him to hold ... and have in usufruct during the lifetime of the grantor ... with the condition that his son is to feed him in the custom and style of yonder place, and look out for his tidiness, cleanliness, lapses, and illnesses, without the grantor or any other person being able to ask Matheo Martínez for rent of any kind on account of the lands and the livestock, for he figures what they can render will be no more than the cost of supporting him.[10]

Looking out for the elderly parents' personal cleanliness and hygiene was a central part of all these exchanges, past and present, between the old and the young. The metaphor for Filomena's failure as a daughter-in-law was the wound that had grown so dirty it was breeding maggots. Even a devoted daughter, however, is capable of losing her patience with elderly parents who can no longer control their bodily functions. One woman told me of how she had taken her ninety-year-old father away from a sister in whose care he had been and brought him to her own house because of just such a loss of patience. When she went to her sister's house one day she had found her father crying. She had asked,

"Why do you cry, Father?" And he had replied, "I dirtied myself and Veronica scolded me. And she changed me in the courtyard and I got cold and she wouldn't let me come in and warm myself by the fire." The guilty sister, regretting her actions, afterwards wanted to take him back, but to no avail. The father remained in the house of the daughter who had come to his rescue until his death a few months later.

It is significant, returning now to our historical example, that old Joseph Martínez put in a clause stating that his son was not to be held responsible for providing a rent of any sort to him for the properties he was giving to Matheo in usufruct. For even the whole of his estate, as the old man realized, could not have yielded enough to pay "rent" and cover the costs of maintaining him. We must always remember that these arrangements of the past were made by peasants who at best were at the bare subsistence level. Here we find another resonance with the idea that it is inappropriate to conceive of the support provided to parents of basic foodstuffs as a kind of rent. In an economy as poor in resources as this one, the rent that offspring could have paid their parents for working their lands would have been quite minimal. But in providing for their parents' subsistence needs they gave them as much as the land could render, they gave what was above and beyond the minimum; in this sense too what they gave was a gift.

Until the middle of this century it was the custom for all the children to work for the house for several years after marrying. But it frequently happened, especially in households consisting of a widow and her children, that one child stayed on in the house longer than the rest: the eldest child to help care for the younger siblings, the youngest child to keep the house afloat after the departure of the elder siblings. Thus the widow Manuela Salas of Santa María, at her death in 1750, leaves to her eldest son, Joseph, "a house with its attached plot ... for having assisted her and worked for her and helped to raise his siblings."[11]

Or in the opposite case, another widow, Micaela Juárez, at her death in 1833 leaves to her youngest son, Mateo, who as a minor had stayed on in the house with his mother after the older children had departed, the following: the kitchen, *plaza de casa*, the granary, and that part of the *corral* which corresponds to him as one of four heirs; several yards of fabric, two shirts, a calf, a yoke with its strap and thong; half of a meadow in the village of Barrio which he was to split with his brother, José, and half a *carga* of wheat and one *carga* of rye. These gifts or *mandas* (bequests) she leaves to him

... on account of the *soldadas* [wages, earnings] for the time he has
been with me and on account of the yields and rents which I owe
to him for the *hacienda* [estate] which I have been holding in trust
for him, this is to be so if said my son does not ask for or demand
soldadas, yields, and rents, for if he should ask for them none of
the above-mentioned *mandas* will be granted him, and he is to enter
the said house through the main doors.[12]

She gives him all this, even assures him of his rightful entrance to his
part of the house, which must have been in back, but not without asking
for something in return: that he have a responsary said for her on all
the holy days for a period of one year, "for that is my will" (*pues es asi
mi voluntad*).

The remuneration Micaela Juárez provides her son, and the conditions
under which she does so, are particularly revealing as to local conceptions
of repayment among close kin. As we see, she was holding lands and
other property in trust for her son, which he had inherited from his
father who died when the boy was still a minor. Thus until he came of
age his mother benefited from the usufruct of his lands and should have,
according to customary practice, paid him a rent for those lands consisting
of a share of their yield. Toribio Mirantes, whom we have met before,
was paid just such a rent by his elder siblings, who worked the lands
he inherited from his father in 1855 when still a minor. In 1858, he and
two other brothers come of legal age and Toribio is paid 10.5 *heminas*
of rye for rent from his rye lands, 5 *heminas* of wheat for rent from his
wheatlands and irrigated plot, and 70 *reales* for rent from his meadows,
though for a period of only two years, since, as his siblings say, "at
present we do not calculate a rent since the grass is held now by said
Toribio."[13]

Toribio was paid straightaway by his siblings as soon as he came of
age, while Mateo's repayment, which was not so easily calculated, was
longer in coming. It is significant that Mateo received the yields and
rents of his lands together with his wages (*soldadas*) for working for the
house in a kind of package deal of his mother's devising, over which he
dared not have haggled lest he lose it all. In this way his mother bestowed
upon him the "gift" that would crown all his labors, and to be sure he
would be worthy of it she did so in a last will and testament, rather
than during her lifetime. And this package she prepared for him did
not come "without strings attached" for it was her will that it be recip-

rocated with the *cargo* (charge or credit) of a return gift—the responsaries her son was to have said for her.

Mateo, to be sure, did not work for his mother for nothing; he got his wages. But they were "wages" in a different sense than the strictly calculated money wages of our day. From the Old Testament we know that a man's labor could earn him a wife, or two, as it did Jacob. Mateo's labor earned him those things that constituted wealth in the peasant context, the house, the calf, and the meadow, and, ultimately, it earned him a wife too, for he married just six months after his mother's death.

In setting up house Mateo must have fared extremely well, for when he married in 1834 he not only had the special bequests his mother left him, but also his rightful inheritance as one of four heirs. His work for "the house" had laid the foundations of his own house. He had a house to which to bring his bride, half a work-team to plow his lands in the calf his mother had left him, a yoke and tools, fabric and seed, and, most important of all, some lands with which to sustain his potential family. This was much more than most newlyweds started off with in the Leonese village community of the past.

Chapter 6

✛

Setting Up House

THERE IS a popular saying that parents-in-law (or, less frequently, parents) are like potatoes, for they do not bear fruit until they are underground (*los suegros son como las patatas, no dan fruto hasta que estan bajo tierra*). This is a reference to the timing of the devolution of inheritance, which in León generally did not take place until at least one parent or even both had died. By this time the offspring were usually married and had formed families of their own, without the benefit of a share of the inheritance to support their fledgling houses. For, in fact, there was little parents could do for their children to help them set up house. They usually needed the family property for themselves to support their own houses, and only in their old age, in the rare cases where they retired, could they afford to let go of it.

In this practice of late transmission a certain mistrust of children found expression. For parents could never be sure whether their children would take care of them in their old age once the inheritance had been distributed, a concern that is still expressed today. The inheritance was their security against the possibility of being divested of house and property by their children, and ending up shivering in a corner like the old father of the thirteenth-century tale.

Micaela Juárez repaid her son, Mateo, what she owed him after her death. This was how it was in most cases. The regeneration of the system, thus, hinged upon the death of the parents. Psychologically this is not an easy social reality to bear. It is for this reason, one supposes, that people prefer to use the referent "parents-in-law" in the sardonic simile cited above rather than "parents." As I was told, this would be *muy feo* (ugly, in bad taste). After all, who would want to wish their parents dead? And yet the folk saying does not lie, they had to be dead to yield fruit for their children and their children's children.

The life of newlyweds

How, then, were offspring able to lay the foundations of their own houses without the immediate aid of the inheritance? To begin with, by continuing to work for the parental house after marriage.[1] Husband and wife each lived in their respective parental houses, worked for their houses, ate in their houses, were clothed and supported by their houses. Only at night were they reunited, when the husband went to his wife's house and they slept together in their matrimonial bed. Since the parents could offer their children little material help, and the children, who had always worked for the house, had no independent income of their own, they simply stayed on in the parental house until such a time as they could set up an independent household. This pattern persisted well into the middle of this century and is vividly remembered by the generation of people now in their forties and fifties. A village woman described her style of life in the early years of her marriage:

I spent six years at my father's and he here . . . here with his mother [a widow] . . . and a brother who was married who was also here, until later on when his mother died and I came down here . . . and that's the way it was with most of us. . . . In my father's house there were two recently married couples, my sister, Dosinda and Cornelio [her husband] sleeping there, and my sister, she died, the one who was married to Baudilio . . . and then my parents and I still there married. Because here there was another brother and his wife and the mother. . . . Since they were here I was there. . . . There weren't enough houses. . . . Since she was here with the mother of my husband, well, I don't know, you almost didn't want to either, what if you don't get along, maybe you come down and then you don't get along with the sister-in-law . . . so you waited to see. . . . And also since my sister had died, there were hardly any women there, just Dosinda, and when my parents died she went there to Cornelio's. . . . You know, Froilán [another villager] was at his father's house for eight, nine years and she with her mother. I have heard

him say it many times, "For eight, nine years I was living in my
father's house, after marriage, and she in her mother's house."[2]

That this residence pattern during the early years of marriage was
widespread in León is evident in the responses to the Ateneo questionnaire from the turn of the century. In places as far apart from each other
in the province as Roderos, Virgen del Camino, Laguna de Negrillos,
and Villablino, one finds great continuity in the observance of this practice. (See Appendix C for map of distribution of responses.)

The response from Roderos indicates that the young couple stayed in
the house of their respective parents for about six years "and after this
period they left the house, especially if their parents had other offspring
to marry." The response from Virgen del Camino in central León points
out that when both bride and groom come from families that have some
capital then each stays in the house of their respective parents. But in
those cases where one of the two will bring little capital to the marriage,
then the new husband or wife goes to work for the house of the one
who has capital, "in this way the parents and the couple save on a hired
assistant."

Similarly, the response from Laguna de Negrillos notes the pattern
of husband and wife living separately for a time in each of their parents'
houses, adding that during this period "they sow some lands for themselves and with what they produce they start to live when they leave."
Finally, the response from Villablino tells us that "at the same time as
they keep on working [for the house] as if they were single, they work
a few small plots which their parents give them, and what these lands
produce is for them, which in the course of a few years amounts to a
small capital." Those who live like this, the respondent noted, are called
baragañeros, the meaning of which remained a mystery to him, since all
he could find out was that baragaña is used to refer to land that is poor
and unproductive and thus little valued.[3] We will consider the meaning
of this term shortly.

These turn-of-the-century responses indicate that the married offspring worked for the houses of their parents, and in return earned a
part of the produce of the family lands. Thus, by continuing to work
for the general benefit of "the house," they gained at the same time,
from the usufruct of the plot or two of land that their parents gave them,
the means by which to form in due time their own houses. And as the
years passed and they built their houses up, they were, so to speak,

expelled from the house to make room for the younger children, as they too came of age and married. The pattern of separate residence was one stage in the family life cycle, as the response from Roderos made clear. It postponed the consolidation of the new family and in turn kept the parental house whole. This would have been true even in those less frequent cases where the poorer spouse came to live in the house of the one of better means, for in the end it was the parental house that was fortified.

Quite a different matter was just how much the parents could afford to give their newlywed children even in usufruct without their own houses threatening to topple down. Due to the cultural preference for treating all children equally, the marriage of the offspring placed a severe strain on the family property. The strain became especially severe toward the end of the nineteenth century and into the middle of this century, when unprecedented population growth doubled and tripled the previous average family size. As a result newlyweds had to turn to other sources besides the family property to be able to gradually build up their own houses. Theirs was a life of toil, hardship, and sacrifice. As a villager put it: "My wife and I married like someone who has nothing. And then we started to work and work and work and to save." (*La mujer y yo nos casamos como aquel que no tiene nada. Y luego empezamos pues a trabajar a trabajar y a trabajar y a ahorrar.*)

Newlyweds rented lands which retired villagers could no longer work, or which the occasional childless couple found too difficult to manage themselves. What was most frequent was to work *de a medias*, literally meaning "by halves," in a sharecropping agreement. Another *labrador* provided the seed, the land, and the tools and in return got half of the total yield, while the young couple, who put in all the labor, kept half of what they produced. The remarks of the village woman we heard from earlier express the distaste of the Leonese *labrador* for working under this arrangement:

My parents had eleven children, all of them they raised by dint of work, by cutting heather in the woodlands, by renting out lands *de a medias*. . . . To Gallegos [8 kilometers away], how many times did I not hear my mother say, that they would go there to weed potatoes, out there; they rented out a plot of land *de a medias*. And how many times did I not hear Aunt Perpetua, who was an aunt of mine, she used to say, "*Las medias* [playing on the second meaning

of the word, which is "socks"] are good for the feet, dear, but not
to give half to the owner." She often said this, "They're good for
the feet, socks, but not to give away half." She held a plot that
produced beans and a half of it for the owner and she only got half
and had to put in all the work, the sweat it cost them, and the
owner got the fruit all clean.[4]

The newlywed couple truly built its house up on borrowed goods.
What they had was the produce of a plot or two of land that their
parents had allowed them to work for themselves, and their half-share
of the produce of the land that they might obtain by working for nonkin
a medias. But the most important source from which newlyweds, above
all, borrowed was the community. In villages such as Santa María where
there existed a large component of communal woodland and/or arable
land, the young couple practically built their house on the back of the
community.

For in these villages once a man took a wife he was entitled to become
a *vecino*, a village citizen, with full rights to a share of the commons. In
Santa María, where the common lands have always been a significant
part of the rural economy, they provided newlyweds with a much-needed
source of income. Again and again in my conversations with village
people it was impressed upon me how high a value an allotment of
arable land once had, or of woodland, from which one could attain
kindling and firewood to sell in the deforested lowland villages. A young
couple, in effect, depended more on the web of use-rights over communal
properties than on absolute ownership to obtain the means to set up their
own house.

The reference to newlyweds being called *baragañeros*, cited earlier in
the Ateneo response from Villablino, is interesting to consider from this
point of view. The respondent had noted that *baragañas* refers to poor
and unproductive lands. I suspect the term carries more historical depth
and meaning than this definition would lead us to believe. In an eighteenth-century tithe book from the neighboring village of Barrillos, the
term *baragaña* had the meaning of recently broken communal land.[5]
Every few years the names of the landholders changed, which would
seem to indicate that the lands were circulated among villagers, that they
did not belong to anyone but were the common property of the village.
Therefore I think that *baragañeros* must have originally referred to that
category of people whose main, even only, source of income derived

from working probably not very productive, but at least freely available, lots of common land. This category would have included the almost landless *vecino*, of whom there were quite a few in the eighteenth century, and, one supposes, by extension the newlywed couple, whose means of support were usually negligible.

The young couple might have felt as if they were going out into the world with nothing, but in truth they often received a *dote* or marriage portion from each set of parents. The *dote* constituted an advance on the inheritance and was always deducted from the total inheritance portion that a son or daughter later received. The portions given to each child were more or less equal. Marriage portions are no longer given, nor have they been for several decades; many people have never heard of the word *dote*, which appears in documents relating to their parents and grandparents.

In the past the marriage portion usually consisted of linens and blankets, particularly for the women, and clothing, new, used, even worn-out, for both the men and the women. Here are two examples. When he married in 1895 Luis Mirantes received as *dote* a cape, several old and new shirts, underclothes, and a new and old pair of pants, a new and an old jacket, a new and an old vest, two pairs of socks, a beehive, a goat, a blanket and sheets, an adze, a trunk, and a cot.[6] When she married in 1911 Joaquina Aller received as her *dote*, besides a straw mattress, sheets, blankets, and a pillow, an entire wardrobe of new and used clothing, much of it in black.[7] The *dote* a man and woman received at marriage may not have provided the means with which to make a living in the world, but at the very least it assured the newlywed couple of their matrimonial bed.

Fraternal households

Aside from the extended households created by the practice of a married son or daughter continuing to work for the house, there also were, and still are, other types of extended households based on fraternal groupings of various sorts. In such households all work together for the common cause; the inheritance is left undivided and worked as a whole, its members forming one house. One such case of a fraternal household was that formed by three brothers of Toribio Mirantes, who lived and worked together. We learn from the inheritance record of Isidoro, one of the brothers, that he is entrusted with 520 *reales*, "for the third part of a pair of oxen, a pair of cows with its calf, the same third part of the cart and the manure including the hay in the hayloft; since the three brothers are used to living in company, it is not divided and as we stated above just the third part of the total value is noted down."[8] The three brothers, rather than split up these goods, preferred, it seems, to hold them as a group in a system of cooperative ownership and use.

Such arrangements were often economically more feasible than setting up house on one's own. This was certainly the case with the two brothers of whom we spoke earlier in relation to house division, the ones who owned the entrance, the sheepfold, and a part of the upper story of their cousin Basilio's house. Their father had died young and their mother had remarried soon after, so that when the brothers came of age they inherited almost the whole of their father's property. These brothers then married sisters. The parents of the sisters still had younger children in the house who were sustained by the family property, so the sisters were not going to inherit for some time. After several years of separate residence, the brothers in their house, the sisters in theirs, the two couples decided to set up house together. The brothers had a house that they had built on land situated at what was then the outskirts of the village; the couples set up a joint household there, living and working together for twelve years.

How did they come up with the idea of setting up a joint household? I asked this question of one of the sisters, who is now in her early sixties. She replied very simply: the house belonged to both brothers and they realized that if they lived and worked together they would earn more and spend less. As she explained, they had their own system of division of labor within their household society. Her husband was one of the village shepherds and he was out all day with the flocks. She would stay home and mind the children, hers and her sister's, wash the clothes, and prepare the meals. Her sister and her brother-in-law worked the lands the two brothers had inherited. This way the sisters and brothers had the capital to sustain them and could save the earnings that the shepherd-brother brought home.

It was a true confraternal household. As my informant told me, they had only one purse (*bolsa*) in the house. Since her sister was out working in the fields, she was the one who did all the shopping in León. Whenever she bought a dress for herself, she bought one for her sister, whatever it was she always bought two, one for each of them, "always the same for the two of them" (*siempre igual para las dos*). And if her sister's husband wore out his pants more than her husband because he was out working the lands, then he got more pants, and if she, with five children, rather than just two like her sister, had to buy more clothes, she bought them; they did not worry about such things (*eso no lo mirabamos*). At the end of their long cooperative stint together the brothers renovated another house and drew lots for their two houses, and all of their property. Everything they split up fraternally, *como buenos hermanos*, as one of the brothers once put it to me.

An arrangement that bears some similarity to this one exists in Santa María today. Again we have a case of two brothers who marry two sisters. But, in addition, the brothers have an unmarried brother and so do the sisters.[9] The brothers have not wanted to split up the inheritance. One of the reasons for this is that they own a tractor and a lot of other machinery in common, the upkeep of which is better managed in a team effort, and also in this way all get the benefit of its use. Theirs is a modern version, we might say, of the arrangement of Isidoro and his two brothers, who co-owned a team of oxen and a team of cows.

One of the sisters, who is married to the eldest brother, lives in the house of the brothers. She has no children. The other sister, who has three children, lives in the house that belonged to her parents with her unmarried brother. Her husband works together with his brothers, but he eats his meals and sleeps at his wife's house, and it is she who attends to him or, as she put it, she is the one who gives him his change of clothes (*yo le pongo la muda*). But both households form a unity in that they work the lands of both families together and take their cows out to pasture in a joint herd. The arrangement works very well, again through the division of labor in the household.

But as the wife of the younger brother with children was quick to point out, the arrangement works so well because her sister has no children of her own. Because of this the childless sister treats the children of the younger couple unselfishly, as if they were hers. Indeed, the children have virtually been raised in their aunt's house. Since the aunt has a bad back, she stays home and cares for the children and gives them their *merienda* (snack), while their mother goes out and works the land with her brother, her husband, and his two brothers.

In another contemporary joint household arrangement, two brothers are involved. Both are married, the elder is seventy and the younger brother just turned sixty-five. The two brothers never split the inheritance

and to this day they work their fields together. The younger brother
and his wife do not have children. The elder brother lives with his wife
in the house that belonged to the parents of the brothers; he has two
daughters, neither of whom currently live in the village. What is so
curious about their arrangement, in the eyes of other villagers, is that
the younger brother, although he sleeps in his wife's house, takes all his
meals in his brother's house and basically is supported by his brother
and his sister-in-law, as if he didn't have a house of his own.

And in a sense he doesn't. For his wife's house is hers. It was passed
on to her some years ago when her mother died and left it to her along
with the charge of a slightly retarded younger brother. Until that time
she and her husband had been living with her husband's brother and
his wife in the brothers' parental house. When she got her mother's
house she went to live there with her retarded brother and her husband
stayed on with his brother. This woman has a younger sister with four
sons who lost her husband to cancer four years ago, and she works with
her in a manner parallel to the way her husband works with his brother.

One of the obvious reasons why the younger brother has remained
with his elder brother is because he doesn't get along with the brother-
in-law who came with his wife's house. This brother-in-law, with the
maliciousness of a child, has been known to say to his sister's husband
if he comes down to her house at mealtimes, to go up there, to his house
to eat! But there is another more fundamental reason why the younger
brother keeps house with his elder brother. Since he has no children
there is no reason really to split up the family property, for to whom
else would he pass his inheritance besides his brother's children? The
same is true of his wife's working together with her widowed sister.
Being childless the couple expects that the property that corresponds to
them as rightful heirs will flow back through the fruitful lines of their
brother and sister, and thereby stay in the family, in its trunk (*que quede
en el tronco*). The younger brother works for the house of his elder
brother rather than for himself since it is through him that the property
will flow down to the next generation, and similarly with his wife and
her sister. For what is a house without progeny? It is a house of mud
wall without a structure, without its beams of whole tree trunks to keep
it standing.

Where there is a sterile branch of the family line, a childless brother
or sister must for all time graft himself or herself to a fruitful line. The
younger brother keeps house with his elder brother for this reason, for

with him, or through him, he is linked into the chain of future generations of his line. The same is true of the extended household encompassing the one fruitful couple, a sterile couple, and two unmarried
brothers, though in this case there is a more subtle merging of family
lines. In the Leonese context, as in the equal inheritance region of western
France, "everything proceeds ... as if marriage merely created a fragile
link between the branches, each stemming from a different lineage, a
link moreover that was without consequences, if it remained without
issue."[10]

Marriage and the production of property

In one sense marriage did create merely a fragile link between two
family lines. Especially where inherited property or property brought to
the marriage was concerned, the general attitude was that if the marriage
was without issue that property should return to the fertile branches of
the family line, to a brother or a sister, or to their progeny. For example,
in their joint testament from 1825, Martina Sánchez and Balthasar Salas
of Santa María, a childless couple, willed that after their death their
property should be "formed into two parts, one part to go to his brothers
and the other part to go to her nieces and nephews."[11]

Or in one of many such examples, Juan de Robles of Villamoros de
las Regueras, marrying for the third time in 1704, made a special bequest
to his future wife, Paula de Ferreras, a widow of Villafeliz, of "five
beams of a house which he has in Villamoros ... so that if she outlives
the donor she may enjoy them for her days ... except that she may not
be allowed to sell or alienate them because after their lifetime if they
have no descendents they are to return to the trunk and legitimate heirs
of the donor."[12] In an egalitarian lineage system such as the Leonese
there was nothing to prevent women from making similar donations to
men (though they were not quite as frequent). Josepha de la Gala from
the village of Marne made a bequest in the same year to her future
husband, Manuel Cañas of Villaturiel, of "the part of the house which
fell to her of the house in which her parents lived and died in Marne,"
and again if the marriage produced no descendents that part of the house
was to return to the trunk of her family and to her legitimate heirs.[13]

But the family line has no claim on the *gananciales*, the property that
husband and wife earn in their lifetime together. This is the yield of

their marriage, it is the harvest that their marriage has sown, and is conceived of as separate from the flow of property down the veins of the family line. We find, for example, that at her death in 1753 Froylana Robles of Santa María left her husband as heir to the estate that she brought to the marriage, "for the days of his life" (*durante los días de su vida*), but the *gananciales* she left to him in perpetuity. As heirs after her husband's days, she left her nephew and niece, Pantaleón and María de Salas, "with the charge of two sung masses in perpetuity founded on the remainder of the property which she brought to said marriage which after the days of said her husband they should split equally."[14] Thus she left her own inherited property to her husband for him to make use of freely during his lifetime, even diminish, but with the stipulation that afterwards it was to go to her nephew and niece, back, in other words, to her family line. But the *gananciales*, over which she had as much of a right as her husband, she relinquished to him unconditionally and in full, without troubling over the claims of her line.

Marriage may, in one sense, have been a fragile link, but looked at from another angle it was the yoke that bound husband and wife into a work-team for life, an image given a less than romantic elaboration in this popular verse:

Ya te pusieron el yugo,	They've already yoked you,
ya te ataron la jamosta,	already knotted you up,
ya no te puedes mover	now you can't even budge
aunque te pique la mosca.[15]	even if you're stung by a fly.

For we must keep in mind that what is passed on in a system of equal inheritance, except in those rare cases where there is only one child, is a fraction of the total—a piece of a house, not a whole house. And the more offspring there are, the smaller each piece will be. To build up a whole from the fragments they bring to the marriage, husband and wife had to work and work and work and save, as that one villager so aptly put it, in order to *gananciar*, that is, increase and multiply manyfold the property that they inherited from their parents. As this same man remarked, "All the capital I have my wife and I bought. Inherited property, nothing, it is a twentieth part of what I have, the rest was all bought."

With the rise in population in the latter part of the nineteenth century the inheritance that a man or woman could obtain from their parents, with few exceptions, became increasingly insufficient, even inconsequential. Of what good was it for husband and wife to amass a splendid estate in their lifetime together if they had seven, eight, or ten children? They might thereby leave each child a little more property, but never enough for it to be really significant. "Who are the poor?" a villager said to me once in a conversation about inheritance, "the children of the rich." He was referring to his wife's grandparents, who had amassed *un capital curioso* in their time only to have it dissipate when it came to be divided among their nine children.

Of course this is not to say that the inheritance was not appreciated or ever came to be considered unimportant, but that a time did come when it constituted, as that villager put it before, as little as "a twentieth part" of a couple's estate. The climax was clearly reached in the period immediately preceding the rural migration of 1960-1970, the point at which the old agrarian regime finally reached its limits.

Certainly there was a strong sense that husband and wife built up a joint estate by means of their joint labor. In a notarized inventory from 1954, for example, the whole estate of husband and wife was said to be conceived of as *ganancial*, for the widow herself stated "that between the spouses the differences in what each had contributed [to the marriage] were minor and that everything they had was like *ganancial*."[16] We have only to think of the numerous purchases of land which *labradores* made, in some cases buying as many as ten, fifteen, even twenty plots of land in a lifetime, to fathom the crucial role that property accumulated in marriage, or *gananciales*, played in the old rural society. All of the couple's energies and savings went into the purchase of more land, to enlarge their estate, to bring yet another *hemina* of land into the house, as a ninety-year-old woman from nearby Devesa expressed it.

The position of women

For their part, women worked as hard, or harder, than men under the yoke of marriage. Turning again to the Ateneo responses from the turn of the century, we find that the role of women in agricultural life and work was certainly as important as was their role in domestic matters. The response from Roderos took a pitying attitude toward the rural woman's labor: "Women work in the fields just as much as their husbands do, it makes one feel pity to see them even mowing with the scythe." As if to symbolize how women never got a respite from their work in the fields, this respondent added an anecdote about a woman

from the village "who while working in the fields gave birth to twins
that in falling hit against their crowns and were killed." The response
from Laguna de Negrillos took a similar tack, noting that economic
position made little difference, for "the wives and daughters of the rich
work at plowing just as much as do those of the poor." The respondent
also added that women involved themselves in all the important economic
decisions of the household: "when the couple decides to buy or sell
something the spouses do so in mutual conformity." A detailed response
from the city of León speaks of the character of the countrywomen from
the surrounding area:

> The women intervene directly in the direction of the children and
> they are the ones in charge of economic matters, acting as the
> principal advisers of their husbands, who do nothing which they
> do not prescribe. This is due to the fact that women are perfectly
> familiar with the business of farming, that a woman is more *la-
> bradora* (if you will excuse the phrase) than a man and in general
> more distrustful, less vulnerable to deceit and fraud. She also devotes
> herself to agricultural tasks during seedtime and when gathering
> the harvest, thereby offering valuable assistance to her husband and
> saving him the wages that would otherwise go to a day laborer.[17]

We must not forget too that since medieval times women have been
property-owners in León and Castile.[18] Rural women disposed of their
property, when they had it, with amazing determination and strength
of will, as some brief examples will serve to indicate. In her testament
from 1784, Baltasara Díez of Barrio de Nuestra Señora left her husband,
Alonso González, a pair of young bulls with their cart, tools, plow, and
thong for tying the yoke; she also left him the bed that came from
Villalón (in Valladolid) with its straw mattress, a pair of sheets "neither
of the worst nor of the best," a blanket with its bedspread over it, a
carga of linseed and half a dozen sheaves of flax, four sheep and six
lambs. All this she left to her husband "under the condition that he not
have any dispute whatsoever with my heirs nor that he ask them for
anything else, for if he should do so it is my will that this bequest be
invalidated."[19] Such was the strength of character of this peasant woman,
telling her husband not to meddle with their children's disposal of the
property if he wanted to keep the gifts she was bestowing upon him.

Or in quite a different case from 1786, Doña Martina González de
Robles of Devesa, a peasant woman of good social and economic standing

who nonetheless was leaving her husband in great debt, made sure to leave him her own property in case he needed it:

> ... and in attention to the fact that at the death of Don Josef my father many debts and quitrents [*censos*] were left behind and that in order to pay and redeem them my husband had to pawn part of his estate and another part he sold ... to compensate him for this injury it is my will in order to pay for the debts which we have since incurred and at present are pending that he sell whatever property of mine, whether moveables or landed property [*raíces*], may be necessary, and for this reason my heirs shall not be able to ask for reclamation at any time.[20]

Here, then, we find the opposite case, of a woman telling her children not to meddle with her husband's disposal of her property, for she wished to pay him back for his loss of property with her own.

Even peasant women of poorer means than Baltasara Díez or Doña Martina González de Robles displayed the same kind of determination where their property, however meager, was concerned. María Gutiérrez of Santa María, for example, in 1718 left to her husband for his lifetime the house in which he lived and a plot of land, which must have been part of her inherited property, as well as "the lands which both bought from Sebastián de la Varga" and "the meadows which belonged to her in the village of Barrillos," with the stipulation that "it all be for the days of his life, no more."[21] In this way she made sure that after his lifetime these goods would go to her daughter, Floriana, her only child. Isabel de Corral, also of Santa María, and of yet lesser means than María Gutiérrez, left her meager bit of landed property and chattels to three grandchildren of her husband by his first wife and to a niece, appropriating these minor treasures in a very specific manner: "to Cristina [a plot in] El Barrial del Fueyo which measures one *hemina* and a frying pan and an iron fire-shovel, to Rafael the plot in Pozobal, to Alonso a goat, to my niece María García the new mantle so that she may sit on my tomb."[22]

So much for the image of the rural Leonese woman as the hardworking *labradora*, the strong-willed owner of her property. Quite another sense of self was usually reserved for the women who in their youth had the misfortune of bearing illegitimate children. "A woman who had illegitimate children in those times," as a villager explained, "had a terrible time getting married, terrible. . . . Those women stayed like that . . . they became old maids (*solteronas*) ... who never married, never had any means. ... They had whatever means their parents had left them, and perhaps their parents were poor and did not even have any land or anything and that was how they remained."[23]

Although a few of the responses of the Ateneo questionnaire suggest that in the countryside it was of little consequence if a woman had children before she married so long as she had some property, the general feeling seems to have been that it severely hampered a woman's chances to marry.[24] A good many women, particularly in this century, were a few months pregnant when they married, but it was one thing to be pregnant and marry and quite another to be pregnant and abandoned. It was the abandoned unmarried mother who suffered the consequences of her deed.

I was told of a woman from Santa María who at the turn of the century was working for a family in the village of Devesa and had a child by the head of the household. As soon as the baby was born she wrapped it in her robe and tossed it into a well. When it surfaced people recognized the woman's robe and she was tried for infanticide. In recent years a woman from Santa María who was working (*sirviendo*) in Madrid killed the child she had by her master, and she too was caught and served a jail sentence.

In the case of another unmarried woman who had her child at home, her father whisked it away as soon as it was born and took it to a hospice. The woman never knew anything more of the child, and later she married a widower some years younger than herself and had children by him. A woman who was rumored to have been made pregnant by her brother-in-law, a topic that found its way into the evening serenades of the *mozos* or young unmarried men, was quickly sent away to another village to learn to sew, thereby saving face; she too later managed to marry.

Sometimes when a village boy abandoned a village girl he had been courting for a long time, he did so to exact vengeance against her family. In the case of the woman whose father whisked her baby away from her, it was well known that her father had joked insultingly about her boyfriend. Referring to his daugher's boyfriend and a peer of his, he said of them when they returned from military service that "they left as lambs [i.e., dolts] and they returned as rams" (*estos se marcharon borros y vinieron carneros*). This greatly angered the boy's family and the boy took revenge by leaving her, "since they were very much engaged and she was sure that they would marry and that was when she had the child by him" (*como eran muy novios y ella estaba muy fiada que se casaban y fue cuando tuvo un hijo con él*). Not that the boy's family had been so kind to the girl or her family either, for his mother used to tell him not to bring home "those girls who are so buttoned up" (*a mí no me traes esas muchachas de tantas embotonaduras*), because she and her sisters wore skirts that buttoned all the way down. In all this there was the usual rivalry between families who knew each other too well, the sense of which is captured in the saying, "I don't make my daughter's bed so she can sleep with your son" (*Yo no le hago la cama a mi hija para que se acueste con tu hijo*).

But if a woman became pregnant by a man who later married her, society forgave them for their impatience. From the same woman who spoke to me in great detail about this subject I learned of an interesting story that reflects so well the sexual mores and intrigues, not to mention the architectonic structure of the old rural house, that I will quote it at length:

> There was a man ... he was married twice. With the first wife, the father of the first wife used to say, "no one jokes around with my daughter, because I stick her in bed, lock the door and the key here, under my pillow and my daughter comes out of her room when I open the door." But then it happened that between sunset and sunrise she was pregnant. ... And when had it happened? ... And then, you know what there was? There was a cathole, have people mentioned the catholes to you before? Look, it is an opening in the door, for the water to drain out, for the cats to come in, at the bottom of the door. In the past they even had them in the bedrooms ... for the cats, for the rats, because in the past the houses, the bedrooms, the majority of them were downstairs and the rats were always around ... and so they made those openings. And imagine what the cathole must have been like that he had to take all his clothes off to get in through the cathole and he entered through the cathole to sleep with her.[25]

This would have occurred around 1887. The couple married, but the parish priest made sure of the capricious husband's repentance. As punishment he had him ring the bells for the Angelus at six o'clock every morning and obligated him to sit up front by the steps of the altar, right under the priest's nose, at every Sunday mass. And for a period of well over two years the man, in fact, did so.

We have seen several images of Leonese women, ranging from the hard-working *labradora* who even mows with the scythe to the independent and strong-willed owner of property, from the unwed mother to the pregnant bride. (See the life history by María Rivero Morán in Appendix A for a personal account of a Leonese woman's life.) A final image is that of the widow who at the death of her husband is liberated, apparently, from the constraints of marriage and society.

I was told a story of a woman who was sitting vigil over her husband's body. While waiting for her neighbors to join her at the wake, she became hungry and fixed herself a stew with sausages which she placed before the open fire to cook. Just as she was about to bite in, the neighbors set foot in the door. Since it is forbidden to eat meat while one is mourning, the widow felt obliged to conceal the stew she had prepared. As she sat facing the fire she could see her cat picking out the choice pieces of sausage from the pot. She lamented before her audience, "Ay, World, World, how you go on taking them all from me, one by one, and the best among them!" (¡*Ay, Mundo, Mundo, como me vas llevando todos uno por uno, y por los mejores*!). Her visitors, who could not see the cat or the stew, assumed she was bemoaning the loss of her husband. In fact, she was speaking to her cat, nicknamed Mundo ("World"), and bemoaning the loss of her sausage.

Here we have an image of a widow pretending to be mourning when she is clearly carrying on perfectly well with life. She obviously has not been shattered by the death of her husband. Her marriage must not have been a particularly happy one or very important to her. Such a marriage would by no means have been typical of most in León, for in general husband and wife both brought property to the marriage, built up a joint estate, together made decisions about raising their children, and in most cases enjoyed a close and cooperative relationship. This is certainly what I have observed myself among the couples I have known. The extreme represented by the widow in the tale serves, however, to point up the contradictions that underlie the usually harmonious relations between women and men.

Perhaps the freest class of women in León, and possibly in most of rural Spain, have long been widows. The widow is given the respect accorded to age, if she is an older person she has usually already borne children and raised them, and in León she becomes a *vecina*, the head of a household in her own right. Her house is then granted use-rights over common properties in her name, rather than in her husband's. She must also take on the burdens of *vecindad*, village citizenship, such as taking part in the communal prestations of labor and participating in the *concejo* or village council, though with the latter she can never do so personally but must send a male surrogate. Thus even the very freest of women still stand below men in a sense. And in the tale the merry widow prepares a feast for herself as if she has cause to celebrate and not to mourn, but she cannot eat it; she becomes a *vecina*, but must send a man to take her place at *concejo*.

Part Three

Chapter 7

The *Concejo* as an Assembly

SINCE THE TIME of the early Reconquest (tenth century), local government in León has been based in the assembly of village citizens known as the *concejo*, or council. According to past and present Leonese usage, it is the *concejo* as a *concejo abierto*, an "open" assembly of all village citizens, every head of a house, representing themselves to themselves, and governing as a single body, that has served as the primary definition.

The *concejo abierto* quickly declined by the thirteenth and fourteenth centuries in the larger towns and market centers of the kingdoms of León and Castile, giving way to *consejos, cabildos*, and *regimientos* ruled by oligarchies of the wealthier townsmen and nobles. But in most rural communities of León and other parts of northern Spain, with their very small populations, it managed to persist until the end of the old regime, and often into the present. The community assembly gradually became a peasant institution and an archaic survival, in Spain and in much of the old European rural world.[1]

In the course of time the *concejo*, like all historic social forms, has acquired several contexts of meaning. The *concejo* is, first of all, an assembly of village citizens in which all matters of common concern are debated and a course of action is chosen by the group as a whole. In a deeper sense it is a corporate body which, though made up of the union of village households, is more than the sum of these households: it is a polity in its own right. Third, it is a juridical or moral presence, with the power to coerce individuals to pay heed to its prescriptions. And last, a point that is rarely made, the *concejo*, as the voice of the village, is a historical actor, a conscious maker of its own history. Let us now turn to an elucidation of these contexts of meaning.

Words and wine

Virtually every village in León has a meeting house for reunions of the *concejo*. During the fall and winter the *concejo* meets indoors, as it also does whenever an important matter is to be broached and voted upon. The feasting that has long been a feature of these meetings takes place in the *casa de concejo* as well. With the coming of spring, and in days of balmy summer weather, the *concejo* simply convenes outside in its customary site, which in Santa María is by the church portal.

The traditional meeting time for the *concejo* is Sunday immediately following the mass. Sunday, as a holy day of rest, is the day when the *labrador* is free to govern. When the matter is of some urgency and importance, the *concejo* will meet on a weekday at the special call of the church bells.

Of the many *concejo* meetings I observed in the course of my stay in Santa María I never once found them to be quiet, efficient, prim, routine affairs. The business of governance was always conducted by open discussion and debate, true to the *concejo abierto* tradition, in which all the men present, frequently talking at once, drowned each other out. Over the din of voices it was often difficult for me to fathom exactly what issue was calling forth so lively an interchange among the various pockets of men. I have to admit that on several occasions I did not learn what went on until afterwards as I strolled home with a villager or two, or sometimes not until much later when I could question my closest informants about it. In fact, I will also confess that the first few times I witnessed the *concejo* meeting by the church portal I had no idea I was in the presence of the old and venerable institution I had set out to study.

Once, at a very stormy assembly concerning the disarray into which the cemetery had fallen in recent years, I overheard a young village man say as he walked out of the *casa de concejo*, "You come out of here the same as before ... everyone talks, but nothing gets done" (*De aquí se sale igual que antes ... se habla pero no se hace nada*). Looking at the matter less cynically, the *concejo*, in its role as an open assembly, is indeed an arena for talk. However, it is also, though much less evidently, an arena for action. It is said of its members, who are known by the term *vecinos*, that they have "*voz y voto*"—a voice and a vote—in the *concejo*. In the protracted discourse of the *vecinos*, which culminates in a vote, the word, slowly and unwillingly, does become deed. But this will be amply exemplified later.

Let us return to the word, really to words, and pause there for a moment. The difficulty I had following the goings-on of the *concejo* (or even identifying it as such at first), as well as the young villager's exasperation with its seemingly interminable fruitless talk, points to the same thing: the disorder of conducting business. And if we look at the historical record, which for the villages is largely inscribed in their ordinances, we find that this disorder has long been a characteristic feature of the community assembly.

In fact the disorder that prevailed at the meetings seems to have been yet worse in past times. And it was words that were often at the root of misrule. The ordinances of Santa María from 1776 ordain that when the *vecinos* are in *concejo* they should not "create disturbances, shout, nor say swearwords which may incite another, nor say 'that is not true,' or concerning the matter at hand that 'it shall or shall not be done in spite of him,' or similar words."[2]

In much the same vein an older set of *ordenanzas* from 1582, which were based on yet an earlier version, for the small villages of La Milla, Güerga, and Quiñones in the southerly Órbigo area of León, stipulate that when the three villages meet in their joint *concejo*, "no one should have the audacity to speak nor do nor say anything discourteous in the *concejo* to any other person, penalty of 100 *maravedis* for the *concejo*."[3]

The 1788 ordinances of Cármenes, a village in the mountainous zone lying north of Santa María, are even more specific: "We ordain and decree that no *vecino*, while in *concejo*, should speak bad words, nor say them to another, penalty of ten *reales*; nor disturb, by giving the lie or saying ugly words, such as blaspheming and swearing to God and to Christ."[4] Those of Villamanín, another mountain village, likewise admonish the *vecinos* to "act with moderation and respect, without raising their voices, speaking bad words, swearing, cursing, blaspheming, getting up from their seats, making gestures with their arms against someone else, uttering threats or any other unchristian expression subversive of peace and good harmony."[5]

Many more examples could be given, but these will suffice to show how widespread and endemic was the phenomenon of disorderly discourse in the *concejo*. The question arises of whether we can assume that the ordinances are providing us with a reflection of actual occurrences. I think it safe to say that it is a lived social reality which informs the various prescriptions and admonitions that surface time and again in village ordinances. Their wealth of detail speaks for itself.[6]

That the men in *concejo* did raise their voices, swear, and lash insults and bitter remarks at one another, and that they did so quite often, seems to be amply demonstrated in the village ordinances. Decorum, certainly, appears not to have been a characteristic feature of the meetings, nor it seems was "peace and good harmony." In the present as in the past, the issues raised in *concejo* could come so close to men's hearts, and be wrought with enough controversy, to fire them up and make them curse all manner of sacred things.

The profane utterances that abounded when the *concejo* met did not fail to reach the ears of church officialdom, who repeatedly forbade them, though to little avail. As early as 1583 the bishop of León, on one of his regular canonical visits to the nearby village of Castro, noted how the people of Castro, "lacking in reverence for the holy name of God, with much disrespect swear to him in their reunions of the *concejo* or in private reunions when playing games and in other ways, due to which his Holiness makes it known to them that the curse which ends in blasphemy is a grave sin and is prohibited by the law of God, laws human, canonical, and pragmatic of these kingdoms."[7]

As a cure for this malady, the bishop proposed that every time a person swore he pay one *maravedí* to the priest, or anyone else he chose, to be spent on wax for the altar of the eucharist, and recite a *pater noster* and an *ave maria*. "By so doing," counseled the bishop, "the good Christian will divest himself of the bad habit of swearing." Those who took his counsel were to be given forty days of dispensation. And as a lesson to those who persisted in their "bad habit," he suggested that during the mass the priest call up, at the moment of the offertory, four or six God-fearing persons "to make accusations of the curses of that week and denounce them before him, and the accused shall pay for each curse eight *maravedis*, half for the funds of this church and the other half for the accuser."[8] Whether the punishments were meted out in the way the bishop ordained we will never know, but clearly, swearing was enough of a "problem" to merit an official reproach.

Bad language was not, in the view of the church, the only threat that the custom of meeting in *concejos* posed to good morals and respectable Christian behavior. Much more serious still was the general rowdiness and turbulence that regularly broke loose whenever the *concejo* met. One reason for it was that feasting and, in particular, wine drinking was a usual feature of the meetings. Fines of various sorts were often paid for in wine or, if in money, were spent on wine, which all the *vecinos* drank together in *concejo*. Wine, and often bread as well, was given to the *vecinos* after they performed community labors in the *hacenderas*. The rites of becoming a *vecino* entailed provisioning a hearty repast of wine, bread, sardines, and in some villages even cheese, for all the men gathered in *concejo*. At the completion of the cycle, when a *vecino* died, his family likewise provided wine and bread for the men of the *concejo* to consume collectively. These are just a few of the occasions on which wine was drunk in *concejo*, and it was certainly not difficult to turn any meeting into just such an occasion. Both the historical record and the recollections of older villagers indicate that "dry" meetings were few and far between.

In the same record of the bishop's visit to Castro in 1583, he notes disapprovingly that in the villages of his diocese the *concejo* has the habit of convening in the taverns, "to spend and drink their fines" (*para gastar y beber sus penas*). The meetings were also all too frequent, being held not only in the afternoon but even in the morning before mass on Sundays and on holy days, "in much disservice to God and with much scandal to good Christians and with much ignominy and infamy and danger to those present at them and to their children and descendents."[9] A century and a half later, in 1726, the bishop of that era, on another visit to Castro, likewise complains that in the same villages, "almost every day they are having *concejos*, not excluding holy days which should be spent praising God our Lord, especially since the *concejos* are not held for the purpose of governing the republic but to satiate their appetite for drink, setting a bad example with their disorder and discord."[10] Or as another bishop succinctly put it in 1740 on a visit to Villasinta, located just a few miles southwest of Santa María, "under the pretext of governing the *Pueblo* they consume themselves in misrule and destruction of their Souls."[11]

The villagers themselves were no less aware of the disorder and discord that excessive wine drinking brought on in *concejo*. "Because there is often much disorder in *concejo* specially after the *vecinos* have had a drink," begins a chapter of the 1776 ordinances from Santa María,

> we ordain and decree that each and every *vecino* be in *concejo* with much silence, modesty, and composure and he who wants to speak shall rise baring his head and shall ask for license from the *Rejidores*, who will order the *Pesquisero* to demand silence of those speaking, so that all may hear the argument which that *vecino* wants to expound, and when he is finished he will sit and cover his head,

and if another *vecino* wants to respond to the proposal, he will
likewise rise with order. . . ."[12]

Here villagers reasoned that if the *vecinos* were going to persist in drinking wine during their *concejo* reunions, at least they should do so with
a semblance of parliamentary protocol!

Some villages did have rules about the amount of wine that could be
drunk in *concejo*. The ordinances from Mataluenga, a village bordering
on the northwestern mountain chain of León, stipulated that "even
should there be many people to punish or wine to drink, they shall not
dare give out wine more than two times."[13] According to Juan Antonio
Posse's account of life in the northeastern Leonese village of Llánaves,
where he was parish priest from 1794 to 1799, the *concejo* never permitted
more than two-and-a-half *cántaros* (jugs) to be given out at a time to its
twenty-three to twenty-six *vecinos*, who during his stay never became
drunk at the meetings. Posse recounted how when he took possession
of the parish his uncle tried to increase the "dose" so there would be
enough to go around for all the men, women, and children present, "but
they didn't permit it under any circumstances, so as not to break with
their customs."[14]

In the course of an extended discussion about the 1776 ordinances
from Santa María, which I sustained over a period of weeks and months
with Leonardo Mirantes, one of my most articulate informants, I learned
that, indeed, until recently wine was frequently given out in *concejo*.
However, my informant felt that the men used to become drunk easily
because they rarely drank wine in their own homes and ate poorly. In
his words: "Since at that time people didn't drink wine because there
wasn't any, they would get drunk a lot. In the time of the ancients [*los
antiguos*], I remember the ancients, my grandparents and all, they would
really tie one on from wine, but that was because they were hankering
after wine and they didn't eat the way we do today, and so it did a lot
more damage."[15] Nowadays wine is hardly ever drunk in the public space
of the *concejo*, he noted, because "each has wine in his own house and
it is not like in those times when one didn't." This remark about the
abandonment of the custom of wine drinking in *concejo* is extremely
suggestive, for its points to its deeper symbolic significance, whose meaning was, understandably, lost upon the church.

Posse, for example, held a philosophical view of the commensality he
often saw taking place during reunions of the *concejo* in the village of

Llánaves. Citing Aristotle, and sounding rather like Durkheim on social solidarity, he remarks, "I looked upon these periodic meals as contributing to the maintenance of union and peace among the *vecinos*."[16]

Díez González, a Leonese jurist who has written extensively on customary law in the mountain villages of northeastern León has a yet more finely tuned interpretation of *concejo* wine. "It was logical," he notes, "for the *concejo*, consisting of the *vecinos*, to collect the fruit of its just suit, and what more natural way is there to show itself 'restored' and satisfied than to consume it." This ancient custom of "drinking the fines" (*beber las penas*, as the sixteenth-century bishop had put it) is in keeping, says Díez González, with the realistic approach to the world the villagers of old had. And also in keeping, he adds, with the conviviality that the gathering of all the *vecinos* in *concejo* called forth, and without which life and work in common would have been impossible. "Blessed be, then, the wine of the *concejo*" (*Bendito sea, pues, el vino concejil*).[17]

From the bishop's condemnation of wine drinking in *concejo* as destructive of souls we have come full circle to the transformation of *concejo* wine into a sacred symbol of communion. Indeed, there is a resonance with the mass in the almost ritual consumption of wine, often in combination with bread, by the *vecinos* in *concejo*. We could say that it made of the *vecinos* one body—the *concejo*. Thus, although the meetings of the *concejo* could be, and often were, disorderly to the point of becoming a reversal of the church service, they nonetheless served the deeper purpose of bringing together the various *vecinos*, each the head of a house, into a common federation, or republic of village households. It was to their union—whether ideal or real was beside the point—that the *vecinos* in *concejo* drank.

Entering the community

Quite aside from symbolism, the question remains: How amid the disorder of meeting in *concejo* did the *vecinos* govern their village republic? Or was there any government at all? Were the bishops correct in reducing the *concejo* meetings to a mere pretense of governance?

Beneath the surface disorder of the meetings there was, indeed, quite an enduring and elaborate structure of customary law—what I refer to here as the "web of use-rights"—by means of which all aspects of community life were not only regulated but brought together into a meaningful order. The *concejo*, as the guardian of this web built up out of the accumulated memories of village ancestors, was highly regarded, and its actions and accords were solemnly upheld by the *vecinos*.

For, more than the sum of its members, the *concejo* was a polity in its own right. In this capacity it not only guarded over the inherited web "of customs and controls,"[18] but governed. Precisely who governed was not a question that could be put to this remarkable institution— although there were officers of the *concejo*—for it was the corporate body of the *concejo* that always had the last word and that, when it acted, acted as one. It is no accident that in the legal parlance of the old regime the phrase commonly used to refer to a village acting as a party to a suit was that of *concejo y vecinos*—the *concejo* and the *vecinos*—for the *concejo* was a thing apart from the *vecinos* who made it up, while together the two formed a single unit.

To be a member of the *concejo* and thus a *vecino*, a person had to acquire rights of *vecindad*—which literally denotes neighborhood but in this case is closer in meaning to citizenship. The *concejo* was essentially a village republic, and this is nowhere more clearly seen than in the rules for acquiring *vecindad*, which favored native sons of the village and put obstacles in the way of outsiders or *forasteros*. And it was eminently patriarchal, a male order, for it was men alone who could acquire *vecindad* for their houses and be present at the meetings of the *concejo*.

The basic prerequisites for becoming a *vecino*, as a *forastero*, were usually marriage, possession of a house, and very frequently land in the village, and permanent residence there throughout the better part of the year. The *concejo* of each village added various other requirements, which could be economic, personal, or moral.

The ordinances of Avelgas, a northwestern mountain village in León, specified that the outsider, in order to "enjoy the rights of the *vecino*," had to have a skill or profession with which to support himself, or be able to raise at least two *fanegas* of grain, one *cuartel* of vegetables, and one *cuartillo* of garden produce.[19] We find in the ordinances of Cármenes, in the northeastern mountain area that is in close proximity to Santa María, a similar requirement, this time phrased in strictly monetary terms: "We declare that it is the custom for any outsider wishing to become a *vecino* in this Place, that he must have a landed estate of 4,000 *maravedises* in this place."[20]

Even with these qualifications *vecindad* was not always granted right away; the *forastero* often had to prove he was not going to become a parasite on the community. In Villanueva de Pontedo, for example, a *forastero* could not enjoy the rights of *vecindad* until he had lived in the village for six months and demonstrated that he could contribute, like any other *vecino*, to payments that the village made to the crown or to its own common fund, and that he would willingly participate, again like an ordinary *vecino*, in such communal prestations of labor as the *facenderas*.[21] The village of Peornedo demanded, along the same lines, that the *forastero*, "before enjoying benefits has to make this his *vecindad* [here in the sense of being a neighbor or resident of a place] for a year and a day, contribute and pay taxes like the rest of the *vecinos* and prove his worth."[22]

The worth of the person wishing to become a *vecino* was calibrated with great care. The ordinances of Omañón, in northwestern León, point out that if the *forastero* "is recognized or reported to be a turbulent man, or a misbehaved one, or a perturber of the common good, he is not to be granted *vecindad*."[23] The 1776 ordinances of Santa María likewise advise that they not admit as *vecino* "any Person of bad opinion and fame and it will suffice [to know] that there was a motive for his having left another *vecindad*."[24]

If after all the tests the *forastero* qualified for *vecindad*, he then had to pay for his *derechos*, or rights. The sum, again, varied from place to place, but everywhere included a repast for the *vecinos* to consume together in *concejo*, and often a monetary fee as well. In Cármenes, the *forastero* entering as *vecino* paid, in 1748, a fee of sixty *reales*, a *fanega* of wheat bread, a ram of three years, and four pounds of white wax formed into two candles for the lamp that continually burned before the sacrament.[25] In Villanueva de Pontedo, Peornedo, and Canseco three *cántaras* of wine were required along with the ram and the bread, and the ordinances of Canseco also specified that the feast be prepared and seasoned in the house of the new *vecino*.[26] It was no minor feast either, when, say, in Omañón the *forastero* had to pay twenty-five *reales*, a hock weighing ten pounds or its equivalent in money, and as much bread as was needed to consume with the meat.[27]

But it was not only the *forasteros* who had to provide such feasts when they became *vecinos*; in many places it was required of native sons too when they acquired *vecindad*. In Santa María, for example, the native son gave to the *concejo* in 1776 three *cántaras* of wine, an *hemina* of wheat bread, and a pair of sardines fried in oil to each *vecino*, while the *forastero* was required to pay twice this amount and a hundred *reales* in cash.[28]

In the neighboring village of Santovenia del Monte, the fee still required in 1874 was three *cántaros* of wine, and for each *vecino* a small loaf of bread, two sardines, and a *cuarterón* of cheese, which the *vecino* newly admitted that year was paying in installments.[29]

That the feast which even native sons had to provide was far from minor is certainly shown in a *concejo* record from 1855 I found in the nearby village of Valdefresno. The six men admitted as *vecinos* that year had asked for a reduction of the customary fee of one *cántaro* of wine for the *concejo* and two ounces of cheese and two pounds of bread for each *vecino*. This *"gracia"* or "pardon" was granted them because, as the document states, they came humbly before the *vecinos* and supplicated them for it. And so each only had to pay the more manageable fee of twenty *reales* which, in the traditional manner, was to be spent on "a refreshment to be had in harmony" (*para un refresco que se gastara en armonia*) by the *vecinos* in *concejo*.[30]

Not every village asked its native sons to pay for their rights of *vecindad*; in some marriage alone was a sufficient qualification. But even in villages where such payment was expected, it was always significantly less for the native son than for the stranger. López Morán, the Leonese jurist, felt that the feast that the native son gave was also qualitatively different from that of the incoming stranger; it was viewed as a "gift" which the new *vecino* offered to his companions in *vecindad*, and not as a payment of a fee.[31] This observation is corroborated by the example of the six villagers from Valdefresno, who were pardoned the major feast, but all the same had to provide a modest refreshment for the *vecinos*. In either case, though, we see how important rites of commensality were to the self-identity of the *concejo*.[32]

The rules of *vecindad*, as these examples serve to show, were quite elaborately conceived, and especially so regarding the admittance of strangers into the circle of the *concejo*. Why were villages so wary of allowing strangers to become *vecinos*? Certainly no village wished to be burdened with vagabonds and landless poor. In an area where the small landholdings that predominated could barely support their tillers, what village was in a position to provide an income for a proletarian population? Thus the outsider had to be able to pay taxes like the other *vecinos* and be in his own employ, as an economically independent farmer or artisan, for no market existed for his labor.

The villages, too, some more, some less, offered "benefits" and "privileges" to citizens of its republic. Simply by virtue of holding *vecindad* a man and his family had rights of use over such communal properties as woods, meadows, and wastes. In villages blessed with extensive and bountiful natural resources, the usufruct of these properties was frequently well worth the price of admission; and freeloaders seem to have abounded. Thus in some places the would-be *vecino* had to live in the community for a while and prove himself a respectable taxpayer and worthy individual before winning rights to village properties. Nor was it just rights to resources that these Leonese villages offered their *vecinos*. In Santa María, where, according to a census from 1798, every *vecino* was an *hidalgo*, strangers apparently came seeking *vecindad* in order to prove they were *hidalgos*. What else are we to infer from the following: "If someone asks for *vecindad* in this place to prove his nobility without desiring to live here, *vecindad* should not be granted him until he produces an authentic document that he will not ask nor demand anything from this *concejo* on account of said *vecindad*."[33]

A village that took in a stranger who turned out to be less than an ideal *vecino* stood to lose much more than its properties. For there was a fine balance, an essential reciprocity, between what a village offered to its *vecinos* as a "gift" and what it expected in return from each and every *vecino*. The *vecino*, for example, had to participate in the communal prestations of labor known as *hacenderas* or *facenderas* for repairing roads and checking boundary markers, attend the meetings of the *concejo*, and take on economic, religious, and political responsibilities when his turn was due. In short, he had to be an active member of the *concejo*, whose task it was to organize all these matters. And only he who lived and worked in the community, and whose own house was bound up in it, was in a position to be a *vecino* on a par with all the other *vecinos*.

The rules of *vecindad* were so deeply rooted in the social and cultural soil of Leonese villages that they have persisted in their bare outlines to the present day. It certainly is no longer as difficult as it was two centuries ago for the outsider to become a *vecino*. Today marriage and an open house and hearth are sufficient qualifications for *vecindad*. We ourselves were frequently told that all we had to do was ask for *vecindad* and it would be granted us (as it was we were given rights to firewood even though we were not *vecinos*, because we were living and working in the village like *vecinos*). Nowadays a token fee of some 150 *pesetas* is paid for *vecindad*, and there is no feasting or wine drinking when a new *vecino* is admitted into the *concejo*.

But to this day, despite the decline in value of rights of *vecindad*, it is still true that a man must be married and have a house in the village in order to be accepted as a *vecino* by the *concejo*. I was told the story of a single man, approaching forty, who, though living in his parents' house, had his own lands and pair of cows and was considered to be economically independent; but when he asked for *vecindad* the *concejo* denied it to him on account of his not being married. His brother protested in *concejo* about it to no avail, and he ended up being fined for speaking brashly. This all took place in 1954. The large number of bachelors in Santa María still living in their parental houses are not *vecinos*; they may go to meetings of the *concejo* and participate in the *hacenderas*, but it is ultimately their fathers who, as the *vecinos*, represent the house in the *concejo* and to the village.

The requirement that a man be married to be a *vecino* harks back to an archaic idea of the *concejo* as a federation, even a democracy, of houses, not of persons. There is only one *vecino* to a house, the pater-familias, in this male order. A single male living in the house of his parents, even if he has property of his own, does not qualify for *vecindad* until, through marriage, he acquires the womb that will make him the head of a family and the fount of a lineage. It has always been marriage that removed men from the society of *mozos* (single young males) and brought them into the adult male world of the *concejo*; but today a category is lacking in which to place most of the bachelors left in Santa María, who are too old to be *mozos* and yet do not qualify to be *vecinos*.

Once *vecindad* is attained it becomes the property of the house. Thus an unmarried man can eventually become a *vecino* by inheriting the *vecindad* of the house after both his parents die. So can an unmarried woman. Women, as widows, inherit the *vecindad* of the house from their husbands. Although no one in Santa María could remember the practice, the 1776 ordinances speak of women paying for their rights of *vecindad* upon marriage so they will be reactivated in widowhood; this payment was known as *alfileres* (pin money) and for both native and nonnative women it consisted of six *azumbres* of wine and twelve pounds of bread, to be paid when their husbands paid for their rights. By paying their *alfileres* women kept their houses tied into the communal web of use-rights. But even as widows women could not attend meetings of the *concejo*, and were required to send a son or neighbor in their place, as they still do today.

Since *vecindad* is in a sense the property of the house, if the *vecino* leaves the village and sets up house elsewhere his rights of *vecindad* are severed from the original house. The *concejo* was quite unforgiving of those native sons who left the village only to return at a later time seeking *vecindad*. In most villages the returning native son had to pay fees of *vecindad* all over again like a *forastero*, despite his being a native son, "for this privilege he already enjoyed" (*pues de este privilejio ya gozo*), as the ordinances of Santa María put it.

Thus *vecindad* was identified with the house, which in turn was identified with the village. All this made for a very closely woven fabric that bound together the village and the houses in it, or again, the *concejo* and the *vecinos*. At certain times it even made of the houses one house and of the *vecinos* one body, the *concejo*.

Vecindad *and the battle for the commons*

One of those times, in Santa María del Monte, occurred at the turn of the eighteenth century. From January of 1700 to October of 1701, the village was caught in a whirlwind of litigation with a prosperous widow from the neighboring village of Villafeliz. The event is recorded in a manuscript still in existence in the village, though all memory of it has long since receded.

The case opens in the city of León with Doña Francisca Díez del Blanco, the widow of Don Marcelo de la Puente, and a woman of "nobility and quality," from Villafeliz, bringing a petition against the *concejo* and *vecinos* of Santa María for not allowing her herds to graze freely in village territories. It was the Doña's claim that her husband had been a *vecino* of Santa María and that the *concejo* had no business denying her rights of *vecindad* as his widow. Her herds had every right to graze in Santa María's lands unperturbed, she claimed, and even so the *concejo* was threatening to take some of her animals in bond by the action known as *prendar*. It was common practice for the *concejo* to take away some item of private property from a guilty party who could not otherwise be brought to pay the penalty for infringement of the *concejo*'s rules. But Doña Francisca would not succumb to penalty or *prenda*. She demanded justice: that her *vecindad* not be questioned, that her herds be allowed to graze undisturbed in Santa María's territory, that any animals taken as *prendas* be returned at no charge to her, and that if the *concejo* had anything to reply to the contrary that it come forth in court and say so.

Litigation is a costly enterprise at any time. Imagine how much more so it is when lawyers' fees have to come out of the pockets of small peasant landholders for whom basic subsistence was a challenge of major proportions in the early eighteenth century.[34] Doña Francisca no doubt expected the case to close fast in her favor with the *concejo* simply failing to organize itself as a body to pay the price of making an appearance in court. She must have been surprised.

The *concejo* responded fearlessly to the first of her challenges as it did to the many others that would follow in the course of the long battle ahead. The *vecinos* demanded that she remove her herds from village lands and that she pay a total of 3,600 *reales* for nine years of encroachments on their pastures. She was no *vecina* of Santa María, they said, nor did she have landed property (*bienes raíces*) in the village, nor had she paid her *alfileres* so her husband's rights of *vecindad* would pass on to her at the hour of his death. What is more, and this was the key failing in the eyes of the *vecinos*, neither she nor her husband had ever had a house in the village or lived there for any length of time, and "to enjoy use-rights residence was required with house and family the better part of the year ... and said Marcelo and his wife had never lived in this place."[35]

Doña Francisca retaliated with a series of accusations intended to prove Marcelo had been a *vecino*. Was it not true, she argued, that he "payed and contributed as a *vecino* and had been charged for his due?" Was it not true that "at the close of last December when he died he was *mayordomo* of the parish church of said place and that for this office and others he had a deputy in the place for his absences"? As a *vecino*, was it not true that Marcelo "would bring blessed bread [*caridad*] when it was his turn"? And since the death of Marcelo and the beginning of the lawsuit, hadn't the *concejo* "assessed and collected from her quotas and assessments as a *vecina*"?[36]

Juan de las Salas Gutiérrez and Juan González, both *vecinos* and the latter *regidor* of Santa María, came forth to answer, and asked that Doña Francisca swear to the truth of their claim: that she had no right to village pastures since she had neither house nor family in Santa María but, rather, in Villafeliz. She insisted, again, that she had inherited rights of *vecindad* from her husband and that she did have a house in Santa María to which to bring blessed bread and satisfy all other burdens of the *concejo* as a proper *vecina*. To her retort she added the complaint that the *vecinos* had taken a few head of cattle from her as *prendas* and this, she felt, was unjust while the lawsuit was pending.

The *concejo* and *vecinos* were fired up. Thus the anger in the sarcastic reply: "It is difficult to pity someone for being deprived of what they never had a title or a right to." For we now learn that the cattle Doña Francisca had been bringing through Santa María's pastures was no modest flock, but a herd of more than eighty head. This was an enormous number by the standards of the day when most *vecinos* had a cow or two and a handful of sheep and goats, which were not always their exclusive property but held in some form of *aparcería* or partnership. And the hungry beasts, in so large a number, were laying waste the communal pastures of the village. Nor was it simply the number of animals that was cause for anger. The widow's animals were ferocious and wild beasts, unlike the tame and domesticated herds of the *vecinos*. Exaggerating a little, perhaps, the two representatives of the *concejo* spoke vividly of how the *vecinos* were afraid to take their own herds to pasture, "fearing for the injury and harm they were experiencing both personally, in being forced to avail themselves of the oaks to save their lives, and in regard to their cattle, some of which were being mistreated and others killed, as all knew."[37]

So much for the upland pastures, to which the cattle not being used for work was sent. But Don Marcelo had also managed to insinuate his animals into the better closed-off meadows which provided sustenance for the beasts of burden. Don Marcelo was in the habit of bringing three pairs of oxen from Villafeliz to the *cotos boyales* (closed ox pastures), when the *vecinos* were not allowed more than a single pair, and those beasts too had laid waste their meadows, "depriving the *vecinos* of the necessary support and sustenance of their work animals" (*pribando a los vecinos del abrigo y substento nezesario para sus labranzas*). Had Doña Francisca been a *vecina* of Santa María she would have had much to account for, the *vecinos* concluded.

Doña Francisca had gotten her way regarding her complaint that the *concejo* not take *prendas* from her while the suit was pending, and the *concejo* had been ordered to return the cattle already taken from her. But immediately after returning the *prendas* what does the *concejo* do, exclaims Doña Francisca, but send out five men to hide in a tree to catch any animals that set foot in their territory. And as soon as her animals enter, again they take a calf and several cows as *prendas*. This is a criminal act, the widow protests, and her animals should be returned to her at once. And so on, in what is but one of a series of replays in which the *vecinos* continuously overturn the Doña's legal victories.

As the case continues, Doña Francisca reiterates again that her husband had left behind a house in Santa María, that he had fulfilled all obligations of the *concejo*, took blessed bread on Sundays, and even had to take his turn guarding *veceras* (common herds). A new detail is provided, however: that she had a house which was open all year long in the territory and wood of Valdelorio—which was all her property—where she kept her cattle and had servants living year-round. Since Valdelorio was surrounded by Santa María's territory, it was impossible for her herds to get to Valdelorio without going through Santa María. Thus she points out: "If she and her husband had not been *vecinos* of said place, every day there would have been lawsuits and dissent and *prendas* of cattle back and forth . . . and her husband had been accepted as a *vecino* without controversy of any sort and had paid for himself and her part the rights he owed to the *concejo* and *vecinos* of said place as was customary and she enjoyed the same *vecindades*, exemptions, and privileges as her husband."[38]

There are several more petitions back and forth between the two parties, but when the case closes in León on the 27th of July of 1700 it closes in favor of the *concejo* of Santa María, with the *alcalde mayor* of the city calling for the immediate removal of Doña Francisca's herds from village territories. Nor were her animals to set foot in those territories again, according to the ruling of the *alcalde*. On the other hand, both parties to the suit would have to pay their own bills, for the *alcalde* made no *condenación de costas*, by means of which he could have forced Doña Francisca to foot the *concejo*'s bill. And as if the debt incurred in bringing the case to León was not bad enough, several months later Doña Francisca appealed to what was then the highest court in León and Old Castile, the *chancillería* of Valladolid, above which stood only the king.

Thus the case is propelled forward, as Doña Francisca, the mother of nine children, continues her battle against the *concejo* and *vecinos* of Santa María. To Valladolid go Vitorio Gutiérrez and Juan de Salas, *regidores* of Santa María, and Juan González, a *vecino*, in the name of the *concejo*'s nineteen *vecinos*. In an aside in the proceedings, the *concejo* is described as meeting at the sound of the bells, "as we are used and accustomed to" (*como thenemos de usso y costumbre*). All the *vecinos* present at the reunion are listed one by one and "in the same accord and feeling" (*de un mismo acuerdo y sentir*) they are said to give their consent to carry on with the case in Valladolid. The reason for including the reunion of the *concejo* in the proceedings is no mere formality: since it is the *concejo* as a juridical person that is pursuing the suit, the *vecinos* are shown coming together as a single body, speaking in a single voice; that the *concejo* is the persona of the village ceases to be a legal fiction, a metaphor, and becomes real.

At this stage we begin to learn the details of how Don Marcelo acquired the *vecindad* that his widow was so anxious to renew for herself. In the words of the *vecinos*, "Although they had admitted said Marcelo de la Puente . . . it had not been voluntarily but out of the fear they had for him, who as a powerful person boasted that he would take away the pastures and rights of use they had in rent and for the bad treatment the servants and shepherds gave their herds if they passed into the territory of Valdelorio where he had his house and all that circumference and private territory."[39]

Although the *concejo* had given Don Marcelo *vecindad*, the *vecinos* continued, he had never lived in Santa María, nor did he have landed property, a house, or a home in the village. In other words, he had not put down roots in Santa María. This sense of putting down roots in a place is captured well in the vivid Spanish term for real estate or landed property, *bienes raíces*, literally "rooted goods." In the eyes of the *vecinos*, this quality of rootedness was the essence of being a *vecino*: it meant forging one's livelihood from one's property in the village, planting one's house and family in its soil. Don Marcelo had bought his *vecindad* but he had not become a *vecino*.

Even when the *vecinos* had placed him in the charge of an office of the *concejo*, he never served it himself but had gotten substitutes to serve in his place. In this too he had failed as a *vecino*, for part of the responsibility of being one entailed serving one's turn as an officer of the *concejo*. For it was only by carrying out these responsibilities that a *vecino* earned the privileges of *vecindad*. And how could Don Marcelo carry them out if he was never around? Had he owned property in the village and had a house and family there, it would still not have been enough. "Not living in said place the better part of the year, he could not nor should not enjoy the effects and emoluments which are produced and caused by said *vecindad* as were rights of use over pastures, for just because he was a *vecino* does not guarantee that it was his right to enjoy them."[40]

Once again the *vecinos* point out in passing that Don Marcelo had not paid for the *alfileres*, his wife's rights of *vecindad*, when he was admitted as a *vecino*, and so she now had no right to them as a widow. But clearly this is not their main point of contention. What has set off their deeper anger and gotten them to turn word into deed is Don Marcelo's and his widow's manipulation of the village's communal resources to their own ends. Don Marcelo "had taken possession of the pastures of said *concejo* in such excess and with so many cattle that they laid waste, ruined, and destroyed them, leaving the poor *vecinos* and natives without those necessary for their conservation."[41] What is more, Don Marcelo's oxen had pastured in the closed oxen meadows of the *concejo*, but the fruits of their labors and—here we hear the parish priest's voice—tithes produced went to Villafeliz where he was, in fact, a *vecino*.

His other cattle, wild as they were, had caused so much damage in the communal pastures that the *vecinos* had been forced to remove their animals and bring them to the sierras and mountains, "where they were at a great disadvantage and grass was scarce, which had brought about the death of many of the cattle and the diminution of their young."[42] The *vecinos* again reminded the court of the danger they themselves were constantly in, with the bulls of Don Marcelo and Doña Francisca coming through the village unbridled. As remuneration for the nine years of pasturage Don Marcelo and his widow had stolen from the village the *vecinos* now asked for 4,500 *reales* and for *condenación de costas*.

Meanwhile Doña Francisca continued to plead her case: that her husband had been a *vecino* of Santa María; that as such he had paid the tributes which had been allotted him; that he was serving as *mayordomo* of the church when he died; that he had a house and stable in Valdelorio, which was within parish limits, and had field hands residing there; and that as a *vecino* he had legitimately brought their cattle to graze in Santa María's pastures. Her argument rested on the point that rights to pastures and other communal properties were a function of *vecindad* and had nothing to do with being housed in the village for any period of time. And since her husband had *vecindad* there was no reason why she, as his widow, shouldn't have it too. Would the court declare, then, that she had a right to the usufruct of communal properties in Santa María "as the *vecina* that she was" (*como tal vecina que era*)?

But the *chancillería* of Valladolid declared otherwise. It upheld the verdict of the *alcalde mayor* of León and again ordered that Doña Francisca remove all her sheep and cattle from the vicinity of Santa María or pay severe penalties, but that there be no *condenación de costas*. Thus the case closed, after almost two years of litigation.

Such forms of corporate litigation were not unusual in old regime Spain. I have recounted the story of this lawsuit in detail not only because of its purely dramatic or literary power (with its echoes of Lope de Vega's *Fuenteovejuna*), but because of the light it sheds on the meaning of the rules of *vecindad* from the "native point of view."

As the case reveals, there were two native points of view regarding *vecindad*—the *concejo*'s and Doña Francisca's. To the *concejo* and *vecinos* of Santa María it was a contradiction in terms to be a *vecino* of two villages at the same time; for *vecindad*, in their view, necessarily implied that house and family were permanently moored in the one and only community in which the paterfamilias was a *vecino*. According to this view, Don Marcelo had been a *vecino* of Santa María in name only for it was in Villafeliz that he was truly a *vecino*. For Doña Francisca, on the other hand, *vecindad* was not a function of house and residence; it was a commodity, which had a definite money value and which, once bought, became the untouchable property of its owner, for him or her to use and pass on at will. Thus there was nothing contradictory, in her view, about holding rights of *vecindad* in two places.

As those opposing views are spun out in the course of the lawsuit we learn a great deal about the economic, religious, and sociopolitical burdens placed upon *vecinos*: that they had to pay tributes of various sorts, participate in the circulation of blessed bread,[43] and take their turns serving as officers of the *concejo* and tending the common herds. Even a man of wealth and power like Don Marcelo had not been able to spare himself such burdens. In those matters the *concejo* had more strength than he, enough to make him, despite his stature, an equal of any other *vecino*.

For it was only on a plane of strict equality that the *concejo* allotted burdens to its *vecinos*; otherwise they would not have tolerated them. The *vecinos* tolerated such burdens too because it was on this plane of equality that the *concejo*, in a manner similar to the allotment of family inheritances, allotted shares of common lands to all *vecinos*. But in this matter Don Marcelo did prove to be the stronger; by virtue of his power he managed to take for his own herds a lion's share of the common pastures and meadows, thereby violating the code of strict equality that was the basis of the *concejo*'s legitimacy as a form of government.

Don Marcelo had carried off this act of exploitation by threatening to wield his power to divest the village of its common lands, a major part of which were being held in rent. Indeed the threat proved to be an excellent strategy for, if we believe the *vecinos*, they suffered for nine years his encroachment upon the commons, which had become usurpation pure and simple when Don Marcelo died at the close of 1699. But it was a temporary defeat, one which was to make the *vecinos* tighten their grip on the commons.

The death of Don Marcelo gave the *vecinos* an excellent opportunity to break the cycle of exploitation he had set in motion and bring the *concejo* back into power. When, with all the confidence of a person whose power is entrenched, Doña Francisca sallied her herds forth into Santa María's pastures as if nothing had changed, she found out that indeed everything had changed. The very same rules of *vecindad* that Don Marcelo had manipulated to sanction his exploitative use of communal grazing rights now became, in the hands of the *concejo*, a shield against the further invasions of Doña Francisca. Although it is she who self-assuredly brings the suit to court, it is the *vecinos* who reveal how unfounded—in the eyes of custom—were her claims.

In all this we see in miniature a drama which, from the sixteenth century, was to be played many times on the stage of history in rural Spain and Europe. The gist of it was everywhere the same: the communities struggling to keep the common lands, under attack by prosperous peasants, seigneurial lords, wealthy townsmen, and the nation-state itself, from becoming the private property of a single individual.[44] In the end was it not the privatization of the commons that had been the goal of Don Marcelo's and Doña Francisca's encroachments all along? And was it not the conservation of its communal character that had inspired the struggle of the *concejo* and *vecinos* of Santa María?

Thus the battle was for the commons. But everything hinged on the question of *vecindad*, that most local of concepts. For the Don and Doña, the mere individualistic purchase of *vecindad* and fulfillment of its burdens by proxy should have been sufficient to grant them access to the commons. Indeed, they also had a house of sorts in the village. But, as the *vecinos* demonstrate, it was not a house in the sense of a household where family and economy were joined. Nor was this so-called house in the settled nucleus of the village; it lay on its borders, off in the wood and meadow of Valdelorio, amidst "all that circumference and private territory." And, most obvious of all, Don Marcelo and Doña Francisca lived in Villafeliz, not in Santa María. Why, then, should they have been entitled to a share of Santa María's common lands? Thus the *vecinos* themselves made the case for the unity of house and village.

What became of Doña Francisca after the case came to an end in 1701 remains a mystery. I found no other documents mentioning her or her husband. Next we hear of Valdelorio is in 1752, in the Catastro de Ensenada, by which time it is said to belong to the Marquise of Valverde, who maintained possession of it until the end of the nineteenth century. Was Doña Francisca forced to sell her property after her defeat in court? Or did one of her offspring marry into noble ranks? Although there is no recollection of Valdelorio ever having belonged to Doña Francisca and Don Marcelo, older villagers do remember that Valdelorio was the property of a marquise. So perhaps their reign was short-lived after all.

But whatever house they built left its mark on the land. From the parish records of Santa María we learn that there were four people living in Valdelorio from 1801 to 1811, a father, daughter, her husband, and their child; by 1814 the husband had become a *vecino* of Santa María, and the father a resident.[45] In 1848, according to Madoz, there was still in Valdelorio "a half-ruined settlement" (*un caserío medio arruinado*).[46] Today all that is left of the house that sparked the lawsuit are the foundations. In its place, however, a myth detailing the origin of the village has grown, to which we will turn in Chapter 15.

The encroachment of Don Marcelo and Doña Francisca on the common lands of Santa María left its mark, in another way, on the village's history. In a document from 1698 and another from 1701, we find the *concejo* and *vecinos* respectively asking the *corregidores* and *regidores* of the city of León, and the Marquises of the estate of Toral and house of Guzmán, that the common lands of Trigalejos and San Pelayo which they were holding in rent be given to them in less tenuous *foros perpetuos* (perpetual leases). In both cases the *concejo* won the *foros* and in so doing practically gained for itself proprietary rights over the vast terrains of pasture and woodland in Trigalejos and San Pelayo (which borders on Valdelorio). In the 1701 document concerning San Pelayo the *vecinos* explain why they desire to hold the land in *foro*: "It is beneficial and convenient for us to have all-embracing rights of use so that no one will be able to go in to graze, cut, or clear in said territory of San Pelayo without the permission and consent of said *concejo* and *vecinos* of Santa María del Monte."[47] The *concejo* and *vecinos* as bearers of each of these *foros* obtain the right, as the 1698 document concerning Trigalejos states, "to be able to *prendar*, penalize, and punish all those persons who break in or attempt to break in from outside to graze their cattle and sheep there."[48]

Surely it is no accident that these *foros perpetuos* over village common lands are won in the very years when Don Marcelo and Doña Francisca were attempting to take advantage of them. The acquisition of *foros* over Trigalejos and San Pelayo, the two major tracts of common pasture, waste, and wood in Santa María gave the *concejo* and *vecinos* total control over these lands, as the passages cited above indicate, and assured them of their perennial right to them. Of course the village now had to pay the city of León six *ducados* a year, and the Marquises of Toral eight *cargas* of rye wheat a year for the *foros*; but judging from the fact that the *foros* were sought after by the *vecinos* themselves, it was not too high a price to pay to keep the commons within the circle of the *concejo*, beyond the reach of grasping outsiders.

Chapter 8

✛

The *Concejo* as a Polity

To A VERY GREAT EXTENT the *concejo* was an acephalous political system. It was the *concejo* and *vecinos* as a single body that ruled in most matters, and especially so in those of some importance to the whole community. And truly no one stood above the *concejo*: it was the pinnacle of local power and authority, as it still is even today in many Leonese villages. All this is true to the tradition of the "open" assembly.

The problem of authority

Although an assembly, and as such ultimately acephalous, the *concejo* has long had leaders and officers of various sorts, so many, in fact, that by the eighteenth century it is virtually a bureaucracy in miniature. Most of those offices, I suspect, were not initiated by the village; it is almost certain that they took form in the long and complex interaction of village and state. But the burgeoning of offices, besides making the *concejo* a little top-heavy at times (especially in the smaller villages of ten and twenty houses), gave it an ever-growing sense of itself as a mini-state, or little republic, a role it accepted with great reluctance.

The most important office by far was that of village headman, the name for which in León has changed from *procurador* in the sixteenth century; *regidor* in the seventeenth, eighteenth, and early nineteenth centuries; *alcalde pedáneo* and later *alcalde de barrio* through to close to the end of the nineteenth century; to *presidente*, the term still in use today. How the headman was chosen varied from village to village until nineteenth-century municipal reforms ushered in a wholly new and homogeneous administrative system, the full implications of which will be discussed later. But basically there were two modes of electing headmen: by turn, through the system known as *vecera*, or by some form of election.

Usually it was in the very smallest villages that the headman was chosen by turn, as in Villamanín or Campo, situated in mountain country just north of Santa María, which had six to eight houses. The ordinances of Villamanín state that "for the governance of this village there should be two *regidores* and a *sobrerregidor*, and these are to be named by turn or *velanda* [another term for *vecera*, but probably stemming from *velar*, to guard or watch over, rather than from *vez* or turn as does *vecera*], and those who are allotted the duty may not excuse themselves under any pretext, and should they do so, the authorities will be notified to compel them and fine them twelve *reales*."[1] Similarly the ordinances of Campo say that "the *regidor* will be by *vecera* each year."[2] Or, in another mountain village lying to the west, in Matalunga, the custom was for the two *procuradores* to be chosen in turn by a two-directional *vecera*: "and one is to follow the *vercera* upward and the other downward," adding, as do virtually all the ordinances, that "these offices are to be taken on without any excuse whatsoever by all who are *vecinos*."[3]

In larger villages, which in León consist of anywhere from fifteen to thirty houses, the headmen were elected in various ways, sometimes representing different neighborhoods in the village, usually the "upper" and "lower" *barrios*. The village of Peornedo, in the north-eastern mountain range, chose its two *regidores* on the first day of the year; they were elected by the elder of the two *regidores* completing his term of office, and two of the eldest *vecinos*. In nearby Canseco, there were three *regidores*, one for each *barrio*, who were chosen by an elder from each of the three *barrios*.[4]

The *regidores* were also elected in Santa María, but in a slightly different manner. In Santa María, according to the 1776 ordinances, it was customary to name all the offices at the end of the year, on Saint Silvester's Day. The bells were rung and the *concejo* came together. Then the younger of the two *regidores* rose and named four *vecinos* who, along with the elder *regidor*, would go to the church portal to elect the various officers. Once outside the elder *regidor* named two *vecinos* for each of the offices and four *vecinos* chosen to make the election proceeded, in order of seniority, to cast their votes. In this way not only were the *regidores* elected, but also the *mayordomo* (steward) of the church, the *mayordomo* of *las ánimas* (the souls in purgatory), the *mayordomo* of Our

Lady, the *estanquero* (reservoir keeper), the *depositario* (treasurer), and the *fiel de fechos* (secretary and village scribe). Once the elections were completed, the five men were to return to the *concejo*, and the eldest of the four *vecinos* chosen to do the voting was to relay the news to all, standing, and with cap in hand.[5]

This customary manner of choosing village officers did live on past the middle of this century in Santa María, but only with one office, that of *mayordomo* of the church, into which were collapsed the other two offices of *mayordomo* of *las ánimas* and *mayordomo* of Our Lady. In reading over the ordinance I have summarized above, Leonardo Mirantes remembered having himself been chosen *mayordomo* by this method: "To name the *mayordomo* of the church in these years past, these years past which is not even ten years ago ... the president would ask two *vecinos* to go out of the *casa de concejo* to name the *mayordomo*. ... I had just returned from Madrid then, there were others, older than me, younger than me, who had been *vecinos* for a longer time, but since I had returned then, well, I was named by order of those men, which is the same as what is being said here."[6]

With the office of headman, as with all other village offices, it was rare to find willing candidates for the job. Each and every office, as the Leonese specialist on customary law Flórez de Quiñones points out, was viewed as "a painful personal prestation" (*una penosa prestación personal*).[7] Indeed, when I naively asked Leonardo, after he had finished telling me how he had been chosen *mayordomo*, whether that was a position of honor, he answered, hardly believing the question: "No, no, no, *mayordomo*, nothing, nothing, it was a sacrifice, because being *mayordomo* one's wife has to sweep the church all year and the *mayordomo* has to go to mass all year, had to go to mass, because in the past we went to mass with *la caridad* which was just on Sundays."[8] It was the *mayordomo* who, until the custom of *la caridad* abruptly came to a halt several years ago, was in charge of cutting the blessed bread up into morsels, so all the parishioners could sanctify themselves by consuming a piece after the mass.

Leonardo was expressing a view which has a long tradition in Leonese village life. The offices, also known, appropriately, as *cargos*, are the burdens of *vecindad*, the sacrifices it entails; they are fulfilled only insofar as they are prestations incumbent upon all *vecinos*. In the same ordinance from Santa María that describes the election of the *regidores* we find a most revealing closing remark: "We also ordain and decree that if one of those newly named for whatever office it may be, has the right to refuse to serve the office allotted him, he should defend his protest before a court of law, without causing disturbances or propounding threats, and without directly blaming the *regidor* or any of those who went out, penalty of four *reales*."9

One of the most difficult of prestations has long been that of headman. The ordinances from Villamanín and Mataluenga cited earlier concerning the rotation of the office of *regidor* do not fail to add a clause stating that no *vecino* dare refuse the duty under any pretext. Or, to cite yet another case, in the village of San Román de la Vega, near the city of Astorga, where the two *regidores* were chosen by village elders for half-year terms, they had to accept the position, "without renouncing it, penalty of two hundred *maravedís*, and if they are rebellious said penalty should be doubled, and based on it said *regidores* named by said men should accept said appointment as required."10

Why should there have been—and continue to be—so much reluctance to take on the office of headman, or, for that matter, any public office? To answer this question, let us see what responsibilities these offices entailed and what made them so undesirable.

The major obligation of the *regidor*, as of the *presidente* today, was to watch over the common interests of the *vecinos*. He had to preside over the *concejo*, maintaining order at the meetings and calling the *vecinos* together whenever a matter of common concern needed to be aired. It was the *regidores* who represented the village in all its dealings with the state, as we saw earlier in the Doña Francisca case, and in villages once under the jurisdiction of ecclesiastical or secular lords, the *regidores* were the key link between the village and the seigneurial establishment.

Thus the headmen were expected to take on significant political responsibilities for the entire village while, at the same time, as ordinary *labradores*, they also had to attend to the needs of their own houses. As I know so well from having been in close daily contact with the current *presidente* of Santa María, this must always have been a difficult balancing act. How many times did I not hear him say that he would have plowed or mowed such and such a field already if he had not had to go to León and attend to *cosas del pueblo* (village matters).11 And, as I also heard him say so often, his actions on behalf of the village were never appreciated; no matter what you do, he would say, you are roundly criticized by all.

Among the worst burdens the headmen had was serving as the village's officers of the law in the days, that is, "when customs were laws," as an informant put it. What this came down to was that the headmen were often put in the uneasy position of having to fine their fellow *vecinos* for failure to comply with one or another of the customary laws of the village. In a small village where everyone knows each other too well and practically every neighbor is a relative, this can be most distasteful. For if a headman fines a fellow *vecino* for violating the rules, this will very likely provoke his anger, and even hatred; but, on the other hand, if he fails to extract fines from his guilty co-villagers, he is not living up to his responsibilities as headman and, if caught, could himself be fined by the *concejo*. Thus to have the power to enforce the laws of custom, as do the men who rule in the village, is to be caught in a knot of contradictions. With all the difficulties power poses in such a community it is not surprising that, at least for some, it is not worth the headaches it inevitably brings.

But the headmen, besides being policemen, have to be tax collectors and village fund-raisers; and extracting money from the Leonese *labrador*, who either does not have it, or has it and hates to let go of it, has probably never been a simple feat. Hints of the hard time headmen had getting the *vecinos* to pay up can be found in many an old ordinance, such as in this one from San Román de la Vega: "For said *regidores* to collect royal tributes, assessments for bridges, and quotas of any kind, they should not call a *concejo* but they themselves should go collect them and for this they should give notice the night before of the hour in which they shall do it and he who does not come to pay shall pay the fine of eight *maravedís*."[12] Warned of the hour and the day in which collection would take place, the *vecinos* could have no excuse for not paying, especially when lack of payment itself had its price. Even with such measures, however, it usually took a great deal more coaxing than this to get the *vecinos* to pay their share of the communal bills, and still does to this day, when villagers live in relative prosperity compared to past times.

Since the headmen deal in money, in the hard-won money of their fellow villagers, no less, they have always had to be scrupulous about keeping accounts. In Mataluenga, where the two *procuradores* were chosen every two months by turn in a simultaneous upward and downward *vecera*, the men had to produce accounts no later than eight days after their terms had ended, or pay the penalty of sixteen *reales*. For this purpose four men were named who, along with the old and new *pro-*

curadores, were to take the accounts down under oath, "so they will take them well and faithfully ... and if it should happen that one of the *procuradores* or accountants does something fraudulent or conceals any rights of this our *concejo*, he who so conceals shall be fined eighteen *reales* for this our *concejo*."[13]

Many more examples could be cited from the ordinances to show just how important were the accounts of how village moneys got spent. But let me just cite an example from the present which I think will prove illuminating, for even when the accounts are properly kept, the actions of the headmen still fall prey to untoward suspicions and accusations. In Santa María the money left over from the installment of a new sewage system was put in a bank account in the name of the village, so it would gain interest and be there whenever the village had need of it. For some people in the village this modern investment scheme is tantamount to losing the money altogether, and they would prefer to see that money redistributed to the *vecinos*, proportionate to what each spent, in keeping with older practices. The year I lived in Santa María a number of village men would not agree to the plan to pave the streets, for which the village would receive substantial government subsidies, because, as one man told the *presidente*, they don't want their money to "disappear" into his hands and never be seen again, implying, in other words, that the *presidente* himself takes possession of it. Ironically, the remark came out of a man whose own father, as *presidente*, was found guilty of pocketing money from village funds when the accounts were drawn up at the end of his term. Such, in short, have been—and, in large part, continue to be—the obligations and duties, even the insults, headmen must bear in many a village in León.

What we must keep in mind about all village offices, from that of headman to *mayordomo*, is that the officeholder receives no remuneration; he is not rewarded for his labors or compensated for time spent. Thus we can understand why the taking on of office might be viewed as a sacrifice. Precisely because it is a sacrifice to hold office, the burden is passed around as equitably as possible. In the smaller villages, as we saw earlier, the burdens of office-holding were circulated from house to house, so that each *vecino*, for example, took his turn being headman; even so, it seems that men looked for excuses not to have to serve.

Similarly, in Santa María today, the three main offices of the Comunidad de Regantes, the village irrigation society, are rotated among the *vecinos*. Every *vecino* takes his turn holding one of these unwelcome posts, unwelcome because abuses of water rights are frequent, and, again, no one enjoys having to fine, or be fined by, a fellow *vecino*. In the same way, the offices of *abad* ("abbott") and *andador* ("messenger") of the village religious confraternity of San Roque are also rotated annually: the first is circulated among the oldest members who have not yet served as *abad* more than once, while the position of *andador* is circulated among the newest entering *vecinos*. It is the *abad* and the *andador* who are responsible for organizing and preparing the feast that is held on August 16 in honor of San Roque. By circulating these offices, then, all the confraternity members share equally in the burden of perpetuating this corporate religious festivity.

Looking again at the old method of election used in Santa María to name the various local officials, in which one *regidor* chose the voters and the other chose the candidates, we can likewise see an ingenious structure for distributing equitably the burdens of power and preventing its monopolization. For there are always individuals who seek out power as an end in itself. The old arrangements for distributing local political offices sought to quell such ambitions by turning power into a type of community resource, like the common lands and woods. Power, rather than becoming the exclusive possession of an individual, was thereby kept circulating around the village.

There were, as I have noted earlier, quite an assortment of offices besides that of headman. From my informant we already heard that being a *mayordomo* meant more housework for the *mayordomo*'s wife and weekly churchgoing for the *mayordomo*, in whom rested a major part of the responsibility over the blessed bread ritual. That there were three *mayordomos* in Santa María in the eighteenth century, rather than just one as in the twentieth century, testifies not only to the greater importance of the church in the past, but also to the fact that there were once enough burdens to keep three men busy. The *estanqueros* of the past, we can safely assume, took charge of the modest irrigation system the village had prior to the building of its own dam, a role filled today by the three main officers of the Comunidad de Regantes. The *depositario*, as the treasurer, had to keep track of the flow of money and goods from penalties and *prendas*, from payments made to crown and church. The *fiel de fechos*, besides being secretary and scribe, very often had to keep a faithful eye (faithful to the community, of course) over the tavernkeeper and, where there was one, over the baker, and guard over the community's weights and measures, to be sure the village would not be deceived in quantity or price.[14] Every office was marked, in short, by its own peculiar burdens.

One office that was surely undesirable, so much so that it was given out at weekly intervals, was that of *pesquisero*, a post that no longer exists. In eighteenth-century Santa María, according to the ordinances of the village from the period, the *pesquisero* "the week it is his turn is like a servant of the *regidores*, or of the *concejo*." It was his duty to bring wine from the tavern when the *regidores* asked him to do so, and to pour it out in *concejo* for all the men, "which he must do equitably not giving more to one than to another and for this he will remove his cap or hat." But the wine pouring was the lighter part of the *pesquisero*'s burden. Far weightier, certainly, must have been his obligation to collect the *prendas* and fines that the *regidores* asked him to get from penalized *vecinos*. The *pesquisero* was to go collect on his own and if after two tries and a doubling of the penalty, he failed, only then would one of the *regidores* accompany him. And if the two of them failed to extract the *prendas*, the matter was to be brought to the attention of the *concejo* and it was to propose the solution.[15]

Indeed, whenever the local authorities were not obeyed it was always the *concejo* that had the last word. Again and again in the ordinances of Santa María we see that the pattern was for the village officers to attempt to extract the fines two times and, failing in their efforts, the *concejo* was to take charge. In the mountain village of Mena the *regidor* could not fine a *vecino* or a *forastero* more than eight *reales* for each infringement; and "when the excesses or transgressions are such that they require a larger fine or punishment this is to be the one established by the greater and better part of the *vecinos* gathered in *concejo*."[16]

In Mataluenga, whose ordinances appear to be at least a hundred years older than those of Santa María, there were two *sacadores* or "extractors" of penalties, fines, and *prendas*; those positions were circulated by *vecera*, as were those of *procuradores* in the same village. When *prendas* needed to be extracted because payments due to the crown or to the *concejo* or fines to be paid in wine had not been delivered, the *sacadores* would go in search of them. If, after one attempt and a penalty of nine *reales*, the *prendas* were not forthcoming, the *sacadores* were obliged to inform the *procuradores* who, in turn, were obliged to ring for *concejo*. Four men then had to go with the *sacadores* to extract the *prendas* required for the unmade payment "and for the nine *reales* incurred the first time and for twelve more *reales* for making the *concejo* gather."[17]

Thus we return to our starting point: that the *concejo* basically represented an acephalous system of government. For in the final analysis we see that the *concejo* itself was the ultimate moral force in the village— not its officers. Of course in everyday life the *concejo* could not be expected to gather on every occasion when a simple decision had to be made, nor could it be present in court at every lawsuit. How would the *vecinos* ever have found time to attend to their own houses? As we saw above, in Mataluenga a fine of twelve *reales* could be imposed on that house which, unnecessarily, forced a gathering of the *concejo*. It was essential, therefore, for the *concejo* to have its officers, for it could not be present in all places at all times; but ultimately the *vecinos* as the single body of the *concejo* ruled. This made for a tense and contradictory social reality, the nature of which was well realized by the headmen or *junta* of nearby Barrio de Nuestra Señora when, in 1964, they ended their "renovation" of custom with the following remarks: "Let us remind you also to fulfill all burdens of *vecindad* and likewise to respect and fulfill agreements, for regrettably the *Junta* has to resort to sanctions against those who are lax, which actions may give rise to hatred and rancor toward those who represent Justice without perhaps voluntarily wanting to represent it."[18]

The democratic ideal

The persistence of so archaic a unit of government as the *concejo abierto* had begun to attract the attention of Spanish scholars at the close of the last century, at the very moment when this as well as many other peasant institutions were collapsing under the weight of liberal reforms. Joaquín Costa, the "regenerationist" jurist, set the tone for a defense of the challenged institutions, especially those taking their inspiration from one or another form of "agrarian collectivism," in the process forging a powerful critique of eighteenth- and nineteenth-century liberal ideology.[19]

Costa's Leonese disciples, also jurists, and native sons of small mountain villages where the tradition of the *concejo abierto* had been strong and long-lived, took up his critique of liberal ideology. They focused on the issue of the municipal reform of the 1830s and on what they perceived to have been its devastating effects on local government. In their eyes the *concejo* was an exemplary model, a Leonese one at that, of social and political life rooted in the democratic ideal. As a result they firmly opposed the reform project fashioned by the Cortes of Cádiz in 1812, in which new municipal units were frequently created by joining together groups of previously autonomous villages to be governed by *ayuntamientos* (municipal seats). This process of bringing separate villages into a con- solidated municipality especially affected the northern provinces of Spain, where in the 1820s more than 50 percent of the population lived in settled nuclei of less than 1,000 people, and where many villages consisted of twenty or fewer households.[20]

A central point of their critique was the formation by the nineteenth- century state of uniform codes of law which were to serve the needs of all the municipalities in the peninsula; they instead defended the previous decentralized customary law, rooted always in the particularities of a local community. Although in the period before the municipal reforms there had existed administrative units larger than the village, these never attempted to eliminate the variety of local custom, nor had they attempted to substitute a representative form of government for what the Leonese jurists characterized as the "direct democracy" of the *concejos*. In the centralized system of government created by the reformers, on the other hand, each village was to elect biennially a *junta administrativa* (admin- istrative committee) consisting of an *alcalde pedáneo* (or *de barrio*) and two or four *vocales* (assistants), depending on the size of the village, to serve as its representatives. The *junta* was responsible to the *alcalde municipal* of the *ayuntamiento*, who in turn represented the entire mu- nicipality in its dealings with the central government. From this point on the *concejo* ceased to have any legal authority of its own.

Though he was convinced that these reforms had devastated the *concejo* as a form of government, Elías López Morán, the pioneer scholar of Leonese customary law, nevertheless emphasized that

> If the legislator, little aware of the necessities and of the social condition of the people for whom he legislates, insists on declaring "centralization!" the *pueblos* will answer with their deeds "auton- omy!!"; if he says: "*Juntas administrativas!*" the *vecinos* of the *pueblos* will continue . . . gathering in their assemblies or *concejos* to take action on what is of interest to them all . . .[21]

Legally the villages were deprived of their traditional right to make ordinances and levy fines, yet as López Morán observed at the turn of the century the *concejos* of León continued to govern themselves ac- cording to the older forms of customary law. At a time when most of their members had become literate, they self-consciously revised and updated the texts in which this customary law had come down to them. Confronted with the "labyrinthine confusion" of the unceasing legislative activity which characterized the nineteenth century, "the *pueblos* took refuge in their customs and in their ordinances as if they were havens of salvation, and they continued ruling themselves by them in what concerned each locality's governance."[22]

There is no doubt that López Morán and other Leonese jurists idealized the democratic nature of the *concejo abierto* in León. Yet they quite accurately pointed to the threat that the new municipal system posed to the traditions of local government and, at the same time, to the seemingly contradictory persistence of the *concejo*. Indeed, in Santa María the *junta administrativa* in the late nineteenth century took it upon itself to act independently of the wishes of the *vecinos* in one particular case which we will consider in greater detail in the discussion of the common lands. And later, during the Franco dictatorship, the legal authority of the *vecinos* was even further eroded, almost to the point of disappearing. Aside from continuing the nineteenth-century policy of not recognizing the *concejo* as a legal body, Franco's state apparatus eliminated elections and imposed the members of the *juntas administrativas* on the villages. Yet even in this period, when its official powers were at their lowest ebb, the *concejo* still continued to meet regularly, impose fines, and govern according to its custom. Its persistence in these years was perhaps in part due to the fact that, whatever the state ordained about the legality of the *concejo*, the Franco regime upheld ideologically everything that was "traditional" and "Christian" in old rural Spain. But certainly the continuation of the *concejo* also owed much to the villagers themselves who, like their ancestors for centuries before them, insisted on governing themselves with or without the state's approval.

Today, though the *junta administrativa* can and at times does act without consulting the *concejo*, it continues to call together the *concejo* when matters of common concern must be decided on. As one of the members of the present *junta* told me, you cannot have both a *junta* and a *concejo* in a democracy; the *junta* of the *presidente* and the two *vocales* represents the *vecinos* who elected them, while the *concejo* is not a legally recognized body, and so the members of the *junta* are not under any obligation to reckon (*contar*) with it. But as he also pointed out, they know better than to ignore the *concejo*, for if they use their legal power to make decisions that turn out to go against the wishes of the *vecinos*, they will have to bear daily the dissatisfactions of their fellow villagers in what is still a small face-to-face community.

One of the reasons why dissatisfaction would be sure to arise in Santa María if the *junta* acted on its own is that the village is presently divided into two factions, as it has been since the years preceding the Civil War. The factionalism originally grew out of the political differences between nationalist and republican sentiments, but it has long since lost its political connotations and is now based in a division into two kinship groups: roughly, the brothers, cousins, and in-laws of the former *presidente* on one side, and those of the current *presidente* on the other. The split is symbolized—some say caused—by the existence of two gathering places in the village where the men come for a few hours on Sunday to smoke, drink a bit, and play cards. These are the village cantina, owned by the former *presidente*, and the Teleclub, which was set up in the late 1960s in an unused room of the schoolhouse, directly above the *concejo* meetinghouse, and which is run cooperatively by villagers drawn mostly from the opposite faction. To this day the former *presidente* and his closest relatives refuse to set foot in the Teleclub, which he claims takes away his business, and the leaders of the other faction reciprocate by boycotting the cantina. At this level the factions are capable of uniting people who have private quarrels among themselves—for instance, Basilio and his sister-in-law, who we saw fighting over the inheritance of Basilio's house in Chapter 3, both boycott the cantina and in general present a common front in opposition to the other faction, though great tension still remains between them.

By the same token, when the village as a whole finds itself in opposition to an outside group, the two factions band once more together to represent Santa María as a whole, a typical example of this being a soccer game between children of the villagers and children from the "urbanization"—there, of course, no distinctions are made between the two sides. If, then, the members of the *junta* attempt to get things done without calling for a *concejo* meeting, they are likely to antagonize members of the former *presidente*'s faction, who will claim that the wishes of the majority were not taken into account. Thus, when the members of the *junta* proposed paving the village streets a few years ago they were immediately and emphatically opposed by the former *presidente*, who listed innumerable reasons why the project would not be beneficial to the *vecinos* and should not go forward. The *alcalde* of the municipality suggested that the *junta* simply declare that the paving would go forward, and collect a special tax, as they are authorized to do, to pay for it. The members of the *junta* decided instead to continue holding *concejo* meetings until they could change the tide of opinion. Eventually they held a clear majority, and the members of the opposing faction—with the single exception of the former *presidente*—finally agreed to the project. The streets were paved in 1983.

The current *presidente* often dwelt on the issue of coming to a consensus in conversations with me about the *concejo*. "The *concejos* are prohibited," he said to me one night, "but we go on having them because they have come down to us from tradition and if we didn't have them the *vecinos* would get very upset." But it is hard to get a clear consensus out of them, "for if there are twenty *vecinos* there, then there are twenty different opinions." In the present the acephalous *concejo* is viewed even by its own *vecinos* in ways reminiscent of the criticism made of it by visiting bishops in centuries past.

Chapter 9

The *Concejo* as

a Moral Presence

DESPITE all the disorder of meeting in *concejo*, there was more government there than could meet the eye of a bishop, or an anthropologist, at first glance. There was almost, surprising as this may seem, too much government, though this was not by any means a permanent state of affairs. Too often assumed as a matter of course, the solidarity of the village community was in the worst of times absent, in the best of times, enforced.

In the historical record for Santa María and many other Leonese villages, broken though it is by gaps, one sees a consistent pattern: the *concejo*, acting through its officers, enforcing solidarity upon a populace ever threatening to go its own way, to cease being a society.[1] Of what use was the inherited web of customs and controls if no one could agree on exactly what constituted it? Thus from the sixteenth century the *concejo* found itself, whether following orders from the higher authority of crown and lord or acting of its own accord, having to set down its ancestral customs on paper in the form of ordinances. We learn, for example, that on the third of February, in the year 1776, "with the noble *concejo* Gathered at the sound of Bells rung" the nineteen *vecinos* of Santa María agreed to make up a book of ordinances; and having gained the approval of six widows and asked for the opinion of the parish priest, they proceeded to "make up said Ordinances, on account of there not being any, and the *Pueblo* governing itself solely by its ancient customs, these being very deteriorated, and derogated, and interpreted by everyone to his own liking."[2]

Ordenanzas de Costumbres
para este lugar de Sta María
del Monte hechas siendo Residores del fran.co Gomez de Cossies
y Benito Gonzalez

En el nombre de la SSma Trinidad Padre, Hijo, y Spiritu Santo, tres
Personas distintas, y un solo Dios verdadero, y de nuestra Patrona la virgen
María Madre de Dios, y Sra Nuestra, cuios ausilios imploramos, para accertar a disponer, hacer, y gobernar, este
nuestro libro de Ordenanzas, siendo todo para mayor honrra, y gloria de Dios
nuestro Señor, bien de nuestras Almas, y buen gobierno para este nuestro Pueblo: amen.

The first page of Santa María's ordinances of 1776

Along with the writing down of ordinances from the sixteenth to the eighteenth century, the recording of *actas de concejo* (acts of the *concejo*) became very widespread in Leonese villages by the last half of the nineteenth century.[3] In these acts, as in the ordinances before, we find villagers consciously embarking upon a reinterpretation, even at times a resuscitation, of their timeworn customs. As a result, various customary forms of social and religious behavior—attendance at *concejo* meetings, funerals, and votive masses; prestations of labor in the *hacenderas*; and the lodging and feeding of the itinerant poor—become enshrined as the laws of the village, to be enforced with fines, penalties, and sanctions of various sorts.

The spirit behind this codification of custom varies through time, of course, but what is particularly interesting is the fact that villagers are continually looking to the past, to earlier forms of behavior, for modes of structuring their economy, society, and culture in the present. And the present not just of the sixteenth, eighteenth, or nineteenth century, but of our own tumultuous century.

The example of a document from the nearby village of Barrio de Nuestra Señora will bring to light the extraordinary contemporaneity of the meaning of custom. The document itself basically consists of a listing of the customary forms of social and religious behavior mentioned above—to pay for rights of *vecindad*, participate in the communal herding of cattle or the *vecera*, attend funerals and votive masses, take part in the blessed bread ritual, be *mayordomo* of the church when it is one's turn, harbor the poor, and attend reunions of the *concejo*. But this traditional list of customs is preceded by a fierce statement of political ideology, which not only situates the customs in time but gives them an entirely new meaning. For this document dates from the last day of the year 1936, only a few months following the outbreak of the Civil War in Spain. The village of Barrio, though in the nationalist zone, was dangerously close (20 kilometers), even on the road to republican mountain country. And its *vecinos*, as if to demonstrate their firm allegiance to the nationalist camp, begin the compilation of their customs "out of the desire to bring to life again ancient customs of a clearly Christian character, interrupted during the five untimely years in which Spain was weighed down by a mournful and malevolent secularism."[4] To show their patriotism to the nation they did not have to look farther afield than to the age-old customary forms of social and religious behavior that had oriented village life for so many years, or in their words, "the good and Christian administration of the *pueblo*." Thus, in the struggle between nationalist and republican forces, custom receives a novel interpretation: it becomes the way of all true Christians, the past serving as a model for the present. Let us now take a closer look at the question of custom.

The obligation to assemble

Attendance at reunions of the *concejo*, which one might assume villagers would have acceded to naturally, seems in fact to have been enforced to some degree in most villages. A set of ordinances from 1582 for La Milla and its territory ordain that when the bells sounded the call to a reunion of the *concejo* all the *vecinos* should come on penalty of two *reales*. Only the *vecino* who found himself at the other side of the river or on the hills of Güerga, both apparently at some distance from the place, could be excused, so long as he had not been there "with the intention of not being in *concejo* and if this persists or it be found that he went there cunningly he shall pay said penalty not coming to *concejo*."⁵

An ordinance from the village of Mataluenga on the same subject states that the *procuradores* should call together the *concejo* "as many times as necessary ... for *repartimientos* [assessments] as well as for *facenderas* [joint labor] and for other things concerning the governance of this Place ... ringing the Bells three times as is customary."⁶ All the *vecinos* were then to gather within a half hour's time. If at least seven *vecinos* had come, the *procuradores* were to take a head count, meanwhile sending two men to walk the length of the main street in search of idlers still, perhaps, at home. On their return the head count was to be taken again and those who had not arrived by this time were to be fined sixteen *maravedís* unless they had not been in the village. A similar ruling existed in Canseco. According to its ordinances from 1761, the *regidor* was to ring the bells for *concejo* three times and with the first man who came he was to go in search of the others, fining them one *azumbre* of wine each for not coming when called. However, any *vecino* who was off in any of the six distant regions of the village named in the ordinance could not be fined, even if he heard the bells.⁷

All these rulings concern reunions of the *concejo* that have been called for a particular purpose, not the regular Sunday gathering of the *concejo* following mass. Thus, those *vecinos* who found themselves in a distant part of the village or away when summoned were excused from attending. But the ordinances hint at the fact that some *vecinos* were wont to stray deliberately to miss the meetings, and that most tended to take their time getting to them, even needing to be fetched.

What of the regular Sunday gatherings? Were these *concejo* reunions attended any more willingly? It is difficult to say, particularly for the period before the last half of the nineteenth century. The ordinances are not explicit about this matter. But in the nineteenth century, and into the twentieth, it seems that even these regular meetings needed some enforcement, at least according to acts from the period. Today most *vecinos* go to *concejo* on Sundays in Santa María, from what I could observe, though there is one *vecino* in particular who never goes to *concejo* and barely participates in the *hacenderas*. One evening I witnessed how the headmen, in calculating what each *vecino* would have to pay for the year's *licencia* (a license for use of pastures the village must pay to the state), added 500 *pesetas* to this man's quota *"por rebelde,"* as they said, for being rebellious. This was like a revelation, for I had no idea until that moment that the system of penalties for nonattendance at *concejo* and at *hacenderas*, which I knew of from village ordinances and acts, was still being enforced in the present.

The regular Sunday meetings of the *concejo*, until very recently, had one major routine purpose: to announce all the faults and penalties of the previous week. Usually those concerning customary forms of behavior were read aloud by the headman, while those concerning infractions on the land were read aloud by the guard or warden of the fields and woods, whose services were paid for by the *concejo*. This was at once a public confession of sin and a public shaming. In some villages the accused *vecino* could state his case and possibly be found innocent by the *concejo*, but in most the guard's word was believed without further ado. It was very embarrassing (*un bochorno*) to have one's name read in *concejo*, as many older people in Santa María told me; the custom of publicizing how one had erred was often worse punishment than the fine.

An ordinance from Villamanín, probably dating from the eighteenth century, states that "the *Regidor* shall be obligated to convene his *vecinos* to take note of the *pesquisa* of the whole week, and all the *vecinos* in the place shall attend."[8] The *pesquisa* was the attendance or roll call that was taken at any of the functions in which the *vecinos* had to participate, from the *hacenderas* to the votive masses. Thus the *pesquisa* of the whole week consisted of a listing of all those who had not been present at the required functions. In a similar way the ordinances of Redilluera from 1726 ordain that there be no *concejo* on weekdays "during the harvest of bread and hay, but on Sundays, to castigate and to draw up agreements on what is needed for the whole week."⁹

This tradition of reading the fines of the week aloud at Sunday's *concejo* reunion was very much alive in Leonese villages at the close of the last century. Reference is often made to the practice in succinct little commandments, such as occurs in this act from Santa María from 1879: "The penalties for ringing of the bells and *pesquisa* of the *concejo* five *céntimos*."¹⁰ In other words, a *vecino* could be fined for failing to attend a *concejo* reunion, which would have meant ignoring the ringing of the bells and missing the *pesquisa*. We find a similar reference to the practice in an act from the nearby village of Santovenia del Monte, written in 1869, which neatly juxtaposes past and present: "On Sundays let the *pesquisas* circulate and the *boletines* be read and he who does not come will be fined two *cuartos*." The *boletines* or bulletin in question is none other than the *Boletín oficial del Estado*, the official journal of the state, which carried weekly news of disentailment, a subject of vital importance to villagers' welfare in this era.¹¹ How fitting that so ancient a custom of the village as the *pesquisa* should blend in the *concejo* with the reading aloud of so modern an organ of national bureaucracy.

In Santa María the fines and *pesquisas* of the week were still being read in *concejo* as recently as ten years ago, a fact I discovered one day while rummaging through the various papers and receipts in the *arca de concejo*, a wooden chest in which all *concejo* documents are kept. There I came across a few slim notebooks that were replete with weekly lists of penalties spanning the period from 1952 to 1973. Most of the penalties listed were for infractions on the land, but there were also frequent listings of penalties for nonattendance at *hacenderas*, masses, and funerals. If its longevity be taken as proof, this archaic system of social control, with its enforcement of solidarity, must have been effective indeed.

Given the fact that the reading of the week's penalties formed a major part of the regular Sunday meetings, it is not surprising to find that attendance at these *concejo* reunions needed to be enforced as much as did the irregular reunions summoned by the church bells. The means of coercion could be mild, on the order of a warning, as in this act from Villamayor written in 1885: "The regular meeting of the *vecinos* is desirable and thus we find that it will be just for it to be every Sunday at 10 o'clock or better yet after mass without any of the *vecinos* being able to excuse themselves unless they have a legitimate reason."[12] A *vecino* who could not be present at the meeting had to state his reason to the *alcalde de barrio*, and in his absence to one of the *vocales* or assistants.

An act from Santa María composed in 1883 put the matter somewhat more firmly: "It has also been agreed that every *vecino* who is in mass on Sunday must go to *concejo* and if not he shall pay ten *céntimos* and he who fails to come at the sound of the bells shall pay ten *céntimos*."[13] Similarly the *concejo* agreement drawn up in 1936 by the *vecinos* of Barrio de Nuestra Señora stipulated that those *vecinos* who did not attend a reunion of the *concejo* when called were to pay a fine of fifteen *céntimos*.[14] Nor were these fines taken lightly; for a number of my informants could well remember that one was penalized for not going to *concejo*, and even today, as we saw earlier, a *vecino* in Santa María does pay a price for being "rebellious."

Hacenderas: *The communal prestation of labor*

Turning now to the prestations of labor incumbent upon all *vecinos* in the communal *hacenderas* or *facenderas*, we see once again the extent to which attendance had to be rigorously enforced by the *concejo*.

All public works, from the building, clearing, and repair of roads, paths, and bridges to the maintenance of community irrigation systems, common pastures, and village boundaries, have long been and in many villages, including Santa María, continue to be executed by calling together an *hacendera*.[15] In every village there were traditionally at least two or three major annual *hacenderas*, whose dates were set for all time, and a number of minor *hacenderas* that were carried out once or twice a month more or less frequently depending on the contingencies of the place and the moment. In Santa María the village cemetery, the school, the houses of the teachers, of the priest, and of the *concejo* itself have all been built by *hacendera*; and in recent years, running water has been installed in village houses, the sewage system constructed, and the streets paved—in short, all of the amenities of modern life have been brought—by means of the institution of the *hacendera*, whose roots reach back to medieval times.

It is a singularly moving experience to witness, from a distance, like a bucolic scene from Brueghel, even a minor *hacendera*—to see, for example, at the beginning of summer all the village men, each with his sickle, hoe, and shovel, gathered together cleaning out the irrigation ditches as a team; or to hear at the height of winter the bells sound and see the men assemble in the village plaza several minutes later for an *hacendera* to clear the streets of snow. What cooperation, what solidarity, one thinks looking on in admiration, and truly our sight does not deceive us, such attributes are there. But a closer, more detached look also reveals dissension, conflict, and the kind of recalcitrance we earlier saw accompanying the taking on of village office. And so too does the testimony of the past.

A Señor Cansada Huerga, writing to López Morán at the turn of the century about the area of La Bañeza and Astorga lying west of the city of León, of which he was a native, gave this description of a typical day of *facendera*:

> The purpose and the day having been set by the *Alcalde de barrio* at a regular *concejo*, the *facendera* gathers in the customary place. ... Along with notice given in *concejo* ... it is convened ... by a characteristic peal of the bells, which the *Alcalde* himself or the guard of the fields repeats several times to goad the lazy, aside from the shouts, excitations, and even insults he directs at them as he passes through the street, and at times even entering the houses by main force, if necessary, "to drag the people out."
>
> When by dint of bell ringing, notices, and threats all the *vecinos* who are to carry out the *facendera* are gathered at last, the *Alcalde de barrio* draws up a list or head count, then gives his orders for the execution of the work. ... Where does he go afterwards? Very simply to punish those who have not responded to the call and have missed the *facendera* of that day. For that purpose, accompanied by one or two persons he has enlisted, he turns back and makes the rounds of all the houses that have not attended, into which he invades followed by his companions, and takes possession, by main force if necessary, of any good, tool, or utensil he comes across, weighing down his companions with them, and all coming to rest in the tavern, where these objects are deposited and held as a *prenda*.[16]

In short, villagers hardly jumped at the chance of participating in an *hacendera*. As we see in this case, the headman virtually had to drag them out of their houses to get them to lend a hand, and even so not all did. Sanctions, like the taking of *prendas*, or pawns, were needed to enforce the solidarity called for in an *hacendera*. Without coercion of one form or another, it seems, few would have gone. This fact is confirmed in numerous records of ordinances and council acts.

An *hacendera* is in essence a pooling of labor, of labor that each *vecino* must contribute as a pure prestation. This labor is a gift in the classic sense defined by Mauss, given not freely, but under obligation. From another angle we could say that it is a "servitude," for when an *hacendera* is called a man's labor ceases to be his own and becomes the property of the community. Indeed, in past times the *hacendera* had been a seigneurial obligation.[17] However we look at it, participation in *hacenderas* has long been one of the major burdens of *vecindad*, and it was and is viewed as exactly that—a burden. Everywhere it must not have been necessary to drag people out of their houses. In most villages, we can assume, the system of reading the fines of the week at Sunday's *concejo*, which exercised a much deeper moral and social coercion, sufficed to shame people into shouldering *hacenderas* and other burdens they owed to the community.

The 1776 ordinances of Santa María speak of an *hacendera* "they call major" (*que llaman mayor*) which was carried out the first Thursday of April every year. All the *vecinos* were obliged to attend, and any who had to be "entreated" (*rogados*) paid a penalty of one *real*. One of the purposes of this *hacendera* was to clean out the *faceras*, or irrigation ditches, of what was then a minute and precious area of irrigated land lying close to the village settlement. Thus even *forasteros*, or strangers, who had land in this area were obliged to attend the *hacendera* on penalty of two *reales*. Along with the obligation to attend the collective *hacendera*, each person had to have the *faceras* bordering on his land made by the following Sunday. Another *hacendera* of the *concejo*, which the *regidor* was obliged to have done on penalty of one *peseta*, was the repairing of a path leading through what was then probably the most important tract of cultivated land in the village.[18]

Even today in Santa María there are still two major annual *hacenderas*. Until recently there was always an *hacendera* the first Thursday of April, as in the eighteenth century. It now takes place on 1 May, which is San José Obrero, a national holiday, and a perfect day for an *hacendera*, since villagers can count on offspring living in León to return to lend a hand. Although all work collectively on cleaning the irrigation ditches, now part of a much expanded irrigated area, each works in proportion to the amount of land he owns and rents. And, as in the eighteenth century, each is responsible for the *faceras* bordering on his land. The other annual *hacendera* is held on Shrove Tuesday, or Carnival, as it is in many villages.[19] This is an all-purpose *hacendera* for work on public roads, paths, and communal properties. In the past it always included the important task of fixing the markers around the village's boundaries.

In the mountain village of Mena there were three obligatory annual *hacenderas*: the first after the snows of winter had ceased, the second between late June and early July, and the third in the first few days of September and again in early October to clear the path leading to the woods.[20] These *hacenderas* neatly corresponded to the timing of the agricultural cycle, as Flórez de Quiñones, who cites this passage, notes. In late June, early July, when the planting season ends and the meadows have to be mowed, the paths have to be clear to allow for the passage of people and carts filled high with hay. In early September it is time to prepare to fertilize the fields and this too necessitates good clear roads. By October firewood must be brought back from the woods, and following the last of the snow the cycle begins again.

We find that the *hacenderas* are attuned not simply to the agricultural cycle, but to the contingencies of nature. Lying on the banks of the river Órbigo, the village of Mataluenga needed to have two *hacenderas* a month to keep the river from overflowing. The *regidores* who were in office from September to the end of April (the offices being rotated twice yearly) were obliged to have these *facenderas* carried out on penalty of sixteen *reales*, "and if more were necessary they should be done so that the territories of this place will not be diminished."[21]

In the past a distinction was made between *hacenderas de carro*, for which carts had to be brought, and *hacenderas de a cuerpo*, to which one went prepared just with the necessary tools. To this day the *hacenderas* demand the prestation not just of a *vecino*'s labor, but of his property as well.

According to another ordinance from the village of Mataluenga, the *procuradores* were obliged to notify the *vecinos* of an upcoming *hacendera* by the Sunday before. On the days assigned to *hacenderas* they were to "ring the bells twice for those for carts, once when the Sun came out and again at eleven." One of the *procuradores* was then to go "in person" (*a cuerpo*) and the other with his cart to the site where the *hacendera* was to begin. An hour later they had to take a head count, charging those who had not come six *reales* if they were supposed to have brought their carts, three *reales* if they were to have gone in person. During the *facenderas* the *procuradores* were to name two men to observe the *vecinos* who had come with their carts "to see if each *vecino* carried as much as his cattle could and he who did not must pay two *reales* penalty for this *concejo* if the two so named declare that they have not carried what their cattle could."[22] In a similar ordinance from San Román de la Vega, near the city of Astorga, the ruling was that "the *vecino* whose turn it is to take ox or cart shall take it on penalty of one hundred *maravedís* and if the cart is not worked with he should be punished and take it another day."[23]

The *hacenderas de carro* were mainly for such tasks as repairing roads and damming rivers, in which large quantities of rocks and wood needed to be hauled; those *de a cuerpo* have always been for the lighter tasks of cleaning out irrigation ditches, water sources, and the like. Nowadays all *hacenderas* are usually *de a cuerpo*; if any hauling needs to be done, tractor-owners are hired by the village to do the work. But, indeed, until not very long ago the old distinction still held, as we can clearly see in the notebooks of penalties from Santa María recorded for the last few decades.

For example, a listing from 1966 cryptically notes: "*Hacenderas* done personal from V's house to C's house. B has a day done and T, V half a day."[24] What this refers to is the personal obligation to keep clean the gutters which, until just two years ago, ran in front of all the houses carrying dirty waters from the stables. As with the *faceras* bordering on his land, every *vecino* was responsible for the gutters bordering on his house. Or, in the same listing, we read: "*Hacenderas* done with carts: V, G, B, H, and in person, C, S, A, L, and from there to H's house they are done."[25] Here we clearly see the distinction between the two types of *hacendera*. The listing of names is by house order, moving toward the right, and it reveals that *vecinos* circulated both the burden of bringing carts to *hacenderas* and going just with one's person.

A listing from 1957 notes: "absentees from the *hacendera* for the firewood of the guards S and P."[26] Until very recently the village gave gifts of firewood from the communal woodland to the Civil Guards living in the municipal seat and, as we see in this example, it was done by *hacendera*. It was convenient and diplomatic, to say the least, to maintain friendly relations with the Civil Guards at a time when their powers were much respected and feared. Again we see the curious way in which so ancient a custom as the *hacendera* is adapted to the political vicissitudes of the present.

In the past as in the present, the *hacenderas* could become arenas for the kind of verbal abuse and general rowdiness that we earlier saw taking place in the reunions of the *concejo*. For instance, the men assemble to clear the streets of snow on a winter day and in matter of minutes, as I observe from my window, they are arguing loudly about whether to start at the bottom or the top of the village; this leads to an argument about why the village is short of water for the first time in the middle of winter; this in turn ends up in criticism of the headmen now in charge, who should be acting more quickly to resolve the problem. An act from Santa María dating back to 1899, which refers to meetings of the *concejo* and to *facenderas*, reflects this state of affairs: "The *vecino* as well as any one else should behave with the proper respect without disturbing the order and if someone violates it by insulting the *presidente* or any other person he pays a penalty of one *peseta* for the first time and if it reoccurs it shall be brought to the attention of a Superior."[27]

Though the ambience of a *concejo* reunion and an *hacendera* bear certain similarities, there is no question that the latter in general carried greater weight. In the same 1899 act we learn that the fine for missing a meeting of the *concejo* was five *céntimos*, while that for missing an *hacendera* was one *peseta*, twenty times that amount. The *hacenderas* were not only less frequent than the meetings of the *concejo*, it was absolutely imperative that they be carried out—so the whole village could irrigate, bring wood from the forest, carry home carts of hay, and save its land from the floods of an undammed river. A meeting of the *concejo* could perhaps be missed every now and then, but not an *hacendera*, on which so much depended.

Perhaps because they were so important, it has always been possible for the *vecino* to send a son or field hand to the *hacendera* in his place. However, those who went as proxies had to be over eighteen, or sixteen in some cases, and their going had to be approved by the headman. As the 1899 act declares, "We do not allow anyone who is not a *vecino* in *concejo* nor in an *hacendera* except by Entreaty [*Súplica*]."[28] An earlier act from 1879, as if to show that this is no joking matter, adds the clause that "he who sends out a person without a supplication even though competent shall pay a half fine."[29] It seems that many houses were wont to send children, for one act from 1883 reminds the *vecinos* that in the *hacenderas* "no young kids will be admitted."[30]

Widows, as *vecinas*, were also obligated to participate in *hacenderas*. In practice they rarely went themselves, but sent a son or field hand of the proper age in their place. A widow who had no one to send in her place had to pay what was known as a *ruego* or a *súplica*, both meaning entreaty or supplication, to the *concejo* every year. In many places the parish priest also had to pay the *ruego* to be excused from *hacenderas*, and so did *vecinos* over sixty-five, and others legitimately impaired from participating.

An act from nearby Santovenia del Monte written in 1878 notes that Josefa Crespa and Sidora González, widows and *vecinas* of the village, asked for the *ruego* and it was granted, freeing them from all the *hacenderas* except the one to clean the waters, probably the springs and ditches.³¹ From another nearby village, Ambasaguas, there is an act written in 1885 that lists seven men who "supplicated the *concejo* so they might be freed of having to attend *concejo* and *facenderas*, except the one for the large irrigation ditch of the village ... for which they charged each one eleven *reales* and freed of having to attend the customary litanies or rogations."³² In both villages we see that no one is excused from an *hacendera* considered to be major. Though unusual, in Ambasaguas the *ruego* also freed a person from going to *concejo* and fulfilling village religious obligations. It is significant that attendance at *hacenderas, concejo* meetings, and litanies are brought together under a single heading of obligatory servitudes from which one could be "freed" only by supplicating the *concejo* for a pardon.

Besides paying the *ruego* there have been other ways in which a *vecino* or a widow could be excused from participating in the *hacenderas*. There is in Santa María an unmarried *vecino* who inherited the *vecindad* of the house at his mother's death. Since he is slightly retarded, he has been given the role of messenger of the *concejo*; when there is to be an important reunion of the *concejo* he is in charge of going from house to house notifying all the *vecinos*. In return for his labors he is excused from participating in *hacenderas* and by the same token he performs a real service for the *concejo*.

Widows, in the past, could similarly be excused from attending *hacenderas* by going from house to house asking for bread for the souls in purgatory (*pan para las ánimas*). The pieces of bread were auctioned after Sunday mass and the money went toward the payment of masses for the dead souls of the village. In the eighteenth century, if the reader will recall, there was an officer of the *concejo* know as the *mayordomo de las ánimas*, and it was he who was in charge of auctioning the bread.[33] Thus the widow who had no one to send to *hacenderas* in her place, and yet could not afford to pay the *ruego*, could comply with the rules of *vecindad* by collecting for the souls of the village dead.

If the *hacenderas* have long been a burden, a servitude to be suffered and borne by all *vecinos*, they have, at the same time, always called forth the commensality and conviviality of the festival. The historical records for the villages are replete with details of wine drinking on days of *hacendera*. From the *concejo* accounts of Ambasaguas we learn, for example, that in 1872 the *concejo* spent eleven-and-a-half *pesetas* on half a *cántara* of wine when the irrigation ditches were cleaned out.[34] Or again from the accounts of Villamayor close to seventeen *pesetas* had been spent in 1868 on refreshments the *concejo* had given out on Epiphany, Carnival, *facenderas*, and votive days.[35] Until recently, we were told, the major *hacenderas* always culminated in a fiesta, with dancing in the village square.

Even today when it is more difficult than ever to form *hacenderas* because, as people say, no one wants to work for nothing anymore, there is wine and sardines for the *vecinos* in *concejo* and much festivity following the *hacenderas* of Carnival and San José Obrero. Of all the occasions on which wine was drunk in *concejo* in the past, only in conjunction with the *hacenderas* does the custom persist. There is still a sense that the labor in common which an *hacendera* involves is distinct from wage labor and should be followed by the eating together of a common meal.

The holiness of the dead

We can readily see that it fell within the domain of the *concejo* to enforce attendance at its reunions and *hacenderas*. But what documentary sources and native reconstructions of the past reveal so clearly is that it was no less within the domain of the *concejo* to enforce attendance at funerals and at votive masses of the village, and to enforce the custom of harboring the wandering poor. It is particularly its role in these matters of religion, morality, and philanthropy that inspired the idea of the "good and Christian administration of the pueblo" coined by the compilers of custom from Barrio de Nuestra Señora in 1936.

One of the most fascinating chapters of Santa María's 1776 ordinances is entitled "The way in which the death of a *vecino* or *vecina* should be observed as a holy day." As soon as a *vecino* or his wife dies, the ordinance begins, "all major work should stop, such as yoking oxen, mowing, digging, cutting . . . and not only are the *vecinos* prohibited from working but so too are any sons of widows and field hands." Unless the head of the household of the deceased gave permission for it, no one was to work on penalty of four *reales* from the moment the person breathed his or her last until he or she was laid to rest. It was the *regidor*'s responsibility to send two *vecinos* at a time to be present at the wake over the body "so that it will not be left alone, penalty of two *reales*, and those in mourning should treat to food and drink the two who sit vigil most of the night." The *regidor* was also obliged to send a *vecino* to dig the grave and carve the sepulcher, "which he should do without resistance, penalty of two *reales*." That fine was to be doubled if a *vecino* or *vecina* missed the funeral mass for no legitimate reason. But by the same token, "to bind the *vecinos* to all of the above, those in mourning should give the *concejo* six *azumbres* of wine and twelve pounds of bread which is like taking leave of *vecindad*."[36]

These mortuary customs, with their reciprocity between house and village and their ideal of solidarity, were so important a part of the social and cultural life of Leonese rural communities that they persisted in more or less their original form until the 1960s and early 1970s. Even today they are practiced, though only in part and without the coercion of penalties. To say these customs have "persisted" is slightly misleading for it implies a passive and automatic acceptance of past traditions. In fact, what both the documents and commentaries of my informants make amply clear is that, if they persisted at all, it was as a result of the conscious agreements of villagers to be bound by them. And this is true not just of the funerary customs, but of the whole web of customs and controls whose various strands are gradually being spun out here.

Consider, for example, the way this 1885 act from Santa María alludes to the text of the 1776 ordinances—indicating that it had obviously been read and scrutinized by a later generation of villagers—and adds new prescriptions for maintaining the old funerary customs under changed conditions:

Concerning attendance at funerals, from the time a *vecino* or *vecina* dies we have agreed that it be fulfilled according to the provisions made in chapter twenty-one of the ordinance and with the same penalties provided for there, and in view of the fact that the cemetery is now situated far from the village and so that the attendance will be the same as we have always seen it, we agree that every *vecino* shall accompany the body until the burial and so soon as they leave the cemetery all the *vecinos* shall wait while the president or person in charge takes count to see if anyone is missing, and if it is just for not going to the cemetery one will be fined fifty *céntimos* of a *peseta* and the person who misses the whole funeral for his own convenience will be fined one *peseta*.[37]

In the nineteenth century, as in the eighteenth, we see that the death of a *vecino* or *vecina* was considered to be a matter of concern to the whole village. But attendance at funerals had to be rigorously enforced, in a manner similar to attendance at reunions of the *concejo* and at *hacenderas*, with head counts and penalties. If left to their own devices, both the 1776 and 1885 rulings seem to say, many villagers might not have bothered to pay their last respects to their neighbors. This fact was clearly recognized by villagers themselves, for why else would they have chosen to be bound by such rulings?

With the introduction of cemeteries in the nineteenth century, a change documented in the 1885 act, it became necessary to enforce attendance not just at the funeral mass but at the procession to the cemetery. In various acts of the period we find that two different fines are levied, depending on whether a person has missed the procession but gone to mass or missed both the procession and the mass. Of course exceptions were made for "persons who cannot be expected to walk on account of the weather or invalids," as an 1899 act from Santa María put it.[38] But it was of great importance that those who could do so participate in the procession, for the dead had to be accompanied by their fellow villagers as far as the grave if, indeed, the custom was to be carried out in the same manner "as we have always seen it."

In the nineteenth century, attendance began to be enforced at the funerals of children as well as adults. Suddenly a child's existence in the world was viewed as having as much importance as an adult's. The change in attitude toward children, the subject of an important and growing historical literature, is shown in many an act from the period. For example, in 1874 the *vecinos* of Ambasaguas decide "in public *concejo* and with the agreement of all the *vecinos* . . . to attend all the funerals of children who have died in this *pueblo* on penalty of a *cuarterón* of white wax to light up the holy sacrament or in its place the value of this wax in money ... for on this we have agreed and signed, and we give power to the authorities to exact the fine from us."[39] The very same penalty was to be exacted from those who missed the funeral of an adult.

In most places, however, children were not quite on a par with adults. We find, for example, that in 1916 the fine for missing the funeral of an adult in Santa María was fifty *céntimos*; for missing the funeral of a child, it was half that amount. In Barrio de Nuestra Señora the very same fines still held in 1936.[40] A more recent accord enacted in Barrio in 1964 states that "attendance at all funerals is obligatory, be they Adults and the same if children."[41] Even in so contemporary a document we get the sense that villagers needed to be reminded of the equal value of the lives of adults and children. Nevertheless, from the nineteenth century the obligation became firmly established for adults to pay their last repects to the deceased children of fellow villagers. The poignancy of such untimely deaths, one imagines, was felt more strongly than ever before in an era of decreasing child mortality. But no matter how we may wish to account for the changed attitude toward children, on the village level the modern acceptance of the child as a person served to strengthen further the meaning of the most traditional of customs. For now the death of any person in the community became an occasion for the symbolic acting out of the solidarity which, in principle, bound together all the houses of the village and made of them a society, a parish truly Christian.

Though some features of the old mortuary customs did change in time, in the end we are left with a very strong sense of the persistence of the whole as a cultural system. Note how this fragment from an act drafted in Santa María in 1890 hardly departs from the rulings of the preceding century: "Concerning attendance at funerals, at the hour of a *vecino* or *vecina*'s death the *presidente* will send two *vecinos* to keep vigil by hours and the day of the funeral we prohibit any *vecino* or *vecina* from yoking the team on penalty of fifty *céntimos*."[42] As in the eighteenth century the community was to be present at the wake and the flow of daily life and work come to a halt the day of the funeral, and again disobedience had its price.

Is the continuity we observe in these death rites merely a continuity of rhetoric or truly one of practice? As we saw earlier, by the end of the nineteenth century most villagers were literate and they not only read their old charters of bylaws but wrote new ones themselves. The acts of the nineteenth century make allusions to earlier documents and borrow many turns of phrase, in a way that makes it possible to even speak of a village literary tradition. We will turn to these themes later. But the continuity with the past is not just literary; records of fines collected and the confirmations of contemporary villagers attest to the living social reality behind the various prescriptions and prohibitions inscribed in village ordinances, acts, and accords.

That fines were, indeed, exacted from those who missed funerals is shown in a somewhat amusing way in this fragment of a 1916 act from Santa María: "Whoever misses the funeral of a child having been notified will pay twenty-five *céntimos* and these fines for funerals whether for bodies large or small will be spent the very same day of the fining."[43] They were to be spent, of course, on wine, in keeping with the old practice of "drinking the fines" in *concejo*.

In Santa María such fines were being levied at least until 1970, as we see in this example: "Absentees from the funeral of F: V, R, F, C," names that were crossed out, indicating that these *vecinos* had paid the prescribed fines.[44] In 1953 there were entries for absentees from two funerals of children: twenty-one *vecinos* had failed to go to the first and thirty-five to the second.[45] One funeral was for twins delivered prematurely at eight months who died the same day they were born and the other for an infant of three months.[46] Most *vecinos* seem to have preferred to shoulder the fine than to halt their work to be present at the funerals of persons gone at so tender an age. In contrast, there were never very many absentees from the funerals of adults.

Fortunately, we need not confine ourselves to written records of penalties to highlight the lived reality of the old funerary customs. Leonardo Mirantes, who helped me to interpret many documents that at first seemed hopelessly obscure, recollected how penalties for nonattendance at funerals were enforced in the recent past:

> ... as soon as the funeral was over we would all go down to say an Our Father there in the house of the *concejo*, as we call it. And then *pesquisa*, as we call it, was taken there, don't you recall that the other day we talked about the *pesquisero*, well, *pesquisa* was taken and whoever had been missing was fined. If there was no legitimate motive ... say that he had been ill, or had to leave on an urgent journey or something of the sort, but he couldn't go to work where people might see him or be at home lying around, if not, if the matter was not made clear, he was fined.[47]

As he pointed out to me, because there were penalties just about everyone went to the funerals. In other villages, where there were no such obligations, just kin went; this was not as good a system, he felt, because the person who had few relations could not be properly accompanied at the hour of his or her greatest need.

Obligatory until recently, attendance at the wake was and still is a duty circulated from house to house *a corrida*, in a circle of turn-taking that moves always toward the right. To describe the practice, my informant put himself in the position of subject: "If a person dies, for example, I die, the wake begins in the upper house. The moment I breathe my last, that they shroud me ... the wake begins in the upper house and they have to stay for two hours ... two people have to stay, an hour each, but two people are there together."[48] The person who completes his or her turn first goes and passes the word on to the next house and so on, until the circle is complete. In this way the burden of keeping the wake going is spread around the village and the dead are never left alone in their last hours among the living.[49]

In the eighteenth century, according to the ordinances of Santa María, it was customary for the family of the deceased to give wine and bread to the *vecinos* for them to consume in *concejo*. We learn from this document that the purpose of the gift was to bind the *vecinos* to the fulfillment of the obligations of funerary custom, while marking the passing of one of their numbers. It was such an integral part of the social-religious complex surrounding death that it appears to have required no enforcement. And again it is the survival, rather than the extinction, of this old practice that we bear witness to. The same informant recalled how the practice was at last abolished in the early 1960s:

> ... In those times the one who died had to give "x" wine and "x" bread and after the funeral we would go eat bread ... this was done away with when F was *presidente* [1958-1962], all that was done away with because, of course, coming from the funeral that you should then have to go to the house of the mourners and ask for a *cántaro* of wine and two loaves of bread to go eat there [in the *casa de concejo*] when many people are wishing to go work somewhere else, because after the funeral is over one can [return to work]. ...That was done away with a few years ago.[50]

Similarly, I was told by Felicísimo Llamazares, another informant well-versed in the customs of the past, that the mourning family gave the *vecinos* half a *cántaro* of wine and a chunk of bread. This, he said, was done away with when Froilán was *presidente*, because it was agreed in *concejo* that after a funeral the *vecinos* no longer wished to assemble to drink wine but to get back to their own work.[51]

Thus the custom of having wine and bread in *concejo* after funerals came to an end, but not because the individual families ceased to provide the customary repast. A distinctly modern view—that it was a waste of precious work time to gather in *concejo* merely to eat the symbolic meal of communion—had supplanted the old receptiveness to the commensality that visiting bishops in previous centuries had found so excessive. When every man had wine in his own house, as my informant had noted, who needed to go to *concejo* anymore for a drink? The custom lost its symbolic meaning at the same time as it lost its basis in material life.

It had been remarkably long-lived, however. So too had been the related custom of having a *vecino* appointed by the headman dig the grave and carve the sepulcher. Leonardo recalled how the *abad* ("abbott") of the village confraternity of San Roque would also select a *vecino* to perform this task when the person who had died was a member of the confraternity. The two *vecinos*, he said, had to be given dinner by the house that was mourning following the funeral, as did the two *vecinos* who in the eighteenth century sat vigil the better part of the night. Not surprisingly, this obligation was done away with in the same period, just preceding the rural exodus of the late 1960s and early 1970s, when population growth had reached its limits, resources were diminishing, urban values were beginning to make themselves felt more strongly, and expectations were rising. Men felt they could no longer afford to spend long hours communing in *concejo* or in the houses of their neighbors, and consequently much, though not all, of the old social-religious order finally gave way.

Holy days and poor relief

Much the same fate befell such other Christian obligations once incumbent upon *vecinos* and their wives as attendance at votive masses of the village and harboring of the wandering poor. Here too we see the remarkably long historical duration of these customs broken in the years preceding the depopulation of the countryside.

The 1776 ordinances from Santa María devote a chapter to the obligation to attend votive masses, litanies, and rogations:

> We ordain and decree that from every house the two senior Persons should go hear the five votive masses of the *concejo* . . . penalty of one *real* for each absence besides the mortal sin they commit in maliciously not attending; under the same penalty the said two senior Persons should attend the litanies and on the Cross of May [3 May] the votive rogation of *concejo*.[52]

The *concejo*, in Santa María and throughout León and Castile, had its own assortment of corporate holy days, established in earlier times, which in many cases continued to be observed into the present century. The votive mass has its origin in a collective vow made to honor a particular saint who, in turn, protects the community from dangers ranging from pestilence to hail and drought. The litanies consist of the Greater Litanies of Saint Mark's Day (25 April), and the Lesser Litanies held on the Monday, Tuesday, and Wednesday before Ascension Day (10 May-17 June).[53] They were, and in Santa María still are, processions to the four ends of the village to bless the land and ask the litany of saints to protect the still nascent crops. On the Cross of May, also at a precarious moment in the agricultural cycle, a similar sort of procession was commonly held. Observance of all these village holy days was obligatory, as the ordinances indicate, and all were financed by the *concejo* in Santa María as in other villages of León.[54]

With the votive masses as with the springtime rogations, there was a sense that these obligations, often taken on by village ancestors in a time beyond recollection, were part of the sacred history of the community. To cease to observe them would thus have constituted not only a rupture in the continuity of past, present, and future, but something of a sacrilege. Read, for example, this ordinance written in 1716 from the village of San Román de la Vega:

> We ordain that since our ancestors took on devotion toward some feast days that occur throughout the year and made a vow to observe them, we command that they be observed and that the mass be said for the pueblo and be payed for by the *vecinos* of this place . . . and if anyone works on these days or on others when this place goes on procession he shall pay a penalty of two hundred *maravedís*,

half to light up the Holy Sacrament and the other half for said *concejo* and for this there should be *pesquisa* and oaths.[55]

For all their sacredness and historical depth, attendance at votive masses and participation in rogations was enforced with head counts and penalties. Sworn testimonies of villagers were often called into account, as the ordinance from San Román de la Vega indicates, to attest to the infringement of the prohibition against working on village holy days.

In general, by the eighteenth and nineteenth centuries the devotional fervor that had inspired the observance of vows and rogations is less evident; instead, we see the routine enforcement of solidarity, though there are lapses where the old fervor returns. Throughout the nineteenth-century acts from Santa María, even those dealing with rights of pasture and organization of grazing on the commons, we see local religiosity being mandated by the *concejo*, as in this act from 1899: "Concerning rogations and masses which this *pueblo* has subject to punishment from time immemorial the *vecino* or *vecina* who is missing will pay a fine of fifty *céntimos* per person."[56] It continues to be enforced into the twentieth century, in Santa María particularly with the springtime rogations. We find *pesquisa* being taken as late as 1966 to see who has missed the litanies: "Absentees from the Rogations: (1st) A, B, R, E; (2nd) A, B, E, V; (3rd) A, R, E. Saint Mark's, M, B, B."[57]

In Barrio de Nuestra Señora, where the headman and *vecinos* undertake a "renovation" of local religiosity in 1964, attendance at votive masses and at rogations is not only called for, but applauded as the way of all true Christians. "The purpose of the attendance which we ask for from all," their charter reads, "is to continue the tradition which our ancestors have set down for us in order to demonstrate to those who do not practice such Christian customs faith and human feeling."[58] This document, like the one drawn up in 1936 by the preceding generation of villagers (cited at the beginning of this chapter), champions the local religiosity of the *pueblo* against the rising tide of national and international secularism. By 1964, however, the threat of increasing secularism can no longer be said to emanate from the republican ideology of the "Reds." It surges from the body of the church itself—from the liberal reforms of the Second Vatican Council, which even today many villagers blame for the loss of religiosity among the young. But, in the end, what is most striking about the document is the curious autonomy we see the village enjoying in León, in this case enabling it even to launch its own miniature Counter-Reformation.

In religious matters local communities have long acted with a sense of their own autonomy, defending, in the words of William Christian, their "own culture and religious customs against clerical intrusions."[59] Villages, after all, chose holy days all their own, whose observance and meaning were confined to their uniquely local history and landscape. This exercise of religious autonomy, as might be expected, did not sit well with church officialdom. In a visit to the village of Castro in 1734 the bishop of León made his dissatisfaction quite clear:

> Inasmuch as his *Ilustrísima* has been informed that in this place and others of this archpriesthood they have introduced the intolerable abuse of observing through a vow of the *concejo*, without it being approved by the bishops, certain days of the year, fining those who work on them and forcing them to believe that they are holy days ... his *Ilustrísima* orders the priest of this church that on the first holy day he should make it clear to his parishioners that they are under no obligation whatsoever to observe the days thus vowed and to abstain from working, nor are they obligated to pay any fine that for said reason the *concejo* charges them with, and that they should only observe the holy days set by the church. ...[60]

To stop this "abuse," the bishop ordered the *concejo* and *vecinos* not to observe their vowed days under penalty of excommunication and a fine of twenty *ducados*. Clearly these threats did not intimidate villagers, for the "abuse" managed to survive almost intact into the present day. Then again, could such threats really have been enforced? The *concejo* as a whole would probably have had to be excommunicated.

Although it did not, perhaps, always conform to church standards, who could deny the religiosity of peasant villages? It was in the villages where basic Christian concepts such as *caritas* or charity often found their clearest, most literal, expression. This is especially evident in the custom, widespread throughout the area of central León, of harboring the wandering poor in village houses. Like other religious customs we have been considering, the harboring of the poor was a prestation which the *vecino* owed to the community. It was an obligatory gift on the same order as attending funerals of neighbors and being present at votive masses and rogations of the village. No *vecino* could escape it.

There were three forms by which the poor were attended to in Leonese villages. One form, known by the term *bagaje*, consisted of the obligation to transport beggars either to the next village or to a hospice, if one existed nearby. One lone act from 1874 in Santa María's *concejo* records testifies to the existence of this practice in the village in the past century:

> ... with the *concejo* gathered in the customary site to treat matters pertinent to the common good of the *vecinos*, one has been that having to contribute with the means necessary for *bagaje* with available beasts of burden and carts, horses and donkeys, all the *vecinos* in common agree to pay whosoever is allotted the lot of having to go in *bagaje* with cart or horse or donkey for the days he is occupied in said service the ordinary wage per day which will be the same for all ... at rates for cart or riding animal, and if someone should suffer any misfortune while carrying out said service which was not his fault we will also remit to him something.[61]

As this act indicates, the obligation to carry out the *bagaje* was distributed by lot and the person so chosen was recompensed for his time, energy, and the use of his animals with a wage paid for by all the *vecinos*. The wage, it seems, was necessary to make the task of carrying out *bagaje* truly just—for would it have been fair for one *vecino* to be transporting a beggar while another was free to work his lands?

In an act from the nearby village of Ambasaguas, we find the obligation of *bagaje* being circulated around the village *a corrida*, in a circle of turn-taking. "With the *concejo* gathered in the customary site," begins this act from 1877, "they agreed to start a new *corrida* for the poor that need to be taken to Lugán only [the next village up the road] and the lots having been cast in public it fell upon Ramón García to start said *corrida* so that it may go on from there." Nobody could be excused from this servitude, the act continues, adding that "if an *hacendera* should take place none will be freed from it, he will continue to owe that *hacendera* and not be fined."[62]

Another form of attending to the poor was through the custom known as *palo de los pobres*, "the stick of the poor," which seems to have been widespread in northern and central León. The stick was made of iron or wood and served as a marker for turn-taking. When beggers came to a village they would ask in whose house the stick had last been. Then they would get the stick and take it to the next house, which was obliged to feed and house them, and so on, in a circle of turn-taking. The burden of harboring the poor was thereby circulated around the village. In larger villages such as Vegas and San Cipriano, where there was more of a stratified population, the poor went only to those houses that could properly attend to them. In smaller villages, such as Santa María, they went to all houses alike, as they did in Barrio de Nuestra Señora according to the 1936 compilation of customs: "All the *vecinos* are obligated to harbor the poor in their respective houses when it is their turn."[63]

Along with these two forms of poor relief, we find yet another—the giving of a feast to the poor on the day of the village fiesta. What more appropriate time to feed the hungry than on the day the patron saint of the village is honored? In the *concejo* accounts of several villages we find references to the expenditures that were made to host the feast, known as a *rancho*. One colorful example can be seen in the accounts from 1865 of the *concejo* of Villamayor, which list the debts incurred by the patronal feast:[64]

For the poor the day of Saint Bernardinus	rs.	ms.
of *titos* [a kind of chick pea] two *heminas* at 13 *reales*	26	
pepper half a pound	1	12
two pounds of oil	4	06
two pounds of salt and three-fourths onions	1	18
. . . for the *rancheros* of the poor one *azumbre* of wine and a box of tobacco	3	26

The feast, as we see from this list of ingredients, consisted mainly of a hearty bean stew, to which some sausage and fatback were usually added; wine and cigars completed the meal. The poor flocked to the villages for these feasts which, we were told, came to an end almost twenty years ago. It had also been the rule to give alms to the poor on the day of the fiesta, a custom which villagers did not always comply with very willingly, judging from these remarks in Barrio de Nuestra Señora's 1964 charter: "For the proper fulfillment of the patronal fiestas [we remind you] not to haggle about Goodwill in giving alms so as to be charitable toward the needy."[65]

Since this discussion may have given the impression that the solidarity of villagers has long been the consequence of rule enforcement alone, let me clarify by way of conclusion my point of view on this subject. I have attempted to show here that "community" should not be assumed as a given, and that villagers themselves never assumed it as a given.

The "Hobbesianism" that may appear to be behind the view that moral community needed to be enforced is less mine than theirs. For what must be kept in mind is that here the enforcement of custom was always internal, a result of the conscious agreement of villagers to be bound by it.

Yet it would be a mistake to think that, since villagers felt the need to enforce their customs, the village itself was not a sufficient moral presence for the majority of people. The rules existed to insure that not merely the majority, but everyone would carry out their vicinal obligations. For in the end it was an idea of justice that lay behind such rulings—and also an ideal of solidarity, as in the death rituals that sought to unite the community, to create brotherhood even perhaps among enemies. The burdens of the community were to be borne equally by all, whether a little poorer or a little richer, whether willing or reluctant. Such, for the Leonese *labrador*, was the nature of community.

Part Four

Chapter 10

The Web of Use-Rights

W E TURN now to the subject of communal property and its attendant forms of cooperation and reciprocity. Here, without a shadow of a doubt, lies the crux of village life in León and in numerous other parts of Spain and Europe. A vast literature bears witness to the scholarly interest that this subject, as complex as it is intriguing, has aroused in the last hundred years.[1] But only infrequently do those pages offer us a glimpse of the local meaning, the sense that peasant villagers themselves gave to this symbolic language of communal rights and usages, in which so many aspects of their view of the world found expression. Before attempting to offer such a glimpse here, a few theoretical clarifications are in order.

"Another way of possessing"

Writing at the close of the nineteenth century on communal practices in rural Spain, the Aragonese jurist Joaquín Costa had referred to them under the general heading of "agrarian collectivism."[2] Although there was an indigenous literature concerning communal property reaching back to the sixteenth century, as Costa himself showed in his *magnum opus*, his work was also part of a contemporary European intellectual trend that viewed individualism in all its forms, and private property in particular, as having evolved from a primitive communism characterized by the ownership in common of all goods.[3] Thus the various communal practices that Costa could still observe in the Spanish countryside of his day he interpreted as relics of an agrarian system once totally collectivist, which had been implanted in peninsular soil in pre-Roman times.[4] The term "agrarian collectivism" referred at once to a golden age when the idea of property did not yet exist and to the corpus of communal practices that had survived the advent of private property.

Although one cannot but admire the exemplary work of Costa, we must look elsewhere if we are to come closer to an understanding of the local meaning given to communal rights and usages by Spanish peasants. The notion of "agrarian collectivism" has the disadvantage of making us think in terms of a simple diametrical opposition between communal and private property, and this all too easily leads to a historically reductionistic view of the transition from one form of ownership to another. From the pen of a historian who writes about the attack on the commons in sixteenth-century Spain, we read, concerning the communal practices that survived into the twentieth century, that "the remaining examples of the old communalism were archaic curiosities out of step with the times, freakish exceptions able somehow to resist the movement toward private ownership."[5] Certainly we will not get very far if we persist in viewing the communal practices that survived to the present day as mere vestiges of an older order without any connection to a coherent system of beliefs and ideas.

On the other hand, the nineteenth-century juridical and historical analyses of communal property, including Costa's for Spain, did bequeath to us a most valuable insight: that an alternative model or idea of property had existed in the Western world, that there had been, in Paolo Grossi's words, "another way of possessing."[6] Next to "property as belonging to" stood "property as function,"[7] or as "use," as I prefer to say. Yet the full implications of this were not clearly seen because the insight emerged in the course of a stormy debate on the origins of private property. Costa's work was part, too, of the polemic that had raged in Spain since the eighteenth century concerning the merits of the communal lands, so vigorously attacked by Jovellanos in his agrarian reform plan of 1793. Now that the intensity of the controversy has ebbed, it is time to take another look at our nineteenth-century bequest.

There is every indication that private and communal property have coexisted in European village communities at least since medieval times.[8] However, though formally distinct, the two forms of property were in practice often meshed in a single system of communal rights and uses. For what was considered property in common included, first of all, communal property in the strict sense of the term: pastures, wastes, woodland, and sometimes arable land, held and administered by the rural community, over which every village citizen had individual rights of use. In addition, it almost always included property that, though private, was opened up, once cleared of its first fruits, for others in the community to use, and that thus for a time became communal. Finally there were customary prestations of mutuality that a variety of agro-pastoral activities called for, that also formed part of the communal system of rights and uses. This meshing together of the common and the private, which was characteristic of a system that was very much "embedded," to use Polanyi's suggestive term, in social relations and cultural conceptions is what I have here chosen to call the "web of use-rights."[9]

In a paper on inheritance systems, E. P. Thompson points out that we let ourselves be deceived by our terms when we think that it was "property," "ownership," or even "the land" that was passed on from generation to generation in old agrarian regimes. From the point of view of the beneficiary, what one inherited was more exactly "a place within a complex gradation of coincident use-rights."[10] For all rights to property, private no less than common, existed not in an absolute realm but within an "inherited grid of customs and controls. . . . The beneficiary inherited both his right *and* the grid within which it was effectual."[11] Later we will consider in depth how such a grid imposed numerous "servitudes" upon the individual family's rights of use over its own property.

The commons too, we often assume, is land over which the village community held exclusive property rights. But this was rarely the case, as Marc Bloch had noted long ago: "It is far more usual to find the commons, like the rest of the village lands, subject to a complex tissue of rights claimed by a whole hierarchy of interested parties."[12] In northern Spain many of the common lands, especially the large tracts of woodland and waste known as *tierras baldías*, had fallen into the hands of seigneurial lords, who granted the villages rights of use over these properties in the form of perpetual leases or *foros*.[13] And if not the property of a lord, the *baldíos* were often the king's: for it had been the practice since the early years of the Reconquest for Castilian monarchs to claim for the crown all property that belonged to no one. The king's subjects, in turn, were entitled to "the use and enjoyment" (*uso y aprovechamiento*) of these common lands.[14]

Though the villages frequently held only the tenure, not the title, to many of their common lands, it was still their assemblies, their *concejos* in León, which were responsible for enforcing the "customs and controls" that regulated their use. The Castilian monarchs saw the importance of local customary law, ordaining at different times that the villages set down their ancestral customs on paper in the form of ordinances. For they recognized that the mode of possessing based on the idea of "property as use" was largely founded in local custom and usage—it did not, could not, exist merely in the abstract. But how could they have failed to recognize this? In medieval French speech, for example, the lands subject to communal rights of use, as Bloch observed, were known as the *coutumes* or "customs" of the village.[15] In other words, custom was conceived of as defining the common.

It is exactly this definition of the common that begins to be challenged in many parts of Europe by the sixteenth century. Emanating from many sources—legal, economic, political, social, and cultural—the spirit of capitalism insinuates itself into the very grain of custom. Already in the Spain of Philip II, long before the disentailment acts of the nineteenth century had been conceived, many of the common lands of the kingdom of Castile were broken up, and with the crown's approval given a price and put on the market. Among the buyers were the overtaxed and indebted *labradores* of the kingdom who could claim no title to much of the land they worked, since it was often borrowed from the commons; at a time when titles were becoming necessary, they purchased them when they could, and even when they could not rather than lose their lands, though it plunged them into still greater debt. Nobles, wealthy townsmen, and prosperous farmers rounded out their estates, frequently enclosing them in *cotos redondos*.[16] In the rest of Europe the new seigneurial class was doing much the same. And legal thought followed in train. "The jurists were now," in the words of Bloch, "hard at work constructing a clear concept of ownership to replace the tissue of superimposed rights over property."[17]

By the eighteenth and nineteenth centuries their task is done. The law was ready to step in to clear up "the messy complexities of coincident use-right."[18] In Spain, Jovellanos was certainly the most eloquent, or in any case most widely known, proponent of the idea that the customary system of communal use-rights was irrational, economically unproductive, barbaric, and unworthy of preservation. Entranced, like many a liberal-minded agrarian reformer of his time, by what Bloch had called the "cult of private ownership,"[19] Jovellanos advocated that the common lands be split up for private ownership and use, and that private property be freed of the many servitudes in which the community had bound it up.[20] In the following century the ideas of Jovellanos and other liberal reformers found their way into the law in Spain and elsewhere in the disentailment acts, which put on the market various properties until then held in mortmain by the church, the nobility, and the communities. If the web of use-rights had not been undone long before disentailment by the forces of money and power, as it had been in much of Estremadura and Andalusia, there was certainly even less of a chance that its threads would hold together afterwards.[21]

The law and, in general, the spirit of the age had succeeded in wrenching property from its social context of custom and use. Costa and other collectivists tried to salvage what they could, for history at least, of the previous system, whose edifice rested, in the words of Marx, "on the *indeterminate* aspect of property."[22] And yet, though the system disappeared in some parts and was dealt a fatal blow in others, where the old marriage of custom and common managed to persist it did so in as coherent a form as it ever seems to have taken in the past, and often in conscious opposition to the new definitions at law.

In Santa María and various of the villages surrounding it, the system of communal rights and usages had a long life, persisting more or less intact until the present day. But the system did not simply persist. It adapted itself to the ebb and flow of history, even fell away at some moments and was revived again at others. And in times of crisis, when one might have expected it to be undermined for good, it often surged up again, as took place during the period of unprecedented population growth lasting from the end of the nineteenth century to the middle of the 1950s. It is only when we view "the old communalism" as merely a jumble of archaic practices, rather than as a coherent system of thought, that we are surprised by its survival into the present.

This system of thought is not easily dissected, however. With this system, as with most systems anthropologists and historians treat, the thought is one with the practice, with its material husk. In the case of the web of use-rights, the conceptual system is wrapped in such very concrete practices as collective crop rotation, the forming of common herds to graze the common pastures, the distribution and use of communal property, and the restrictions placed on private property that made it subject to common use. We will, therefore, be paying close attention to the intricacies of these practices.

For purposes of analysis, though, it may be helpful to pretend for a moment that we can set aside the material husk of the practices and peer through to the thought encased within. By doing this we may discover three interrelated motifs: 1) that there is, or should be, a sharing of goods within the community, even when this involves the imposition of "servitudes"; 2) that there exists a flow of reciprocities and obligations around the village, that things go round, in the local idiom, *a corrida*; and 3) that *vecindad*, or village citizenship, confers upon the house the right to receive *suertes*, lots or gifts, from the common bank of goods.

Although we can draw out such motifs we should not deceive ourselves into thinking that we have discovered the meaning of the system. What we have here are just preliminary frames with which to organize the finely woven diversity of threads that make up the web of use-rights. The deeper we get into the material the less helpful such atemporal summations will be, for its complexities only become apparent when viewed in practice and in historical process.

Servitudes

The old Leonese agrarian regime was founded on a combination of agricultural production, mostly based in cereals, and animal husbandry. The fertility of the soil was maintained by fallowing: one year the land was cropped, the next year it was left uncropped to rest and rejuvenate. Since hay was not sown as a crop, fodder was always in short supply, and so stubble left on the land after harvesting became pasture for cattle and other beasts. This double-faceted use of the land as arable and pasture eventually came to be organized collectively, though at different times in different places, through the introduction of what is known as the "common-field system," or, in Spain, the system of *dos hojas* (meaning two sides, like the two sides of a page), or *dos pagos*, or *año y vez*.[23]

In accordance with this system, the fields were brought together into two or three large units. Cereals were grown following a schedule of crop rotation that the community fixed. Once the last ear of grain had been gleaned, the livestock of all the households could be turned upon the land and it could be grazed irrespective of boundaries, as though it were a vast common pasture. In this arrangement, which is at once economic and social, we see the meshing of private and common interests that was so characteristic of the old system of communal rights and uses. The manure of the grazing animals fertilizes each individual plot as it fertilizes the whole, and the stubble of all the plots together provides sustenance for each household's beasts while doing so for the common herd.

The common-field system has often been thought of as an immemorial fixture of the rural landscape of Europe. But historians are now discovering that the system had not fully crystallized in many areas until the thirteenth and fourteenth centuries, and in León and Castile perhaps not until the fifteenth and sixteenth centuries.[24]

A set of ordinances from Tierra de Avila composed in 1487 indicate that not all places in its jurisdiction followed a common-field system at the time, and those places that did were having a difficult time enforcing it. Some people, the ordinance reads, "maliciously" sow their fields on the *hoja* that is supposed to remain fallow and open to the herds, in order to later accuse their cattle-owning neighbors of laying waste their crop and reap the fines. But the ordinance, which appears to have been written at a moment of transition to a system of collective crop rotation, clearly takes the side of the herders, and declares that the *vecinos* be allowed to graze their animals on the open fields, even where there is land sown, and not be fined. Anyone daring to ask for a fine is to return it doubled.[25] Similarly an ordinance of 1555 from Portillo, in the province of Valladolid, states that: "the year that one *suerte* is sown, the other one not be, so that the one that is sown be well guarded and in those remaining the cattle be able to roam freely and the damages be avoided which every day are being done because of the sowing in scattered plots, which the herders cannot guard, and the owners of cattle are much hurt by the lack of order."[26]

Order was eventually established in most parts, or a greater semblance of it anyway. Santa María's ordinances from 1776 provide a picture of a system of *dos hojas* whose contours were already more or less fixed. In Santa María, the long main street of the village, along which the houses are strung, served as the dividing line between one *hoja* and another, or between the cultivated "side" and the fallow "side" (see Map 5). The system of *dos hojas* was thus an expanded version of the basic symmetrical organization of space that characterizes the settlement. The *dos hojas* also represented an organization of time, and one side, the *bago* or furlong known as El Truébano, used to be sown in odd years, while the other *bago* of Los Tragüezos was sown in even years.[27]

The side or furlong that was sown was closed off; it was said to be *coto*, or in its "closed time," as the old English expression went.[28] The year a furlong was *coto*, as some villagers explained, it was closed to all

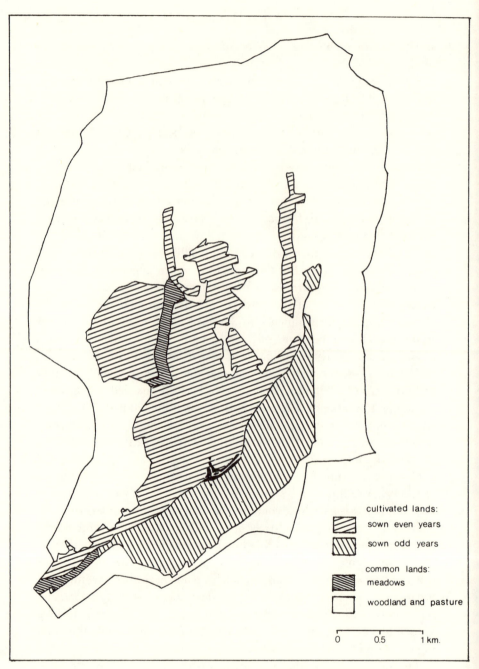

cultivated lands:

sown even years

sown odd years

common lands:

meadows

woodland and pasture

0   0.5   1 km.

Map 5. The *dos hojas* system of crop rotation

herds and flocks, to the passage of carts, and even of people. This closed time was signaled by the lifting up of hedges (*sebes*) around the edges of the sown side. Year after year, throughout the late nineteenth and into the middle part of this century, lots of woodland were made available to villagers in order that they might "close the borders and conserve the crops" (*para cerrar las fronteras y conservar los frutos*). Thus the ordinances speak of *cotos* being "broken" by the entrance of sheep or cattle, a transgression that was fined by the *concejo*: "We ordain and decree that any cattle that breaks *cotos* and *bagos* pay for ... the damage done."[29]

The following year the other *hoja* was *coto* and the previously closed *hoja* was *descotado*, or open. When the "open time" began, again as in the old English expression,[30] the hedges were removed and the space became a common pasture for the livestock of the village, what is known in Spanish as *la derrota de las mieses*. The restrictions on rights of passage now fell upon the *hoja* that was *coto* that year. Formed into a vast enclosure, the lands sown could be protected more easily from the trespass of people and beasts, while all the lands lying fallow could be grazed indiscriminately by the herds of the village.

This alternation of enclosure in common and pasture in common formed part of a larger system of open and closed fields that was administered by the *concejo*. Apart from the grain fields that fell within the *dos hojas* system, there were the kitchen gardens and private meadows, to which different rules of enclosure applied.

In Santa María the area of La Viña, a small irrigated tract lying near the settlement, was to be kept closed at all times. Each house holding land in La Viña had to help keep a hedge around the entire area all year long, and the house that failed to do so, according to the ordinances from 1776, was to be fined six *reales*. The purpose of these mandatory enclosures was to reserve the plots in La Viña for the more intensive cultivation gardening requires or, as the ordinances put it, "so that all kinds of crops may be planted there."[31] Its year-round enclosure meant that people could not bring cattle to graze in La Viña, even on their own land.

A hundred years later the special status of La Viña was still respected. An act of the *concejo* from 1885, while alluding back to the ordinances of the previous century, reminded the *vecinos*: "La Viña is to remain closed all year and all around as provided for in chapter sixteen of the ordinance penalty of fifty *céntimos* of a *peseta* the first time any border is found open, and the second according to the will of the *concejo*, and

the borders noted down here will be checked every month to punish
them if they remain open."[32] To this day La Viña is kept closed all
through the year, though in the present it is but a fragment of a much
larger area of irrigated terrain.

In contrast, on the private meadows there was until recently a prohibition of permanent enclosure. With the meadows as with other private
properties, their enclosure in a land tenure system of small, scattered,
and intermingled plots would in almost every case have blocked off the
passage of herds and people. The eighteenth-century ordinances of Santa
María point this out, and ordain that no *vecino* take it upon himself to
enclose any meadow without first informing the *concejo*. It was the *concejo*
that then sent out four *vecinos* to determine whether the meadow, if
hedged, would impede the path of herds and people, and if it did it was
to remain open.[33] The rule applied to those meadows from which the
owner kept just the first coat, or cutting, of grass in late June (*primer
pelo*). In addition, there were a few enclosed meadows from which, as
the ordinances put it, the owner was "privileged" to also keep the second
cutting of grass in September (*el otoño*). But on Saint Andrew's Day
they too were to be opened "so that all the livestock may graze on them,
and remain open until the first of March, penalty of four *reales*."[34] Whatever was left on the private meadows after their owners had mowed
them thus became communal grazing land.

There were other reasons why the permanent enclosure of meadows
might be prohibited. We find quite a different rationale for this prohibition in a fascinating record of litigation that took place in 1871
between Baltasara Salas, a *vecina* of Santa María, and the village of Santa
María acting as a corporate body. Baltasara Salas had on her own authority enclosed a meadow that was located amidst other meadows on
the very site the village customarily used as a common threshing ground.
According to the council record, an individual could not clear or close
his or her property in the vicinity of these meadows nor prevent the
community from placing its threshing ground anywhere within that site.
Many *vecinos*, so the record tells us, had nowhere else to thresh.[35] Thus
we can see why the matter was of enough consequence for all the *vecinos*
to agree to pay the costs of going to court.

In short, the individual family's rights of use over its own property
were not unlimited and free, but tied into the tangled web of communal
usufruct. Roman law, not without a hint of prejudice, invented the term
"servitudes" for these rights of use given to others over property not

their own.[36] So tightly woven was the land of Baltasara Salas into the communal system of use-rights that to have freed it of its "servitude" would have meant tearing the whole web. For the threads of the web were frail and easily ripped: just one field out of order in the *dos hojas* of crop and pasture, just one meadow enclosed when it was supposed to be open, could wreak havoc.

A kind of gleaning

The *concejo*, acting on behalf of the majority of *vecinos*, constantly sought to bring the private into the realm of the common or, more exactly, to redistribute limited goods more equitably than the system of private property alone would have allowed. This effort is particularly evident in the practice known by the term *apañar*, which literally means to take hold of or gather by the hand. In the rural Leonese context to *apañar* was to engage in gleaning of sorts, though what was gathered was not grain left behind after reaping, but various useful plants and weeds with which to feed a family's cows, rabbits, pigs, and chickens. Beginning in late February, before spring was on its way, and continuing until Saint Peter's Day in June, people would go *apañar* milk thistle (*cardo lechero*), chicory (*achicoria*), fennel flower (*neguilla*), and other wild plants that sprouted up around the tender shoots of wheat, in the meadows, and in the baulks and ridges separating individual plots of land.

As in the communal grazing of the *hoja* left to rest, people were able to *apañar*, by hand or with the sickle, in and around the lands of others as well as in the common meadows during the appointed time. The meshing of private and common interests evident in the system of *dos hojas* is likewise in evidence in the practice of going to *apañar*. The person who goes to *apañar* brings back edible plants for the family's animals and, at the same time, rids the land of weeds. Some plants, like chicory, stifle the growth of grass; by pulling them up the *apañador* provides a real service for the owner of the land. One would frequently hear in the past people saying, "Why don't you go *apañar* chicory on my meadow?"

On the other hand, the private meadows were open to the *apañadores* for only a short time. People could *apañar* on the private meadows only until the first of March, and stiff penalties were set for anyone daring to do so later on, in April or May. Yet, as Santa María's ordinances point out, even if a *vecino* wished to *apañar* in one of his own meadows he had to bring the matter to the attention of the *concejo* on penalty of two *reales*, a stiffer fine than any that was brought against the *apañadores*.[37] For by making public his intention to *apañar* his meadow, an owner could not turn around later and make false accusations of damage done on his property.

The practice of going to *apañar* had its basis in a form of economy, yet it does not fail to reflect a certain attitude of mind. In Santa María the practice was subject to communal regulation until the construction of the village dam in 1955 brought more land under cultivation, which could be used to plant grass, clover, and alfalfa. Before the dam was built the early spring months were the hardest to endure, because it was just then that the supplies of hay and other fodder crops brought home during the previous summer were running low. The two basketfuls of plants and weeds that the *apañador* brought home daily helped to tide over many a family during this time of scarcity in the agricultural cycle.

In this way we can more or less explain the function that the practice served. But in the first place, what is significant is the fact that the plants which grew wild in the landscape, no matter whether on private or common land, were conceived of as the property of any person who chose to gather them. They were there for the taking. When the *concejo*, perhaps under the influence of the better-off *vecinos*, made an attempt to charge people for exercising their right to *apañar* there was, at least early on, a good deal of protest. This, anyway, is what we can infer from an act of 1870 that states, "we also agree ... that the *apañadores* who before payed, seeing how much commotion and discord there was, we have decided to let them go free of charge."[38]

Payment for the right to *apañar* did eventually become the established mode, however, even though the sum charged was always a very small one. And, as time went on, more and more people started closing off their lands to the *apañadores*, making private what had long been considered common. They would put up a few shafts of rye on their plot and everybody then knew that the plot was *coto*, that it was closed to communal use. But the *apañadores*, I was told, would frequently knock down the shafts in protest, especially if that person had animals that grazed on everybody's fallow.

It is unusual to find records of the exact numbers of people who went to *apañar*, and only one such listing from 1901 survives in Santa María's council records. Out of a total of sixty *vecinos*, forty-one had *apañadores* gathering grasses in the spring of 1901 and twenty had *apañadores* gathering chicory; some *vecinos* had two or three *apañadores* gathering at once. For, in general, it was only the young and women who went to *apañar*. So we can say that about 70 percent of the population at the turn of the century had need of the humble weeds of nature.[39] The commentaries of contemporary informants lead me to believe that the percentage steadily increased as families grew larger toward the middle of this century. Nevertheless, there were people who did not need to *apañar* and could afford to flaunt their independence from the community by closing off their lands to the *apañadores*.

People also went to *apañar* in the common meadows reserved for the exclusive grazing of beasts of burden. It was thus crucial that these meadows be allowed continually to replenish themselves. One of the tasks of the warden of the fields and woods hired yearly by the *concejo* was to see to it that the *apañadores* ceased their labors by Saint Peter's Day. With so many young people in the village going to *apañar* in the 1920s and 1930s this was no easy task, as the following story shows.

Once, on the very day that the communal herd or *vecera* was to begin grazing in the meadow of Los Tragüezos, a group of young men and women went there to *apañar*. The men made large piles of the grass they had cut with their sickles, while the women filled up their baskets to heaping. When the *vecera* got to where they were, you should have seen the commotion there was, my storyteller recounted, and all the blame fell on the guard who, people said, had let us *apañar* the whole valley. But then on the day of the procession to the *ermita* or shrine of Villasfrías, when the young people thought they would again be able to trick the guard, he managed to outsmart them. "They all saw that he was going with the *casa* and all dressed up for las Villasfrías ... Hey *tío* Joaquín went to las Villasfrías, *tío* Joaquín went to las Villasfrías. Let's go down, let's go to the valley, let's go to the valley. They went to the valley. But instead of going to las Villasfrías, he went and turned back ... and planted himself there in the valley of los Tragüezos. ... When we were all there, a few young men and women, down comes the guard and fines us all two *reales*."[40]

This anecdote, so rich in its evocation of the lived nature of custom, also reveals the extent to which the commons, indeed all property, had constantly to be kept under close supervision. It was not just the young who tried to take advantage of the system, however. What the young did in jest, their elders sometimes attempted to get away with in earnest.

Yet to be caught stealing from the common bank of goods, seeking an unfair advantage over one's fellow *vecinos*, was one of the greatest shames that could befall an adult member of the community.

The system of servitudes and rights of use over private and communal property existed by common agreement to foster a sharing of goods within the community. To go against the ideal of shared communal goods was to invite the envy of one's fellow villagers, as my informant explained to me. When the guard would announce in the public arena of the *concejo* that so-and-so had, say, broken a *coto*, that is, taken animals to graze in a closed field, his fellows would think to themselves, in his words, "Why, hell, the saint, someone who was a little like that, Mr. Sanctimonious and with his cows in such and such a place! The envy there was, that someone else should take his cows to graze and one's own should be in the stable." Precisely to avoid such envy, "so there wouldn't be envies that you entered and that I didn't enter and that somebody else did, everything was *coto* until the same day."[41] In other ways too the quest for equality that surfaces time and again in the old communal regulation of agriculture is but the sublimation of envy.

Chapter 11

✛

The Common Herds

I T WAS NOT just the land that was entangled in the web of use-rights but also the animals belonging to every family. In Santa María, as in other Leonese villages, the various classes of animals—the oxen, the young cows and calves, the mares and donkeys, the sheep and goats, even the pigs—went to pasture on the common stubble and fallow, on the common meadows and woods, in common herds. Each house sent its animals to graze with all the others and each house took turns playing the part of herder. This system of communal herding is the *vecera*.

A system of communal herding

The term *vecera*, clearly from the Spanish word *vez* for turn, in rural Leonese usage refers to the herd itself and to the system of turn-taking employed in herding. The meaning of *vecera* is sometimes extended to refer to any system in which obligations and rights are circulated from one house to another in turn. But the concept of a villagewide circulation, circuit, or flow is more frequently expressed in the generic term, *la corrida*, which is used both as an adverb to refer to things going round *a corrida*, and as a noun to refer to a completed circuit or *corrida* of turn-taking (see Map 6).[1]

Though much changed, the *vecera* of the cows still exists in Santa María, as well as in a handful of nearby villages. Beginning in May and continuing until early September, it involves most of the households who own cattle. There are, however, several houses that do not participate and take their cattle to graze on private meadows. But they are still required by custom to wait until the *vecera* has gone out before going

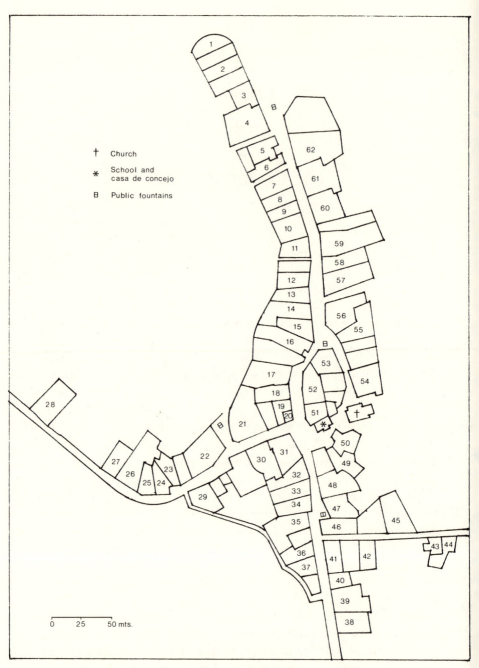

Map 6. The *corrida* in Santa María del Monte: a generalized model of house rotation. The *vecera* begins in house 48 and ends in house 47 every year.

1. Balbino and Hilaria with a cart of oats. Part of the *urbanización* of Montesol is visible in the background.

2. Nieves and Germiniano winnowing chick peas

3. Sixto and Inés finishing off the milking of the cows. Most families now use milking machines.

4. An evening meal in the kitchen

5. Members of the village religious confraternity of San Roque in the *casa de concejo*. The land consolidation maps are on the wall.

6. Sixto demonstrating how a wheatsheaf was gathered between thumb and forefinger when grains were harvested with a sickle

7. Inés with *ceranda* (sieve)

8. Láutico and Julita with their youngest grandchild

9. Hermelinda with newborn piglets

10. Aurelio, the village shepherd, with sheep grazing on the fallows

11. Sweeping the threshing ground

12. The oak doors of an old house, where the village blacksmith lived

13. A bedroom in a village house lit by the afternoon sun

14. A wall in the *portal* of a house hung with scythes, yokes, and other farming implements

15. Sifting chick peas

16. Harvesting with the combine

17. Fuencisla in her kitchen garden

20. The owner of the more traditional part of the house that was split in half in Villamayor (Diagram 6)

out themselves. And should a house whose cows are not in the *vecera* wish to take them to graze on the common meadows, it may do so only after the *vecera* has done so. The *vecera* always has precedence.

Every two beasts counts for a day or turn guarding the *vecera*. The house that has three cows guards a day in one *corrida* and two in the next. Any member of the house may go, and both men and women do. The *vecera* is always taken to graze by two herders at a time, who are usually next-door neighbors. The herders for the day must ring the church bells at approximately four o'clock, following the midday meal, to signal the beginning of the *vecera*. The other participants then know that it is time to let their cows out. A quarter of an hour later the beasts emerge from the houses and assemble along the main street of the village, with one herder bringing the herd in from the rear and another leading it forward. At dusk the herders taking their turn that day return with the *vecera* to the village. Thoroughly domesticated, the cows find their way home themselves; if their owner is not there they wait by the door to be let in. The house that has completed its turn must then pass the word on to the next house in line so that it will know to herd the next day.

The *vecera* is still, as it was in past times, a cooperative institution, whose main purpose is to spread the burden of herding around the community during the most intensive period of the agricultural cycle, when every house has all it can do just to bring the harvest in. But the rules governing the *vecera* have grown decidedly lax in the last few years; in fact, they have almost completely fallen away. The *vecera* goes to graze in the best common meadows of Los Tragüezos and El Coto, which in the past were reserved for the exclusive pasture of the oxen and cows that served as beasts of burden. There is also no limit on the number of cows a house can send to the *vecera*, while in the past the number was always strictly controlled. Finally, participation in the *veceras* is nowadays completely voluntary. Only in the precedence which the common herd of the *vecera* still enjoys over the animals taken to graze privately do we find preserved a memory of the meaning and sense that the *vecera* once had.

For what we notice first of all in eighteenth- and nineteenth-century village sources, and find confirmed in the recollections of elder villagers, is that participation in the various *veceras* of the past was usually obligatory. In very few places could a house take its animals to graze apart

from the common herds, and even where it could this never freed any
house of its obligation to guard the *vecera*.

A set of ordinances from Oseja de Sajambre, close to the border with
Asturias, where there were separate *veceras* for the goats and sheep,
stipulated in 1701 that all the *vecinos* must take part in these *veceras*.
The one deviation from the norm that the *concejo* allowed was in cases
where a *vecino* had more than seventy head of cattle. Only then could
a *vecino* separate his animals from the common herd, though still "guarding a day in each *corrida*, even if he does not include them [his animals]
in the *veceras* mentioned." As occurs in Santa María in the present day,
"in the case of the person who wishes to separate his [animals], when
he takes them to pasture, he must wait until the ones from the village
leave, penalty of a *ducado* whoever does not observe it thus."[2]

In Salce, a northwestern mountain village, no *vecino* who had pigs
could take them to pasture, or even let them out of his house, except in
vecera with all the other pigs of the *pueblo*. Again, the *vecino* who did
not want his animals included in the *vecera* was still linked, forcibly,
into the chain of turn-taking: "he who has them and does not send them
to it must guard this *vecera* penalty of four *reales* . . . unless he has them
locked up in the house." There was also a *vecera* for the calves in Salce.
Those *vecinos* whose calves had difficulty following the *vecera* might
have the burden of taking a turn being herder of the common flock
lifted from their shoulders, but only after four men appointed by the
concejo ascertained that the calves were truly unable to go. If the four
men found the calves fit, the *vecino* in question had to serve his turn as
herder, even if he kept his animals out of the *vecera*. The *veceras* of the
past too continued well into the cold winter months: "and this *vecera* is
to remain standing until rigorously impeded by snow."[3]

Almost two hundred years later, in 1873, the *concejo* of nearby Ambasaguas still conceives of drawing up an act "to set a fine of four *reales*
for each pair [of cows] that goes about alone away from the pastures
where the *vecera* goes, and one *real* for any cattle that goes about alone
or apart from the *vecera*, such as mares, donkeys, etc."[4] In another nearby
village, Santovenia del Monte, an interesting accord is made in 1878
concerning the *veceras* of the calves and donkeys. The *vecino* who does
not want to send his animals to the *veceras* does not have to, but heaven
forbid he should later change his mind, for "if someday he wishes to
introduce them into the *vecera* they will not be admitted." Similarly, if
a *vecino* buys any cattle and "waits too long to introduce them, if more

Going out with the *vecera* in the afternoon

than eight days pass, later even if he wants to introduce them they will not be admitted."[5] Even though participation in the *veceras* appears not to be obligatory any longer in this period, the *concejo* still sees fit to punish those who absent themselves by imposing fines and closing off the *vecera* to newcomers after a certain date.

Taking a turn herding the *vecera* was a prestation that the *vecino* owed to the community. It was a burden, obligation, or servitude on the same order as performing public works in the *hacenderas*, being present at the wake and funeral of fellow *vecinos*, and taking one's proper turn harboring the poor. No *vecino* could escape it. Even Don Marcelo de la Puente, the powerful cattle-owner that we met in an earlier chapter, had to take his turn guarding the *vecera* in seventeenth-century Santa María.

Like the prohibition of permanent enclosure on private meadows, the *vecera* imposed certain limitations on the free exercise of individual property rights. Like the system of *dos hojas*, which brought together the cultivated fields into one *hoja* and the fields lying fallow into another *hoja*, blurring boundaries and distinctions, the various *veceras* joined together the animals of every house into common herds. In fact, the practice of communal herding went hand in hand with the common-field system: just as it was easier to protect the crops from the trespass of people and beasts if everyone followed the same order of rotation, so too if everyone's cattle grazed in common herds rather than individually and at random. At the close of the nineteenth century, the mountain village of Canseco specifically acknowledged this relationship. Its *concejo* declared that whoever did not want to be bound to the communal rotation of crop and fallow would have their cattle separated from everyone else's, "and at no time will any *vecino* be able to take charge of herding them; nor should a *vecino* take on cattle of any kind for them, and for each time he does so he will pay the fine that has been set."[6]

But how does one explain the fact that the *vecino* who fenced off his animals from the common herd still had to serve a turn as its herder? It was as though the *corrida*, the circle of turn-taking, could not be broken, and every house formed a vital link in the chain of reciprocities. If any house was passed over, it seems, the principle of the *corrida* was violated.

Indeed, the conception of the *corrida* that people continue to have today is of just such a ring, with all the houses in the village following one after another in an uninterrupted sequence. This became especially clear to me when I was told the story of the lapse of the custom of bringing bread to church on Sundays *a corrida* by the various houses in turn for the blessed bread ritual (*la caridad*). Since this custom has already been described in detail elsewhere,[7] let me just say in brief what it consisted of in Santa María.

Every Sunday a different female head of a household would take a turn bringing to mass a two-kilo round loaf of bread (*la hogaza*) for the priest and a one-kilo loaf to be consumed by all the congregants in the blessed bread ritual. The priest would bless the bread during the mass and then the *vecino* who was taking his turn being *mayordomo* or steward of the church would cut up the one-kilo loaf into morsels (*migas*), like the ones used to make Leonese garlic soup, and place them in a basket. At the end of the mass the congregants each took a morsel of "the soup" on their way out, crossed themselves, and ate it. A piece of the blessed bread was always saved and the woman who had brought the bread would pass it on to the neighbor who lived in the house to her left, to distinguish it from other *corridas*, and she, in turn, would bring the bread the following week, and so on, week after week.

One Sunday sometime in 1976 the man who was serving as *mayordomo* that year failed to attend mass. Since it is the *mayordomo* who must cut the bread into morsels, no blessed bread was given out that day, and the priest took both loaves home. Consequently, the woman who had brought the bread did not have a piece to pass on to her next-door neighbor. Her neighbor, in turn, refused to bring the bread the following week since she had not been given the customary piece from the sanctified loaf of the week before. At the next week's mass, when again no bread was brought, the priest chided his parishioners for having allowed such a good custom to be lost. But it was too late, the damage was done; one of the connecting links in the chain of reciprocities had broken; the sequence, like a torn string of pearls, had come undone. People blame the priest for not having cut the bread himself or gotten another person to cut it the day the *mayordomo* was absent. Since there was no bread to give and no bread to take, in other words, no exchange of reciprocities, how could the *corrida* go on? This was how *la corrida de la caridad* came to an end in Santa María.

This digression may help to throw light on our original query: why the *vecino* whose animals grazed separately was still under obligation to herd his neighbor's animals in the *vecera* when the *corrida* came around to his house. As in the cycle of blessed bread exchanges, every house had to take its turn in sequence for the *corrida* to be able to go on. It made no difference whether a *vecino*'s animals were actually *in* the *vecera*, what mattered was that the *vecera* keep flowing round, uninterrupted, from house to house, *a corrida*. Just one house left out and the chain fell apart.

Although no longer compulsory, the *vecera* of the cows in Santa María is tinged still with this sense of what an *a corrida* progression signifies. Thus, as I was told by various people, if one sends one's cows to the *vecera* the first day it begins, then one is under obligation to herd the *vecera* when one's turn is due for the entire season, even if later one withdraws one's animals from it. Not sending them from the start, one does not owe this prestation of labor. But once one's house is looped up in the chain of reciprocities it cannot be unfastened until the cycle is complete. In the present, as in the past, the only way a house can ever break out of the *corrida* is if its cows die or if they are sold. Only then, in the expression of the past, could a house "cast the *corrida* out" (*echar la corrida fuera*).

To keep the *vecera* flowing some villages kept a written record of where the *corrida* had last been. A note in the *concejo* records of Villamayor from 1867 reads: "The *vecera* of the oxen ended in the house of Juan Torices, which will be taken into account so that it may begin in the house that follows." Or again the following year there is this reckoning of sequence: "The *vecera* of the oxen this year of 1868 ended up in the house of Manuel Bardal and Melchor de Robles, they guarded a day and owe another one."[8] But for the most part such records were not necessary. People usually remembered who was next in line in the *corrida*. A number of villages, like Santa María today, begin and end the *vecera* in the same house every year, so there will not be any doubt about how the sequence should go.

When we consider that the practice of communal herding in *veceras* made every *vecino* responsible for the animals of all his neighbors, if only for a day at a time, we can readily understand why it was often necessary for the *concejo* to enforce the participation of all the *vecinos*. Not surprisingly, the rules surrounding the question of the liability of the herder were worked out to the last detail.

The most elemental requirement the herder had to fulfill was, of course, to make sure that the animals with which he had been entrusted "returned to the *pueblo* in a healthy, usual, and normal state, in accordance with how they had been handed over to him in the morning," as an ordinance from the mountain village of Mena put it.[9] The herder "should not dare club or stone [the animals in the *veceras*] penalty of eight *reales* and if it happens that by stoning or clubbing a herder maims or breaks the leg of an animal, he must pay what it is appraised for, the owner losing the fourth part," admonish a set of ordinances from the village of Mataluenga.[10]

Many villages ruled that the shepherd who left behind an animal was to go in search of it with its owner. But in this matter the owner also took part in the liability. For these cases Santa María's ordinances from 1776 had set forth the following course of action. The owner had first to bring the loss of the animal to the herder's attention, then take a walk around the village to see if it appeared—a calf or lamb could well end up in a different house by accident, as often happens today. If the animal did not appear, the owner was to let the herder know and the two of them go in search of the lost animal. If, however, the owner failed "to do what has been said and some misfortune occurs then it shall be the Owner's loss."[11]

But the greatest peril to herd, herder and owner alike, especially in villages covered with scrub forest, was always the wolf. A village like Santa María where, I was told, wolves frequently found their way into the settlement at nighttime, had naturally come to devise very minute prescriptions through the years for dealing with losses caused by the attack of these most hated creatures from the wild.[12] First of all, as the village's eighteenth-century ordinances put it, "though an animal be maimed by the wolf, so long as it returns on its own foot to the place even if it falls dead at the Door of the Owner the herder should not pay anything at all."[13] If, on the other hand, the wolf killed the animal in the forest, "but didn't eat any of it," then the herder had to pay the difference between what its value would have been alive and what its value was dead. In cases where the wolf had "eaten something" the herder was to pay for the injuries caused. When the animal that was killed or maimed turned out to be a mare, then the herder was liable for its full value, perhaps because, as today, its meat was not happily consumed by humans.

In effect, so long as the animal made it back to the village settlement the herder was not responsible for what became of it afterwards. When out in the pastures and wastes, though, it was incumbent upon the herders to do everything in their power to defend the animals in their charge from the ravages of a wolf. The herder thus had to be a capable person. A *vecino* did not himself have to go out with the *vecera*; his wife could go, or he could send one of his children. But whoever took the turn for the house had to be over the age of sixteen "and not dumb, maimed, nor crippled" (*y no bobo, manco, ni tullido*) added the ordinances of Mataluenga.[14]

For the herder not only had to defend the *vecera* from the wolf but, as a person of age and sense, be capable of swearing to the truth of how mishaps had occurred. Where an animal caused injury to another, it was the owner of the animal who paid the damages and not the herder. The herder thus had to be old enough and mature enough to be able to say, on oath, whose animal was to blame. The account of incapable people was not to be believed, and if mishaps occurred while the *vecera* was in their charge it was their houses that had to pay for them. So ordained the ordinances of Mataluenga where, no matter what, the house always lost a fourth part of the value of any animal that was wounded or killed in any of the three *veceras* for cows, mares, and pigs that existed there.

Every village adopted slightly different rules. In Oseja de Sajambre at the beginning of the eighteenth century, the herder of the *vecera* was liable for all losses, repaying "a goat for a goat and a sheep for a sheep" (*cabra por cabra y oveja por oveja*).[15] The liability of the herder was not always so great, nor were all mishaps, as we have seen, made the herder's responsibility. Yet there was much to take on in being herder and much to lose. Even as late as 1944 in Santa María the herders of the *vecera* for the work-animals, by common agreement, were to go with the owner in search of a lost animal and payment for injuries or losses were to be borne by them. Significantly, the *concejo* record of this agreement ends with the words, "and if a *vecino* does not sign this obligation then we will not guard animals for him."[16] Here people felt it necessary to bind themselves to the *vecera* with their names so they would truly live up to the obligations it imposed.

The turn toward hiring herders

With the rise in population in the nineteenth century, an important change occurs in the old system of taking all the village animals to graze in *veceras*. The animals still continue to graze in common herds as before, but instead of being guarded by all the houses in a circle of herding turns, they now begin to be supervised by individual herders hired by the community. In particular it is the calves and nonworking cows, the

sheep and the goats, the mares and the donkeys that become the charge
of individual herders. The herding of pigs ceases altogether, perhaps
somewhat earlier in the century, as they come to be stable-fed rather
than grazed on the roots and plants of the woods. With the oxen or
cows that served as work-animals, the *vecera* continues in the old way.
It was as if these animals, being too important to entrust to any one
person, were still best cared for by all the owners in turn, while animals
that were not required for daily labors could be sent further away, to
the less fertile pastures, where it was a greater burden for the *vecinos*,
who had other pressing chores, to take them. And truly in this period
another kind of community had taken shape: it is no longer a little circle
of twenty *vecinos*, who can circulate the herding of all the animals among
themselves without much difficulty, but a much larger village; and with
greater numbers of people it becomes possible for all the *vecinos* to join
together to pay for the services of a herder, where before it would not
have been feasible.

"We the *concejo* and *vecinos* of this village of Villamayor say that on
account of our having relinquished the *vecera* of the cows we have passed
them on to Manuel de Laíz *vecino* of the aforesaid village."[17] So begins
an act from nearby Villamayor drawn up in 1847. One has the impression
that the practice of hiring individual herders is just taking form. But by
the 1860s it is certainly well established in many villages, where for
almost the next hundred years it becomes an annual routine for the
concejo and *vecinos* to contract their herders.

Who were the herders? They were usually *vecinos* of the community
that hired them. Moreover, the same people often continued as herders
year after year. In Santa María, the herd of calves and untamed cows
known as the *vacada* was the charge of Isidro de Robles for almost every
year during a twenty-five year period extending from 1868 to 1893. Isidro
de Robles was a native of nearby Solanilla who had married into Santa
María just four years before he became herder. It was to become his
lifetime occupation, for he died three years after giving up herding.[18] As
an outsider he had little land in the village and for this reason, perhaps,
he became a herder. Not that the herders were necessarily short of land.
Sometimes it was ill health, a lack of strength to guide the plow, which
determined a person's calling, as occurred with the father of a village
woman who was herder for many years in the early part of this century.
(See life history of María Rivero Morán in Appendix A for an account
of the *vaquero*'s lifestyle.) Many a man, since the herders were almost

always male, simply preferred the freer lifestyle of the shepherd to having to earn his daily bread by the sweat of his brow.

Since the shepherd was a member of the community, but one who being out every day with the village flocks could not farm, he was paid in grain and even given his stew daily by each of the houses in turn. For taking charge of the *vacada* in 1869, Isidro de Robles was paid a *celemín* of rye per cow (for the first pair a family sent to the *vacada* and half that amount for all other pairs) and given by each of the houses in turn three pounds of bread daily and his *puchero regular*, in León consisting of a stew of chick peas or beans with fatback and a piece of sausage. The arrangement began and ended on Saint Peter's Day in late June and during this time Isidro took responsibility for any misfortune that befell the animals in his charge. It was his obligation to recompense the owners for their animals if they were bitten or killed by the wolf. And as surety Isidro gave his own brother, Ignacio de Robles.[19]

When Felipe Torices took charge of the herd of mares and donkeys in late October of the same year, the village agreed to pay him 119 *reales* and to provide again the customary fare of three pounds of bread and his daily *puchero*. He too was liable for the animals in his charge, but not any more so than the various houses had been when they took their mares and donkeys to pasture by turn. As in the ordinances from Santa María, the agreement Felipe Torices makes with the village states as a first condition "that if the wolf kills a mare or donkey I shall pay for it and if it bites one and it returns home on its foot I shall not have to pay anything."[20]

For his labor the herder not only received payment, but was granted the liberty of not having to fulfill the various burdens of being a *vecino*. Thus in an agreement dating from 1870, once again involving Isidro de Robles, who by then was receiving for every cow a *celemín*-and-a-half of rye and eight *reales*, "the *concejo* frees him of *hacenderas*, litanies, or masses of the *concejo*."[21] Without this specific grant, Isidro, as a *vecino*, would have been required to carry out vicinal burdens or pay the *ruego*, or pardon, for not doing so.

So far we have been looking at the shift to a system of hiring herders from the herder's point of view. In truth the system was centered not around the herder but, as before with the practice of attending to all flocks by *vecera*, on the ring of houses that exchanged reciprocities in a flow of turn-taking around the village. It was the village collectivity, represented always by the *concejo*, that hired the herders, and the new system no less than the old was a communal arrangement in which all the houses, forcibly, were bound up.

As we noted earlier, the practice of taking the oxen and work-animals to graze in *vecera* by the various houses was never abandoned. It was the herd of calves and untamed cows, the *vacada*, that in this period became the charge of an individual herder or *vaquero*. On the one hand, then, we have a continuing pattern of turn-taking with respect to the herding of the *vecera*, and on the other, a new pattern of turn-taking to provide the shepherd with his daily bread and sustenance. We have already seen how in the past a *vecino* who grazed his animals separately still had to take a turn supervising the common herd of the *vecera*. In a similar way participation in the *vacada* and the *corrida* of giving food to the herder took on an obligatory character.

To understand fully this aspect of the *vacada*, we must first consider the organization of grazing on the common stubble and on the common meadows and woods. In Santa María, as in other nearby villages, the community had devised a kind of hierarchy of grazing rights. The oxen or work-animals were accorded the special privilege of grazing before any of the other animals; in addition, the best common meadows, the *cotos boyales* or ox pastures, were closed to all other beasts and reserved for their exclusive use. The high status accorded these animals was a mark of their indispensability: a household could not farm without its pair of oxen or work-cows, which provided traction for plow and threshing sled. Next in line after the work-animals were the untamed cows and calves which grazed in upland pastures, as did the herd of mares and donkeys. Finally, at the bottom of the hierarchy were the flocks of sheep and goats, the *rebaños*, which grazed in the poorer wastes and woodland pastures situated at the furthest extreme from the settlement.

The use of the ox pastures was always stinted, to use the English expression, that is, a limit was placed on the number of cattle a household could send to graze there. In the eighteenth century, each household in Santa María was allowed a single pair of oxen; all other cattle had to graze in the upland pastures. But during the plowing, harvesting, and sowing seasons, a house could bring down another pair of cows from the upland pastures to the ox pastures if they needed it to work their land. It was understood always that the ox pastures were strictly for animals that were needed in agricultural labors—a house had to work with the animals it had brought to these pastures for three days in every week at least, and it was fined, according to the 1776 ordinances, half a *real* per head per day for failing to do so.[22]

In the second half of the nineteenth century the rules governing the use of the common meadow and upland pastures became exceedingly more intricate. With the unprecedented rise in population that characterized the period, there was a new demand for land, a question we will shortly treat in detail, and for pasture, as people acquired two and three pairs of cattle to cultivate much larger extensions of terrain. The number of work-animals now permitted a household on the reserved common meadow or ox pastures was made relative to the amount of land it worked. Thus, in an accord from 1885 a pair of cattle was allowed to every household that had "something to cultivate," a pair and a half to every household that worked thirty *heminas*, two pairs for forty-six *heminas*, two and a half pairs for sixty-two *heminas*, and three pairs for seventy-four *heminas*.[23] By 1890 the number of cattle allowed to a household was being calculated according to what each paid in *contribución* or taxes; again a pair was allowed every *vecino*, a pair and a half for twelve *pesetas* paid in taxes, two pairs for eighteen *pesetas*, five cattle for twenty-five *pesetas*, and three pairs for thirty-two *pesetas*.[24] As in the previous century, if these cattle were not yoked and working for a continuous period of time they were fined and had to return to the upland pastures with the *vacada*.

Thus the *vecera* of the work-animals grazing on the reserved common meadow and the *vacada* of the untamed cows and calves grazing in the upland pastures formed a single system. At a time of growing population and diminishing resources, the limitations on the number of cattle a house could include in the *vecera* were ecologically essential lest the ox pastures be overgrazed. Clearly in this matter those houses that owned and worked more land were advantaged, for more of their animals got to graze the finer grasses the village had to offer. On the other hand the system was proportional on all counts: those houses that, being better off, sent more cows to the *vacada* had to pay that much more grain and money in support of the herder; and since each cow counted for a day in the *corrida* of providing the herder's bread and stew, they owed that many more days of giving food. One man who had been a shepherd remembered how sometimes he ate at one house for a month or more, practically losing track of the number of days he had been going there.

Of course all the houses tried to get away with sending as many cattle as they could to the ox pastures, not only for the better grazing they offered, but to get out of the obligation of giving the herder his daily fare. In the eighteenth century, as we saw, there was a limit of one pair per household, though an influential personage like Don Marcelo de la Puente had managed to insinuate three pairs. By the late nineteenth century, when two and three pairs were being granted entrance to the ox pastures, it became more difficult than ever to enforce the rules.

Already in an act from 1868 drawn up in Santa María we can glimpse the conflicts and problems that were surfacing. According to this act, there had been a reunion of the *concejo* to discuss "the manner in which each *vecino* is to send his pairs to graze in the ox pastures and which [animals] are to be kept in the *vacada*." The consensus had been that six *vecinos* be named to convene with the *alcalde pedáneo*, or headman, and his four assistants to draw up an accord "for the good of this *pueblo*." They decided upon the following. Pointing out how many people brought two pairs to the ox pastures when in fact they only worked with one, these men reminded their fellow villagers that only cattle yoked and working four days during the week would be allowed to graze there. Toward this end they advocated social control: "to know whether this is being complied with *pesquisa* will be taken in *concejo* ... the *alcalde pedáneo* asking if anyone knows of a *vecino* who has not complied."

If a house needed to bring a cow it had in *vacada* in the upland pastures down to the ox pastures, it could do so during the seasons of intense agricultural work so long as it was before the first of March. That house only had to continue feeding the herder until Saint Peter's. But if a house failed to bring down its cows by this date it had to continue giving food to the herder until New Year's. By the same token, a house that brought cows to the *vacada* as of Saint Peter's and sold them or took them down to the ox pastures was to continue providing food until New Year's to the herder in the name of those animals. The accord ends by stating, in a manner reminiscent of the old rules concerning participation in the *veceras*, that all cows, except those needed to work the land, would be considered part of the *vacada*, even if they never left home. "And so that this accord will stand as an ordinance in this matter we have agreed that it be read in public *concejo* so that no one may allege ignorance of it."[25]

Numerous acts of this kind could be cited. They abound in the latter part of the nineteenth century, bearing witness, almost certainly, to the tensions arising from the complicated system of communal payment and feeding of the hired herders. In fact, an act from Santa María drawn up in 1873 begins by acknowledging that the *vecinos* found themselves divided about the *vacada*. Making up a new agreement, they adapt an older tradition of cultural practice to the changed circumstances of their time. With renewed vigor the principle that all the houses must be linked, if forcibly, into the *corrida* of turn-taking, now to provide the herder with his bread and stew, is brought forward: "... all the *vecinos* ... have been reconciled to all the cows except the first pair being kept subject to the *vacada* and to providing food for the *vaquero* even if they never send them there and these cows that never go to the *vacada* will not pay the wage but they will provide food always."

In the same act it was agreed that if a house sent a cow to the *vacada* for three days it would have to provide food during the entire *corrida* and pay its share of the herder's wage. Once in the *corrida*, as we have seen before, there was no getting out. On the other hand, when a house sold a cow or lost one that had been in the *vacada* it no longer had to keep providing food to the herder. The same principle held if a house lost its pair of work-animals or sold them and found it necessary to bring up a cow or two from the *vacada* to the ox pastures. In both cases the *corrida* was halted, it was said to have expired at the house that fell out of the circle, in the local expression, *levantando corrida vencida*. Significantly, in either situation the house that fell out of the *corrida* of providing food remained under obligation to contribute to the herder's wage. This accord, finally, granted the individual houses a strangely binding kind of freedom: "It was also decided that the *vecino* who wants to be freed from the *vacada* will also be freed or separated from every *vecera* of the *concejo*."[26] In other words, a house could choose not to participate in the *vacada*, but at the price of being cast out of the entire system of herding in common.

These rules and practices, including the *corrida* of providing food to the herder, remained in force until the end of the 1950s in Santa María and neighboring villages. By then the system of grazing the work-animals in the ox pastures and the calves and cows in the upland pastures began to fall apart. It gave way finally to the present system where cows that work and do not work are alike taken in *vecera* to the old ox pastures, a system in which all the houses are no longer bound up. When people can take their cows to the now abundant private meadows, so few and far between in past times, they need not worry about turning down the gift, which must eventually be repaid with a herding turn, of the common pastures.

The village bull

To complete the picture of the old system of herding in common, let us briefly consider two related customs: the choosing, in the words of the old ordinances, of "fathers for every class of livestock" in the village, and the hiring by the *concejo* of a castrator for the village animals not selected for breeding.

Santa María's 1776 ordinances devote a chapter to the selection of stud-animals. For "the good governance of this *Pueblo*" begins the ordinance, every year come Saint James and Saint Anne the village should choose a bull, boar, he-goat, and ram for its cows, pigs, goats, and sheep. The *regidor* or headman was obliged to name "two intelligent men" to go from house to house in search of the best male animals. The animals that these men selected were not to be castrated until they had served their year's term, and until the selection was made, "no one should castrate a male animal no matter how puny it may be without the permission of the *concejo*." The chosen animals, we learn, were formed into a *vecera* and theirs was the privilege of grazing not in the upland pastures, but with the oxen in the reserved pastures.[27]

In Oseja de Sajambre, according to its ordinances from 1701, the owners of the two or three bull calves chosen yearly for breeding paid a penalty of seven *reales* every time they yoked their animals during the period of their service. Again, in return for this prestation the owners were rewarded by being allowed to send their animals to graze in the better pastures reserved for the oxen.[28] Moreover, as the ordinances of Canesco from 1761 point out, the bull of the village, like its stallion and boar, could not be impounded; they roamed freely, their owners did not have to account for "penalty and damage" (*pena y daño*).[29]

With the passing of the years these customs fell into disuse in some parts, only to be revived again at a later time. This is the impression one forms in looking over nineteenth-century acts that deal with the subject. For example, in 1871 we find the *vecinos* of the neighboring village of Villamayor gathered in *concejo* "agreeing unanimously once again" to revise the "immemorial custom of naming a stud for the cows on the first of March of every year." The council record of this reunion informs us that "this has not taken place for several years for certain reasons on account of which several owners of cattle have suffered harm." Beginning that year and "so on successively in years to come," it is agreed that the *concejo* will choose a committee from among the *vecinos* (how many we are not told) to select the best bull of the village, "without its owner being able to put forth any kind of pretext or excuse." In the event that the owner of the bull so chosen ever wishes to sell it, the *vecinos* agree, the *pueblo* will always have preference over other buyers, so long as the funds are there. For borrowing this bull the community, in turn, would recompense the owner by allowing him to send his animal to the ox pastures and by releasing him from the twin burden of taking a herding turn in the *vecera* and paying his share of the wage of the *vaquero*.[30]

A similar revision of the custom of free bull took place in Santa María in 1877. An act drawn up in that year reports that the owners of the bull-calves of the village had refused to participate unless the conditions were set down in writing. The new ruling restated the privilege of the free bull to roam freely through the common fields and meadows and the obligation of its owner to not castrate or sell the bull without the permission of the *concejo*. But for all its freedom the bull was no longer to be allowed to get away with everything: "if said bull-calf does damage to private properties its owner will be obliged to pay for it without exception as with any other cow that does damage and it won't do any good to say that it is the bull of the *concejo* for the *concejo* can only rule in the *concejil*." As in the past, the owner of the bull-calf was to be free of all burdens relating to the herding of his animal: if the calf had been in the *vacada*, all the owners of cattle were to take turns providing food on its account, while the *concejo* was to pay its share of the wage; if it had been in the *vecera*, the owner did not have to guard the *corridas* that fell to his house.[31]

The custom of free bull is a classic example of the servitudes that weighed down private property in an old rural society. The property of an individual house, the bull chosen for breeding, or rather its seed, became for a time the common possession of all the houses. It represented, as did other servitudes, an attempt to redistribute limited goods more equitably than the system of private property would ever have allowed. Where the owner of the calf would certainly have preferred to castrate his animal and thereby be in possession of a hardy ox to pull his plow, he was forced by the community to make his bull available to all his neighbors' cows.

On the other hand, the owner was well recompensed for lending his bull to the community, especially in more recent times with the development of regional cattle markets. Various people pointed out that the better-off *vecinos* often made it a habit to buy a good calf in the cattle fair in León which, if chosen to be a stud, grew fat on the common meadows and later could be sold at a profit. In fact, it was the profit motive, conspiring with the intense political factionalism preceding the Civil War, which led to the downfall of the custom in Santa María. As one informant explained:

> The bull of the *pueblo* was free, it roamed all over. But a moment came when the thing fell apart. The grandfather of these kids here had one bull, and he was on the Señorito's side, and another fellow up there, E's father, had another. That's where it fell apart—"This bull's better," "that one's is better"—and from that it started falling apart and afterwards it ended completely, because everyone took sides and that's where the politics of ending with the bull came from. And afterwards there were whatever bulls there were, but each one in his own house and one did as one liked, but there was no longer a bull of the *pueblo*.[32]

Where there were common herds and a common bull, ram, he-goat, and boar, it comes as no surprise that there should also have been village-hired castrators. They were hired every four or six years and typically received, along with a money payment, "the customary rights," which consisted in Santa María of an *azumbre* of wine for every visit. The village also agreed in 1873 to give the castrator two carts of wood every year.[33] The one or two castrators hired had to make three visits yearly, in March, July, and September, and it was their obligation to castrate all animals of cloven hoof in the village. An obligation drawn up in Santa María in 1869 added the provision that "if there are more than four pigs to castrate and we are given the message we are to come in the middle of the month of November ... and if not the contract will be null."[34] Inserted into another obligation from 1879 was the clause, "and if there should be a donkey, he is to castrate it for a *peseta* as long as it is not over four years old."[35] These were customary agreements that were as binding upon the village as they were upon the person who was hired to serve the varied needs of all the houses.

"Today for you, tomorrow for me"

Of all the animals a *labrador* owns, in the past as well as in the present it is the oxen and cows that represent the most significant investment. Having considered the range of practices relating to the old system of

herding in common, let us conclude with a discussion of an institution
that epitomizes it—the mutual aid society formed by all the owners of
cattle to insure one another for losses of their animals. In Santa María
such a society exists today. It is known as the cow company (*compañia
de vacas*) and involves all the *vecinos* who own cattle. If any member
loses a cow through sudden illness or accident, the other members pay
a certain amount of money per kilo for the meat of the animal corresponding to the number of cattle each owns; this sum is paid even if it
turns out that the meat cannot be eaten.

During my first visit to Santa María in the summer of 1978, a cow
belonging to a member of the company died suddenly late one afternoon
as it grazed unguarded with two other cows in the owner's private
meadow. People said that the cow had become full of air and lost its
breath as it ate, until its belly burst. At dusk the carcass of the young
black cow, spotted in white, was hauled away in a tractor and the
veterinarian sent for. The next day, the meat having been found fit to
eat, the animal was butchered and within hours the beef had been
distributed around the village.

Two principles of reciprocal exchange found expression in the butchering and distribution of the meat: one, the *corrida*, which we have
already discussed in detail here; and another, the making of equivalent
suertes or lots from which one chooses one's luck, at the heart of all
distribution of property, familial and communal. Three *vecinos* assist the
house on whom the misfortune has befallen in butchering the cow,
weighing the meat, and making the equivalent lots. The obligation to
provide assistance in these matters is circulated *a corrida*, three neighboring houses taking a turn at a time. Once the meat is arranged in
equivalent shares, each of which is assigned a number, the women of
the member households cast lots to receive their shares, one for every
cow they own. Some time later the money is collected from all the houses
and given to the unlucky owners of the dead cow.

I had gone with the woman of the house where I was living that
summer to pick up the meat. There were maybe sixty or seventy piles
of beef laid out on big sheets of yellow plastic, cut out from the bags in
which fertilizer comes, in the *corral* of the house that had lost the cow.
Women were coming and going, picking out their numbers from the
bowl, taking their shares home in basins, pails, and bags, assuring those
who were just arriving that there was still plenty of meat left.

The woman of the house that had lost the cow began chatting with

us. Were they supposed to get a ration being the owners of the cow?
She did not know, but they had gone ahead and taken the head and
tongue. My companion responded that this was natural and expected,
the owners always keep the head and tongue, and sometimes they also
take their ration. For that they would wait and see, the woman said, if
anything was left after the *vecinos* had gotten their shares. Then she
motioned us into the kitchen and pointed to the pot where the head and
tongue were soaking in water. We're going to make use of this, what
else can we do? And my companion, consolingly, of course, the tongue
is very good, it's very flavorful.

We stepped into the *portal* and prepared to take our leave. Seeing us
there, the man of the house came over. After a few polite words, he
remarked that they felt the loss deeply, but so it goes. It can happen to
anyone, answered my companion as we stepped out the old oak door,
tomorrow it could happen to us.

This idea, clearly, lies at the heart of the institution of the cow company. One never knows when misfortune will strike, and if it knocks
at one's neighbor's door today, it might knock at one's own door tomorrow. Misfortune, like death, spares no one. Yet the money the owners
of the dead cow receive from their neighbors, which in 1978 was set at
a hundred *pesetas* a kilo, is hardly enough to buy another one. It is a
small aid, though still it is more than one would be likely to get from
a butcher. It is also a fair arrangement from the point of view of the
other members, for they buy the meat at fraction of what it costs in the
store. Of course the point is that, as members of the company, they must
buy the meat whether they want it or not—this is what is crucial, since
most Leonese *labradores*, who in their life and work spend much of their
time around their cows, are not especially fond of beef and could easily
pass up a steak for homemade sausages or sardines. Thus the meat is
truly purchased in the spirit of the gift, not in a utilitarian attempt to
profit from another's loss. There is also a certain sense that the order of
things is set right in these acts of neighborly cooperation, as if, by coming
to the aid of one's neighbor, equality were somehow restored in the eyes
of God; or looked at from a different perspective, as if the gift were the
talisman that keeps envy and evil away from one's own house.

In any case, mutual aid societies of this kind are not unique to Santa
María, nor are they recent creations. They once existed in various parts
of Spain, from Aragon to Galicia, the Basque country to Soria.[36] In Santa
María the earliest reference I found to the cow company was an act

from 1893; there the *vecinos* signed an obligation stating that each would take the part that corresponded to him "of any cattle which in this *pueblo* suffers damage, as well as pay for it, the owner keeping the hide and the offal."[37] It was also in existence in the same period in the old Leonese town of Sahagún.[38] But there is no question that it has a still greater historical depth, reaching back at least as far as the seventeenth century.

An ordinance drafted in 1623 from the village of Acebedo, in the northeastern mountains of León, speaks not of a cow company as such, but of the obligation of the *concejo* to come to the assistance of any *vecino* who has lost an ox: "considering ... that the death of an ox is for any *vecino* a source of much harm and damage and more so if it happens to a poor person ... we ordain that to aid him in his loss this *concejo* aid him with two *ducados* from its *propios*."[39] The kernel of the cow company is here. And if we look at an undated ordinance which could certainly have been written at any time in the eighteenth century, perhaps even earlier, we can see clearly the idea of such a company forming. This ordinance is drawn up in Chozas de Abajo, a village near the city of León and not far from Santa María. In its rich detail many of the themes that came up in our discussion of the present-day cow company are transmuted into a peasant poetics:

> We ordain that if from the first of May to Michaelmas a *vecino*'s cattle suffers damage or has a disease that is not harmful to the lifeblood of man even if he eats its meat, bearing in mind that the Lord asks that we be charitable with our fellow men that cattle should be killed and distributed among the *vecinos* at one-and-a-half times the value it would have in the marketplace, and with the condition that this distribution is to be made by four men named by the *Concejo*, and if someone does not want to take the meat, if it is known that he has the means he is to be obliged to take it, because this is a mutual contract and as is often said, today for you and tomorrow for me, besides among many little falls to each and one does a good deed.[40]

Here the incipient company is to exist just during the months of the harvest, from the beginning of the haymaking to the bringing in of the last of the wheat and beans. Clearly this is the most precarious time of the year for the *labrador*, and it is when the loss of an ox or cow would be felt most deeply. Participation in the company is obligatory, at least for all the *vecinos* who are known can afford it.

Again we are in the presence of a servitude that is imposed on the individual houses in the common interest. But what is especially intriguing about this text is the world view it expresses. In the same breath the *vecinos* are admonished to be charitable to one another as fellow Christians and reminded of the place that each occupies in the chain of reciprocities. Probably even then, however, it was the sounding of the second message that, as in the present, was heard and heeded—"today for you and tomorrow for me."

Chapter 12

The Common Lands

"From you I have learned that equality is a necessary result of the common lands," wrote Juan Antonio Posse of Llánaves, the village in the northwestern mountains of León where he was parish priest at the end of the eighteenth century. "For you live in a land men can scarcely inhabit," he continued, casting a dire prophecy, "do not forget that your fate is writ in keeping the lands communal, and that as soon as you lose this community you will be reduced to a desert in which only vultures and wild beasts will dwell."[1] It would be difficult to find a more evocative statement in support of the common lands. Posse, who was priest of Llánaves during the twelve-yearly drawing of lots for the communal grain fields, had come to see this institution as the source of "union, peace, and all the virtues that men joined together in society ought to have."[2]

Between Posse's desert and ideal society lies the reality of the common lands. Not that Posse's account is altogether lacking in truth. Where the communal inheritance was extensive and access to it was on equal terms for all *vecinos*, one does indeed find a good deal of social cohesion and even unity. Such was the case in Santa María at the beginning of the eighteenth century, as we have already seen, when the *concejo* and *vecinos* defended their common lands against the encroachments of Doña Francisca, the wealthy cattle-owner from neighboring Villafeliz. It was the case too, as we will see, in the second half of the nineteenth century when, in the height of population pressure, the village turned to its common woods to meet the subsistence crisis. There were, of course, moments of dissension, and in general the trend was, in fact, toward privatization. But never did things in Santa María and other Leonese villages reach the fearful point of no return Posse had foreseen.

Communal grain fields, gardens, meadows

In Santa María, as elsewhere in León, there was common land available
to village households for kitchen gardens (*huertos*). I found evidence of
this in the village ordinances from the eighteenth century, which was
further confirmed by the commentaries of older villagers who remembered that there had once been such common land. Felicísimo Llamazares
heard his grandparents say that the land known as La Viña Abajo "next
to the house of the shoemaker was divided into *suertes* [lots]; every few
years they drew for them, kitchen gardens for each to have four onions
... a son couldn't inherit there, one had to leave it for the *vecinos*."[3]
These gardens are now all in private hands.

The ordinances tell us that every *vecino* had to keep his garden closed
with a live hedge (*cierro vivo*), probably to shield it from the trespass of
wandering animals and *veceras*, and plant cabbage for home consumption
at least once a year. We also learn that these kitchen gardens were a
scarce good in a village with little irrigated land; though at the time
there were still enough plots to go around for all the *vecinos*, there would
no longer be enough if the population grew:

> ... since there is no place to make more gardens without causing
> grave detriment, even should there come to be more *vecinos* than
> there are gardens, no more shall be made until one is vacated; and
> should there be more *vecinos* than vacant gardens, the gardens shall
> be provided first to the *vecinos* of longest standing who do not hold
> one, and those who are left without one should wait until one is
> vacated, and not cause altercations or run to the courts, on penalty
> of remaining without a garden and paying twenty *reales* for expenses
> of the *común*.[4]

It is clear that the kitchen gardens were held by each of the *vecinos*
during his lifetime, returning at death to the community, which could
then allot a vacant garden to the *vecino* who, in order of seniority, was
lacking one. With characteristic realism, the ordinances even make provisions for handling the discord that *vecinos* impatiently waiting for a
garden might cause.

In other villages where there was apparently more land available for
gardening, the *vecinos* were often under obligation to keep a kitchen
garden. This was the case in the mountain village of Mataluenga, where
every *vecino* was expected to have "a kitchen garden to plant vegetables

for home consumption" and where the *vecino* "who does not have a kitchen garden of his own may make one in unoccupied terrain of the *concejo*." Those who failed to keep a kitchen garden "from the first of March until Saint John," stipulated the ordinance, "should be fined and pay to this our *concejo* for the first time two *reales*, the second four, and the third eight."[5] Similarly, in the mountain village of Omañón "every *vecino* and resident with an open door should or can close off a kitchen garden in terrain of the *concejo*, where it will not block the highway and cattle paths."[6]

Significantly, in both Mataluenga and Omañón the *vecino* who borrowed land from the commons to make a garden could keep it enclosed only for a period of three years. At the end of this period the hedges around the terrain tentatively staked out for private use had to be thrown down and the land returned to its original state as part of the common patrimony. The practice in Santa María of allotting kitchen gardens to the *vecinos* to make use of in their lifetime likewise served to keep this land within the domain of the commons. Though given over to private use, by remaining within a communal framework of circulation of goods the gardens could not become the private property of any family. Yet, the fact is that in the course of time these gardens ceased to be part of the common inheritance in a process whose history is, unfortunately, obscure. Only the extreme fragmentation of the land in La Viña, where hardly anyone is without at least a miniscule *cachín* in which to plant "four onions," bears testimony to its once having been communal.[7]

We have already spoken of the communal ox pastures and upland pastures where the common herds grazed. In addition, many villages distributed portions of communal meadow and threshing ground for private use. The nearby village of Valdefresno, for example, in 1858 divided up four *heminas* of meadow into *suertes*, or lots, to go around for each of the twenty-nine *vecinos* then living there. Two conditions, or servitudes, were placed on this land: that "it not be broken up into arable now nor at any other time," and that "it should only serve as private meadow and pasture every year from the first of March until the twenty-fourth of June of every year and from the twenty-fourth of June until the first of March ... it should serve as common pasture for common use."[8] Thus the *vecinos* of Valdefresno kept this land within the framework of the collective web of use-rights.

In another nearby village, Santovenia del Monte, lots were cast in 1869 for the lower part of the communal threshing ground. Again certain limitations were placed on it. On those *suertes*, the record of the drawing tells us, that fell below the one Esteban had drawn the *vecinos* would be allowed to bring an animal to pasture if tied to a post. But the *vecinos* who had drawn *suertes* falling above the one Esteban had drawn would only be able to make use of them with sickle or scythe until Saint Peter's. These *suertes* probably lay closer to the sown lands. In both cases, however, if the *suertes* were ever needed to make more room for cattle paths and the passage of *veceras*, they were to be relinquished again to the *concejo*. Furthermore, they were not to be enclosed or broken up into arable.[9]

Meadows were in short supply until well into the middle of this century in most of León, so it is not surprising to find in both our examples a prohibition against breaking up the lots into arable land. But more than this, what emerges is a clear sense that the *suertes* are only borrowed from the common bank of goods, to which they must ultimately return. With the vast range of lands held in common but subject to private use, we find the same effort constantly being made to keep the commons common. In late eighteenth-century Llánaves, as we know from Posse's account, there were communal grain fields distributed by lot every twelve years among the *vecinos*. If during this period a *vecino* passed away his *suerte* returned, like the kitchen gardens in Santa María, to the *concejo* and was given to the *vecino* of longest standing who was without one. The twelve-yearly circulation of these lands around the community was infrequent enough to give every *vecino* the time to cultivate his plot with care and frequent enough to keep them from losing their original character as commons.[10]

The clearing of the woods

Many different types of land made up what was conceived of as the commons. But in terms of pure extension none was as important in the rural economy of Santa María certainly, and other Leonese villages lying north of it, than the communal wastes (*baldíos*) and woods (*monte*). In Santa María, where the common woods escaped the privatization of nineteenth-century disentailment, they came to play at the end of that century and into the next a crucial double role in the social economy of the village.[11] On the one hand, the woods were cleared to create arable land for a growing population; on the other, the wood itself became an important source of supplementary income, especially for families with little land to work. Surrounded as it is by formidable extensions of bush, heath, and oak woods, Santa María del Monte proved to be an excellent setting in which to study these historical processes that bound up the destiny of the people with the *monte* of the village's name.

The breaking up of common woodland to create arable land for a hungry populace is vividly recorded in an act drawn up in Santa María in early April of 1869:

> ... due to the fact that in this our village the number of *vecinos* has increased and on the contrary there are many *vecinos* short of land to sow to support their families and seeing that the village has terrain to clear ... it was agreed to mark out *suertes* ... with the condition that the *suerte* corresponding to each *vecino* be held by him for the days of his life, remaining afterwards for the *concejo*, so that the *concejo* may dispose of it and give it to the next *vecino*.[12]

Acutely conscious of the problem of demographic pressure on the land, village people took matters into their own hands by organizing the clearing of part of their forest to bring more land under cultivation. As was the case with the kitchen gardens, these *suertes* of land were to be held for the days of a *vecino*'s life and afterwards they were to return to the *concejo*. So urgent was the need for land that, the act tells us, the clearances were to begin "that very day" following the selection of *partidores* to go into the forest to mark out the plots. This course of action, the *vecinos* understood, was not in keeping with the law. The land they had agreed to clear lay in an area that they were simultaneously trying to have exempted from disentailment on the grounds that it was needed for communal grazing. This act thus represented an obligation binding on all the houses of the community to bear responsibility for the assarts, "in proof of which" (*en prueba de ello*), as it reads, all forty-two *vecinos* signed their names, for themselves, or in a few cases by asking a witness, *un testigo a ruego*, to sign in their stead.

The land clearances had probably begun several years before, for these *suertes*, we are told, were to be marked out next to another set already in existence. Since earlier records than this one from 1869 are lacking, we cannot be sure exactly when the clearances began. But one thing is certain: they picked up momentum as the century wore on and the consequences of population growth increasingly made themselves felt. An act drawn up in Santa María in 1880 provides another portrait of a

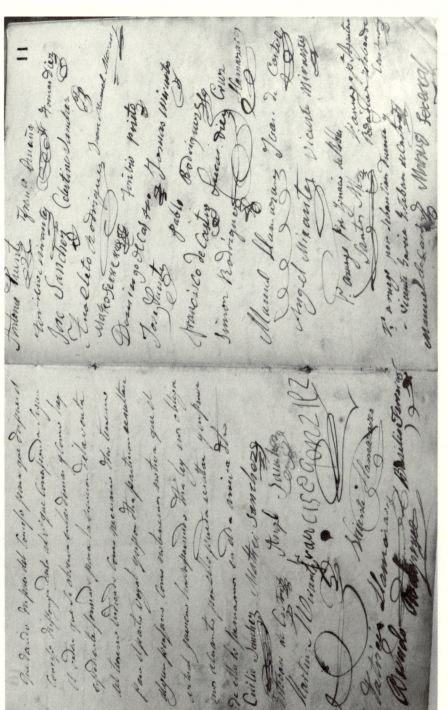

A page from Santa María's *actas de concejo*. In this act from 1869 the *vecinos* agree to clear land in their communal woods to meet the subsistence crisis brought on by the major population growth of the last century.

people so much in need of land from which to gather the rye for their daily black bread that they are willing to take to the woods with mattock and billhook, even at the risk of being apprehended and fined by the law. The first part of the act takes the form of a dialogue between the hesitant headman, aware that he ought to be representing the legality of the state, and a community united in its resolution not to be left destitute while there is land to be had:

> ... the community in one voice asking the *señor presidente* that to be spared some hardships in the present year *suertes* be marked out for land clearance, and the *señor presidente* heeding the declarations of the *vecinos* and seeing their unanimity he told them that they were not authorized to do so, but the *señor presidente*, seeing the arguments put forth by the *vecinos*, came around to their side, agreeing in unison with everyone to name people to mark them out so lots might be cast for them.

It had been a "sterile year" and the resources of both the *concejo* and the *vecinos* were few. Thus it was agreed that two-and-a-half *pesetas* would be paid to the *concejo* for the *suertes*, since their holders would make something of a profit from them by selling the wood. Once again all the *vecinos* who wanted a *suerte* had to sign the document in testimony of their collective responsibility:

> ... and we bind ourselves all the *vecinos* and each on his own with our persons and our goods, present and future, to pay all the costs and damages that may come from said *suertes*, and in order for this document to have all the necessary force ... we sign it, he who can, and he who cannot will ask a witness to ... without signing no one will be able to make use of them.[13]

When again in 1887 the community "finds itself short of land to sow" and decides to clear another patch of the common woods, this time the lots are to be cast "for always" (*para siempre*).[14] As we have seen, previously the lots had been cast for the lifetime of the *vecinos*, or in the local idiom, *por vida*, so that at their death they reverted to the *concejo* and the *vecinos*. From this moment the *vecinos* begin to press for a distribution of land that will endure beyond their lifetimes and continue to flow down the veins of their lineages. In 1890 the *vecinos* redistribute land already cleared years before, "which used to be given out by lot a *suerte* for each *vecino* every eight years, and now the whole community in one voice said to give them out for always." Taking cognizance of their deed, all the *vecinos* in the customary manner etch their names onto the document, thereby obliging themselves to bear the burden "should something happen or they be denounced because of said terrain since there is no authorization."[15]

Much the same scenario is acted out in 1891 when the *vecinos* undertake another redistribution of land brought into cultivation "many years ago," very likely in the generation of their fathers. The two *suertes* every *vecino* held in this patch "for life" were now to be given out one apiece, "for always."[16] An act from 1894, in which a similar redistribution is documented, expresses the shift from temporary to permanent possession more forcefully: whereas before every *vecino* held two *suertes* for life, "on this day the *vecinos* in one voice said that two be given out to every *vecino* and lots be drawn giving *to each his own* for always" (my italics). In all these cases where the *suertes* are given out for permanent possession, there is no longer any question of paying the *concejo* for them. Usually, as in this instance, the sum, a modest one of two-and-a-half *pesetas*, is to be paid in two installments, one at the time of the drawing and another later on.[17]

Thus the people of Santa María responded to the crisis of subsistence that an increase in their numbers had provoked by turning to their common woods for fresh land. This in itself was nothing remarkable. What is significant is that they chose to act as a community and take responsibility as a community for any misfortunes that ensued, whether from the illegal assarts or the equally illegal distributions of cleared common land for permanent possession. Moreover, they felt it was necessary to fix their actions in writing. Was it ultimately a lack of trust that inspired this curious recourse to the written word, as if no one could be sure whether his neighbor would live up to the terms of the agreement? Perhaps. After all, as we have seen, written contracts were not unknown within the more intimate domain of the family. But I suspect there were other reasons having to do with the historical juncture in which the people found themselves as the nineteenth century drew to a close.

The nineteenth century had been a period of tumult and revolt; nevertheless, major reforms were enacted which, though legal in nature, had much broader implications for the economy and society of rural Spain. The state via its modern bureaucratic apparatus was changing the land tenure system of the country and invading the farthest reaches of local life ever more effectively. The people of Santa María, when they wrote up in legal language acts that they knew very well to be illegal, were expressing their own local understanding of what was necessary at that historical moment, as well as their awareness that their local understanding was at odds with the views of the state.

For the first time in their history they were writing their own documents, since most *vecinos* were now literate, and using these documents as symbols of their solidarity. In so doing they showed how thorough was their knowledge of forms of cultural expression found in the world outside the village. A number of the documents dating from this era employ, for example, the term *in solidum*, from the Latin meaning "for the whole" and the root of our modern "solidarity." Thus in 1908, when the *vecinos* again distribute *suertes* of communal arable land among themselves, the record of the act states, in what had become the set mode, that "if by Fortune there should be any denouncements because of said *suertes*, we oblige ourselves together and conjointly and each for himself and *ensolido* [*sic*] to pay all the costs they may give rise to and thus consenting we all sign." But a note is appended to this act, which reads: "This term which says each one for himself and *ensolido* isn't valid, it has to be all together and conjointly."[18] Villagers were thus not only aware of forms of expression developed in the larger society—which they freely borrowed to portray their own social persona—but also kept up with changes in those forms, bringing them back always to a local context of interpretation and use.

In putting uncultivated wastes and woods to grain, the people of Santa María were invoking a long tradition of land clearance which in Spain, as in Europe, begins well before the nineteenth century.

The work of colonizing the vast depopulated spaces of a peninsula still only partially reconquered by the first kings of Spain in the early Middle Ages had been accomplished by granting settlers many privileges and freedoms in the use of unworked land. Though retaining eminent domain, the crown gave settlers rights of *pressura* and *scalio*, which allowed them to take possession of those unoccupied lands that were within their means to clear and cultivate.[19] Throughout Europe the period from the early eleventh to the late thirteenth century was a time of large-scale land clearance in which many expanses of heath and forest were sacrificed to plow and hoe.[20] Yet, as Marc Bloch has noted, much virgin woodland and waste was left unscathed by the great medieval clearances.[21] These sometimes formidable unworked spaces left outside the dominion of agriculture constituted a reserve of common land over which village households had rights of use.

In Castile, as is well known, the work of deforestation begun by the settlers was continued in the twelfth and thirteenth centuries by the transhumant herds of the Mesta, which damaged many a tree with their teeth and hooves. With the passing of time what forest and scrub was left in the countryside had retreated to the hills and mountains; not surprisingly the Spanish term *monte* for woodland derived from the Latin *mons* for hill or mountain.[22]

When a rapid increase in population growth during the sixteenth century created land hunger throughout the kingdom of Castile, an anxious peasantry turned to its reserves of common pasture, waste, and, in particular, *monte* for virgin land. One chronicler could already note in 1553 that "there was beginning to be a shortage of *montes*, because in Castile they were all being plowed for sowing."[23] That denuded treeless austerity that we have come to associate with the landscape of Castile had taken form.

Two interrelated aspects of land clearance in sixteenth century Castile are evident in the work of recent historians. The first is that the population increase that began toward the middle of the century led people to expand the cultivated area at the expense of the commons.[24] The second is that the monarchy was aware of the breaking of communal ground and responded to it by ordering in some cases that the land marked out for cultivation be returned to its natural state; at the same time the Royal Treasury, realizing that the demand for these plowed wastelands could provide an important source of revenue, proceeded to sell legal titles to the occupiers of these lands as well as to the moneyed classes intent on rounding out their estates.[25] Many humble peasants, in the view of Angel García Sanz, were forced to acquire titles to the lands they had staked out for cultivation at the risk of losing them, and to do so they often had little choice but to take on *censos* (quitrents) using what little property they had, their houses even, as collateral.[26] Another possible view, which informs the work of David Vassberg, is that "the peasants coveted these lands for themselves" and that it was this "current of individualism" that "contributed to the erosion of communalism and its substitution by the institution of private property."[27]

This aside on the history of land clearance in Spain, summary though it is, shows that the people of Santa María were not doing anything new when they turned to the commons for fresh arable land at the close of

the last century. What is historically significant is that as late as the
nineteenth century and well into the twentieth, as we shall see, they
could still reinvent not only the great medieval clearances but the sixteenth-century ones, which, in the view of Vassberg and others, were
supposed to have done away with most of the commons. Although the
southern plains of León had suffered from the same sort of merciless
deforestation as the two Castiles, the northern hills and mountains, with
Santa María in the interstices, remained well wooded. In these areas,
which were precisely the most economically backward, there were still
vast extensions of unplowed, if marginal, common land to turn to when
the nineteenth-century crisis of subsistence set in. But where the common
patrimony had already been eaten away in large part by the forces of
money and power—and, though one doubts it, by the covetousness of
peasants—there was nowhere to turn. In Andalusian agro-towns, for
example, always more stratified than the small villages of central León,
a rural proletarian class took form in the nineteenth century and gave
expression to centuries of desperation in rural rebellion.[28]

The sources of conflict

Although the people of Santa María were able to keep the forces of
proletarianization at bay, the village was no paradise during the years
when the population was growing and resources were dwindling by the
day—and these were long years, stretching from the second half of the
nineteenth century to past the middle of the twentieth, broken at last
by the migration of vast numbers of village people to urban centers. The
breaking of common land began in the nineteenth century in a spirit of
community and mutuality, but it was not to last. Already as the turn of
the century drew near there were conflicts, and they failed to diminish
in the 1920s and 1930s when common land was again broken, by then
with the legal authorization of the state, to meet what had become an
interminable crisis of subsistence.

When the first generation of *vecinos* started making *suertes* of common
land in the 1860s and early 1880s they were always given out *por vida*,
that is, for the lifetime use of the holder, so that after his passing they
reverted again to the community. In the late 1880s and 1890s the next
generation of *vecinos* began to press for a distribution of land *para siempre*,
for always, which, like family property, would flow down the veins of

the lineage rather than form part of a communal system of circulating goods around the village. Must we attribute such a shift to the covetousness of the people or to an emergent ethos of individualism? We are left with the problem of interpretation. In this case it seems clear that we must look for an understanding of this historical shift in the conception people had not only of communal property but of private, or family, property.

That so much *monte* had remained intact until the nineteenth century is significant.[29] It was not until people became painfully aware of the fact that the cultivated area of the village had to be expanded that they began to clear the woods, brush, and thicket and sow grain on the new lands. They borrowed these lands from the common bank of goods when they found that their own privately held properties were no longer sufficient to support themselves and their families. I prefer to speak of land "borrowed" from the commons, rather than "usurped" as some might say, implying that the land is taken wrongfully or without right. The common woods, in local terms, formed part of a web of use-rights encompassing goods, obligations, and reciprocities. Within this web, the woodlands were locally conceived of as a reserve or common bank from which the *vecinos* who formed the community could "withdraw" land when they found that their own, private properties were no longer sufficient to support themselves and their families. Though according to the laws of the nineteenth-century Spanish state they were in the wrong—as they were only too aware—when they clear land from the commons the *vecinos* have in mind a higher law, the right to subsistence.[30] Even so they are realistic and, expecting to be apprehended by the lawyer's law, they represent their solidarity to themselves in documents of their own making.

When, with the passing of time, the *vecinos* insisted on turning the land borrowed from the commons into private property, it seems they did so out of a realization that the family inheritance, so pitifully shrunken by the growth of their numbers, might eventually disappear altogether. Here we return to the old distinction in Spanish rural society between the *labrador*, who is a property-owning, self-sustaining farmer, and the *jornalero* who, owning little or no property, is condemned to work for others for a wage. For Leonese *labradores* the imperative has long been to pass on not just to one, but to all descendents the status and the freedom that comes with ownership, with being a *labrador*. Perhaps for the first time in their history, as they stood poised on the shifting sands of rising population and diminishing resources, the *vecinos* of Santa María realized that they were on the brink of falling down into the ranks of the *jornalero* class. It was their awareness of this possibility—and not covetousness or an emergent individualism—that made them want to keep forever the property they had originally thought only to borrow from the commons.

Yet as the turn of the century drew near, the *vecinos* were no longer as united as they had been in the initial phases of the crisis. The *monte* that at one time had brought the *vecinos* together *in solidum* began to tear them apart. One source of conflict, whose repercussions we will see later, was whether too much of the *monte* was being sacrificed to the plow. It involved, on the one hand, the somewhat better-off *vecinos*, who owned substantial flocks of sheep and goats and feared that the clearances were doing away with too much valuable pasture, and on the other, the poorer *vecinos*, who were often newlyweds just starting out in life and in desperate need of land to work. Its resolution, if it can be called that, was unforeseen and laced with irony.

Another source of conflict, which emerged on the eve of the Civil War, revolved around the question of whether the *suertes* of common land being distributed at the time were to be given out *por vida* or *para siempre*. What entitles a person to receive a *suerte*, in the past as in the present, is the right of *vecindad*. Once a man has married and set up house in the village he may become a *vecino*, but not before then. This rule has the force not of law but of custom, for according to various of my informants by law a man may be a *vecino* when he reaches the age of twenty-three, regardless of whether he is married. During those years preceding the war there were a number of older *mozos*, I was told, who were twenty-three and yet could not be *vecinos* because they had not married. In the late 1920s an extensive tract of common land had been cleared in the hills of La Lomba, and in the years from 1932 to 1936, when war was imminent, the *vecinos* prepared to clear another stretch of land in the nearby valley of Muñegro. The old *mozos* who would not be entitled to *suertes* in Muñegro because they were not *vecinos* began to raise havoc in *concejo*. They demanded a return to the distribution of *suertes* for the lifetime use of the holder, *por vida*. This way if they married a few years after the casting of *suertes* they would be entitled to them when the older *vecinos* died. But a distribution *para siempre* would leave them out of the circle for all time.

The demands of the *mozos* fell on deaf ears, not so much because the *vecinos* did not want to listen but because in the discordant years leading up to the war the *concejo* had come to be dominated by a clique of *cuatro ricos* (four, that is, a few rich men), of whom the most prominent was *tío* Maximino, a man of some economic and political clout. *Tío* Maximino was a native of nearby San Cipriano who had married into Santa María around 1910. His father-in-law had "a good capital" in the village and his nephew, who was mayor in the municipal seat of Vegas, was a member of the Falange. He himself was a somewhat fanatical Catholic, in the view of some, in whose company one had to take care not to use profane language, and even more so after the war when blasphemy became a criminal act punishable by fines and enforced churchgoing. Let us hear the story, though, as it was told to me by an informant:

> . . . when they marked them out [the *suertes* in Muñegro] there were two or three here who wanted a *suerte* and they stirred things up saying that they had to be *por vida*. But there were a few, a few like that, three or four elders who governed a little better or a little worse as I say, but who had power then, well, they had their fathers-in-law with them and of course if the father-in-law dies, for example, one who had in his house a father-in-law who was already seventy or in his sixties and about to die, well, casting them *por vida* when he died he would lose the *suerte*. And if it stayed as it was, *para siempre*, that *suerte* would be inherited by the children and grandchildren and whoever. And at that time there were a few, one of whom was E, another the father of L and those and another two or three, E of Castro who is still there, well, around the year 1931, 1932 or around then they went from one place to another with denunciations, because they wanted them to be cast *por vida*, but since *tío* Maximino was the one who was in control here in the *pueblo* . . . well, he was always hanging around the municipal seat, he was the one who bossed everyone about . . . whatever he said, if you uttered a curse he would fine you and you had to pay. He would make you go to church afterwards for three or four months . . .[31]

In a slightly different version of the story told to me by another informant, we learn that the *mozos* were tricked into thinking that the *suertes* would be distributed *por vida*:

> At that time there were in the *pueblo* eight or ten older *mozos* . . . who had the right to be *vecinos* from the age of twenty-three. But the *pueblo* follows a trajectory, that until one marries one cannot

be admitted as a *vecino*. . . . Well, since there were so many of those *vecinos*, already they are protesting and already there are quarrels to mark them out, there are quarrels in *concejo* and such, and they thought to tell them yes, that they would give them out *por vida*. That they would give them out *por vida* and in that way when someone passed away upon his death it would go to the others. . . . And it turned out that yes, yes, they said that but they deceived them. Those *mozos* were deceived. Afterwards they came, and they didn't get them. Someone would die, someone would leave . . . and the others they went round there, they denounced them, they took them to court in León. But since the *junta administrativa* was on the other side, and didn't pay attention to them, they got nothing out of it. They had to leave things as they were.[32]

Though the old *mozos*, who later married and found themselves deprived of a *suerte* in Muñegro, had been defeated in their battle with the *cuatro ricos*, the younger couples in need of land to work had scored a minor victory. For it was the younger *vecinos* who, wanting the land to be worked, had done the paperwork required by the state bureaucracy to gain permission to clear land. It was in the year 1931, as my informant put it to me, during the Republic, that people began to wake up a little and see that "those *montes* were only being used by those who had a lot of sheep and goats. And then young people came in, among them my father . . . and they marked out *suertes* of land." Those were the years "when the village began to raise its head," for the virgin land gave a great deal of rye.[33] The village was gathering a larger harvest than ever before and working more land than people could remember ever having been worked. There were eighty-four *vecinos* then, four times as many as there had been in the eighteenth century.

During these years of plenty a few of the younger *vecinos* bought *suertes* from unmarried women and widows and others unable to work or clear the lands. The valley of Muñegro is held in common jointly by Santa María and the village of Barrillos. Many of the lands marked out for clearing were farther away from Barrillos and people from there sold their *suertes* to people from Santa María. My informant recounted how his father bought several *suertes*, for he, like everyone else in the village, was under the impression that the *monte* belonged to the village and that the village could dispose of it as it wished. In this way he and others of his generation whose means were little got through the hard times and even prospered.

But this is not the whole story of the *suertes* of La Lomba and Muñegro. In the next generation, some thirty years after the *suertes* were given out *para siempre*, the work of Maximino and his companions was irreversibly undone when a surveyor from Hacienda (the Ministry of Finance) came to draw up a new cadaster. Upon reaching La Lomba the *vecinos* who were accompanying the surveyor began to say, "Well these, they said they were *por vida* and then afterwards between *tío* Maximino and the other four. . . ." As a result, the surveyor put the lands down as part of the commons. At first no one fretted about this classification. Since *montes* had always been free of tax in the past, those who held *suertes* were glad to be able to go on as they always had. But things had changed. The *montes* too had begun to be taxed and as communal property it was the village as a body that had to be the taxpayer. When the tax receipts began to arrive a few years later in the name of the village, it was no longer possible for some people to continue to hold on to the *suertes* as if they were private property. They had to let go of them—at first with much raising of voices in *concejo*, for some had bought *suertes* and others had received them as part of their inheritance, and they blamed the men who had gone with the surveyor for not having told him that those lands were private. Yet, in the end, "no one wanted to kick up a row. Some lost a little more, some lost a little less, and well, enough."[34]

The *suertes* were redrawn, and from the mid-1960s on they were distributed for ten-yearly periods, as they continue to be. Though these lands found their way back to the commons, numerous others remain in the hands of village families. In what was to be a prelude to the migration out, the *suertes* which in the early years of being cultivated gave so much rye stopped producing in the 1950s and 1960s, and today mostly lie abandoned. Yet many *vecinos* would have succumbed to famine or sunk to the ranks of the landless poor long before if it had not been possible to enlarge the impoverished family inheritance by borrowing from the common inheritance of the village. The abandoned lands, many of which are reverting to brush and woods, bear silent testimony to a society of survivors.[35]

Chapter 13

✝

The Common Woods

THE LAST of the clearances was carried out in 1955 and 1956 in a final effort to make the land produce enough bread for all—and not only in Santa María but throughout central León.[1] Though much land was cleared and the arable area considerably expanded in what was almost a century-long crisis of subsistence, the woods of Santa María, as of other wooded villages to the north of it, were never fully conquered by the plow. It was in the woods, after all, that the calves and untamed cows, the sheep and goats, the mules and donkeys, found grazing in the form of leaves, undergrowth, and shoots. And the number of animals that grazed in the woods had increased together with the rise in human population, making it even more essential that the ecology of forest grazing not be thrown awry by too many clearances. The woods, of course, were essential to the continuance of human life, for their products lit the hearth and warmed the bake-ovens in which the family's bread was made. They were also, and above all in this period, the source of a livelihood for numerous village families.

The woodlanders

Shares of communal oak, heather branches, and heather trunks were given out by lot, *echando suertes*, as people say, in the same way as with *suertes* of arable land. *Suertes* of woodland are still distributed in this manner in the present. Wood continues to be needed for the hearth since every house has not only a gas stove but a woodstove, which keeps the kitchen warm in winter and cooks the beans slowly in summer when the women are out in the fields all day with their husbands. Yet several people who have trees on plots of their own no longer go to the *monte* for firewood or even take a *suerte*, and no one conceives of forging a livelihood anymore from the common forest. "Nowadays," remarked a village man, "no one goes to the *monte* unless it burns" (*hoy ya no se va al monte, no siendo que se queme*). Yet just thirty and forty years before the village had been full of woodspeople, who like their forefathers wove fagots of heather, pulled out the trunks of heather bushes, chopped wood, and made charcoal for fuel to sell in León and in lowland villages with scarce wood or scrub.

Villagers became woodspeople for the same reason that they cleared patches of the commons—the population had grown, was growing, and there was no longer enough land for everyone. Unlike the *suertes* of arable land, there was never any question that the *suertes* of wood were for the temporary use of the holder, a fact that points to a fundamental distinction between communal plowlands and woodlands: that land which with one's labor is made to yield fruit falls more easily into the private domain than land which, still in the state of nature, produces without intervention from human hand. What villagers received when they drew lots for their shares of common woodland was the use of the wood on those shares for a specified period of time, usually six months to a year. It is clear that villagers were not indiscriminately turning into private property all of their commons; what they sought was to maintain the balance between property belonging to the village as a whole and property belonging to the individual households, a balance that had been thrown off by the demographic expansion. Thus the *vecinos* never thought to make the *suertes* of wood *para siempre*. On the other hand, the *suertes* of arable land fell clearly within the realm of subsistence, while those of the common wood—though its products were used in hearth and home and to enclose the fields during the "closed time"— had a commodity aspect, and this posed numerous problems for the community.

Forasteros, that is, strangers, or simply persons from other villages were rarely allowed in the common wood of Santa María since they were wont to lay waste a commons not theirs. They had to go to the village and buy heather and firewood that already had been cut, or purchase it in such market centers as Puente Villarente and Mansilla de las Mulas, where the wood was brought to be sold by villagers. However, in an exceptional case allowances were made, as we learn from this act drawn up in March of 1880:

... seeing the miserable year in which we find ourselves and so that all the poor might have somewhere to turn, if the village agrees ... they can sell [wood] to strangers under the condition that to cut it as well as to carry it off the *vecino* must be there with them ... setting aside Tuesdays and Fridays of each week for the carts of the strangers to enter, not permitting the carts to enter the cutting site before sunrise or after sunset.

Thus the *vecino* who sold the wood from his *suerte* had to take responsibility for any damages done to heather bushes and oaks if he granted a *forastero* permission to go into the *monte* on his own. By setting aside two days of the week for the sales, the community, as well as the village guard of the fields and woods, was able to keep an eye on the traffic flowing in and out of the forest. And naturally at night no carts could be allowed in the woods; stiff fines were always reserved for those who fetched wood during the hours when their neighbors were in bed, for a person who hides his actions under the cover of night cannot be up to any good.

In this act, as in virtually all others drawn up before 1900 concerning the making of *suertes* of communal woodland, we find that same self-awareness we have seen before in the acts referring to the assarts, of the kind of state forming in those years and of the legality to which it now expected local communities to conform. The year 1880, we know, saw the *vecinos* clearing land without legal authorization, for it had been a "sterile" year. But the *vecinos* did, indeed, obtain legal license to cut wood from the commons that year. Even so they were aware that they would again be acting illegally, "seeing that we will not be able to cut or comply with the regulations set by the law." Therefore, as before, all the *vecinos* must sign the written agreement to symbolize their solidarity: "We the *vecinos* all oblige ourselves by common consent that if anything should happen to pay what it may cost all conjointly, for this felling of wood has been given out equally to all the *vecinos*, two *suertes* to a *vecino*."

By the last quarter of the nineteenth century it had become the rule to levy a charge on the use of communal resources, from meadows to pastures to woods. People did not take to the idea very easily, for in past times, as eighteenth-century ordinances make clear, rights of use over the commons had always been exercised freely. The acts consistently call attention to the tardiness of the *vecinos* in paying for their rights to *suertes*. In the act from 1880 we learn, for example, "that since in past fellings there has been much delay in paying the charge placed on them, at the very least everyone should be reminded that no *vecino* may make use of the lots without paying the four *reales* with which they have been burdened."² Forty years later the idea of paying for use-rights had not taken hold; an act drawn up in 1919 to distribute *suertes* of wood admonished that the charge of one *peseta* be paid "before drawing a number and we also point out that no one may draw a number without paying overdue debts and by common consent we sign. . . ."³

It is no accident that these old rights of use begin to be paid for, though with much nagging of the *vecinos* to be sure, in the nineteenth century, or that today the practice has become well established. The villages were now, more than at any other time in the past, being burdened with taxes, licenses, and permits for use of their commons, for the state had become the overseer of the web of use-rights. Finding itself in need of funds, the *concejo* had little choice but to set a price on the use of *suertes* and other communal properties.

The acts referring to the making of *suertes* of wood are so numerous that it would be tedious to cite even a small portion of them, and in general they all follow very much the same form. It was the custom to *levantar acta*, as people say, to draw up an act, whenever a communal felling was to take place, a custom that in recent years has been lost. From the end of the nineteenth to the middle of the present century these fellings were regularly carried out twice a year, once in late winter, usually in February, and again in late fall, usually in November, and there are acts preserved for this entire period. In reading through them one cannot help but note a shift in rhetoric from the earlier acts to those drawn up in the 1930s, a shift that seems to reflect a change in attitude about the relationship of the community to its commons.

As was the case with the land clearances, there were several occasions, particularly before the turn of the century, when the *vecinos* joined together to fell wood without obtaining permission from the state. Thus when the *vecinos* decide in 1879 to distribute among themselves wood left over from earlier cuttings "in order to close the boundaries and conserve the crops and also for households to use," they again individually etch their names onto the document in proof of their solidarity: "In case the Law does not uphold us for not doing this at an opportune time or for not having the authorization of a License, we the *vecinos* oblige ourselves to respond with our persons and goods (present and future) to all the damages which may come of this cutting."⁴ Even when the *vecinos* do obtain a license to cut wood in their commons they still feel the necessity of expressing their solidarity should something somehow go wrong. Thus when the *vecinos* proceed in 1890 to distribute *suertes* of wood among themselves, having obtained the required license, they do not fail to note in the document that "if anything should happen or if it be necessary to pay any denouncement for not cutting in accordance with the Law, we oblige ourselves together and conjointly and each on his own *en solidum* to pay whatever costs this may give rise to."[5] By the 1930s, though, this expression of solidarity drops out of the acts and one finds instead, as in this act drawn up in the first year of the Civil War, statements such as "if any of us be the cause of a suit, it will be up to him to pay all the costs it gives rise to in court."[6] This is a far cry from the "all together and conjointly" rhetoric of the earlier acts. It seems to coincide with the same loss of unity we already saw emerging in the 1930s with the land clearances.

But if the *vecinos* were acting less as a community and more as separate individuals by the 1930s (not surprisingly given the divisive political atmosphere of those years), there is no question that it was the communal system of use-rights to wood that allowed many of them to raise up their houses. There is hardly a person over forty in the village who does not remember how his or her early years of marriage were spent forging a livelihood from the common forest. In the words of Láutico Robles:

> We married, we spent three years, one in the house of his father and the other in the house of her father, each in the house of his and her parents ... and then afterwards, I came here, well then afterwards to raise the children I had to bring them up faithfully with that, going to the *monte*, cutting heather, cutting wood, making charcoal, then afterwards with it cut and ready take it to the *pueblos* beyond, to Villamoros, to the Puente Villarente. .... And that way, well, we spent, what can I tell you, perhaps ten years at the least, the least, the least, well, eighteen, twenty years.[7]

Since most of the terrain of Santa María is poor and fit at best to grow rye, while the few good wheatlands were in those years all too scarce, people took the wood to the lowlands to sell and bring back wheat and wine:

> ... You went with a cart of wood and earned five *duros* and you brought back five *heminas* of bread, of wheat, here wheat was not

gathered. You went at another time and earned five *duros* and you brought back a wineskin, a *colambre* as we call it, of wine, a *colambre* of five *arrobas* and you went sacrificing yourself.

These are just two voices from among many, for though a handful of villagers were spared even a part-time existence as woodspeople, the majority had been forced to deal in the wood that fell to them as part of their communal inheritance. Even if one had to pay a *peseta* or two for the use of the *suerte*, this was a pittance compared to the earnings one could garner from selling its heather and wood. "For if," Leonardo Mirantes added, "a *suerte* fell to me that had a thousand fagots of heather and I cut them and earned 500 *reales*, [those were] 500 *reales* that were mine by dint of my labor."[8] In this sense the *suerte* was virtually a gift won in the lottery of life.

The conservation of the woods

With so many clearances and so much felling of wood, the conservation of the *monte* understandably became a matter of grave concern to the village. It was a question not simply of conservation, though, but of seeing to it that the wealth of the forest, which now had to be distributed among more *vecinos* than ever before, would stretch around the whole community. Thus there emerged a complex set of rules and regulations governing the use of communal woodlands. As we have already noted, *forasteros* or strangers were rarely allowed in the common wood; and when they did enter, they were frequently blamed for making havoc there. An accord concerning the woods drawn up in 1879 begins with a remark about "the disorder there was in the *monte* because a few *vecinos* had let in the carts of *forasteros*, that this was a state of abandon."[9] Yet clearly the *forasteros* were not entirely to blame for the disorder in the *monte*. The *vecinos* themselves were as often at fault.

A ruling from 1870, for example, limits every *vecino* to a cart either of heather trunks or heather branches every fifteen days, and of the latter to no more than seventy fagots a trip. "These are to be regular fagots according to custom and if it is known that someone is being malicious, whether in bringing more than seventy fagots or in making them big, he shall pay twenty *reales* and half will go to the one who catches him." Even where there were two *vecinos* living in a single house, say, a father and a son, only two carts a month were to be allowed them. The ruling covered the period from the first of January to the end of October, and only in cases of dire need were carts to be allowed into the woods in November or December. Anyone who wished to bring a *forastero* to his *suerte* was to let the headman and the guard know beforehand and have the *forastero* bring his cart through the *pueblo*.[10] By 1885, however, *forasteros* were not being allowed in the common wood under any circumstances, a rule that held into this century. In the words of the 1885 accord, "the *vecino* who wants to give a cart to an outsider is to take it with his pair to the *pueblo* where that person lives." And sixty *vecinos* affixed their signatures to the document, bearing testimony to its contents.[11] In short, the *vecinos* could not do whatever they pleased with their *suertes*; there were rules, of their own devising, about how much one could bring back from the forest at a time and how often, and in what manner one was to traffic in the wood that fell to one.

The common woods and pastures were of such importance that a guard was hired by the village every year from among the *vecinos* to watch over them, as was true in virtually all the villages of the area. In a contract between the guard and the village drawn up, again, in 1870, we see the extent to which the *vecinos* sought to regulate the *monte* and how difficult this task often was. The guard was expected to go into the woods every day. Like the village herders, he took on a certain amount of responsibility in guarding over the commons. The community set a fine of 30 *reales* for every illicit cart of heather trunks and heathers the guard caught; this was if the guilty person "resisted or made demands," but if he acceded uncomplainingly then he paid only 20 *reales*. The fine for a cart caught at night was 40 *reales*, while for a cart of wood the fine was 60 *reales* during the day and 70 *reales* after the sun set. But if the guard failed to go to the *monte* on a particular day and it turned out "that during that day carts left the *monte*, for each one that we find out about he is to pay the penalty that the person who did the damage owes, and besides for each day that he does not go watch over the *monte* he is to pay 4 *reales*, and this is to be seen every week." The guard was also held responsible for any trees missing from the cutting site, as well as any felled wood, and to this end the *monte* was to be checked three times a year by a person named by the guard and another named by the *concejo*.[12] And in places where no one apparently wished to be a full-time guard, for obvious reasons, the job was circulated—as in Ambasaguas in 1887, when the *vecinos* decide "to name a warden *a la corrida* of the *pueblo* to guard the *monte*, on account of its having been abandoned by a number of *vecinos*."[13]

The king and the village

This tradition of drawing up a local code of rules and regulations to conserve the woodlands of the community originates long before the nineteenth century when, about to fall away, it reaches its apogee. It goes back to an old interaction of the state and local communities, an interaction that by the sixteenth century is fully formed in all its features. One can see certain aspects of this interaction in an interesting set of documents preserved in the *concejo* archives of Santa María and of neighboring Villamayor.

In 1518, the deforestation of Castile plainly in evidence, Charles V in the company of his mother Juana issued a decree, to be sent to the cities, towns, and villages of their kingdom, ordering that the *montes* be reforested with new plantings, and that ordinances be drawn up locally to keep the common woods from being laid waste.[14] After the royal decree was confirmed by the Cortes of Valladolid in 1537, it made its way to the city of León where, in 1547, its contents were read aloud by two of the city's heralds in the plaza of Santa María del Camino, on a market day, "in the presence of many *vecinos* of said city and other parts." It reached the villages somewhat later, but reach them it did, for ordinances were made up by the *vecinos* of Santa María in 1588 and by the *vecinos* of Villamayor in 1599 responding to the king's letter calling for the woodlands of the kingdom to be better guarded and cared for. A copy of this letter, "written on paper and sealed with the royal seal of red wax," took its place beside the local ordinances of both villages, heading them, the decrees of king and village thereby joined in a single document.

The royal decree had expressed concern about

the great disorder there was in the uprooting, cutting, and felling of the *montes* . . . and the great need there was and there is in these our kingdoms of *montes* and pinewoods and other trees, both for the pasture and support of cattle and for wood for these our kingdoms and dominions, for this is one of the things which is necessary for the sustenance and maintenance of the people ... and if not remedied you might find yourselves with the passing of time greatly in need. ...

To remedy the situation the decree ordained that oaks and pines be planted where they would least interfere with farmlands, and willows and poplars be planted along the banks of rivers. Old and new trees were to be properly looked after, a guard being hired for the task, to prevent people from pulling, cutting, or uprooting the *montes*. The guard's wage would be paid by the town *propios* where there were any, and otherwise it was to be collected by making an assessment of the means of each *vecino*, in other words, by *repartimiento*. Every city, town, and village of the kingdom had, finally, to draw up ordinances of its own, against which no appeal would be heard, so that what was locally enacted would be, and here the king speaks directly to his subjects, "complied with and carried out and observed in the manner in which you ordain and decree."[15]

The ordinances that the *vecinos* of Santa María and Villamayor draw up are similar and yet not exactly the same. In both cases the *vecinos* of each place, the greater part of whom journeyed to León to draw up their ordinances before a scribe, note that they have been unable to guard their *montes* properly; people from neighboring villages cut and uproot the trees and bushes in their woods during the day as well as during the night, and the fines that they customarily levy are too low to make them, or even the *vecinos* themselves, cease laying waste the *monte*. Hence for both villages the ordinances are primarily a catalogue of fines (set high enough, it seems, to deter wasteful woodlanders) for various crimes against their common woods.

Villamayor's ordinances provide a detailed account of the varieties of trees and bushes that existed in the village woods, which included oaks, hawthorns, furzes, rockroses, willows, brooms, osiers, heather, and thyme. The composition of Santa María's woods could not have been very different, for all these trees and bushes are found in its landscape today. In any case, the ordinances of Villamayor, like those of Santa María, set fines for the cutting, clearing, and uprooting of trees and bushes without the permission of the *concejo*, fines that are almost always doubled if these acts are committed at night. There are specific fines for carrying out varying amounts of wood, whether by cart, by horse or mule, or strapped to the shoulder. Although the ordinances of both villages set steep fines for making charcoal in their woods, which range in degree from one *ducado* to twelve *ducados* depending on how much has been made and whether by day or by night, those of Villamayor are especially severe with people who cause fires in the *monte*; against such people were to be levied "all of the highest penalties established by the laws of these kingdoms."[16] And in both villages whatever trees or bushes had been cut or dug out of the woods were to be left there by the guilty parties for the *concejo* to use as it chose, and where witnesses to these crimes were lacking, the guard was to be believed simply by his oath. Both villages, finally, ask that the law and the courts take their ordinances seriously, for if not nothing will come of their efforts. The ordinances of Santa María place special emphasis on this:

> ... if a person leaves the district of said place taking anything from it with him, whether by cart, by beast or in any other fashion stated above, someone is to go to his house and by the Path to ask him for the fine which he has incurred or for a *prenda* [pledge], and if he does not give it of his own will, that in such a case it be asked of him before any Justice or *Alcalde* of the land and the Magistrate of the City of León, by virtue of it, of whom we shall ask and implore that Justice be done us, because otherwise we will not be able to guard and conserve our *Montes* and Trees as his Majesty ordains. ...[17]

Aside from what they tell us about the precarious condition of wood-lands in the sixteenth century, what is interesting about these documents is the glimpse they give of an older sort of relationship between state and village. In contrast to the kind of state that was forming in the nineteenth century, its predecessor had recognized the importance of the local context of custom and use; thus even when promulgating decrees of a general nature, the kings never failed to call upon the cities, towns, and villages of their kingdom to make up their own particularistic ordinances suited to the exigencies of the locale. This tradition of enacting local ordinances certainly far outlasted its time in numerous Leonese villages where, taking on a life of its own, it continued well into our century.

Chapter 14

The State and the Commons

SO FAR we have been focusing on the purely local view of the clearings and cuttings in the common woods in nineteenth-century León, and on the local awareness of the laws of the state regarding the commons. Yet, at the same time, the state was carrying out reforms that were invading all aspects of local life ever more effectively. One such reform was disentailment, a phenomenon that in Spain is still ideologically tinted and subjectively understood. There is a continuing scholarly debate on the subject, which boils down to the question of whether disentailment was responsible for major transformations in landholding patterns and rural social structure, and for the subsequent class polarization and peasant unrest that emerged in some regions.[1] My aim, however, in the next few pages will be to delve as deeply as the sources permit into the question of local reactions to disentailment in Santa María and nearby villages. Given the presence of strong and richly elaborated traditions of community and commons, our Leonese example forms a striking contrast to those that have been documented for other regions.

Disentailment and the villages

Two major reforms had been enacted in the nineteenth century by a central state rationalizing, in the midst of great social and political dis-order, its bureaucratic apparatus. The first, the municipal reforms of the 1830s that established the present-day provincial and municipal bound-aries, we have already discussed. The second, whose local ramifications we will now consider, were the acts of *desamortización*, or disentailment, promulgated with respect mainly to ecclesiastical properties and tithes by Juan Alvarez Mendizábal in 1836-1837 and generalized to include municipal and other properties by Pascual Madoz in 1855.

The purpose of these acts of disentailment was to free for the market property held in mortmain by the church, the nobility, and the villages, where it was presumably lying stagnant, and to remove the feudal remnants of quitrents (*censos*) and perpetual leaseholds (*foros*) which still fettered persons, properties, and communities. The liberal reformers of the era hoped thereby to reduce the public debt, weaken the influence of the church, and create a rural society of small landowners. As the century wore on and the less happy consequences of the disentailment reforms surfaced, they came under increasing attack. In particular there was much dissent about the sale of communal village properties, which were viewed as having been the mainstay of the rural economy in many regions, the strongest case for this argument being made by Costa and his collaborators at the close of the last century.

The Ley Madoz, as it is known in Spain, called for the alienation of all village properties with the exception of those that fell under the category of *bienes de aprovechamiento comunal*, properties subject to communal rights of use. The law thus distinguished between two different types of corporately held property: *propios*, which were lands that the communities gave out in rent and that therefore produced income; and true *bienes comunales*, which were used freely and communally by the *vecinos* as members of the community. *Propios*, the law inexorably declared, should be alienated, but *bienes comunales* were to be exempted from disentailment. It was, of course, in the state's interest to disentail as much property as possible, since the revenue from the sales of disentailed land went to meet the national debt; this fact was one of the reasons for insisting on the distinction between *propios* and *bienes comunales*. Another was the search for an absolute distinction between private and communal property, "to replace the tissue of superimposed rights over property," to quote Marc Bloch again, that characterized the old regime. As the Spanish historian of law Alejandro Nieto astutely observes, because the law of Madoz made this distinction, it became necessary to define clearly in subsequent legislation (and I would add in practice) what was meant by *bienes comunales*, since so much hinged on the concept.[2]

For a village to have its communal properties exempted from disentailment, the municipal seat had to write a letter on its behalf to the Ministry of Finance, stating that those properties were being used communally and had been since 1835. The *vecinos* of Santa María requested such an exemption in 1895 for all of their common pastures, wastes, and woods.³ We can safely assume that it was granted since these properties never went on the market, though pieces of some did end up in the hands of individual *vecinos* through purely local processes, as we have already seen. Other villages, however, were not so lucky.

With the disentailment reforms the state not only created new definitions of property, it sought to enforce them, sending inspectors out to the villages to see that the reforms were properly put into practice. The properties that were put up for sale by virtue of the laws of disentailment were regularly listed in the official organ of the state bureaucracy, the *Boletín oficial del Estado*, with the details of their location, quality, size, type, and the minimum bid that would start the auction. Before being entered in the *Boletín*, though, the properties in question were measured; and if the servant of the state who had carried out the survey discovered that lands purported to be truly communal had been cleared, split up into *suertes*, or, worst of all evils, become private property, the report could be very harsh. These unpublished records are naturally much more interesting than the neutral descriptions that eventually appear in the *Boletín*, for they tell us a good deal about the kind of state that had taken form, and its relationship to local communities.

Thus, to choose one among many examples, there is this report on part of the *monte* in nearby Villafeliz dating from 1875:

> ... having proceeded with the measurement, demarcation of boundaries, and assessment of the lands which, set in the *monte* of Villafeliz, have been distributed in *suertes* and cleared arbitrarily by the inhabitants under the cloak of the exemption which they have requested but not obtained, lands which come from their *propios* and do not produce revenue for the State, we have verified it with all possible exactitude.⁴

Or, in reference to a terrain composed of forty-nine plots in another nearby village, we have this:

> ... the lands which in the district of Villasinta corresponded to its *propios* and after having been granted an exemption for some of them under the heading of pasture they have been sold, cleared, and distributed among the *vecinos* without satisfying the 20 percent [tax on sale of *propios*] and without producing any revenue at all for the State.⁵

About another plot from the *propios* of Villasinta the inspector reports that "it was sold by the *concejo* defrauding the interests of the State and it does not produce revenue."[6] Finally, concerning a meadowland in Villaseca, we are told that it "corresponded to the commons of the *vecinos* and it has been cleared and distribued arbitrarily among them without producing any revenue for the State."[7] More examples could be supplied, but these will, perhaps, suffice to show with what stern coldness state officials looked upon the clearings and distributions of common lands that villagers throughout central León were carrying out to survive the subsistence crisis.

The *vecinos* of Santa María had been fortunate indeed in not being caught for, as we have seen, they were guilty of the same "crimes" other nearby villages paid the price for. Perhaps because the wooded area of the village is so very large, the clearings were harder to detect in Santa María. In addition, a royal decree enacted in 1862 allowed for the exemption of *montes* of pine, oak, and beech consisting of at least 100 hectares, whose status was to be noted in what became known as the *Catálogo de Montes*.[8] Santa María's *monte* consists of over a thousand hectares, much of it oak woods, so it was certainly eligible for such an exemption, though it appears, if the memory of my informants serves them well, that it was not enshrined in the *Catálogo* until much later.

At any rate, what we must not fail to note is that the *vecinos* of Santa María, no less than their neighbors from other villages, clearly did not make the same distinction between true and only apparent communal property that the state had contrived to suit its quest for revenues to meet the national debt. Nieto makes this point especially well:

> ... lack of understanding of the laws must in fact have been quite grievous and this distinction between commons and *propios* was hardly ever grasped by the villages. ... For the villages this amounted to insignificant subtleties: the municipal patrimony, in all its variety, was one, as the classics had understood and as it had been put into practice traditionally: what today was used communally and freely, tomorrow was rented to outsiders or to the *vecinos* themselves.[9]

Indeed, in all the villages of the area and elsewhere in Spain a traditional method of raising funds for public works and debts has been to rent or even sell lands from the commons. In Santa María, for example, there is an area known as the *suertes* of La Campana. It is composed of what originally had been fifty-nine plots of land, which had been cleared in 1899 and distributed among the *vecinos* at 4 *pesetas* apiece to pay a debt of 236 *pesetas* for casting the church bells of the village, so essential for summoning the *vecinos* not just to mass but to *concejo, hacenderas,* and *veceras*.[10] Though they are still referred to as *suertes*, these lands are now private. More recently, in the 1950s, a few fragments of common meadow were sold in *concejo* to raise funds to build a new school and house for the teacher. Villagers see no contradiction between this use of communal property and, say, the grazing of the common herds on village meadows; both form part of a single system that, "in all its variety," is the commons.

The meshing of what, to the law, were different types of commons is especially clear in an act from the neighboring village of Santovenia del Monte. It concerns the sale, in 1907, of 3½ *heminas* of communal woodland to Santiago de la Puente, a *vecino* of the village. This land is sold, the act tells us, because the village needed to come up with 75 *pesetas* for a tax stamp (*póliza*) that had to be affixed to its petition to exempt the *monte* from sale. State officials would not have looked kindly upon such actions, and yet for the *vecinos* it was clearly a logical way to proceed. But like their neighbors in Santa María, the *vecinos* of Santovenia were well aware that their local understanding of the commons was at odds with the definitions at law; and so the village agreed to return the 75 *pesetas* to Santiago de la Puente if the sale of the land was reported to the authorities. Interestingly, the purchase of this piece of communal woodland did not free it from the web of use-rights:

> Santiago de la Puente does not have nor will have the right in said piece of terrain to break or clear, he can only cut the wood to his taste and disposition as his own for always, both he and his heirs, but he will not be able to impede the village's grazing, or rather that of its animals, in complete freedom always. . . .[11]

The legacy of disentailment

In Santa María virtually all the properties that had belonged to the parish church and ecclesiastical landlords in León were bought by *vecinos* of the village.[12] A *mayorazgo* (entailed estate) consisting of various lands scattered through Santa María, Barrillos, Barrio, Gallegos, Sopeña, and

Villanueva, which had been founded in the eighteenth century by Don Tomas Robles, then the biggest landowner of Barrillos, was bought by the notary public of that village when it came up for sale in the next century. His widow later sold the fifty lands belonging to the *mayorazgo* in Santa María to three *vecinos*, who split the costs ("getting the money from wherever they could") and the properties equally.[13] (Indeed, disentailment did not bring absentee landlords into the village; rather, it speeded their disappearance.) But it was not just individual *vecinos* who bought lands put on the market by disentailment. The village as a whole joined together to buy properties that it had traditionally administered or held in perpetual leasehold, displaying again the kind of solidarity that marked the early land clearances.

An interesting pair of documents in the *concejo* archive of Santa María tell of how the *vecinos* agreed, in 1874, to buy the Charity of March (*Caridad de Marzo*) and of how, after purchasing it in 1875, the land was split up among them into equal lots. What was the Charity of March? It consisted of seven properties—three rye lands, three wheatlands, and an irrigated meadow—which the *concejo* had traditionally administered, the rent from these lands going, in the eighteenth century, toward the payment of a yearly mass on Our Lady of March and the rest toward bread and wine to give to the poor at the church door. There were several other such *caridades*, among them the Charity of April (*Caridad de Abril*), also known as the Charity of Palm Sunday (*Caridad de Ramos*) since it paid for a mass and charity toward the poor on Palm Sunday, and the Charity of August (*Caridad de Agosto*), founded on three different endowments, all of which paid for masses on Our Lady of August and gave to the poor the income that was left over.[14] The *caridades* were essentially groups of lands bequeathed at one time, it appears, to the *concejo* rather than to the church, another testimony to the strength of that institution in León; they existed also, among other places, in Santovenia del Monte, Villamayor, and Vegas.[15] Until 1871 the *caridades* in Santa María were rented out to *vecinos* for four years, two harvests (because of the alternation of cropping and fallow), all of which were still paid for in wheat and rye.[16]

In 1874, "the *concejo* having gathered in the customary house to treat matters pertaining to the common good," the *vecinos* decide that, the Charity of March "having been put up for sale," two or three of their number be named to go to León and bid for it, "with the understanding that these lands will be for all the *vecinos* who want them." For the state, of course, the Charity of March fell under the rubric of *propios*, since it was corporately held land that was used by individuals rather than by a social group and it produced rent. (Yet it was rent that, as we have seen, was recycled back into the society, through the charities, and the cosmos, through the masses.) As such it formed part of the web of use-rights and the *vecinos* were determined that it remain within that web. Thus they agreed in the same obligation to join together to buy any other *caridades* that came up for sale, such as that of Saint Andrew (*Caridad de San Andrés*), which they purchased in 1882, and that of Saint Pelagius (*Caridad de San Pelayo*), which appears to have been passed on to the *concejo* when the old confraternity of that saint became defunct.

In deciding to repurchase this *caridad* from the state, the *vecinos* also committed themselves in a more far-reaching way: ". . . we also oblige ourselves that if a *forastero* should get or buy said lands no *vecino* may rent them nor buy them nor exchange them under the condition that whoever does this will be obliged to pay the *concejo* the amount of 200 *reales* and also the *vecinos* will look at him most sternly." In other words, the Charity of March was to be for all or none of the *vecinos*. The agreement states that, if they get the Charity, any new irrigation ditches or borders that are needed will be made by the *vecinos* who draw the lots requiring them. And should any of the payments be delayed because of "some lazy person" (*algún perezoso*), it will be the responsibility of that person to pay whatever costs or damages come of his tardiness. Finally, it is agreed that if the *vecinos* acquire the lands belonging to the Charity of Saint Pelagius they will continue to pay for the mass on the saint's day and bring him one or two pounds of wax.[17]

The act drawn up four months later tells us that the *vecinos* have bought the lands of the old Charity of March and that they have named a commission of four *vecinos* to split them up into equal shares together with other lands that the *concejo* has available to it. The commission assesses the shares at 70 *reales* each, and decides on the new ditches and borders that need to be made, making a detailed list. It is not clear exactly which lands besides those of the Charity have entered into the distribution, but the *concejo* apparently also acquired the two lands of Saint Pelagius—one situated close to the settlement in La Viña and still known by the saint's name, and another in the vast wooded area of San Pelayo. The latter had been the site of a monastery in early medieval times, the memory of which was preserved in the confraternity of Saint Pelagius, which planted its shrine there, and whose legacy, in turn, was carried on in the Charity of that saint. I say that the *concejo* must have acquired these lands, for the *vecinos* agree to pay the six *reales* for the yearly mass of the saint, which falls between Saint John's and Saint Peter's. And since the mass has its origin in a monastery cum confraternity cum Charity, all religious brotherhoods of sorts, it was to be followed, not surprisingly, by the ritual sharing in *concejo* of a *cántara* of wine, "for all those that attend the mass to enjoy together, and he who does not attend will not enjoy this refreshment."[18]

Certainly the most important purchase the village made in the era of disentailment was that of the old perpetual leasehold or *foro* over the vast extension of common woods known as San Pelayo, that most historical of points in its landscape. Previously renting out this extensive terrain, the village had acquired the *foro* in 1701 from the marquises of the estate of Toral and house of Guzmán after a long battle over the commons with the local cattle-owner Don Marcelo de la Puente and his widow Doña Francisca; it was the encroachments of these prosperous cattle-owners that impelled the *vecinos* to seek, as I have suggested, the perpetual rights of use that a *foro* guaranteed. Now in 1896 their descendents found themselves, at last, in a position to become the full owners, no longer just the users, of the woods of San Pelayo.

The village preserves among its old papers a "deed of the alienation of a *foro*" executed by the countess of Peñaranda de Bracamonte (a descendent of the house of Guzmán) in favor of eighteen *vecinos* of Santa María, the grandfathers of most of the present *vecinos*. In what is a curious case of historical serendipity, the *vecinos* chose as their lawyer the Leonese-born Gumersindo de Azcárate, who wrote on "the vestiges of primitive communism" at the turn of the century, and their case was heard and inscribed by none other than Joaquín Costa, notary of the Colegio de Madrid and champion of "agrarian collectivism." Our celebrities aside, the village, represented by eighteen of its *vecinos* and, in turn, by Azcárate, bought for 4,500 *pesetas* the old *foro* of thirty-two *fanegas* of rye, which had essentially amounted to a feudal due, thereby acquiring proprietary rights over the age-old common *monte* of San Pelayo.[19]

In buying the Charity of March and the old *foro* over the woods of San Pelayo, the village had managed to act in unison, with the very kind of community that had inspired Posse to write so idyllically about the common lands. Particularly, the acquisition of full legal title to the woods of San Pelayo was a significant victory for the *vecinos*; for the first time in the village's history this major portion of their commons was truly theirs. But the victory was to be short-lived.

During the final years of the century, the divisions in the village concerning the use of the *monte* had grown ever sharper. On the one hand, there were the better-off *vecinos* who looked to the woods for the grazing they could offer their substantial flocks of sheep and goats; on the other hand, there were the poorer *vecinos*, many of them newlyweds in need of land to work and wood to sell, for whom the woods offered their one and only livelihood. The spirit of the conflict is captured by Sixto Mirantes, one of my most historically knowledgeable informants:

> And of course back then there were so many people—everybody who got married had lots of children, eight, nine, seven, six, five. . . . Back then one didn't live like now, nowadays when no one goes to the *monte* unless it burns. . . . And, of course, they'd cast a *suerte*, . . . and so someone who had eight or ten children and all would say, "Hey, won't you sell me your *suerte*?" "Sure, look, go on, go cut it." And generally speaking it was the ones who had the most [children] who would go gathering, and making charcoal, and cutting heather. But when these other people saw this, [the ones who had] about 300 or 400 goats, and maybe some 3,000 sheep— "Hell! They're doing away," I remember hearing that man named P. over there say, "they're doing away with the *monte*! It can't be! And then what about the cattle?"[20]

In those years the *vecinos* of the *junta administrativa* were on the side of the herders. For fear that the woodspeople would use up the *monte*, the *junta* decided, in the interpretation provided by the same informant and others, to have the woods of San Pelayo listed in the *Catálogo de Montes*.

The *Católogo*, we noted earlier, was a listing of all the *montes* that were to be exempted from disentailment. But in time another distinction developed, that between *montes* of *utilidad pública* (public use) and *montes* of *libre disposición* (free use). Although with both types it is ultimately the state, through the organ of the national conservation agency, ICONA (Instituto Nacional para la Conservación de la Naturaleza, originally known as the Jefatura de Montes), that has the last word about any clearings, cuttings, or uses of the woods, those of *libre disposición*, as the name indicates, are freer; since they depend less directly on the state, authorizations for clearances and fellings are granted more easily in them, whereas in the case of *montes* of *utilidad pública* these are harder to get, and for using the *monte*, even to graze the village herds, a license must be obtained and paid for year after year. And it is the *montes* of *utilidad pública* that are inscribed in the *Catálogo*.

Of course what the *junta administrativa* wanted was to make it difficult for the woodspeople to continue clearing and cutting in the common woods, so there would be plenty of pasture left for their herds. But what they failed to realize was that the insertion of the woods of San Pelayo in the *Catálogo* was tantamount to giving the *monte*, purchased at so dear a price just a few years before, away to the state:

> And it was then ... that they went to Montes and catalogued it. To get back at the others, because they said that the *monte* was going to get used up—and of course it was, because those *suertes* over there past Los Tragüezos, those are *suertes* marked out from the *monte*. And up there, all that next to Valdelorio are also *suertes*. "Hell," this one said, "they're doing away with the *monte*." Sure they were doing away with the *monte*, man, these people, of course, the people who had less, that was all they wanted. There were people to work it. "There you go, take a *suerte* and clear it, plow it, and make it produce." Hey, well, of course they were using it up. So [the others] went there and catalogued it. And since they put it in the *Catálogo de Montes* now it's theirs [the state's]. But they shouldn't have done it! The *junta administrativa* we had in those days did it. For as I've told you here we had an exemption from sale of that *monte*, with a deed of payment.... Now the owner of it, absolutely, is the state. The Jefatura de Montes is the owner of it.[21]

Although my informant here speaks of these events as if he had lived through them himself, the fact is that all this had to have occurred before he was born, in the generation of his father. (He was uncertain of the exact date of the cataloguing.) But he is a person for whom the past is vividly present, so it may be that he heard the story from his father or from his elders, whom he greatly enjoyed being with, and combined it with elements of his own recollection of the conflict between herding and agricultural interests in the village. Certainly it is true that when the first definitive edition of the *Catálogo de Montes* ("and other wooded areas exempted from disentailment for reasons of public use") was published in 1901 the *monte* of San Pelayo was listed there. Though earlier unpublished versions of the *Catálogo* had appeared in 1863, 1877, and 1881, these remained incomplete listings, and it was not until after the royal decree of 1897 that the *Catálogo* was prepared in earnest.[22] Thus the *monte* of San Pelayo would have found its way into the *Catálogo* some time between 1897 and 1901, that is, after the purchase of the *foro* and before the publication of the *Catálogo*. These are the historic years of my informant's tale.

Of course this, like all tales, like all histories, is an interpretive reading of events. For if it is a story of how the village, ironically, gave its own woods away to the state, it is also an interpretation of why the village is no longer able to dispose of this extensive portion of its commons as it sees fit. Though this informant provided the most fully formed account of how the woods of San Pelayo got caught in the state's stranglehold, he is by no means alone in thinking that the village hardly has any control anymore over its own commons.

Leonardo Mirantes also spoke to me of how the village had been "deluded" (*nos estaba en un engaño*) about the woods of San Pelayo: "These *montes* belong to the state. We can make use of them, but we cannot clear, nor sell, nor do anything with those *montes*. Not even cut when we want to. You have to get permission, understand?" In the same conversation he spoke of the confusion that the distinction between *montes* of *utilidad pública* and *montes* of *libre disposición* had engendered. The *monte* of La Lomba, where *suertes* were given out "for always" in the charged political climate of the 1930s, is of *libre disposición* and "with these the *pueblo* can do what it likes, the *pueblo*, what it cannot do is divide it up, that is precisely what it cannot do, though they used to think that they could. They cannot do so, divide it up now *para siempre*. . . ."[23] Villagers had taken the term *libre disposición* to mean that they had complete freedom to dispose of the woodland of La Lomba as they wished, but it turned out that this *monte* was not very "free" either. Indeed, it has been a most painful lesson for many of them, especially the older *vecinos* who remember a time when the village had more control over its commons and things were less bureaucratized, to learn that they can no longer act independently as a village, but must forever be at the mercy of the state.

The people of Santa María and other nearby villages which I studied were not passive victims of the disentailment reforms. They perceived the threat to their common lands, defined as they were by custom, that was posed by the state's attempt to establish a new and absolute definition of the commons. This attempt at redefining the nature of communal landholding went hand in hand with the attempt to establish an equally absolute definition of private property and thereby to rationalize the old agrarian regime, doing away with the tissue of superimposed use-rights long sanctioned by custom. At the same time, village people clearly understood that the state's program represented a modern version—legitimated, to be sure, by legal and ideological justifications—of the old forms of encroachment on their commons, and they fought back, as in earlier centuries they had fought back, in long and costly corporate litigation, when the state tried to cash in early on its reform program by selling off the lands it stripped of communal status. That they could fight back was itself significant, for there were other parts of Spain where this would have been out of the question, and where the battle for the commons, of which disentailment was a continuation, was fought not with paper but with blood. Or not fought at all, the church and common lands falling into the hands of a few proprietors and the greater part of the population eventually succumbing to proletarianization with resentment.

Until more detailed research is carried out on the reaction of local communities to disentailment along the lines suggested here, it will be impossible to say whether the case of Santa María and surrounding villages in central León modifies the general findings for the rest of Spain. At the moment what can be said is that here we have an example of a people who withstood the threat that disentailment might have posed to their livelihood without rising in arms or falling into the ranks of the rural proletariat. In truth disentailment changed little in these Leonese villages.

Much had to do with the nature of community in León, which even at the close of the nineteenth century was still imbued with a residue of an older ethos, that of the small medieval settlement where you either "worked together or died separately." Thus we find villagers in the period assuming joint responsibility for the privatization of communal woodlands—in documents of their own making—and seeking exemptions from sale of their commons, or buying it back, not as individuals but as a community. But the ethos had also begun to change and conflict was arising in the community as a result of population growth. It was these conflicts that, in the view of many, reversed the victory the village had earlier won in the battle for their commons when one faction effectively signed the *monte* over to the state. But in a sense the cards were stacked against the village from the start, for only the state was to be the victor this time. Since the years of disentailment, the commons has gradually been severed from the old social context of custom and use; it is the state, much grown in power, and not the village that now oversees the web of use-rights.[24]

Part Five

Chapter 15

✛

The Presence of the Past

IN 1725 Miguel de Salas Celis, parish priest of Trobajo del Cerecedo and native of Santa María del Monte, had notarized his intention to endow the tomb of his parents, "and on it place a memorial stone with their coat of arms in order that in said tomb shall be buried all the descendents of his parents only through the line of Salas and Celis."[1] Offering an endowment to the parish church fund of six *reales* "a year perpetually and forever and ever," which he founded on a meadow and a rye land, he seems to have expected that the family line stemming from his progenitors would, in the biblical sense, be fruitful and multiply, their progeny and all their descendents resting in the one spot together until the end of time.

The vicissitudes of history and of time's passage are such that the memorial stone below the altar commemorating the endowment has come down to us perfectly preserved, but no one in Santa María today has any recollection whatsoever of the Salas Celis family.[2] The chiseled writing on the stone is in an old and unfamiliar hand made more incomprehensible by the numerous abbreviations. In the minds of village people, who tend to attribute to any old monument or manuscript more age than in fact it has, there is no doubt that it was written in Latin and that it dates from the time the village was founded. Yet the message is in Spanish and certainly does not date back to remote times.[3]

With the disappearance in the 1830s of the old practice of burying the parishioners in the body of their church, the meaning of a family tombstone in such a setting is lost upon contemporary villagers.[4] When the old wooden floor of the church was replaced with modern tiles some years ago and skulls and bones appeared from underneath, people had difficulty understanding whose they were or what they were doing there.

In a conversation I had with a village woman I sought, without success, to convince her that the skulls and bones were the remains of people who had once lived in the parish. "We thought," she said, "that they had to be the relics of saints."

History as it is locally conceived

We have looked for the presence of the past in the forms of house and family, community and commons. I would like to embark now on a different sort of journey through time, one in which we will often have to retrace our steps. For we have yet to see how history itself is conceived by the people of Santa María and the villages surrounding it, what their sense of the past is, and what meaning they give to the written word; in short, to what extent and in what ways is the past present for the people whose history, in many different guises, has filled these pages?

There are two levels at which we can look for history as it is locally conceived: the legendary, with its roots in oral tradition, and the documentary, steeped in the village's own literary tradition of making and keeping written records. At the level of legend, history becomes a tale of origins, of the place and the people; though based in historical fact, it is a tale that the historical imagination of generations of villagers has spun and elaborated, weaving and unweaving the Penelopean tapestry. And new tales are continually being woven as old historical contexts recede into the past. Thus the elaborations on the Salas Celis tombstone and the bones of bygone parishioners.

Running parallel to this legendary level of history is the level of history as inscribed in local texts preserved in the village from times past and surrounded, often, with an aura of the sacrosanct. The villages of Spain have long been tied into the written tradition of the larger society, many of them since the medieval days of charters and *cartas pueblas*. But without a doubt it is in the sixteenth century, during the reign of Phillip II, that the villages find themselves ever more in touch with the literate world. For it is in this period of expansion overseas and growing bureaucratization at home that, as John Elliott puts it, "government by the spoken word" is gradually replaced "with government by the written word—government by paper."[5] Or as Jean Vilar notes in a recent article, this is the era par excellence of the quest for statistical knowledge, which is sought with an eye toward implementing new fiscal policies, and also as an end in itself.[6] Hence the remarkable geographic questionnaire sent out to all the towns and villages of the kingdom of Castile in the years 1575-1580, which surveyed information on matters ranging from local economic to local religious life.[7]

But it is not just by responding to questionnaires before a royal scribe—as again happens in the eighteenth century with the equally remarkable statistical inquiry known as the Catastro de Ensenada—that the villages gain fluency in the ways of the written word. In the sixteenth century the villages begin to have their ancestral customs set down on paper in the form of ordinances for their own local governance, at the impulsion, frequently, of the central state. This tradition is carried on into the nineteenth century and beyond with the recording of council acts by villagers, already literate, who are reading the old texts of ordinances passed on to them by their ancestors and self-consciously writing their history as they make it.

Let us return now to the legendary level, where we began. The example of the memorial stone in the church which has outlived the family it was intended to honor, and which in the present can no longer be understood except as a deposit left behind by the first settlers of the village, points to one of the ways in which the past is present—or not so much present as represented. Similarly with the skulls and bones found under the floor of the church; the context for their original meaning having been lost, they become, in a reworked version of the past, the relics of saints.

The people of Santa María, like their neighbors in nearby villages, are much concerned with history, though they conceive of it in the same way as they do the Holy Scriptures, mainly as a source of explanation for the origin of things. The questions people most frequently put to the past are: how did their community come into existence and who were its first settlers? When I told people in Santa María that I had come there to write a history of the village, they took that to mean that I was interested in the foundation and early settlement of their community. And so I was told, by many different storytellers and on many different occasions, the legend of how Santa María was founded and settled.

It is a legend that, again, shows how present the past is and how, at the same time, the past is reworked to shed light on the origin of things. In the woods of San Pelayo, the story goes, existed a monastery, and in the woods of Valdelorio, a convent. There was a path through the woods that linked up the monastery and the convent and that was much used, for every day the monks went to sing mass to the nuns—a detail that greatly amuses people. It was the servants and field hands of the monks (the nuns appear not to have needed any) who founded the village in its present location, and it was the monks who gave them the patron of "the sweet name of Mary" (*el Dulce nombre de María*) as they wished their servants to be as devoted to the Virgin as they themselves were. Many people, in telling the story, add that the first houses were those two lying closest to the church, for the rest was all woods. After the monastery and the convent fell away, for reasons not entirely clear—some people link their disappearance to the invasion of the Moors—the village continued to grow and to call itself Santa María, after its patron; and since in those days the woods reached right up to the houses, the first settlers thought to add, "del Monte."

In the woods of San Pelayo, the story continues, lies hidden a buried treasure—gold coins in the hide of a bull—which the monks left when the Moors came, or which the Moors left when the monks came, people are not sure. Many have gone digging around in search of the treasure but no one has ever found it. I once heard a woman say, as we stood washing at the public fountain, that it's a pity they haven't brought in a steam shovel to dig up the ground there. This remark came from a woman who, having left the village twenty years ago for the industrial heartland of the Basque country, could envision more effective "archaeological" methods than haphazard digging with pick and shovel. Yet clearly the legend of buried treasure has not lost any of its hold over her imagination.[8]

When people tell this legend, which being a story of origins is set in a remote and distant past, they tend to mix together biblical and medieval times. A number of people told me that the village was founded after the Flood, and that was why it was built on a hill, just as in trying to understand the great mystery of the world's diverse languages they refer to the tower of Babel. Everyone knows, too, that the Moors inhabited Spain, but most villagers have no more than a hazy idea of when they lived in this area. This is understandable since the Moorish presence in León and in northwestern Spain generally was not very strong nor very long-lived. As a result, the distant past is symbolized by the presence of the Moors (*cuando andaban los Moros por aquí*) in medieval times and fused with the events of an equally distant biblical era. Mythically speaking this fusion of eras is wholly appropriate for both are times of creation: of the world, and of the village (the world as the villager knows it).

The legend, for all its mythical accretions, is indeed based in a solid core of historical experience. In fact, it is impressive to see how fully the presence of so distant a past is preserved in this tale of origins. Evoked in it is the flavor of the medieval past, particularly the early ecclesiastical settlement of the area. In the years following the Reconquest, monastic communities sprung up throughout central León, most of them Benedictine, and villages were often founded under their auspices or took root near them. The early Benedictine monastery of Saints Cosmas and Damian was situated in the woods of the nearby village of Canaleja, and not very far from another Benedictine community—that of San Pelayo del Monte—about which not much more is known than its existence in the thirteenth century.[9] That this monastery is the one which figures so prominently in the legend of how Santa María was founded and settled there can be little doubt; and it was of particular interest to me to learn that a historical memory of the monastery of San Pelayo del Monte is still preserved both in the legend and in the place name of the woods of San Pelayo. What became of the monastery is not entirely clear from the records. Like many monastic communities nestled in the woods and countryside of León it seems to have disappeared during the passage to early modern times (being reincarnated, as frequently happened, in a village confraternity or Charity), its properties and domains falling to the monastery of San Claudio in León.[10]

But if the existence of a monastery in the woods of San Pelayo is accurately remembered and recounted, the story of the convent of Valdelorio, so far as I have been able to discover, is apocryphal. As we have seen, there had been an isolated house and barn in Valdelorio at the turn of the eighteenth century. The buildings and the surrounding woods of Valdelorio had belonged to the prosperous cattleowner Don Marcelo de la Puente from Villafeliz and they later passed to his widow Doña Francisca; she, as we know, brought a lawsuit against the *concejo* and *vecinos* of Santa María in 1701 when she was denied the pasturage rights in the village's commons which her husband had secured for their formidable herd by reason of his power and influence. Curiously enough, no one remembers Doña Francisca or the lawsuit, which is less than three hundred years old, while a monastery that fell out of existence some seven hundred years ago is still vivid in the thought of present-day villagers.

The foundations of a building can clearly by seen in the woods of Valdelorio, as they can in the woods of San Pelayo. Though from the old monastery of San Pelayo a massive stone baptismal fount was brought to the parish, as a number of people remember hearing their ancestors say, crosses have been found in both sites. The discovery of crosses in Valdelorio, and the fact that the lawsuit with Doña Francisca did not leave any mark on the historical consciousness of the people—perhaps because it is not the stuff of which legends are made?—makes it susceptible to interpretation as an old religious site. Here we see the workings of the people's historical imagination, and their sense of structure and symmetry. It is not another monastery that people posit as having existed in Valdelorio but a convent, embellishing the story with the detail about the monks going to sing mass to the nuns, for the sexes are segregated at opposite ends of the woods. The idea of these two celibate communities coming together for mass, and perhaps for other things, gives the story its touch of humor.

The interest villagers have in interpreting the origin of their social world through historical legend also leads them to seek explanations for the disappearance of other nearby villages that are believed, or known, to have existed in a past beyond recollection. I was told the story of how there had once existed a village between Santa María and Villamayor called San Justo, which was located in the woods of Trigalejos. The story seeks to provide an explanation for why the common land of Trigalejos is today the joint property of both villages: it is after San Justo disappears that its lands are split between Santa María and Villamayor. All the historical record tells us is that the *concejo* and *vecinos* of Santa María had been renting the woods of Trigalejos from the city of León since the early seventeenth century; and that in 1698 the village acquired a *foro* or perpetual leasehold over Trigalejos, agreeing in the same year, as noted in a separate document, to share these woods and the *foro* of six *ducados* yearly with Villamayor.[11]

So perhaps there never was a San Justo. But that is not as important as the fact that the story bears witness to a true historical phenomenon— the *despoblado*, the disappeared village.[12] The depopulated village is not, after all, a new figure in the Leonese countryside. It appears at the dawn of early modern times, in the seventeenth century, and again in our own century. The presence of these *despoblados*, a constant reminder of the tenuousness of the *pueblo*'s existence, did not fail to leave an imprint on the historical thinking of the *pueblos* that did survive.

It is interesting that the story I heard in Santa María of how San Justo disappeared is also told in Secos to account for the disappearance of nearby Moral, which we know without a doubt was a *despoblado* in the seventeenth century.[13] I suspect the story forms part of a larger stock of folklore motifs, but this will require further study. In any case, here is the story as it was told to me in Santa María and again in Secos by a woman conversant in the legends of the past:

> Moral before, in the past, was the *pueblo*; instead of Villafruela, Moral was the *pueblo*. And it is said that once in the past the *caridad* was brought to church. You know what the *caridad* is—bread. Bread, the round loaf, the bread, which here is still brought. ... And there was a spring, which still exists, above Moral, and it is said that she went for water, the one whose turn it was to bring the *caridad*, and she brought back a salamander in the pail. And she kneaded with that water. With that water, but she didn't see it. And since they all used to go to church, to mass, all who ate, they gave out the *caridad* in the church. All those who ate the *caridad* died.[14]

The blessed bread ritual, as we noted earlier, involved all the houses of the village in a systematic circulation of reciprocities. Each week a different female head of a household took a turn bringing the bread to Sunday mass, from which a piece was always saved. The woman who had brought the bread passed on this piece to the female head of the house next door to hers, and so on, in a continual progression that tied together all the houses of the village. At the end of the mass the congregants took a piece of the bread, which had been cut into morsels by the *mayordomo*, crossed themselves, recited an Our Father if they wished, and ate it.

That this appropriation of the sacraments by villagers constituted, in their own eyes, a symbolic representation of their sense of oneness as a community of Christians, united in the body of Christ, is clearly shown in the legend of the disappeared village. All the parishioners eat the poisoned bread, partaking together of communion, and all die. In one stroke the whole community is wiped away. When I mentioned this legend once to the parish priest of Villafruela, he dismissed it as a piece of anticlerical lore. But I am not so sure it is. Rather than viewing the legend as reflecting badly on the official religion, as the village priest did, I would suggest that it be seen as a meditation on the meaning of community for these villages. A certain ambivalence is apparent here: on the one hand, the image of the poisoned bread of communion seems to express a distrust of community; on the other, the fate of the village that, eating as one body, dies as one body, harks back to that sense of the village as a whole that is evoked by the story of how Santa María originated, according to some people, from a single family.

We see in these tales that, despite a centuries-old immersion in the written tradition of the larger society, there is still a place for legend and the historical imagination in the Leonese village. I make this point, obvious though it may seem, to demonstrate that literacy itself need not interfere with, or significantly alter, the cultural construction of pasts that invest the present with meaning. Nor need it change the way in which time is reckoned; for, as we have noted, the legendary past is not set in a specific time but in the long ago transpired age of the Flood and the Moors. Yet there can be little doubt, keeping in mind these reservations, that centuries of contact with the written word, initiated long before villagers themselves became literate, left a particular kind of imprint on the historical consciousness of the people. To this subject we now turn.

Ageless custom

With the creation of greatly expanded bureaucratic structures in the age of Phillip II, and the substitution of government by the spoken word with government by the written word, the villages of Spain begin to be drawn into the world of literacy. Clearly, in the sixteenth century, it is a world into which the average villager has not yet been initiated. The printed tax survey sent out to the villages in 1597 reaches villagers in León who are still unfamiliar with even the basic forms of accounting with pen and paper. When asked to state what each *vecino* has paid in *alcabala* (tax on sales) during the previous five years, and how the *alcabala* has been calculated, the two *vecinos* representing Santa María (like those representing Represa, Villamayor, Santa Colomba, and a host of other places) tell of how they name on the first day of every year "two inspectors [*fieles*], who do not know how to read or write, and who note down the *alcabala* on a stick of wood swearing an oath and in that way they collect said *alcabala*. . . ." At the end of the year the *vecinos*, we are told, gathered in the customary place and publicly drew up accounts of what each person owed of the *alcabala*.[15] After the collection, the accounting stick, having served its purpose, was disposed of. As a result, says the response from Armunia, now a suburb of León, "they cannot give a very accurate report of what each person has had to pay" in the five years past.[16] The economic information that this rudimentary recording device kept track of was surely not very dear to the hearts of villagers, and one can readily understand why they felt no qualms about throwing away these records.

It was quite a different matter with the village ordinances, which preserved on paper the ancestral customary laws of a particular locality. These records, far from being ever thrown away, were held in a kind of veneration, cherished and saved until they virtually fell apart from the wear and tear of the years. This attitude was based not so much in notions about the magical character of the written word, though they too would have played a part in it, as in the historical fact that, until the nineteenth century, "customs were laws" (*los costumbres eran leyes*, as an informant put it).

The concept of customary law had developed out of the late Roman and medieval idea that peasant customs, whose authority and legitimacy were sanctioned by tradition, could have legal force.[17] Yet for long periods these customs remained unwritten, inscribed only in "the memory of men, as far as it extends," as Marc Bloch citing from a medieval text put it.[18] Although in the larger towns and cities of Castile the process of codification begins in the late Middle Ages, in the villages it appears that customs were not committed to paper until the sixteenth century, and often not until much later.[19] The reign of memory had a longer life in the villages, and it was never superseded even after their customs were set down in writing.

Earlier we noted how, when the kings of Castile promulgated decrees of a general nature, they never failed to call upon the cities, towns, and villages of their kingdom to make up particularistic ordinances suited to the exigencies of the locale. Our examples, a set of ordinances from Santa María and Villamayor regarding the conservation of the common woods, were drawn up at the close of the sixteenth century in belated response to the call of Charles V for such locally enacted laws. At other times villages were called upon to draw up broader sorts of ordinances founded in their customs, for their *buen gobierno*, their good governance. In some cases the villages themselves took the initiative in codifying their customs, for it was only by being codified, properly approved, and signed that custom had the force of law before the courts. But impelled

one thing is clear: the local community was looked upon, even
~~e~~ as high up as the king, as a kind of mini-state, or little republic,
with the power to make and enforce its own laws.

Of course it goes without saying that the communities were never
autonomous entities operating in their own closed little worlds. The
process by which the villages came to codify their customs is a case in
point. It takes place in the course of a long interaction between the state
and local communities. Yet, once begun, it is a process that takes on a
life of its own. Thus the curious spectacle of Leonese villages like Santa
María continuing to record their customs and their council acts into this
century, long after the state has annulled their power to do so. But we
are skipping ahead here. Let us attempt, as far as it is possible, to trace
the history of the written tradition of the village.

There are, I think, two layers to this tradition, an older one encompassing the period from the late sixteenth to the early nineteenth century,
and a more recent one, which begins unfolding around the 1830s and
is carried on into the Civil War years. In large part what distinguishes
the two layers from one another is the question of literacy: in the first
period the great majority of villagers are illiterate, while in the second
almost all (of the men that is) are literate. But also there is a subtle shift
in the way the written word and the document is perceived; and in the
later period the flowering of literacy in the village is accompanied by
the growth of self-consciousness about making history.

The earlier period is characterized, above all, by a constant recycling
of the texts of the old ordinances; a constant effort at keeping these
"preserved communications," to borrow a term that Jack Goody uses in
the pioneering work *Literacy in Traditional Societies*,[20] from being destroyed by the ravages of time. For example, the ordinances concerning
the conservation of the woods which the *vecinos* of Santa María had
drawn up before a scribe in 1588 were recopied in 1664 and again in
1773 in the presence of the *alcalde mayor* of León, who signs the copies
to invest them with the necessary legal authority. "Torn and worm-
eaten in substantial parts" with the passing of the years, the original text
was twice recycled so its meaning would not be lost to later generations
of villagers. For although the vessel in which the communication is
preserved must constantly be renewed, the communication itself does
not age; across the centuries the word continues to signify.

We can find many similar examples of villages having their tattered
charters recopied. In the process their contents are sometimes refor-

mulated or expanded upon but always the contrast is made between the
evanescent nature of paper, ink, and binding and the immemorial and
ageless nature of custom. From Villapodambre we have this interesting
example of the *concejo* agreeing in 1659 to recopy the old ordinances of
the village

> . . . since the ordinances by which said place and its *vecinos* for
> their good preservation rule and govern themselves were written
> up in a bound book which, with the wear of time and its passing
> from one *vecino* to another, has broken and been destroyed so that
> it cannot be read, and also because they were missing a few chapters
> and others needed to be reformed.[21]

Or from the village of Canseco we hear, in 1761, that the *vecinos* decide
to recopy the text of their old ordinances for "with the passing of time
they have gotten so crumpled and deteriorated that one can hardly make
out some of their chapters." By recopying the old text "the laudable
customs which until now have been observed will not be shadowed
over."[22] In the northwestern mountains of León, the village of Curueña
still sees fit to recopy its old ordinances in 1841, "on account of their
being torn, broken, and virtually rendered useless . . . for otherwise it
will come to pass that the best and soundest customs of said *pueblo* will
be annulled and ruined."[23]

The recopying of ordinances, just as they were on the verge of falling
into hopeless illegibility, could not have been entirely a task of mere
reduplication. In places where the text was worn out beyond recognition
it would have been necessary, again, to invoke "the memory of men, as
far as it extends." And, indeed, whether villagers were codifying their
customs for the first time or recopying an old text of ordinances, they
generally called upon three or four of the eldest *vecinos* to assist in the
task of recalling the ancestral customs of the place. Once set down on
paper, the text of ordinances was read aloud in *concejo* so all the *vecinos*
might hear and approve them. Though memory was invoked to draft
the texts, it is clear that once the customs became fixed on paper they
lost a certain fluidity and flexibility; they were much less susceptible to
change and to nuances of interpretation. Villagers themselves recognized
this, but they did not always think it was a bad thing. In fact, they seem
at times to have welcomed the order that the creation of ordinances from
the flux of customs—inscribed in so inconstant a vessel as "the memory
of men"—imposed.

Custom itself had a way of succumbing to the wear of time if it was not put down in writing. Thus the ordinances of Santa María drawn up in 1776 begin, in a passage we have heard before, by stating that the *vecinos* have agreed to make up ordinances "on account of there not being any, and the *Pueblo* governing itself solely by its ancient customs, these being very deteriorated, and derogated, and interpreted by everyone to his own liking." A similar sort of statement is made by the *vecinos* of Santovenia de la Valdoncina in 1635 when they, too, come to the realization that their customs need to be preserved in a form less inconstant than the memory of men:

> . . . in said Place from time immemorial to the present they have governed and ordered themselves in accordance with the customs that have existed and exist in said Place, and because they do not have them down as written ordinances approved by the Justice of this Very Noble and Very Loyal city of León, there have been some lawsuits, doubts, and differences among the *vecinos*.[24]

Or again, going back to a still earlier period, when ordinances were drawn up for all the villages falling under the jurisdiction of the old Concejo of Bernesga de Arriba in 1547, we hear how

> it is useful for [the valley] to have ordinances and a manner in which to live and be ruled on account of the great disorder and little guard which the *vecinos* of said valley have, due to which . . . said places and their *vecinos* suffer great harm and they expect with each day to come to be greatly diminished.[25]

The written word is thus extolled for its ability to fix the rules of social existence in the community, where litigiousness, quarrels, and all manner of differences of opinion are the stuff of everyday life. Besides being able to preserve for a time the communications of the ancestors, villagers seemed to hope that the "technology of writing," to borrow another term from Jack Goody, would create order and solidarity out of the disorder and dissolution that so often, by their own accounts, threatened to tear the village community apart. Perhaps they were not being overoptimistic; once set on paper customs became ordinances, acquiring all the force of law. Unlike free-floating customs and usages, the written word did have, in a society where bureaucratic structures emerged early on, an extraordinary power.

Before the nineteenth century the parish priest was frequently present at these acts of codification and, in places that lay distant from the office of a notary and no one else was literate, he often served as the scribe, writing down the customs as the elder *vecinos* called them up from memory. Even in places where a handful of villagers were literate, particularly by the eighteenth century, the priest was called upon to serve as a witness and as often as not he left his mark, as in the preambles to the ordinances, which always invoke the Trinity and the Virgin Mary, and in exhortations to the *vecinos* to swear less and be better Christians. All this begins to change around the 1830s, when more and more villagers start becoming literate themselves and writing up council acts on their own.

Literacy has hesitant beginnings in Santa María during the early eighteenth century, when the possession of this technology is limited to priests and to certain other families related to them. The priest we heard from at the start of this chapter, Miguel de Salas Celis, had a brother, Juan, who was literate. Juan de Salas Celis, in fact, was involved in the village's attempt to obtain perpetual leaseholds over the common lands of Trigalejos and San Pelayo at the turn of the eighteenth century; his neat signature appears on the documents granting the village these lease-holds. The *fiel de fechos*, or village scribe, who wrote down and read aloud in *concejo* the ordinances of Santa María in 1776 was Juan Antonio Rodríguez, a grandson of Juan de Salas Celis; and he also had a brother, an uncle, and a granduncle who were priests. These little enclaves of literacy expand soon after the turn of the nineteenth century as rural schools gradually start springing up in the villages. Madoz tells us that there was a primary school in Santa María in 1848, which "twenty children of both sexes attend," just as there were schools by this time in other nearby villages.[26] By 1860, only 25 percent of males over five are illiterate in the municipality of Vegas del Condado, to which Santa María belongs. Literacy is now, however, the province of men, for 70 percent of the women were still illiterate.[27]

The rereading of custom

With the spread of literacy, and the municipal reforms of the 1830s, Santa María and other nearby villages begin recording the minutes of their *concejo* reunions in acts which are kept in a bound pad known as the *libro de actas de concejo*. We have encountered many of these acts here; they abound for the second half of the nineteenth and first half of the twentieth century, as do the "kitchen documents" recording acts of inheritance. These testify to the initiation of villagers into the world of writing, and to their new-found enchantment with the written word. I have frequently made use of both kinds of records in documenting the historical patterns of house and family, community and commons, for they express in a profoundly local idiom the sense of a past now fading and yet still in some ways very present.

Whereas in the period before the spread of literacy the villages were concerned above all to keep recycling the old texts of ordinances, in the nineteenth century there is a turn toward revising and renovating, re-suscitating and reinterpreting the customs inscribed in these texts handed down from the ancestors. The old texts are still reread and scrutinized, but they are no longer recopied more or less verbatim. Yet in this era of legal, social, and political flux the villages of León continued ruling themselves according to their old customs and ordinances, as López Morán had seen, taking refuge in them, in his words, "as if they were havens of salvation."

Indeed, there was a return to the customs of the past in this era or, more exactly, a self-conscious attempt to maintain them under changed conditions. This is especially evident in the case of certain customary social and religious forms of behavior, such as the obligation to attend the funeral of fellow *vecinos* and *vecinas* which, as we saw, was the subject of an act drawn up in Santa María in 1885. This act alludes to the text of the 1776 ordinances, even citing the specific chapter that makes reference to the subject, and it makes provisions for carrying out the old obligation in "the same way as we have always seen it" by having the *vecinos* accompany the dead to the grave, which now meant that they had to go in procession to the recently built cemetery lying at some distance from the settlement.

An even more explicit example of a village seeking to keep alive past traditions in a most self-conscious manner can be seen in the document drawn up by the *vecinos* of Barrio de Nuestra Señora in 1936 following the outbreak of the Civil War; it is a document that speaks of the community's desire "to bring to life again ancient customs of a clearly Christian character." These are such customs as attending the funerals of fellow *vecinos* and the village's votive masses, participating in the communal herding of cattle by *vecera*, taking part in the blessed bread ritual, and harboring the poor when it is one's turn.

In the historical context of the war the observance of what in another context might have been simply old customs took on political meaning; it became a question of ideology, of marching in step with the religious crusade of the Nationalists, or so at least was it perceived by the *vecinos* of Barrio. The village of Barrio was much divided by the war, and clearly these divisions left their mark, for again in 1964 the next generation of villagers makes up a similar sort of charter "to continue the tradition which our ancestors have set down for us in order to demonstrate to those who do not practice such Christian customs faith and human feeling." Here we can detect a pattern of "inventing tradition" for novel purposes, which has been so much a part of how the past is used since the end of the last century.[28] Aside from the interest in seeing how villagers reinterpreted custom in a contemporary context, what is intriguing about these documents is that no one asked the *vecinos* of Barrio, in either case, to draw up such charters; they did so quite on their own, compelling those who wished to express their solidarity with the cause to affix their names to them.

This brings us to a characteristic feature of the documents written in the years when most village men had become literate—the importance of the signature. In the ordinances of the past one found, at best, the signatures of the local scribe and one or two literate villagers. The acts, in contrast, are nearly always etched with the signatures of all the *vecinos*. Many of them appear to have been written at the reunions of the *concejo*, where they would have been read aloud to all the *vecinos* present, with each then signing his name as the fountain pen circulated from hand to hand.

As we have noted in passing, the signature acquired an extraordinary symbolic power in the second half of the nineteenth century. In those years villagers had taken it upon themselves to carry out clearings and fellings on their common lands to survive a crisis of subsistence brought on by unprecedented population growth. It was in this very period too that the state was carrying out disentailment reforms and invading the farthest reaches of local life ever more effectively. Particularly where the commons was concerned, the state now called for the alienation of all village properties that were not true *bienes comunales*, properties used freely and communally by all the *vecinos*. This historical conjuncture— a severe, seemingly interminable, crisis of subsistence and the emergence of a modern bureaucratic state intent on transforming and redefining the old categories of property and land use—could not have been more

unfortunate for the villages. At a time when they were desperately in
need of their reserves of common land, these were suddenly being torn
from them and made subject to new legal strictures. Forced to choose
between famine and proletarianization or disobedience of the law, the
villages took the latter path, cutting and clearing in their commons
surreptitiously, and hoping to escape the notice of those cadres of state
officials trained in a modern sort of surveillance.

Hence the signature, affixed to a peculiarly local document. In Santa
María the various clearances and fellings carried out before the turn of
the century were often illegal, as we have seen, actions that the *vecinos*
nevertheless inscribed in written documents. Rather than trying to bury
all traces of their frankly illegal deeds, the *vecinos* wrote it all down in
the form of contractual obligations binding on each of them and on the
community as a whole. The document stood as proof of their solidarity,
proof that clearly they would never have dared present before a court
of law; but as a "preserved communication" it served as a reminder and
a symbol of their collective responsibility. Signing their names they bound
their persons "together and conjointly," for the state had become too
powerful a force to combat each on his own. Thus the writing of documents by villagers grew out of their self-awareness of the kind of state
that was forming in those years and of the legality to which it now
expected local communities to conform; the written word, made strong
with the signatures of all the *vecinos*, served as a kind of shield.

Having made its way into the village, the written word gets into the
house. Here we should pause for a moment to consider the contrast
between the "kitchen documents," drawn up by particular houses in the
inheritance process, and the acts of the *concejo*, representing the agreements and acts of the community as a whole. To introduce my discussion
of the idiom of equal inheritance, I had called attention to the fact that
the "kitchen documents," or personal inheritance records, are not kept
past three or four generations; once they lose their contextual meaning
they lose their power over the individuals involved, and become no more
than "old papers" concerning agreements buried and no longer binding.
This, in any case, is the attitude I found people to have about the old
inheritance records in their possession, with few exceptions. On first sight
this may seem puzzling, given that the records of the *concejo* are fairly
well preserved and probably contain just about all the documentation
the village has produced in the last four hundred years. Why, then,
should the home documents be treated any differently?

The rationale must be sought in the fluid nature of the house in León, or to put it another way, in the fact that the nature of family lines is noncorporate, in contrast to the corporacy of the village polity. With partible inheritance the house—in the broad sense in which people speak of it, as not only the physical structure that houses the family, but the lands, the animals, and the goods—is divided in each generation. As we have seen, the house is in continual flux, forever being broken up into fragments and recombined into new wholes. What constitutes "the house" at any given moment in time is an elusive link in the chain of a family line that recedes back into an unrecoverable past while it moves without ceasing toward an ever-unfolding future. This sense of the house as an entity in flux, whose stability is as short-lived as the span of a couple's married life, bears directly on the fact that home documents quickly become anachronistic.

There is an idea that all the family papers should remain in the trunk (*en el tronco*), that is, in the house of the parents. Once in a while the offspring will take their *hijuelas* with them, but this rarely occurs. Thus any one family often has not only its own inheritance records but those of brothers and sisters, aunts and uncles, not to mention parents, grandparents, and great-grandparents. This is why I was usually able to see quite clearly what there was to divide and how exactly it got divided up among all the siblings. But this element of constancy in the records lasts for a few generations of a family line, for a point is soon reached when memory cannot extend far enough to rescue ancestors from oblivion. Inscribed with the names of people lost to memory, the records of inheritance transactions are necessarily transient, since in every generation a new division is called for. And after two or three generations the particular agreements enacted and set down on paper in what, with the passing of the years, begins to seem like a distant time, cease to describe the reality of a house redivided and reunited many times since. When a woman who lives in a house considered to be one of the first to have been founded in the village gave me the old inheritance records she had, she said to me that maybe I would find something in them about the people who settled the village. They dated back to 1824, and this to her already seemed like a distant past.

The *concejo* records, in contrast, express a sense of permanence, of continuity between past and present. Stashed away in the wooden chest of the *concejo*, they are passed around from one headman to another, as they were in past times. Unlike the home documents, which are as mortal as the people they concern, no one would think to destroy the *concejo* records once a certain number of years have elapsed (though, as I have noted, in some villages the documents have disappeared because of factionalism between the incumbent and the new headman). For they are the legacy of the village as a whole, the customs, laws, and wisdom that have come down to it as part of its communal inheritance.

But if they are conserved, they are rarely read or consulted anymore, as they were in the late nineteenth century when an earlier generation still looked upon the 1776 ordinances, which they cited in the new acts they drew up, as a model for organizing aspects of their economic and religious life. Today the *vecinos* do not even write their own acts. The Franco regime initiated a policy of having the *alcalde* of the municipal seat check the local acts of the villages every few years. In time the acts started to be drawn up less frequently, and when they were drawn up they concerned the material progress made by the village: the building of the public fountain, the installment of streetlamps, the bringing of running water to the houses, and more recently, though whether it is progress we have yet to see, the collective agreement to go ahead with the consolidation of parcels plan.

During the last few years, it is bureaucracy pure and simple that has found its way into what were once the local records of the village. This was epitomized for me one night when I went over to the house of the *presidente* and found him and one of the *vocales* troubled over how they were going to write up an act concerning the inclusion of a few pieces of the commons in the consolidation of parcels plan. The lawyer had given them a typewritten example of what they were supposed to write, in proper legal language, but he had failed to tell them how to begin the act! Though better schooled than their ancestors, the villagers of today hesitate to write up any documents of their own; and who can blame them, their documents are no longer written for themselves but for an audience of critical officials.

In an earlier era, as we saw, the village's records of customs were continually recycled, for their meaning seemed not to age. By the mid-nineteenth century, though the villages were still orienting themselves, more self-consciously than ever before, according to the customs inscribed in their old records, they were also writing, for the first time, their own history—a collective one—as it came into being. This is the beauty of the acts dating from the years of the first clearances and fellings—aside from their role as symbols of solidarity, they are pure chronicles, set down on paper for the record, to leave a mark, a ripple, in time. Requested by no one, inspected by no one, these chronicles serve to remind us that peasants have not been a people without history.

Long after the birth of the modern Spanish state, the *vecinos* of Santa María, and of many of the villages surrounding it, continued to think in terms of the "little republic" ideal. They continued to draw up ordinances and bring to life old customs, record their acts and levy fines for transgressions purely customary, such as absenting oneself from *hacenderas* or votive masses of the village. But in recent years, history—that larger history which the peasantry has never been more than "a part" of, as A. L. Kroeber, Robert Redfield, and others had seen, though the irony of the concept escaped their notice—has caught up with them, overwhelming that other, local history of their own making. It is now that peasants in Santa María—and elsewhere in rural Spain and Europe—are no longer making a history of their own that we have begun, with hindsight, to salvage what we can from the wreck of oblivion.

Epilogue

AFTER a three-year absence, I returned to Santa María in August of 1984. As we approached the village by highway I fell into the kind of reverie one experiences when returning to a landscape one has known well, and remembered and forgotten at the same time. I looked out at the familiar valleys and heather bushes, the yellow fields brimming with stalks of rye, the burnt-red soil, the fallows overgrown with wild flowers and weeds, the strange wavelike patterns sewn into the hillsides by erosion, water, time. Coming closer, I began to notice the unfamiliar, to see things that tested the vision I had cultivated through the years and summoned up in recollection.

I had expected, of course, to find the layout of the land changed. I had been in correspondence with several people in the village and their letters had charted the gradual, but imminent, progression toward land consolidation. Information about the changes that were taking place had come to me in bits and pieces: first, that the new parcels had been given out by the engineers and that, no, not everyone was satisfied but there was no going back anymore; then, that the government's bulldozers were at work carving out the new plots from the old and that everything was in shambles; and finally, that there were roads now that led out to all of the village's fields, that you could go to any of them by car. But it had been difficult for me to imagine exactly how the landscape had been altered. As we drew closer I could see, with the sort of intensity that only first impressions can call up, that the village was out in the open, visible from every direction, exposed, almost naked. There had been more trees, more hedges, more gardens; now there were large fields of barley and oats reaching right up to the houses, practically touching them. This impression had not yet coalesced when we rounded the curve and turned into Santa María.

After a few moments of driving down the newly asphalted road I saw Germiniano coming along with his old wooden cart, leading his yoked cows forward with the long thin stick they call an *ahijada*. We stopped and I thought to myself that perhaps things had not changed that much after all. He recognized us, bellowing a hearty greeting, and saying, "you haven't forgotten about this place, have you?" His son, who is a seminary student in Madrid, appeared next, with Nieves, his mother, following behind on donkey, and we all chatted briefly about the weather, the crops, how long it had been since we returned to Santa María. Then they were off, rushing in the way people do there to the field still untended, because, as they say, the summer is short and the harvest won't wait.

We drove on and stopped again after a few yards, just at the entrance to the village. It was still the early part of the afternoon and people had already eaten and rested and were now emerging from their houses to go work in the fields. In a matter of moments we had attracted a little crowd around us, between those going to the fields and those who had seen the excitement from their kitchen windows and stepped out the door. I was in the midst of answering, yet again, questions about how long we would be staying and where, when a village woman appeared on the scene and asked, after a warm greeting, in which house we would be staying. Before I had a chance to answer someone interjected, "At your house." And she, taking the joke in stride, said that it would be fine with her. "Don't think we wouldn't manage," she retorted.

I had noticed, while enjoying this sort of old-style conviviality and garnering of information, that there were several teenagers, clearly not from the village, in fashionable gear and haircuts, cruising up and down the sloping village street on bicycles and mopeds. They were from the *urbanización* across the highway, I was told: strangers. As I was to see during the course of the summer, there were more strangers in the village than ever before, more cars whizzing by at top speed, enough to give me the sense that, at least during the vacation season, the village no longer belonged to its rightful owners, the people who forge their living from its land, who endure its cold lonely winters, and who expect to return to its earth when they die.

Much has changed in Santa María since my first visit to the village six years ago. I would go so far as to say that if I had begun my research in 1984, rather than in 1978, I could not have written the kind of book I did. Not that the changes now in evidence were unforeseeable years ago, or that "the presence of the past" has suddenly receded into the mists of time, but Santa María today is a different kind of village, and its people, to some extent, a different people. Nor is this simply my own perception of things; it is theirs too. One remark I heard this past summer brought it all home for me—"This isn't Santa María del Monte [*del monte*, of the woods] anymore, now it's Santa María del Condado [*del condado*, of the county or earldom, from *conde*, count or earl]."

This remark was intended to be both metaphoric and ironic, for the village has officially been known as Santa María del Condado for several years. With the municipal reforms of the last century, Santa María was incorporated into the municipality of Vegas del Condado. Yet it was still known by its original historic name, Santa María del Monte, until the middle of this century. What forced people to start referring to the village as Santa María del Condado was the existence of another Santa María del Monte (de Cea) in the province of León; this homonymy, in a modern age, caused too much confusion in the delivery of the mail to both places. So people started writing Santa María del Monte del Condado on their correspondence. But this was a rather cumbersome and long appellation, and after awhile it was reduced to Santa María del Condado. Eventually the name spread to other official contexts and then to everyday discourse. Today, a traveler on the highway from León to Boñar will see no sign for Santa María del Monte; for years now, the sign that points to the village has read Santa María del Condado.

Yet, looking at this queston of names metaphorically, that Santa María is no longer "of the woods" but "of the earldom" means much more than a mere turn toward a convenient address for mail delivery and other official business. It means, first of all, that in the present Santa María truly deserves the noble title of its recently adopted name. Being "of the earldom," now that the name is an anachronism, does not evoke images of a place unfree and subject to feudal domination, but rather a place of some note.

In the past the people of Santa María were often made to feel that their village was inferior by people from the nearby riverside villages, where the land was fertile and productive, money circulated more freely, and some people at least lived very well. Santa María, in contrast, was a forgotten village, where the land barely gave rye, money was almost unheard of, and the woods surrounding (and isolating) the village were one of the main sources of a livelihood.

All of this has changed now with the consolidation of the old scattered plots, which cost over 30 million *pesetas* to carry out; the creation of an *urbanización* right across from the village, which in the summertime fills

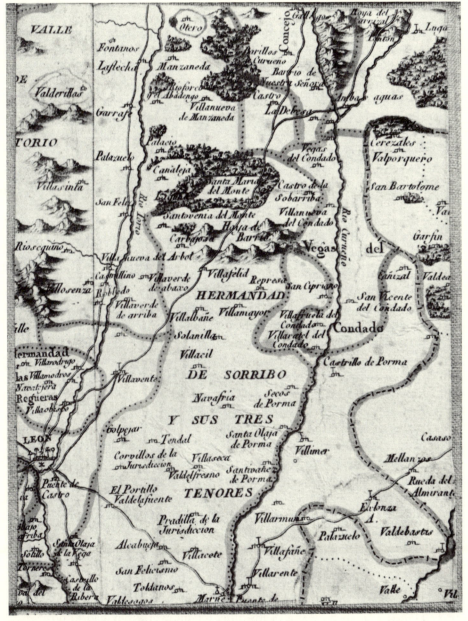

Detail from Tomás López, *Mapa geográfico de una parte de la provincia de León* (1786). Note how Santa María del Monte is shown surrounded by woods.

up with vacationers; and the village's own attainment of the urban comforts, from a sewage system to a public telephone. Nowadays, with artificial fertilizers, the irrigation of a ring of fields surrounding the village with a communally built dam, and the growth of cattle-raising, the people of Santa María live well, as well as most in the riverside villages. The existence of a weekend retreat, interestingly called Montesol ("Sunnywoods"), on land that once belonged to the village, testifies to the fact that Santa María is far from forgotten. One can even say that the village has thereby been made a part of the urban movement to return to the countryside, so widespread in rapidly industrialized Spain; that it has been made a part of modern history.

Even my own modest research into the history of Santa María has helped to rid the village of its inferiority complex. While I was there this past summer, an article appeared in the Leonese daily about my research with a headline that put Santa María in the limelight, and an article I had written in Spanish, analyzing and transcribing the village's 1776 bylaws, was published, copies of which I distributed liberally. This generated a good deal of excitement. The new priest, who commutes to the village twice a week to say mass, spoke admiringly of the bylaws concerning religious activity in his sermon, not just in the one he gave in Santa María, but in the ones he gave in the other three villages he attends. He was very impressed by the fact that there was so much historical material available in Santa María and said as much to us in a conversation which a village woman we know well overheard. After he had left, she turned to me and, with some pride, said, "he thought only they had history there in the riverside villages [where the priest himself is from], but now he sees that we have just as much, more!"

In comparison with past times, then, Santa María is an important village, a prosperous village, a village with a history and a future. It is, in this sense of having risen in status, "of the earldom," not "of the woods." But there is also irony in that status, only recently acquired, for those people in Santa María who lived through the era when it was still "of the woods." I remember explaining, in 1978, that I had come to Santa María to study the way of life of the village and being told by Hilaria that theirs was a brutish life, for the work they had to do was "brutal, very brutal." A number of times I heard the phrase, "The land is a very spoiled girl" (*la tierra es muy señorita*); in other words, the land will not do a thing for you, you have to work and slave "for her." And work, knowing *how* to work, was the essence of the old regime, the essence too of what it meant to be "of the woods." When I went back to Santa María this past summer the remark I heard most frequently, almost daily, was that nowadays no one wants to work anymore, no one knows *how* to work anymore. People want to live like earls, not like woodcutters.

August, as I remembered it, was the month of greatest agricultural activity in the year; all month long one would see people returning from the fields with carts full to brimming with stalks of rye, the new Leonese breed of cows, intended for milk, plodding along with the load, and the village threshing grounds bustling with the work of the harvest. There were a number of people you could not see unless you went looking for them in the fields or the threshing grounds; and it was not unusual for some families to be threshing and winnowing, with machines twenty and thirty years old, almost until midnight. The threshing grounds were crowded with people, carts, cows, piles of hay and grain; a young man from the village, who runs a bar in Madrid with his brothers, rushed past me on one occasion, saying, "This is worse than New York City, what do you think, Ruth?" Theirs was hard, exhausting work, yet everyone was quick to point out that, though they worked hard, their parents and grandparents, not to mention those who came before, had worked harder. For, in a past not too distant, the rye was mown with the sickle, threshed with the threshing sledge, winnowed with the wind; they, at least, had it a little easier. Still, to bring in one or two hundred bushels of grain with not much more than the labor of the family, a team of cows, and some outdated machinery was no easy task.

Returning to the village this past August and finding the threshing grounds virtually deserted, I innocently asked people whether they had already brought in the rye harvest, or were they somehow starting late this year? I was told, by everyone, that the rye had not yet been touched, that they were waiting for the combine harvester to arrive; some had made arrangements with the cooperative from Villamayor, and some with individuals from Villaseca and Barrio de Nuestra Señora who owned combines. The combines were to arrive any day now, people kept saying, as the first week, then the second week of August passed by. People always spoke of the combines alone, not the men with the combines, as if those imposing machines had a life of their own. It was strange to see people waiting for the harvest to be brought home for them; strange, as one man said, "that it should be August and not a soul in the fields or in the threshing grounds." When the combines arrived, just after the middle of the month, everyone breathed easier; there had been a great deal of anxiety in the air till then—what if hail had fallen or too much sun scorched the grain, so many things could have happened.

"In four days," a young man told me, "they harvested what they used to harvest in two months." He was raised in the Basque country, where his family migrated in the 1960s, and though only twenty-two could remember coming back to the village when he was a child to help bring in the harvest of his grandparents, with sickle, scythe, and threshing sledge. The changes he has seen in his short lifetime, he said, amounted to a progression from "the stone age to modern times."

Naturally I would not go so far as to say that; but then he too was speaking metaphorically, and indeed in the last fifteen years, even in the last three years, the village has undergone a great transformation. In 1981 a few people had tentatively called upon the combine to harvest a field or two, but before then no one had at all. Since then everyone has used the combine for the rye harvest, if not for the barley, oats, and wheat, which are grown in smaller quantities, though this past summer many even sent the combine in to do those harvests. "You can't work the way we used to any more," Leonardo said to me as we stood around after mass one Sunday talking. Sixto, standing next to him, chuckling, added, "These days no one *wants* to work the way we used to!"

Until 1981 there were three tractors in the village; now there are seven. Of these, five are operated by unmarried men ranging in age from twenty-five to forty-three. They are the ones who, with their siblings or parents, raise ten or twenty head of cattle, and work as much land as strength and time will allow, renting out parcels from the retired people in the village or from those who have emigrated to the cities. Even the people who continue to work in a more traditional way, with a team of cows (oxen having been given up in the 1930s), recognize that theirs is a dying way of life, and that the future of Santa María as a farming village depends on increasing mechanization.

One morning, while taking a walk through the deserted threshing grounds, which afford a splendid view of the Cantabrian peaks on the horizon, two men from the village came along, brothers, each leading a pair of cows yoked together. Both teams were made up of an older cow accustomed to the yoke and a calf wearing it for the first time. Froilán and Emiliano led the cows around the threshing grounds for an hour or so; this, they told me, was to get the calves used to the yoke. I followed along, and we talked about how it would soon be impossible to find any beasts of burden in the village; one of the men remarked that when his neighbor, who works with a tractor, needs a team he always borrows one from him. A certain patience is required to train a team, a certain sense of time and work and the bringing of things to fruition—which is rapidly being lost.

Especially symptomatic of this loss is the village's unanimous acceptance of the government's consolidation of the old miniature and scattered plots, which were part not only of a land tenure system but also of a cultural system. It must be said that the current attitude toward the reform was a long time in the making, and that between the approval of the plan in the village council and the actual land reform more than six years elapsed. For the older people, who are the majority in the village, there is no question that the three, four, or five fields the engineers gave them just don't add up to the forty, fifty, and sixty plots that they had accumulated through inheritance, destiny, and their own hard work. They, at least, have accepted land consolidation—which in northern Europe ceased to be an issue two centuries ago—with a mixture of resignation and defeat, a sense of its historical inevitability.

Consolidation itself is the final stage of a long process of economic, social, demographic, and cultural change, in which the history of a village "of the woods" and the larger national history of Spain sometimes intersect. One can trace it back to the unprecedented population growth of the nineteenth century, which took place in an era when the state was actively and ever more successfully interfering in village affairs with disentailment and other rationalizing reforms. This process of change continued in the 1920s and 1930s, a period of heavy emigration to Argentina and Mexico, when the modernization of agriculture was just beginning to take hold in Spain; it was in this period, in Santa María, that people began to harvest rye with the scythe rather than the sickle, and to winnow with machines. Then, with the Civil War, things came to a sudden halt, and the countryside returned to the bastion of traditionalism, to survive. The late industrialization of Spain kept people in the villages until the end of the 1960s and 1970s, but from then on the movement to urban centers grew in strength and numbers, and became irreversible.

Those who left continued to return to their native villages to lend a hand with the harvest during the summer, to slaughter the family pig around Saint Martin's, to celebrate the birth of Christ in December, and

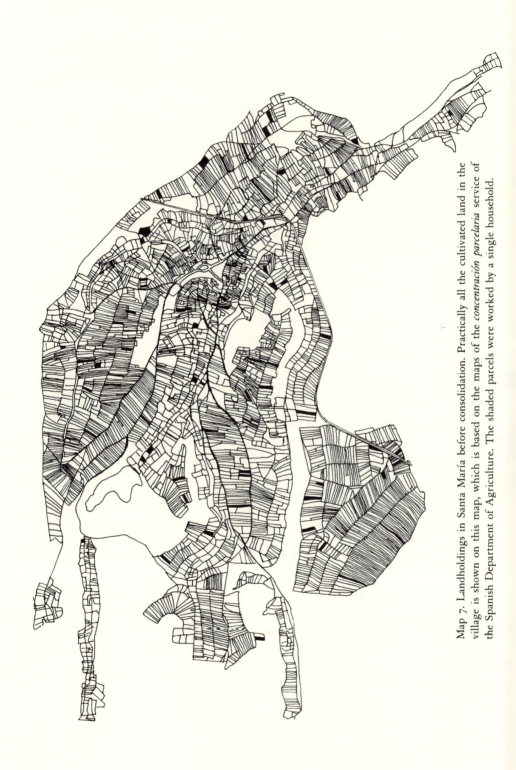

Map 7. Landholdings in Santa María before consolidation. Practically all the cultivated land in the village is shown on this map, which is based on the maps of the *concentración parcelaria* service of the Spanish Department of Agriculture. The shaded parcels were worked by a single household.

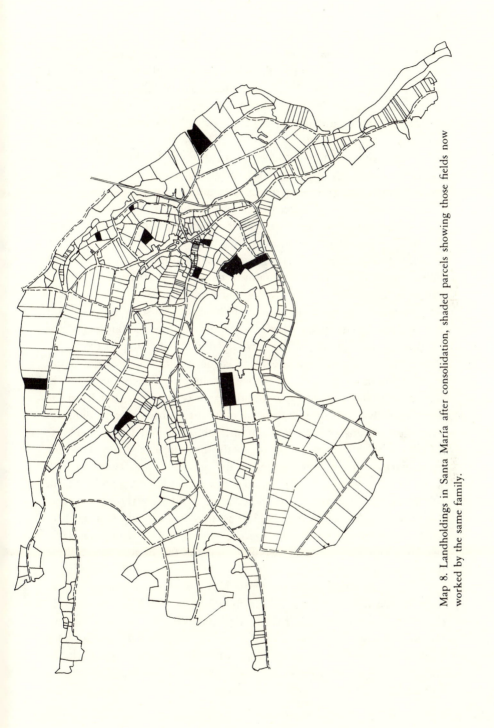

Map 8. Landholdings in Santa María after consolidation, shaded parcels showing those fields now worked by the same family.

commemorate His death during Holy Week. Their bonds to the countryside remained strong, and consequently urban styles and preferences
were quickly integrated into village life, hastening the disappearance of
the old agrarian regime. At the same time, as the village was emptied
of its excess population those who stayed behind were able to prosper,
working the best lands intensively and raising cattle to be not beasts of
burden but a steady source of income. Now, with the general aging of
the village population, and the social security checks the state sends in
regularly, there are fewer and fewer people involved in agricultural
production, opening the way for tractors and combines.

This entire historical trajectory, described here in a nutshell, culminates in the consolidation of the scattered parcels in the old land tenure
system by government engineers and planners, to create a more rational,
efficient, and comfortable arrangement than had ever existed before. It
culminates, too, in a certain amount of chaos and destruction—so often
said to be necessary to bring a new world into being.

We went one morning to observe the irrigation of some hillside lands
that lie close to the village dam. One could still see the borders of the
old small plots engraved in the new landscape, as if a map of the layout
of the fields in the past had been placed on top of a map of the layout
of the fields in the present. There we encountered Felicisimo, who was
beginning to irrigate with the runoff that was flowing down from the
fields above his. He had carved out a miniature garden plot, grown lush
with string beans on runners, onions, cabbages, and potatoes, in the
middle of a large inert meadow, in the middle of a wasteland. The
upper part of the field was higher on the slope and it was covered with
weeds and dry grass. It could produce if it were plowed, he told us, but
he's not going to bring in the plow; if his children want to, they can,
but they probably won't either. He said they had already worked very
hard all winter—the new plots were given out at the beginning of the
year—cutting down trees and pulling out the old hedges to refashion
their new plots.

I asked him whether he was pleased with the consolidation that had
been carried out. He shrugged his shoulders and said that he thought
that in the long run it was for the best. He had fifty plots and his children
no longer knew where most of them were; now with five they can keep
track of their property more easily. Not that they will ever work the
land, he added, but, who knows, and he cited a proverb: *Por los años
mil, las aguas vuelven a ir por donde solían ir* ("Every thousand years the

waters flow again where they once flowed"). He explained that you can force water to go in a certain direction, but after awhile, if you leave it alone, it goes on flowing the way it used to. Thus the analogy: "In other words, in twenty, thirty, one hundred years maybe those people who left will return to where they used to be, which is in the *pueblos*."

This is wishful thinking, of course, for it seems clear that, save for an economic disaster, those who left the villages are not going to return to cultivate the land. It is precisely such a realization that is behind people's approval of consolidation. The scattered plots of the past, which formed part of a web of persons, rights, and obligations, are no longer a meaningful inheritance to pass on to one's urban offspring. An entire age has passed, people realize, and with it a cultural system writ in land.

Yet for the older people, and even for those not so old, like my twenty-two-year-old informant, the presence of the past continues to exert a certain hold on the imagination. The wastefulness of the new regime as opposed to the old is often noted; how in the past every ear of wheat, every stick of wood mattered, and how today thoroughness is sacrificed for speed. Those who are accustomed to working in the old style still approach the land with the sort of patience I spoke of earlier, slowly and coaxingly, intensively, giving it attention every day without fail. The tiny yet lush garden in the midst of an overlarge field, one too large to work in the old way, is an example of such an attitude. For the large fields demand an extensive manner of working the land; as people point out, the very idea of plowing one of the new fields with a donkey or pair of cows is exhausting. Thus some carve out their human-sized plots out of the new large ones, and these are worked to the fullest and nothing is wasted. But no one has any doubt that a dehumanized landscape is more suited to the requirements of the modern world.

With consolidation the fields were not only made larger; the irrigation canals were widened, the old roads enlarged and new ones plowed into existence with bulldozers where there had once been cultivated land. To accomplish all this, to make every field have access to a road, a real road, for cars, not just a footpath, many, many trees were cut down that used to border on paths. The tree-lined paths that lead to the two communal meadows, once reserved for oxen and beasts of burden, are now completely bare. When people received their new parcels they cut down the trees and hedges that ended up within them, and many even removed the borders of foliage and knitted twigs and put up barbed wire fences. A number of people spoke of how strange the village seems now, how

foreign. New trees will be planted as time goes on, but for the moment
it is the bareness that impresses. One has a very palpable sense of the
destruction of a landscape; and of the loss of a way of life associated
with the woods.

A slogan about consolidation that has become popular is that "those
who lose win" (*el que pierde gana*). In other words, even if the fields the
engineers gave you do not total up in acreage to what you had before,
they are still worth more to you because all your property is now brought
together. Here people have in mind not just the time-saving aspect of
having a few large plots as opposed to many small ones, but its monetary
advantage. Those who are too old to work in agriculture, like those who
no longer live in the village, lease their fields to the handful of tractor-
owning families; now they can charge a proper rent for them because
they no longer have *cachines*, little pieces everywhere, but *buenas parcelas*,
good-sized parcels. For those who remain in the village and manage
some, if not all, of their property, the large new parcels are more convenient since there are no longer enough people around to attend to
different fields at one time. And, again, since no one wants to work hard
anymore, the consolidated fields—though certainly not large by American standards—are a must for the combine.

Yet, for all its apparent conveniences and advantages, consolidation
has produced certain inequalities and irrationalities. As one man put it,
"they say that those who lose win, but there are some who win 50,000
and some who win 500,000." The reference here is to the real estate
value of the land, and to a very particular set of events that point to the
element of chance in the outcome of consolidation. Just after the fields
were consolidated a woman who no longer lives in the village managed
to sell a plot located on the edge of the settlement for 500,000 *pesetas*.
Another woman, expecting to earn as much, put up for sale a plot she
had just received with consolidation, which was located at some distance
from the settlement; and she, to her disappointment, could not find
anybody who would pay more than 50,000 *pesetas* for her property. The
plot near the settlement could, and probably will, serve one day as the
location for a summer house, since it is easily linked into the water and
sewage system that already exists in the village. The plot that lies at a
distance from the settlement has value only as agricultural land, and
such land is not hard to come by.

Thus the engineers have unwittingly created a kind of inequality in
landed values that makes some people the holders of potentially very

marketable land and others of virtually unsaleable land. When the engineers rated all of the village's lands, with the help of a few villagers, they took only the productive value of the land into account; the plots people have received with consolidation are no doubt as productive as the ones they had before, but their real estate value is another matter. Now that there is a summer retreat right across the highway from the village and the offspring of villagers themselves desire a summer home, a *chalet*, the demand for land near the settlement has grown and will continue to grow. Those fortunate enough to have received parcels close to the village houses will benefit enormously, while those who have not will be no poorer, but no richer either. It is no wonder people use images from the lottery to talk about consolidation, speaking always of how so-and-so "won" or "lucked into" certain properties.

Quite apart from the new inequalities relating to real estate, there are other, perhaps less dramatic, inequities that have come about since consolidation. One of the rationales behind the old agrarian regime had been that everyone ought to have land of every type—at least a meadow, a garden plot, a field to grow rye, a field to grow chick peas, maybe even a field for wheat or oats. The plots were scattered, partly through the effects of destiny and inheritance, but also because of the idea that it was better not to have all of the harvest in one small area which a sudden burst of hail or frost could destroy. The scattering and mixing of the plots of every family created a kind of web that forcibly brought people together into a community.

The aim of the engineers who drew up the plans for consolidation was to fashion nice, square fields out of the long thin strips and jagged, hardly regular, plots that had existed before. This, as village people noted, was more easily done on paper and on a flat desk than on the land; a few of the new fields are on slopes that are hard to work, whereas in the past all the plots had been molded to the land's curves and contours. The notion that everyone ought to have a little bit of land of every type made no sense to the engineers, and they instead gave people their new fields where they had previously had the greatest concentration of plots. When we were at the threshing grounds one day with two women who were sifting chick peas with a sieve, one of them noted that they had very few chick peas this year. Had it not been a good harvest, I asked. No, it wasn't that, she told me; it was just that, with consolidation, they no longer had the type of land appropriate for growing chick peas. They had gotten many fields good for grain, sandy land, but hardly any of the thick clayey land that was ideal for chick peas. Before, she said, you had a bit of every kind of land. Now there are people who don't even have a little land close to home to plant "four onions."

Areas that had been extremely fragmented, like Tras las Casas, where chick peas and garlic were grown, or especially El Pical, once a collection of lush miniature gardens, are now the property of a few families. These are areas that are close to the settlement, where every family used to have some land, and which everyone recognizes now should not have been consolidated. A kind of equity reigned before, which had taken form slowly through the years, and a single gesture across a page has erased it. In El Pical, where there are fifteen plots now, there had been fifty-one. The intensively worked gardens have disappeared and been replaced with expanses of barley and oats that are harvested with the combine. Only La Viña Arriba, another patch of tiny gardens, was not consolidated, because all who had land there rallied together to have it excluded on grounds that it was too close to the settlement. With the other areas near the houses there was a failure of solidarity.

Now that every field has access to a road there is no longer any need, or excuse, to cross a neighbor's field to reach one's own. So long as all the fields formed part of a mosaic it was understood that such crossing over was inevitable, and this made for conflicts and arguments as much as it did for reciprocity and a certain sense of community. On the one hand, there were always problems with passing teams and carts causing damage to the crops, for which a rancorous neighbor was sure to ask for recompense. Yet, on the other hand, there was a sense that no one, whatever degree of self-importance he or she possessed, could remain aloof from his or her neighbors. The very layout of the land prevented it. Consolidation, of course, represents the very opposite of such a conception; it frees the landholder of all servitudes, all ties to the community, and makes each field a world unto itself. It even makes self-importance possible, so that all can think themselves earls.

The day after we arrived in the village we went with the *vecera*, the communal herd of cows, to the common meadow of El Coto. (In general the village's common lands have remained intact despite consolidation.) We followed the straight path, now considerably wider but shadeless, and soon arrived at the meadow. Balbino, a friend and informant of many years, was there and we slipped into conversation easily. How were his daughters and his sons, we asked. All were fine; the two married daughters were on vacation, one in Cadiz, the other in Alicante, and the eldest daughter, a nurse, was working as usual; the older son was studying to be an agricultural engineer, the younger son was in the army. We were somewhat taken aback to hear that his daughters were on vacation; in previous years they returned every summer to help with the harvest. And the harvest? I asked. They didn't have that much sown this year, he said, and most of what they had, except for the barley and oats, would be harvested with the combine.

There is an irony to the fact that there is no longer much manual work to be done in the village at harvest time. Balbino went on to talk about the *paro*, the terrible unemployment in the country, which had reached 20 percent, and about how gloomy things looked for the young. Would his sons find work, he wondered. Now they can't even return to the village, because mechanization has made the family system of working the land almost obsolete. It's not like before, he said, when you mowed everything with the scythe and you had a lot of *cachines* everywhere. Then a family with five or six offspring could live off the land. Today not only can they not return to the village, but there is no work to be had in the cities. Suddenly, he shook his head. "Spain is lost"— *España está perdida*. These were words I was to hear again, from other people, in the course of the summer, sometimes with reference to the current political regime, but usually, as here, to speak of the poignancy of Spain's loss of its rural past.

This is a time of transition for Spain. The political transition from dictatorship to democracy is only one, and the most apparent, of the transitions taking place. In the interstices another transition has been unfolding, which in the long run of Spanish history is of great moment: the transformation of a rural society into an industrial society. That transformation, now in its final stages, is one of the forces behind the economic crisis so painfully visible in Spain today, for unemployment, inflation, declining opportunities. More subtle, but no less important, are the social and cultural changes, even rifts, that have occurred, which one can observe from the vantage point of a microcosm like Santa María.

I noted at the start that, after a summer in Santa María, I had begun to get the feeling that the place somehow belonged less to its inhabitants than to the outsiders who now pass through on vacations. The creation of an urbanization across the highway, "Sunnywoods," has had something to do with this situation, for its people go to Santa María to buy milk, rabbits, and eggs, and a few to attend mass on Sundays. Though

one or two ties of friendship have developed between the people of Santa
María and the people of Montesol, there is enough antagonism to make
for some fierce name-calling when soccer teams from both places play
against each other, as they did at the village fiesta. Montesol, with its
prefabricated houses and orange-yellow streetlights, which cast an eerie
glow on the horizon every night, has become an indelible part of the
landscape and social reality of Santa María.

Yet its people are not the only outsiders who have entered the village's
orbit. In Santa María itself, two houses have been bought by outsiders,
two that are village property have been rented for yearlong use, and one,
this past August, was let to an Asturian couple at what village people
thought an exorbitant price by an emigrant from the village. The number
will no doubt increase as times goes on. Then there are the city people
who pass through on weekends, to picnic by the village dam, or in its
meadows, leaving refuse behind as souvenirs.

Curiously enough, however, given the number of outsiders who come
and go in the summertime, no one in the village has tried to capitalize
on the situation in a big way. There are no hotels, no restaurants, no
shops, just a small canteen, as it is known, which is associated with one
faction in the village, and a Teleclub, which is associated with the other
faction in the village, and is open for business most evenings and Sundays
throughout the summer. Only in the riverside villages, which are close
to highway intersections, like Barrio de Nuestra Señora or Puente Villarente, does one finds such commerce, and particularly the discothèques
which young people frequent—but then these villages have always been
more in contact with outsiders than Santa María, once secluded by its
woods.

The fact that people from Santa María do not particularly cater to
the outsiders that come and go through the village says something, I
think, about the community and the values that still persist there. There
is more to this indifference than simply a lack of funds. Attitudes toward
time, work, and the land are changing, as we have seen, but for all that
something of the old European peasant ethic has remained intact. This
is the same ethic that is behind what John Berger has called the French
peasantry's "in-built resistance to consumerism" as well as what Juliet
Du Boulay has characterized as the Greek villager's "basic reluctance to
buy and sell at all."[1]

This ethic finds its clearest expression when village people over forty
criticize what they consider to be the core values of the younger urban
generation, and of the new Spain. I remember a woman being critical

of her daughter and son-in-law, both of whom have white-collar jobs, because they felt they earned too little. After they left I came to drop off the scraps for the pigs and she repeated their complaint to another woman who happened to be there. "It's all vice"—*todo es vicio*—she said; rather than be happy with what they have they want more.

If there is one word that epitomizes for the old the way of life of the young it has to be *vicio*. The vices of the young are that they want too much, spend too much, and still don't have enough. It is often said of the young that they don't know how to enjoy themselves without spending money. They have to go to the discothèques to dance, people will say, instead of getting a dance going in the village square on Sundays, as was the custom in the past.

For people long accustomed to the moral economy of the village, with its customary forms of reciprocity, cooperation, and exchange, the materialism of their own offspring easily takes on the appearance of greed, ambition for ambition's sake, vice. Yet, while the older generation decries the money culture that their children have adopted, they are the first to admit that many features of that culture, if not its core values, have found a place in village life. There is more money in the village today than ever before and, as people frequently note, more prosperity, perhaps too much prosperity for everybody's good. Virgilio put it this way: "Today since everybody has more, everybody wants to be more" (*Es que ahora al todos tener más, todos queremos ser más*). And María added, "There is more arrogance now, one takes care of things alone in one's own house, one doesn't ask anything of one's neighbors" (*Ahora hay más orgullo, se arregla uno solo en casa, no se va a pedir nada al vecino*). Though they are not outside the money culture, the older people at least have an awareness of the moral and social implications of having too much— for they remember a time when there was too little—an awareness that is generally lacking in their urbanized offspring.

Yet the contradictory prosperity of Spain seems here to stay. Already those who are inheriting the earth in Santa María have started to build spacious *chalets*, swimming pools surrounded by cement walls, and rose gardens. Their ancestors were woodcutters, but they will be earls. Such is the shape of things to come. Or so it appears.

This book is about a different Spain, an old rural Spain that I caught sight of as it was retreating from view, in which the past was more of a presence than the future. In years to come it is not to Santa María del Monte that I will return but, more and more so, to Santa María del Condado.

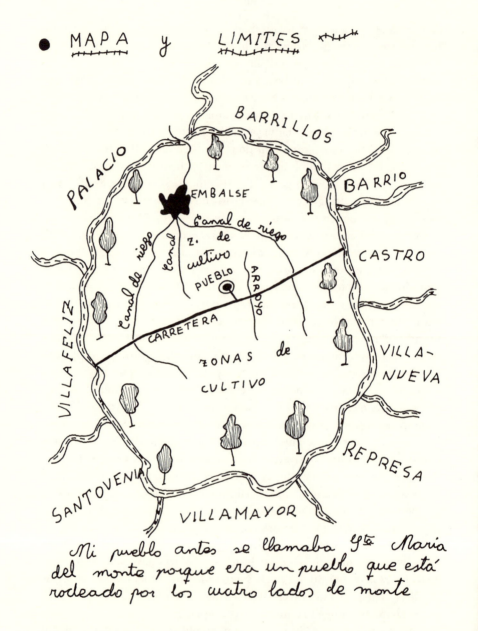

Map 9. A local vision of Santa María around 1970, surrounded by trees and other villages, as drawn by Leandro Carral, then in the eighth grade. The caption reads: "My village used to be called Santa María del Monte because it was a village that is surrounded on all four sides by woods."

Appendix A

✛

Two Life Histories from Santa María

What follows are two life histories I collected in Santa María in the summer of 1984. In the course of fieldwork I gathered many life histories, through both informal conversations and taped interviews. But it occurred to me later on, as I wrote this book, that it would be an interesting project to get people to write down their life histories themselves, in the form of texts. So when I went back to Santa María in 1984 I asked two people, a man and a woman, to write their personal *historias* down for me. Both did so willingly, apologizing for mistakes in grammar and spelling, but clearly enthused by the task, for they are people who have thought their lives through, so that the personal past has crystallized into a story. Since this book is built up out of local family and village texts, I have thought to include these two personal documents, which give a sense of how individuals, rather than collectivities, construct their own past. Another sort of history could be written about Santa María and its people based on such texts, and I hope to write it some day.

The authors of these texts spent a good many years away from the village and in this sense their experience is not really typical of most people from Santa María who are in the same age group. Leonardo, who was seventy-eight, spent twenty-six years in Madrid, working as a milkman, returning to the village in middle age, while María, who was sixty-three, spent her childhood living in a few different villages and several years of her adult life in the mining town of Ciñera. But by virtue of having been away, both have a perspective on life in the village in the past and on their own childhoods that makes their accounts especially perceptive.

Leonardo was the oldest of six children and not only had to take care of his siblings but also work at his father's side in the fields from the ages of nine or ten. His account of his life is organized around the comparison of the hardships of his childhood in the rural world of the village and what he conceived of as a much easier life in Madrid. The work he had to do in Madrid delivering milk would have been "hard work for someone who doesn't know how to work, but for me it was like sewing and singing," he writes. This comparison leads him back, at the end of the account, to how the village itself has changed since he returned in the 1950s to take up life as a farmer once again. Here Leonardo's story ends, and he concludes by remarking that the *pueblo* has all the comforts of the city now and is no longer the *pueblo* he left in his youth. His last sentence about how the *pueblo* receives "all those who visit us as if we were all one family," is in part a reference to us, the anthropologists—how we, though strangers, have come to be received like family—but more generally refers to the openness of the *pueblo* to the outside world in the present in comparison to the closed community of the past.

María organizes her account around the theme of her life as a calvary, where the series of mishaps and disasters that she suffers—losing her mother as an infant, being treated harshly by her stepmother's family, working at hard physical labor from the age of ten, marrying young, losing her husband who died in shame for a robbery he never committed, supporting her young children as a widow, keeping the family together after her second marriage—become for her stations of her own cross. She views herself as a woman of strength and independence, from her tomboyish climbing of trees as a girl to the way she took the family to the mining town of Ciñera after her second marriage when she saw that her mild-mannered husband refused to exercise paternal control. It is her endurance that she emphasizes, giving a sense of what life was like in the old rural world of the village from a woman's point of view. Together with Leonardo's account, it forms a portrait of a way of life that both of them, like so many others of their generation, have lived to see disappear.

Life history of Leonardo Mirantes Rodríguez

A little history of a Leonese farmer born on the sixth of November in the year 1906. My childhood passed like that of all children except that since I was the oldest of six siblings I had much to do, especially babysitting, which is why my childhood was not a happy one, because when I was nine or ten years old, and not very developed, I already used to go help my father with the farming chores, for my mother when not pregnant was with the little ones and even though she wanted to she couldn't help us; for the same reason I lost a lot of days at school but thanks to the teacher Don Quintin who gave us classes from six until eight in the evening, and I had a great passion for it, and that was where I learned to read, count, and write. In this manner my childhood passed and by the year 1920 I would go hoe in the *ribera* [the riverside villages to the north] earning 5 or 6 *reales* a day and a meal, working from sunup to sundown in the spring, and in the winter going to the woods to cut heather with my father to take to the bakers, who in those days would pay a *real* for each pair of fagots and now they cost 36 *pesetas* a fagot and no one wants to go cut them.

In those years I also worked on the highway that was being built from Barrio to La Vecilla; there we worked nine hours [a day] and they paid those who received the most 15 *reales* and those who received the least 13 and in that group was I, very happy because at the end of the week I would bring home almost 80 *reales*. I also used to go mow with the scythe in the mountains, thirty kilometers from here; there they paid us 20 *reales* a day and food and drink, which was what mattered most to us. This happened to me in the years from 1920 to 1927.

In the year 1927 I thought of emigrating to Madrid in search of work and with the help of some relatives of my grandmother. And here is where the important part begins. I had never left the house and didn't know what a train was because I had never ridden one. My father took me to León and placed a cousin of his in charge of taking me to the station and he gave me instructions for when I arrived in Madrid to take a taxi, which I had no idea what it was, and that he [the taxi driver] would take me to the address that I gave him and he explained everything I had to do. But I was carrying some sausages that my grandmother had given me to take to her relatives and I was carrying them in the suitcase, but they had filled me with so much fear that I wouldn't let the suitcase out of my hand. I got to Madrid and came out with everyone; I didn't take a taxi because I had never ridden in one and suspected that it would take me to an unknown place, this because they had filled me with so much fear, but I did take a horse and buggy, because I felt it would be safer and in this way I arrived at the house of my boss, who was my boss for twenty-six years. Here my history changes and a new life begins for me which has been much better than my previous one.

Leonardo in front of the Puerta de Alcala in Madrid after arriving to take up
work as a milkman (1927)

In Madrid I started working as a milkman delivering to the houses,
very hard work for someone who doesn't know how to work, but for
me it was like sewing and singing; there I started to wake up, to be
associated with many good people, especially my boss and companions
who always gave me good advice; because of that, even though we didn't
have a single day free, not even Sundays, we lived very peacefully until

Leonardo in his kitchen garden

the year 1931 when the Second Republic was proclaimed, then we had a little more freedom. I found myself a girlfriend and was no longer so bored, and in the year 1934 I was married to Ramona, the wife who thank God I have today, and there we got an apartment for 40 *pesetas* where we spent our best honeymoon. I earned 7 *pesetas* and 75 *centimos* a day and we lived very happily; then we took on a lodger to sleep and do his clothes for a *peseta* a day. But here the good part ended because on the 18th of July of 1936 the Civil War began and for us the work ended because there was no milk to give out; then they took us to the front as militiamen of the worker's union [Union General de Trabajadores]. I was at the front in Madrid, Casa de Campo, Clínico, and Villaverde, and during this time I would return, with permission, to see my wife, but in May of 1938 they took me to the front in Teruel; there we had a bad time of it, but I can still talk about it, for a few companions we never saw again.

I ended up as a prisoner, luckily, because they brought me to León, to San Marcos [the monastery], which was then a concentration camp, but in ten days I was back at my parents' house; of my wife I knew nothing because the two zones were cut off, so that until the war ended I was here in the *pueblo* and she in Valencia with a sister cashing the pension that was left to me as a widow or missing person until the war ended. I went to look for her in Madrid and in her parents' house in Teruel without finding her after the war ended.

After all this we began again like the first day. The boss called me and we returned to Madrid. We worked well, my wife helped me with the deliveries, earning some money when she could and at the same time doing her chores at home. In this way [we continued] until the year 1950 when the company began to decline due to the fact that the boss was sixty years old and he married someone who was twenty-seven; she let the business go downhill. And we in the year 1953 returned to the *pueblo*, working at agriculture which I always liked a lot, and now having a good time here because we have all the comforts, because this is no longer the *pueblo* that I left in the years of my youth but a *pueblo* with more culture and receiving all those who visit us as if we were all one family. This is my little history.

Goodbye until always.
[Santa María del Condado, 6 September 1984]

Life history of María Rivero Morán

Santa María del Condado, 3 September 1984.
My name is María Rivero Morán. I was born in Villaseca de Laciana on the 26th of May in 1921. From that day sixty-three years and three months and a few days have passed which have been my calvary. I had an older sister who died before I was born, then another was on her way when my mother became ill and the sickness advanced with her

pregnancy. My mother died with the girl in her arms and I was left, a year-and-a-half old, with my father and a mute sister of my father's, who helped my father raise me.

A few days after my mother died my father came to Santa María with the two of us. To earn our bread he took on the *vacada* [the herding of the village's calves and unyoked cows]; all day he was in the woods and valleys. My aunt would take me with her to bring him his meal in the woods. During the summer the flies bit up the calves and they would hide in between the trees and not come out, and this even though they put bells on the wilder ones; and my aunt would carry me in her arms, putting me down to run tie up the calves. One day I began to follow a path between heather and brush and many sticks. Afterwards they couldn't find me and night was setting in. At last they found me; this happened in Los Alamos.

After a year they took it [the *vacada*] away from him because of envy. We had to go to Barrillos. After about nine months they had a son who died because she gave him her breast. The day of the anniversary of their engagement my stepmother, as they say here, died. During the time that she lived, my stepmother's stepmother and half sister that she had, she was with her father and her stepmother and her half sister and a brother of hers who was called Evaristo. She loved me but those two bitches couldn't stand the sight of me. That Velarmina [her stepmother's half sister] did me much harm. She would pinch me and be left with the piece of flesh in her hand. The grandmother would grab me under her arm and pretend that she was going to throw me to the pigs; I was left unconscious. My father arrived, he had to give his wife a purge, and he saw me in that state. He suffered a lot. Another day I fell in the village fountain and a woman pulled me out; the water jug weighed more than I did. When I got home they wrapped me in a skirt and put me in bed. My father couldn't even love me in front of them, they used to say that he didn't love his wife, that he loved me more. We both suffered. Then she died and my father stayed there another year; afterwards back again to Castro. He remained there another six years. My aunt rented a house; during the summer she would go home very early at three o'clock in the morning and my father was with the calves.

They would leave me in bed with a fried egg for breakfast. I would eat it and go out the window. I would go wherever I wanted to, [to snatch] nests, to climb the poplars. For fear of being hit the boys my age didn't dare to, and I would do it since my father couldn't see me.

But when he would return they would tell him; he would get upset, but there was nothing he could do. When I was a little older I would go *apañar* [mow with the sickle] for a calf my father bought which cost 14 *duros*; after a year he sold it and it brought him 64 *duros*. I was maimed from lugging the sacks. I would throw them over my shoulder and would put my hand on my left side and my ribs sank. My father took me to León to La Portuguesa, someone who fixed bones. He took me three or four times, since my bones were so tender; I was ten years old.

My father would return at ten o'clock in the morning. He would go out again at three o'clock in the afternoon until the evening. In the afternoon I would take him his five o'clock [meal], a small can of sardines and a *cuartillo* of wine and a little bit of bread for the two of us; my aunt was given food for the day. Afterwards we came back here to Santa María and he would go to Castro every day. During the summer he left the house at half past two in the morning to ring the bells at three o'clock and he would return at ten o'clock to nap and let the sheep rest in Castro. He returned again to Santa María at three o'clock in the afternoon to ring the bells and would sleep once more; this was during the summer. In the winter he would leave in the morning and return in the evening; this until he returned to Santa María and the calves here. He bought a cow and we would form a team with a neighbor. I had to go plow and do more than I could, and go help him take the *vacada* to the woods and in the afternoon go find him. During the summer there were many storms. One day we were caught in one in Las Cruces. We had to come back through the rye fields because it was hailing; the cold seemed to cut through me. I was soaked through many times.

I was growing up. When I was fourteen years old I found myself a boyfriend. I was married at sixteen and a half. A year later my husband, Eliseo, that was his name, became ill. After a year of being married we had our first child, whose name was Andrés. I was in labor for three days and was very ill; afterwards my breasts weren't well, they broke open, they had to hand-feed me. After four months he [Andrés] died; then Luis came after two years and then Valentina after two years, a little more. We were married for eight years and for seven [he, Eliseo, was] ill. He was operated on his stomach and was fine, but because of a calumny that was raised against us, that he had robbed three *heminas* of wheat from some cousins, the *guardia* [civil guards] came; they hit him and my father, they put handcuffs on Eliseo which left their mark on him during his life. He was so struck with grief that it finished him off. I was very ill the day Valentina was born. The guards came, I was very upset; what if the child died from drinking my milk? The guards in the *portal*, I and the girl very ill. They wanted to take Eliseo and my father to jail, all because of a misunderstanding. I rose above it, but he wasn't able to: he died.

I was left with my father and my two children, three years a widow, all the weight of the house on me. The children were small and my father was ill. He would go with the *vacada*. I had to go harvest rye and cut hay, chop wood, pull out heather trunks to sell, and cut heather branches, sticks, and young trees to get something to eat. Once, going with branches and young trees down a valley called Vallincueva of Represa, upon turning the path the yoke broke in half and one cow was left with the cart, pulled off the ground; that is, it was just hanging there. The world seemed to be falling on me. My cousin Isolina was with me. Turning, we saw another team and two people; they were coming from plowing. Seeing me so young and in such straits, they felt compassion for me and consoled me, saying that they would remove the yoke from their cows and that I should continue on my way. They took the broken yoke and their cows unyoked and the plow on their shoulders. They were from Represa; they used to call them Los Cuberos. Later, after about two hundred meters, there was a canal. It was very horrible, the only thing left was the width of the cart; the cows with that large yoke were frightened, all the weight fell back and they were lifted up from their heads. I didn't think this would end happily, but I saw a man with a team and he helped me. We went out to the highway of Moral. Then it was nightfall; we slept in an inn in Santibañez, in a manger a half-meter wide, Isolina and I, we both had to face the same side if not we couldn't sleep. The following day we went to Puente Villarente. I had already sold my load.

The year after my husband died I went to the mines, to work at unloading coal. I was there for two months; the boss wanted to get involved with me, and I came back to Santa María. I went to [work on] the highway gathering rocks; I also had to leave that for similar reasons. After three years I married Virgilio. He is a brother of the other one [her first husband]. We have a son named José Antonio. When Luis was growing up, he and his father, which is how they call him, didn't get along. His father wouldn't tell him what to do. I would say to Virgilio, tell the boy, the two of you go together to the fields; he would say that

María in her pear grove

he can go where he likes, I know where I have to go. It's not that, I would say, you have to go together wherever you need to. If the boy would say, let's go to a certain place, he would say, you go. In other words, I could see how things were going, and I decided to go to Ciñera where I had cousins. I got excited about it. Their father went first to the mines; he was there for three days and returned home again. We went on in this way for a year, until one day, doing accounts, we were worse and worse off. He asked me if I could go look for work for him. I went. Luis entered the mine and he [her husband] worked in construction. I didn't want to be separated from my children or my husband, so I found work for both of them. Then Valentina, José, and I went, because my father had died and my aunt before my father.

After a year there I became ill. I had many complications. Just after marrying Virgilio I was operated on my appendix. When I was fifteen I noticed a bulge in my right side; it kept getting larger. Ever since I had Valentina I've suffered a lot from colic; every so often I would get an attack, for two days I would be ill. Then trying to raise the children. But it got worse and worse until I couldn't manage anymore. In 1978, in September, they operated on me twice; the following year they operated again, in October once more, in the same place, removing my appendix and uterus.

Today I am taking a lot of medication. I take it for my circulation and pressure, for the colon to aid my digestion, for my nerves, and two spoonfuls of syrup when I go to sleep to make a bowel movement. They say that it has to be this way as long as I live. This is what I remember; there are many other things I don't remember because I've lost much of my memory. But my children are three, two sons and a daughter, two daughters-in-law and a son-in-law, and five grandsons and three granddaughters, who are all wonderful. They are worth all I have struggled. They all esteem me, that is, they esteem my husband and me. And it's been twenty years since my husband suffered a thrombosis. He's doing fairly well; from that time he's had a pension. I thank God for letting me write these lines.

María Rivero.

Appendix B

Population and Economy

Table 1

The People of Santa María del Monte, 1978 and 1984

Total residents '78	'84	Names and relations	Remarks
2	—	Cornelio M = Dosinda S	Moved to León after retirement; visit frequently
—	2	Temines S, Bernardina R (mother)	Moved back from Bilbao in 1981
3	3	Heriberto G = Ana M, Joaquín (son)	Parents retired; son owns tractor
2	1	Maria Cruz C [= †Cosme S]	Husband died in 1978
2	2	Bienvenido M = Felipa R	Nearing retirement
3	3	Dionisio G, Irene and Matías (children)	Widower of many years; his children were raised in his sister's household, below
2	2	Froilán M = Hermelinda G	Nearing retirement
2	2	Evangelina S, Ángeles S (niece)	
4	5	Victoriano C = Otilia R, Aurelio and Carlos (sons), Miguel (grandson)	Parents retired; Carlos works with a tractor; Aurelio is the village shepherd; a daughter died in 1978 and her son returned to live in the village

Table 1 cont.

Total residents '78	'84	Names and relations	Remarks
3	3	Secundino M = Aracelis Ll, Santiago (son)	Parents retired; son owns tractor
3	3	Maria Amparo R, José Antonio and José Luis M (sons)	Widow; older son works with tractor; he married in 1981, but wife and son live in wife's natal village
2	2	Felicísimo Ll = Geronima M	Former shepherd; retired
2	—	Emilio M = Adoración S	Moved to León after retirement; visit frequently
3	3	Fernando R, Inés R (sister) = Sixto M.	Soon to retire; Sixto was one of my best informants
3	2	Germán C = Maximina S	Youngest son went to study in Madrid in 1981
2	1	Paulino A [= †Natividad C]	Retired; wife died in 1982
5	5	Petronila P; children: Clara, Delmiro, Amable, and Aladino C.	Widow since 1956; youngest son is bedridden
2	—	Eladio A = Cónsula C	Retired; live half the year with their children in Madrid
2	2	Nicanor Ll = Victoria M	Retired; children have built a summer home in their share of the house
5	7	Ángel G; Agustín G (son) = Anita F, Ana María, Ángel, Miguel, and José (grandchildren)	Retired widower; son owns tractor; one of two village families with young children
2	2	Nicéforo C = Bonifacia C	Retired; once was the village shoemaker
4	2	Balbino Ll = Hilaria C	Nearing retirement; village *presidente* since 1979; two youngest sons have moved to León to study; I lived with this family in summer 1978

Table 1 cont.

Total residents		Names and	
'78	'84	relations	Remarks
8	9	Teógenes S = Emilia R; Ceferino S (brother); Arístides S (brother) = Vicenta R (sister of E.), Luz del Mar, Alberto and Almudena (children); Constantino R (brother of E.)	This complicated double household is second in village with young children; together, they own two tractors and work close to a sixth of the village's arable land
3	4	Láutico R = Julita Ll, Manuel and Juan (sons)	Father now retired; sons work with tractor; Juan returned from Paris in 1980
2	2	Luis P = Honorina M	Retired
2	2	Vitaliano Ll = Evarista M	Retired
3	3	Venerable P = Isolina P, Miguel (son)	Nearing retirement; former blacksmith
2	2	Baudilio Ll = Natividad M	Retired
1	—	Aurora P	Retired; now lives in León with son, who rents out the house in the summer
2	2	Fuencisla M, Nicanora C (daughter)	Widow
1	—	[†Jose P]	Widower, died 1980; left no direct heirs, inheritance now disputed among 48 nephews and nieces
2	2	Olegario S = Felicidad R	Retired
3	3	María Jesús = Juan, María Ester (daughter)	Schoolteacher for the five village children
2	2	Victorino S = Ester M	Nearing retirement; *presidente* from 1963 to 1979; they own the village cantina
3	2	Germiniano C = Nieves M	Youngest daughter moved to Madrid in 1979
2	2	Virgilio Ll = María R	He is retired; their children have all built summer houses on their shares of the house property

Table 1 cont.

Total residents '78	'84	Names and relations	Remarks
4	4	Hermógenes S = Guadalupe G, Carmen, Julia (daughters)	Daughters now have jobs in León
2	—	Mónica C [= †Secundino S]	Husband, the former cartwright, died in 1980; she now spends half the year with her daughter in Bilbao
4	3	Anibal M = Victoria S, Felipe (son)	Other son left to study in Carrion de los Condes in 1983
2	2	Justa Ll, Saturnina Ll (daughter)	Widow of many years; her husband was tailor; lives with oldest, unmarried daughter
2	—	Don Efigenio M, Humilde M (sister)	Former village priest; moved to his home town of Barrillos in 1982; new priest lives outside of the village, says mass on Sundays and Thursdays only
2	2	Leonardo M = Ramona	Retired; one of my most reflective informants
2	2	Epigmenio C = Amalia M	Son is building a summer house in the village

Table 2

Landholdings Worked by the Households of Santa María del Monte, before and after Consolidation

Household size	Before		After		% owned	Remarks
	Hectares	Parcels	Hectares	Parcels		
9	66.1	484	60.1	53	30	2 tractors
4	27.9	238	28.9	25	30	tractor
5	23.8	170	23.6	24	25	tractor
7	25.0	202	23.7	22	35	tractor
3	22.1	182	19.0	15	65	tractor
3	17.1	129	16.5	16	20	tractor
4	14.8	133	13.6	18	70	
5	16.3	139	16.8	11	65	
3	15.3	107	14.8	20	30	
3	12.1	104	13.0	9	45	
2	13.3	106	12.3	16	40	
2*	10.2	104	8.9	11	50	
3	10.7	90	8.9	13	27	
2	8.8	81	9.7	10	100	retired
2	7.2	59	6.8	10	75	
2	6.1	57	6.1	9	65	
2	6.8	50	6.0	8	95	
2	7.7	59	8.0	8	100	
3	7.3	61	6.5	7	100	
2	7.0	57	5.9	8	100	retired
4	6.2	60	3.9	10	25	
2	5.0	38	4.2	4	55	retired
2	5.0	40	5.3	6	100	retired
4	3.4	38	3.4	5	100	living in León
2	3.9	39	3.2	5	100	retired
1	4.3	44	3.3	7	50	retired

NOTE: The landholdings listed include both the parcels *owned* by the household and others rented or, more often, borrowed from relatives or friends. The column "% owned" indicates the approximate percentage actually owned by members of the household. This and the following tables are based on the maps and lists of property-owners compiled in the course of land consolidation by the Instituto de Reforma y Desarrollo Agrario (IRYDA) of León, as well as on personal observation.

* This is the household whose lands are shaded in Maps 7 and 8.

Table 3

Land Distribution in Santa María del Monte, Classified by Size of Holdings
(1978 and 1984)

	<1 hectare	1-2.99	3-4.99	5-9.99	10-15.99	Total
1978						
No. of holdings	29	64	30	18	7	148
Total no. of parcels	156	1,059	870	995	601	3,681
Total area of holdings (hectares)	15.23	128.12	110.10	121.09	84.98	459.52
1984						
No. of holdings	41	68	23	16	6	154
Total no. of parcels	61	210	92	97	41	497
Total area of holdings (hectares)	20.61	139.10	88.66	103.81	70.17	422.35

Table 4

Land Use, Santa María del Monte
(1978)

	Hectares	% of total area
Cultivated land (private ownership)	476	21.8
Meadowlands	30	1.4
Woodlands	1,662	76.2
House sites and dam	13	0.6
Total	2,181	100.0

Appendix C

Distribution of Responses to
the Ateneo Questionnaire of 1901-1902
in the Province of León

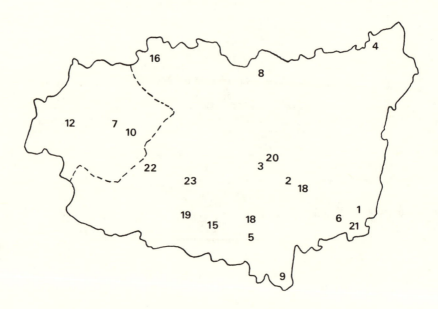

The Ateneo questionnaire sought out information on customs and practices relating to birth, marriage, and death in all the provinces of Spain. The responses are remarkable documents. Unfortunately not all of them are extant. Only a copy of the responses, written on thousands of thin slips of paper, survives in the Museo Nacional de Ethnología in Madrid. For a history and an analysis of the questionnaire and responses, see Lisón Tolosana, "Una gran encuesta de 1901-1902." The responses for León are:

1. Sahagún	13. Mansilla de las Mulas
2. Roderos	14. Various places (unspecified)
3. Virgen del Camino	15. La Bañeza
4. Oseja de Sajambre	16. Villablino
5. Laguna de Negrillos	17. El Bierzo (general)
6. Gordaliza del Pino	18. Pobladura de Pelayo García
7. Congosto	19. Destriana
8. Rodiezmo	20. León
9. Valderas	21. Grajal
10. Bembibre	22. Rabanal del Camino
12. Villafranca del Bierzo	23. Astorga

The numbers are those given in the responses themselves. There was no number 11; number 14 includes responses from unspecified villages throughout the province; number 17, El Bierzo, refers to the western region of León bordering on Galicia (marked by the dotted line on the map).

Afterword

✛

A LATE Midwestern spring—yellows and reds at last, the forsythia in tangles, tulips raising their heads. I am tweezing the dried branches around the green vines. As I work I worry because I really don't know what I am doing. I never expected to have a garden of my own. I grew up on an undistinguished edge of New York City in a series of noisy apartments smelling of onions and green peppers frying in olive oil. I don't recall my parents having any houseplants until I was a teenager, when they went out and got two tall lanky, palmy things at 20th Street and Seventh Avenue to match the glass and chrome modern furniture they had saved for years to buy. This garden in Michigan came with the house that came with the job as professor that came with the dissertation that came with the life shared with people in Santa María.

Why didn't I listen better when people in Santa María talked about how they took care of their gardens? I am remembering how carefully people in Santa María tended their fields, their wheat, their rye, their garbanzos. They were consummate gardeners, and out of their gardens came huge cabbage heads, garlic that was fruity enough to eat raw, tomatoes as sweet as mangos, and roses so opulent they were embarrassing. And I am remembering how unhelpful I was to them.

The Englishwoman who lived here before has left me this inheritance: an undulating garden full of violets, peonies, daisies, and lilies, as well as a miniature vegetable plot. I am doing my best to tend to my "four flowers," as people would say in Santa María. This is my second spring in this garden. My first spring I didn't dare touch anything. I couldn't seem to keep the names of the different flowers straight in my head. But this year it has all started to make sense, and my mind is wild with the names of plants. A few days after cutting back the vines, I bring home samplings of "leopard's bane," "bleeding heart," phlox called "orange perfection" and "the king," "snow in summer," "evening primrose," "dragon's blood," and "lady's mantle." I tell the names to my son Gabriel, almost five, and he repeats them to his friends: "Look! Do you know what that plant is called? It's called 'don't forget me.' " People from Santa María always close their letters with the words, "Goodbye from these friends who don't forget you."

I am remembering how fascinating it was to learn from people in Santa María a whole language in Spanish associated with the agricultural world that I had not known before: the names for tools—*arado* (plow), *escabuche* (hoe), *hoz* (sickle), *guadaña* (scythe)—the names for crops—*avena* (oats), *cebada* (barley), *centeno* (rye), *trigo* (wheat)—the name for the bread that always came in a round loaf as big as the circle between your arms—*la hogaza*. Although Spanish was my mother tongue, I had to start from scratch in this new language.

As I worked in my garden, I began delicately. I didn't want to get my hands dirty. At first I didn't touch the soil. I remembered how leathery my skin felt after I helped harvest potatoes in Santa María. I tried to just use my hoe. But when one of the little pansy plants would not stand straight in the space I had dug out, I gingerly patted it into place with my hands. With that, I lost the fear of getting dirt under my fingernails. I put my hands to work.

A few days later I went to have my yearly physical with a nurse-practitioner employed by the university. We got to talking about our gardens and she told me that this year she would wait until the middle of May to plant anything. She had lost much of her garden the year before, planting too early. I remembered how people in Santa María worried about the first cutting of hay left to dry in the fields in May. Would it rain and the neatly arranged piles of hay turn to worthless mush? I remembered the stories of people who couldn't sleep from worrying about their tender crops. Now, every day, I have been checking the weather and going out to see the plants I have put in the soil. Will the basil make it? I am told it is not "frost hardy." Did I not wait long enough to plant the tomatoes? On my way out of the office, the nurse-practitioner reminded me that on my birthday this year, when I turn thirty-five, I must call to make an appointment for my first mammogram.

I begin this afterword in a pastoral mood not unlike that which suffuses this book as a whole. That mood soon passes as the days get suddenly cold, windy, and rainy, and I return to my desk to think of what to write here. It is time to open the folder in which I have kept the reviews of this book and sit down to read them again, one by one, as the sun goes in and out of the clouds.

Over the years I have had ambivalent feelings about my first fieldwork
in Santa María and the writing of this book. I have felt ashamed of the
blindnesses of that early stab at fieldwork. I have felt ashamed, too, of the
silences, cowardices, and repressions I now see in the book. But more
than anything else, it is the separation I made between my work and my
life that bothers me; the links certainly were there, but they were sub-
merged in the intellectual project. I find myself no longer willing, nor
able, to maintain such a separation between my personal and ethnographic voices. In my efforts to come to terms with this book, I want to
reflect upon the reasons why I wrote it as I did and what it meant at a
time in my life when I was coming of age emotionally and intellectually.[1]

Despite my self-criticism, this afterword should not be read as a mea
culpa. It is meant to be a meditation on the conditions under which we
come to know—and not know—what we know.[2] For there was much
that I knew then that I didn't allow myself to know, that I kept deliberately at the periphery of my field of vision. It is those sanctioned igno-
rances that I now want to recover. What for? Paradoxically, to write both
for and against history, to be accountable and to be free, to reveal my
shame and to assuage it. For a long time I tried to disown this book, and
yet I am glad it is being given the chance of a second life in paperback.
With this coda, I want to reclaim it and, no longer ashamed, let it go.

I dedicated this book, with its focus on the traditions and memories of
those who were structurally in a grandparent relation to me, to my own
four grandparents. While my motives were not altogether clear to me at
the time, I have come to believe that my quest to understand "the presence of the past" in Santa María was a link in the quest to recover, even
stabilize, my own migratory family past, which during the last three generations has been marked by a series of diasporas and exiles. My grandparents had always been, for me, a key link in this quest. Both sets of
grandparents migrated to Cuba shortly after the 1924 Immigration and
Nationality Act closed the door to Jewish emigration to the United States
from southern and eastern Europe. My maternal grandparents, who were
Yiddish speakers, became fluent in Spanish. Even after they migrated to
the United States following the Cuban revolution, their primary language, the language of the family, was Spanish. I had an even more direct, if ambivalent, link to Spain on my father's side of the family: my
paternal grandparents, who came from Turkey, were Sephardic, descen-
dants of Spanish Jews expelled in 1492, who spoke Spanish with the
rhythms of Ladino, or Judeo-Spanish. There is a town in western Spain

called Béjar, a likely place of origin for my last name, and working in Spain for me was partly about a desire for memory, a community of memory, in which I would find that sense of being rooted in a place that had been so absent in the recent history of my family. As one reviewer noted, my book provides not so much a strong sense of time as of place.[3] It seems odd to me now to think that there I was, a child of a confluence of diasporas, and that it was precisely this diasporan consciousness that I denied and made invisible in my first fieldwork in Santa María.

When I was growing up, I urged my grandparents to tell me stories about their past, and through those stories I tried to construct, or imagine, a community of memory. In my early twenties, when I went to Santa María to do my fieldwork, I likewise sought out the stories of village elders and tried to understand the meaning of the recent changes in Spanish life from their vantage point. It is a common pattern for women ethnographers to position themselves in the daughter role in relation to the people with whom they work.[4] Instead, I took on the granddaughter role, and so thoroughly identified myself with the elderly generation of peasants that one reviewer expressed a sense of confusion about which interpretations were mine and which were those of my subjects.[5]

I had very little interest in the stories of the younger generation of village people who had left for the city and were much closer to me in age. In the same way, at home I was unmoved by the stories my parents or their generation had to tell of their lives in Cuba and of their emigration with their young families—of which I, too, had been a part—to the United States. This was narrow-minded of me, to be sure, and showed how limited a notion of communities of memory I had, but I was convinced at the time that only the grandparent generation could link me, two generations later, to a past that would otherwise be cast away in what I called "the wreck of oblivion."

So obsessed was I with not forgetting that I focused my attention on the ways in which the past was still a presence in Santa María. Moreover, my sense of attachment as a granddaughter was sufficiently intense that I experienced the loss of many of the old rural worldviews, and the tender mortality of those who held them, as a personal loss. Unwittingly, I became enmeshed in an "allegory of salvage" by which, as an anthropologist, I sought to capture, authorize, and redeem the disappearing past in the text that inscribed that disappearance; and, inevitably, there was more than a touch of "imperialist nostalgia" in the way in which I mourned the passing of an age in Santa María from the outpost of rootless (but not yet postmodern) urbanity.[6] It is in the epilogue, in particular, that I am most guilty of invoking the historical scenario of "a relatively recent period of authenticity ... followed by a deluge of corruption, transformation, modernization."[7]

But, on the whole, it seems to me that I was groping toward a more subtle understanding of the way in which the present is continually being formed and transformed in a complex negotiation with the inherited structures of the past. In the discussions of the division of the house and the web of use-rights, I made a clear effort to go beyond notions of inevitable modernization in order to articulate a perspective on the relations between system and agency, structure and process, hegemony and resistance, the terms of analysis which have since become central to the recent convergence of anthropology and history. That such a contribution was at least implicit in my work was evident to an anthropologist surveying the range of ethnographic studies carried out in the 1980s, which sought to understand the emergence of different forms of political economy in response to capitalist development strategies that underdeveloped as much as they developed particular regions.[8]

Ultimately, though, and undeniably, the text that emerged from my work was an unclassifiable kind of collage of past and present that went against the grain of conventional ways of writing both ethnography and history. A historian, who was sympathetic to this blurring of genres and historical moments, wrote about the book: "This is not your ordinary social anthropology, for Behar is more concerned with the past than with the present. ... This is not your ordinary history either. Our attention is directed to the soul of this community more than its body."[9] My aim had been to blend ethnography and history to create a hybrid text that would eliminate the border between the disciplines, but the mixture was not to everyone's liking. The harshest criticism I received from both disciplinary sides was that I had done neither good history nor good anthropology.

In retrospect, I worry less about the issue of whether the book fell between the cracks of the two disciplines than about the fact that I didn't go far enough in working through the implications of my efforts to make the telling of stories the core of my text. Even so, the stories made their way into the book surreptitiously, whether in the telling of the Doña Francisca saga, or the account of the haunting of Filomena by her own past actions, or the narrative of how the village forged its own history in its confrontation with the centralizing Spanish state. I am thankful for the reader who perhaps did not intend to compliment me when he wrote, "the author . . . is certainly a good story-teller and the book feels at times more like a romantic tale than a stodgy monograph."[10]

If the person I am now were writing this book there would be a more conscious and explicit effort to attend to storytelling as a form of knowledge and writing.[11] I can now envision quite a different book based entirely on life histories. It was only toward the end of my first period of fieldwork that I began to realize belatedly that such a thing would have been possible. After my return visit to Santa María in 1984, I quickly added two life histories as an appendix to the book, a move I knew to be inadequate, but which I felt at least gave the text an open-ended quality, a sense of possibilities still left to explore. Yet I followed those histories with a second appendix on population and economy, reflecting the marked ambivalence I felt between reflexive storytelling and social science modes of representation. By the time this book was going to press in 1985, I was in Mexico, beginning new work focusing on the speaking voice and the telling of life histories. This Mexican work later influenced the more self-reflexive turn of my recent writing on Spain. Like many anthropologists of my generation, I have been inspired by the discussions of the last few years about the ways in which ethnography might be rethought and revitalized, and in my current work I find myself increasingly using blended narratives that fuse ethnographic, reflexive, and feminist voices.[12]

Why was I so obsessed with local village and family documents, with the written word, when I wrote this book? For certainly I was obsessed, excessively so some readers pointed out, with the figure of the "literate peasant" and with the archives kept by rural people. One's old obsessions are not always easy to explain. To start with, this is a book by a young woman who was in the process of trying to figure out what it might mean to be an anthropologist. A recent convert to anthropology, I had arrived in the field after rebelling against the exclusions of the "great books" tradition I had been steeped in as a literature student. My understanding of Spain was based on what I had been taught about Spanish literature of the "Golden Age," and I had spent a semester in Madrid in order to "perfect" my Cuban Spanish. In anthropology I expected to find something more than venerated books. That something more was life experience, the stuff, as I saw it then, that went into, and came before, the making of books. So what did I do? I went to a Spanish village and discovered that country people, too, had literary texts of their own! The last thing I had expected to find in Santa María, as an anthropologist, were texts, and I think I was thrilled at the idea of being a literary renegade purposely working on elucidating the meanings of the sort of writing that I knew would not have counted as literature.

Yet in Santa María I found myself in a realm of Spanish society that neither life nor literature had prepared me for. Cutting myself loose (or so I thought) from my literary and personal moorings, I took on such subjects as family inheritance, village political organization, and communal land tenure. At the time I felt that I was taking on "hard" subjects, the sort of subjects that did not come easily to me, the sort of subjects that I considered most outside of myself.

Although the anthropology of women had emerged by the mid-1970s, I chose not to study women in any detail. I didn't want to be viewed as a woman who only studies women, a subject that I characterized at the time as too "easy" and too close to me (and since there was not yet much institutional support for women's studies, these views remained unchallenged). In reflecting on my work now in the context of reading and teaching works of ethnographic writing by women, it seems to me that for academic women the burden of authorship is always very heavy. The need to earn credentials in order to be taken seriously has placed women, until recently, in an uneasy position with regard both to studying women as subjects and to experimenting with self-reflexive and personal voices in their writing.[13]

I dealt with my uneasiness by writing a general village ethnography in which my own presence and existential concerns were muted. I tried to offer a vision of gender that was balanced and relaxed, nothing too "strident." A vague feminist debt compelled me to include a short, dutiful section on the position of women, but the greater part of my efforts were focused on the male world of the *concejo*, for which I sought out elderly male interlocutors to talk to about the practices of the past and the meaning of the documents that their ancestors had left behind. Positioned as I was in the granddaughter role, and yet also securely part of a couple, *la pareja*, with my husband David Frye, it was possible for me to work with men as easily as I worked with women. This perhaps made me less attuned to the construction of gender as an issue than I would have been in a more sex-segregated society. Yet I think there is no escaping from the fact that I glossed over the difficult issues of male dominance in the *concejo* and the control of sexuality through social and religious norms. Lacking the confidence to undertake a critique of the honor and shame

paradigm that had so unabashedly stereotyped and orientalized Mediterranean gender relations, the most I allowed myself to do at the time was
to say politely that the paradigm was not relevant to Leonese gender
relations. But, as a reviewer noted, it would have been much more useful
intellectually to have challenged the paradigm itself.[14]

Another important absence in the book, as reviewers repeatedly
pointed out, was religion, a subject I dealt with only briefly and then
rather distantly. On my return to Santa María in 1987 I decided to fill
this gap in my work, and talked with village people and local priests
about how their religious views had been shaped by the Spanish Civil
War and, more recently, by the collapse of the Franco regime. In addition, I sought out narratives about their attitudes toward death.[15]

Why had I not focused on religion earlier? At the time, I felt very
uncomfortable about religion. Uncomfortable is actually too soft a word
—what I felt was tremendous anger that I dealt with by adopting an
attitude of studied indifference. The anger stemmed from a family feud
about my relationship with David. In all the years I was working in Santa
María with him, my family refused to accept David because he was not
Jewish. My father, who disowned me for a year, told me I was not to
bring David home. It took my paternal grandmother's death to change
things. Abuela died while we were nearing the end of our year's stay in
Santa María in 1981. It saddened us that David had not been allowed the
chance to meet Abuela and he wrote a long letter of condolence to my
father. To our surprise, when we got back to New York at the end of the
summer, my father welcomed David and apologized to him; my mother
had kept the folded and refolded letter in her handbag like a prized
possession.

But at the time I was doing my first fieldwork, no such reconciliation
had yet taken place, and I wanted to have nothing to do with religion
and its intolerances. The ethnographer is a "positioned subject," whose
own "lived experience both enables and inhibits particular kinds of insights."[16] In my case, I deliberately turned away from the study of religion, burying myself instead in the details of inheritance and the common
lands: a denial that inscribed a displacement (though my interest in the
relation between parents and children was perhaps a partial effort to not
turn away totally from the life experiences in which I was caught at the
time).

In addition to the unresolved personal issues, there was a more general
intellectual problem at the root of my discomfort with religion that also

remained unresolved for me. At the time I was doing my research, there was a highly developed anthropological tradition of studying "primitive religion," but only recently had anthropologists begun to work on the "great religions" and, in particular, on Catholicism.[17] At the time, I think I knew more about Zande witchcraft, as described in the famous work of British anthropologist Evans-Pritchard, than about the significance of the Trinity or the practice of Jewish mourning customs.[18]

While my personal situation led me to reject religion as anything even remotely positive, it still felt odd to me to be living in such a thoroughly Catholic country, where the idea of other religions was, just ten years ago, something that most village people could barely fathom. I was never quite sure how best to position myself, but I tried in my role as ethnographer to participate in every aspect of village religious life, short of taking communion. I couldn't find much wisdom on these matters in the work of anthropologists, who had plumbed deeply into the symbolism of a wide range of religious rituals in the former colonies of Europe while remaining silent about the problems of studying the Christian European world.

Spain, after all, had enforced religious orthodoxy by expelling its Jews at the end of the fifteenth century and its Muslims just over a hundred years later, by carrying out a vast missionary campaign in the New World, and by fusing Church and state power during the Franco period. How was one to go about studying this complex knot of religion, politics, and national memory? How was one to do so without lapsing into the black legends that "have made Spain over according to the outsiders' images," or invoking the national character stereotypes that have led to "inadvertent dehumanization"?[19] The answer, at the time, escaped me; this was a subject I characterized not as "hard" or "easy," but as simply beyond my reach, and I looked the other way.

The cover photograph I chose for the book, showing my friends Hilaria Carral and Balbino Llamazares posing on either side of a cart of oats, together with the set of photographs inside the book, provides a striking visual record of what I allowed myself to see and not to see during the period of my first fieldwork. When I showed Hilaria and Balbino the cover in 1987, they said that they must look really poor to people in the United States. I realized that I had very few pictures of them other than in peasant guise; I had rarely photographed them in their street clothes or Sunday best. Only as peasants could they fit into my argument and be

made visible there. I think that what one does as a photographer is intimately related to what one does as an anthropologist. I have very few
pictures of the younger urban generation of people from Santa María,
who might have posed for me next to their cars, or in the bars or factories
where they work, or in their small spotless apartments with the parquet
floors, the macramé bedspreads, and the baroque ornaments. As long as
I positioned myself to see only what was on the verge of passing away,
this first generation of urbanites remained invisible to my camera.

As I noted in the opening pages of the book, I arrived in Santa María
at a time when the people who stayed behind in the village were trying
to understand the presence of the past in the present. What I saw less
clearly was that this was also a time, just after the death of Franco, when
everything having to do with rural life and rural traditionalism was being
denigrated and devalued. The rural exodus, Vatican II, and the undoing
of all forms of censorship and repression inherited from the Franco regime had created the conditions for changing, or even eliminating,
"anachronistic" customs in the name of modernity. As I look back now,
it seems to me that the countryside was in the process of being reconcep-
tualized as a site for play rather than work. The creation during the early
1980s of Montesol on the other side of the highway from Santa María del
Monte, which I, as a defender of the realm of traditional, found utterly
disdainful, served as a dramatic, discomforting example of how new conceptions of the countryside were coming in to challenge the old.

By showing an interest in the old ways and allying myself with the
older generation in the role of sympathetic granddaughter-anthropolo-
gist, I gave a certain validity and importance to the realm of the traditional in Santa María at the very moment when it was being depreciated
ideologically. Anthropologists have a tradition of identifying with the
plight of those they perceive to be marginalized, and I was no exception.
My identification with the Santa María elders and farming families certainly boosted people's self-confidence and made them feel that, if they
had nothing else, at least they had "history." But, inevitably, I think I also
heightened people's own sense of being mired in the past, of being backward and underdeveloped.[20]

Only later, upon my return to Santa María in 1987, did I begin to see
a rather different perspective emerging with the realm of the traditional
being reclaimed by the politics of regional autonomy and the search for
authentic local cultures.[21] People in Santa María told me that, in the years
I had been away, reporters had come, asking to hear traditional wedding

songs and to see the old farming implements. No longer would the foreign anthropologist be the only one who made rural people self-conscious
about themselves as "other." In the fifty years since the end of the Civil
War, Spain has changed from a society where half the population was
employed in farm work to one where only fifteen percent of its people
still work the land. Under these conditions, the ethnographic salvage mission has taken on a new immediacy in the wider society, which now looks
to the realm of the traditional (if at all) with the folkloric curiosity and
distance of people gazing at an exhibition of gleaming artifacts cleaned
of dirt and sweat.

It did not occur to me at the time I was doing my fieldwork that the
rural traditionalism I was seeing might itself have been a peculiar kind
of artifact of the early Franco period and its nationalist glorification of
rural life. "The common image of the country [as] an image of the past
and the common image of the city [as] as an image of the future" was
inverted in Francoist ideology, which blamed cities for infecting the nation with the vices of modernism and called for a return to peasant life
and rural Catholic values.[22] Ironically, the postwar hunger and scarcity
of an isolated Spain led the Franco regime in the 1960s toward a program
of rapid industrialization aided by foreign investment (largely from the
United States in exchange for four naval bases), the opening up of the
nation to tourism, and the remittances of emigrants gone to work in
northern Europe.

The peasants who had been the object of so much romanticism were
transformed into a marginal people, whose values and culture offered
little worthy of emulation to a modern, urban Spain. In Santa María, the
people I knew seemed to be plagued not by nostalgia but by a sense of
having lived anachronistically for so long. They had stuck to the old rural
values lauded by early Francoist ideology, but what good had it done
them? The new Spain was turning out to be urban, consumerist, and
hedonist—exactly the opposite of the old rural Spain.[23]

This book, whatever else it may be, remains as a partial (in both senses
of the word) portrait of those people who stuck to a rural way of life and
a rural set of values long after most of Spain had moved on. It also remains as a shadow portrait of the anthropologist who thought it important to listen to what those people had to say. The people of Santa María
and I have since moved on, too. I could not photograph Hilaria and Balbino on either side of a cart of oats anymore; they now live in the city of
León, where they help their children and grandchildren run a quintes-

sentially Spanish breakfast place, a *churrería*. Departures and deaths have led to the closing of other homes, some of which have been transformed from farmhouses into vacation homes. I am told that the village fiesta in late August, when everyone tries to return from wherever they may be, gets bigger and more elaborate each year.

The image of Spain currently being exported abroad is that of "the new Spain." In the last few years there has been a spate of articles in the American media about how Spain is "letting its hair down," many of them written in connection with the work of filmmaker Pedro Almodóvar, who is described in *Newsweek* as "a taboo-smashing director [who] revels in the new Spain."[24] In the same article, Almodóvar is quoted as saying in regard to the Francoist past, "I deny the existence of that past. There's something I hate about memories in general, even sentimental memories. They don't allow you to develop, to move on. I deliberately construct a past that belongs to me. In that past, Franco doesn't exist." The notion of obliterating the past, of moving on, of not standing still, is the philosophy behind the new social movement in Madrid that is often summarized in the phrase, "la Movida." Almodóvar is said to be "the personification and spiritual godfather" of "la Movida," a movement that celebrates "life after Franco, sexual freedom, punk rockers, sunshine, great food, good times, and the general explosion of creative expression that a nation experiences when moving from a dark past of repression into the light of freedom."[25]

For Almodóvar, the key feature of the new Spanish mentality is the unmooring of the individual from all forms of repressive power and their punitive moralisms in the quest to recuperate "the inclination toward sensuality, something typically Mediterranean."[26] Although Almodóvar idealizes Mediterranean sensuality and sets his films in a hypermodern Madrid, he was born in a rural Castilian town in La Mancha, a place where, as he has said, "the absence of pleasure is total, absolute."[27] Against such peasant austerity, he sets out to imagine a new Spain devoid of Franco and the recently outgrown rural past.

An essential part of becoming modern for Almodóvar and others of the younger generation in Spain involved leaving their village communities behind and denying all historical legacies. This book offers a counterimage, dwelling on the life of those village communities that were left behind, erring too much on the side of not forgetting. Perhaps because I never had a village to leave nor return to, it seemed to me that to choose to remember nothing of what those villages were like would have been too annihilating.

For my part, I am glad to have lived in a little village before I knew what would become of me, before I knew I would one day try to take care of a garden of my own. If I had listened better to my friends in Santa María, maybe the tomatoes and the basil would be thriving now. Chamomile, so rampant in Santa María, will not prosper in my garden no matter where I put it. The thyme I've planted in a few places seems to be doing well, though. Thyme grows wild in the hills around Santa María; maybe after a few years it will also grow wild here.

Ann Arbor, 1991

Notes

✝

Introduction

1. See Johannes Fabian, *Time and the Other: How Anthropology Makes Its Object*.

2. Both Evans-Pritchard and Kroeber were early spokesmen for the convergence of anthropology and history; see E. E. Evans-Pritchard, "Anthropology and History," and A. L. Kroeber, *An Anthropologist Looks at History*. For an evaluation of the interrelations between anthropology and history, see Keith Thomas, "History and Anthropology," and "The Tools and the Job"; I. M. Lewis, "Introduction" to *History and Social Anthropology*; Pierre Goubert, "Local History"; Alan Macfarlane, "History, Anthropology, and the Study of Communities"; Emmanuel Le Roy Ladurie, "Recent Historical 'Discoveries' "; Bernard S. Cohn, "Anthropology and History: Towards a Rapprochement"; Natalie Zemon Davis, "Anthropology and History: The Possibilities of the Past"; Carlo Ginzburg, "Anthropology and History: A Comment"; and Lawrence Stone, *The Past and the Present*, pp. 3-44 and 74-96. Of interest too is Marc Bloch's *The Historian's Craft* for its insights on sociological history.

A few prominent examples of ethnographic history are Emmanuel Le Roy Ladurie, *Montaillou*, Natalie Zemon Davis, *Society and Culture in Early Modern France*, William A. Christian, Jr., *Local Religion in Sixteenth-Century Spain*, and Carlo Ginzburg, *The Cheese and the Worms*.

Despite the convergence of anthropology and history in recent years, there is still room for misunderstanding, as shown in the words of even so perceptive a historian as E. P. Thompson, who points out that "the discipline of history is, above all, the discipline of context; each fact can be given meaning only within an ensemble of other meanings." Curiously, he seems to think that this characterizes history as opposed to anthropology or sociology, which he does not distinguish very well, when in fact it is what history and anthropology should have in common. Cf.

E. P. Thompson, "Anthropology and the Discipline of Historical Context," p. 45.

3. For a historical approach to tribal society, see Renato Rosaldo, *Ilongot Headhunting, 1883-1974: A Study in Society and History*. In *Bwiti: An Ethnography of the Religious Imagination in Africa*, James W. Fernandez studies the development of the Bwiti cult in the light of colonial history and Fang interpretations of the past. For an ethnohistorical study of the involvement of peasants in anarchist rebellion, see Jerome Mintz, *The Anarchists of Casas Viejas*. For a global study emphasizing the interconnections between the history of Europe and that of the non-Western world, see Eric Wolf, *Europe and the People without History*.

4. For some examples, see Maurice Bloch, "The Past and the Present in the Present"; Jane Schneider, "Peacocks and Penguins: The Political Economy of European Cloth and Colors"; Sydel Silverman, "On the Uses of History in Anthropology: The *Palio* of Siena"; Clifford Geertz, *Negara: The Theater-State in Nineteenth-Century Bali*; Joan F. Mira, *Vivir y hacer historia: estudios desde la antropología social*; Marshall Sahlins, *Historical Metaphors and Mythical Realities: Structure in the Early History of the Sandwich Islands Kingdom*; J.D.Y. Peel, "Making History: The Past in the Ijesha Present"; Frank Salomon, "Shamanism and Politics in Late-Colonial Ecuador"; Gillian Feeley-Harnik, "The Political Economy of Death: Communications and Change in Malagasy Colonial History"; and Richard Price, *First-Time: The Historical Vision of an Afro-American People*.

5. Archivo de San Isidoro de León, Documento real, no. 325.

6. Though the village is now called, for most purposes, Santa María del Condado, after the municipality of Vegas del Condado to which it now belongs, I use the village's old historical name here of Santa María del Monte. For a discussion of what this change of name means, metaphorically, to people in Santa María today, see the Epilogue.

7. For such a critique, see John Davis, *The People of the Mediterranean: An Essay in Comparative Social Anthropology*. Henk Driessen makes a similar critique of Andalusian studies in "Anthropologists in Andalusia: The Use of Comparison and History." In his essay, "La fábula de Alcalá y la realidad histórica en Grazalema," Ginés Serrán Pagán offers a suggestive historical consideration of Julian Pitt-River's *The People of the Sierra*. Carmelo Lisón Tolosana's *Belmonte de los Caballeros* is one of the few accounts, for Spain, that integrates historical materials into the ethnographic study of social structure and economic life.

8. See, for example, the work of Susan Tax Freeman, *Neighbors: The Social Contract in a Castilian Hamlet*; Joseph Aceves, *Social Change in a Spanish Village*; Richard Barrett, *Benabarre: The Modernization of a Spanish Village*; Stanley H. Brandes, *Migration, Kinship and Community: Tradition and Transition in a Spanish Village*; William A. Douglass, *Echalar and Murélaga: Opportunity and Rural Exodus in Two Spanish Basque Villages*; Joseph Aceves and William Douglass, *The Changing Faces of Rural Spain*; and Davydd Greenwood, *Unrewarding Wealth: The Commercialization and Collapse of Agriculture in a Spanish Basque Town*.

9. See the personal accounts of Richard Muir, *The English Village* and Pierre-Jakez Hélias, *The Horse of Pride: Life in a Breton Village*, and Frederic O. Sargent on "The Persistence of Communal Tenure in French Agriculture."

10. Marc Bloch, *French Rural History: An Essay on Its Basic Characteristics*, p. 247.

11. Fernand Braudel, "History and the Social Sciences," p. 20.

12. Arno V. Mayer, *The Persistence of the Old Regime: Europe to the Great War*, pp. 4-5. Cf. Albert Soboul, "Persistence of 'Feudalism' in the Rural Society of Nineteenth-Century France," and Dietrich Gerhard, *Old Europe: A Study of Continuity, 1000-1800*.

13. Davis, "Anthropology and History," p. 275.

14. Antonio Domínguez Ortiz, *Sociedad y estado en el siglo XVIII español*, p. 410. There were, of course, regional variations to the enclosure movement in England, and the debate continues as to its consequences. Among many others, see the useful introduction to the subject by J. D. Chambers and G. E. Mingay, *The Agricultural Revolution, 1750-1880*. Although the "enlightened" ideas surrounding the agricultural revolution did reach Spain, and were much discussed in the "Sociedades Económicas," they had little practical effect on agricultural life until the nineteenth century. On this subject, see the classic study by Richard Herr, *The Eighteenth Century Revolution in Spain*. Bartolomé Bennassar notes, "in interior Spain the technical relations of production changed little and slowly" (*The Spanish Character*, p. 63). For an excellent study of agrarian reform in Spain in this century, see Susan Friend Harding, *Remaking Ibieca: Rural Life in Aragon under Franco*. I would like to thank Susan Harding for allowing me to read her work while still in manuscript.

15. Bloch, *French Rural History*, p. 197.

16. See, for example, Fernand Braudel, *Capitalism and Material Life,*

1400-1800, p. 232 and David Gilmore, "Anthropology of the Mediterranean Area," p. 177.

17. Let me emphasize that these remarks pertain to *central* León. In
the rich agricultural plateaus, toward Old Castile to the south, such as
El Páramo, Los Oteros, and Tierra de Campos, villages are larger and
economic divisions are more marked than those which occur further
north.

18. For further discussion of this peasant ethos in the context of early
ethnographic conceptualizations of the peasantry, see Robert Redfield,
The Little Community and Peasant Society and Culture, pp. 61-66.

19. See Freeman, *Neighbors*; Randall McGuire and Robert McC. Netting, "Leveling peasants? The Maintenance of Equality in a Swiss Alpine
Community"; Lisón Tolosana, *Belmonte*; and David Gilmore, *The People
of the Plain*.

20. For a further elaboration of the contrasts, see Julian Pitt-Rivers,
"Introduction," *Mediterranean Countrymen: Essays in the Social Anthropology of the Mediterranean*, and for an elaboration of the unifying features
of European social organization, see Susan Tax Freeman, "Introduction,"
to "Studies in Rural European Social Organization."

21. On the dangers of generalizing about the Mediterranean, see James
W. Fernandez, "Consciousness and Class in Southern Spain" and Michael Herzfeld, "The Horns of the Mediterraneanist Dilemma."

Chapter 1.
A Portrait of a Landscape and of a People

1. Conversation with Manuel Robles, 29 June 1981. Just as we reached
the meadow, I wrote these remarks down in a little pad I usually carried
around with me. They are necessarily inexact, but the turns of phrase,
which were still fresh in my mind, are those of my informant. The
original Spanish of this and all other quotes in the book can be found
in Ruth Behar, "The Presence of the Past: A Historical Ethnography of
a Leonese Village."

2. For a description of the method of harvesting grain with the sickle,
and for other aspects of the traditional technology of country life, see
Dorothy Hartley, *Lost Country Life*, pp. 175-176; for León, see the description in José Antonio Fernández Flórez, "El 'Becerro de presentaciones,'" pp. 330-331. José Millán Urdiales mentions that the sickle passed

out of use in the grain harvest in the 1920s in the nearby area of Gradefes as well (*El habla de Villacidayo* [*León*], p. 39). For a history of the association of sickles with women's work and the scythe with men's work, see Michael Roberts, "Sickles and Scythes: Women's Work and Men's Work at Harvest Time." For the resistance to the use of the scythe in the grain harvest in France, see Bloch, *French Rural History*, p. 47, and for its slow acceptance in most of Europe by the nineteenth century, see Braudel, *Capitalism and Material Life*, p. 245.

3. William A. Christian, Jr., *Person and God in a Spanish Valley*, pp. 22-23.

4. My sources on the Reconquest and repopulation of Spain are Claudio Sánchez Albornoz, *Despoblación y repoblación*; Luis García de Valdeavellano, *Curso*; and J. González, "Reconquista y repoblación." For an insightful discussion of the frontier in Spanish history and its later repercussions see Teofilo Ruiz, "Expansión y crisis." For the role of women in the Reconquest of Spain see Heath Dillard, "Women in Reconquest Castile."

On settlement by *pressura* and *scalio* see García de Valdeavellano, *Curso*, pp. 239-241 and José María Mínguez Fernández, *El dominio del monasterio de Sahagún*, pp. 67-84.

5. Seigneurial properties, of course, existed, as shown in García de Valdeavellano, *Curso*, pp. 235-236, but they overlaid the system of small proprietorship and were made up of many small properties scattered about various villages. García de Valdeavellano discusses the different settlement patterns of the north and south of Spain, which are certainly at the heart of the distinction between the *labrador* of the north and the *jornalero* of the south.

6. Casildo Ferreras Chasco, *El Norte de la Meseta Leonesa*, p. 203. For the wider context of land fragmentation in northwestern Spain see T. Lynn Smith, "Fragmentation of Agricultural Land in Spain."

7. Ferreras Chasco, *El Norte*, pp. 245-246.

8. Ibid., p. 243.

9. For an excellent study of the periodic agrarian crises of the old regime in Spain see Gonzalo Anes, *Las crisis agrarias en la España moderna*, and for the crises of mortality see Vicente Pérez Moreda, *Las crisis de mortalidad en la España interior*. Angel García Sanz has produced a detailed study of these crises for the area of Segovia (*Desarrollo y crisis del Antiguo Régimen en Castilla la Vieja*). See Domínguez Ortiz, *Sociedad y estado* for a concise statement on the problems of the rural world in

the eighteenth century which takes into account not only the short-term crises but the long-term cycles that were the theme of Emmanuel Le Roy Ladurie's now classic work, *The Peasants of Languedoc*.

For the annual figures of births and deaths in Santa María del Monte, see Behar, "Presence," p. 416.

10. Behar, "Presence," pp. 416 and 419.

11. For the epidemic and famine of 1803-1804 see Pérez Moreda, *Las crisis de mortalidad*, pp. 374-390; Anes, *Las crisis agrarias*, pp. 401-423; and García Sanz, *Desarrollo y crisis*, p. 88.

For the phenomenon of the deserted village in France, see Jean-Marie Pesez and Emmanuel Le Roy Ladurie, "The Deserted Villages of France." I know of a number of depopulated villages in central León—Otero, Villanueva de Manzaneda, and Villazulema, all in the Torío River valley, which have disappeared since the eighteenth century, while Villamoña, San Martino, and Santiago de Villafría had disappeared much earlier—but they are far outnumbered by the villages that have continued in unbroken existence since the early Middle Ages. In the final chapter I discuss a legend concerning the village of Moral, which was depopulated in the seventeenth century and revived in the nineteenth.

12. Behar, "Presence," pp. 425-426.

13. Ibid., pp. 416-417, 421-424.

14. Taped interview with Felicísimo Llamazares, 31 March 1981.

15. There had been an earlier wave of emigration in the 1910s and 1920s to Argentina and Mexico, but the numbers who left were not large enough to halt the rise of the population in central León (the effects of this emigration were felt more sharply in the mountain villages lying to the north) and, unlike the later emigrants to Europe, those who left in this era rarely returned to Spain.

16. Behar, "Presence," p. 427. See Ferreras Chasco, *El Norte*, pp. 173-192, for an analysis of this demographic shift in the whole area of north-central León.

17. AGS, Expedientes de Hacienda (1597), leg. 112.

18. Ibid., leg. 113.

19. For this observation I would like to thank Teofilo Ruiz, who has often pointed out to me the medieval reverberations of contemporary forms of village life in León and Burgos. It is possible too that the anti-commercial ethic reflected in certain traditional forms of mutuality among Leonese peasants may be related to the uniquely Spanish concern for "purity of blood." The notion of "purity of blood" referred to the lack of any Jewish or Moorish blood, and the Jews and Moors were

associated with commerce and money. The peasants of northern Spain were largely outside the money economy and thus "pure of blood." This is a hypothesis that would require further study. See Bennassar, *The Spanish Character*, pp. 213-236 and 261-262, on the theme of "purity of blood" and Noel Salomon, *Recherches sur le thème paysan*, pp. 805-842, on the literary elaboration of the idea of the "pure" villager in the work of the Spanish playwright Lope de Vega.

20. Susan Tax Freeman, *The Pasiegos*, p. 239.

21. Christian, *Person and God*, p. 171.

22. Max Weber, "Capitalism and Rural Society in Germany," p. 370.

23. Taped interview with Sixto Mirantes, 5 June 1981. It will be noted that "four" (*cuatro*) is used locally with the meaning of "a couple, a few."

24. Taped interview with Láutico Robles, 12 March 1981.

25. Apeos de eredades, Santa María del Monte parish archive, 1716; AHDL, Fondo general, ms. 14259. As for the fortunes of the Salas Celis family, it is interesting to note that when Paula died in 1700 she left money to have three funeral services performed, each headed by eight priests, and followed by a further sixty masses for her soul; when Domingo died in 1707 his heirs could manage no more than fifty memorial masses "for lack of means and for owing [still!] the marriage portion of Paula de Celis his legitimate wife." Libro de difuntos, 1665-1822, Santa María del Monte.

26. Ibid.

27. Actas de concejo, 21 November 1869, Santa María del Monte.

28. Actas de concejo, 2 May 1869. In 1865 we know that there were fifteen households with two pairs each and seventeen with one, plus one with half a pair, four with one and a half and two with three pairs (Amillaramiento, 1865, Vegas del Condado municipal archive).

29. Actas de concejo, 5 October 1899, Santa María del Monte.

30. E. P. Thompson, "The Grid of Inheritance," p. 345.

31. For the cereal monoculture of León and Old Castile, and the predominance of rye in the poorest and coldest areas, see Domínguez Ortiz, *Sociedad y estado*, p. 178; for the poverty of most soils in León, and for the importance of rye even today in the northern half of the province, see Ministerio de Agricultura, *Mapas provinciales de suelos*, 1: 506-515. For the distribution of wheat, barley, and rye in central León in 1797, see Behar, "Presence," p. 420.

32. On the traditional rural economy of European villages, see George Casper Homans, *English Villagers of the Thirteenth Century*; B. H. Slicher van Bath, *The Agrarian History of Western Europe*; Bloch, *French Rural*

History; and Georges Duby, *Rural Economy and Country Life in the Medieval West*. The Leonese agrarian economy is discussed historically by Ferreras Chasco, *El Norte*.

33. AHN, Clero, 5516 (Apeos generales de Santa María del Monte, 1766). For livestock in central León in 1752, see Behar, "Presence," p. 420.

34. AHN, Clero, 5516; Libro de tazmía, 1779-1834, Barrillos; Apeo de las heredades, 1775, Canaleja; AHN, Hacienda, 7458 and 7462 (Provincial summary of the Catastro de Ensenada, "Número de ganados por especies y pueblos"). On the history of the family pig see Jean-Jacques Hémardinquer, "The Family Pig of the Ancien Régime: Myth or Fact?"

35. Apeos, 1721, Vegas del Condado. It is clear from this document that wine was not produced locally but imported.

36. AHN, Hacienda, 7457 (Provincial summary of the Catastro de Ensenada, "Número de individuos que deben pagar lo personal, por oficios y pueblos").

37. Ibid.; AGS, DGR, 1ª Remesa, 329 (Respuestas generales to the Catastro de Ensenada for the city of León); RAH, Censo de Aranda (1769) and Floridablanca (1787). In the responses to the Catastro de Ensenada survey, carried out in 1751-1753, the village of Villaobispo is included with the figures for the city of León, a fact which has probably inflated the number of *labradores* listed for the city.

38. See the articles for Ambasaguas, Barrillos, Devesa, and Santa Colomba de Curueño in Pascual Madoz, *Diccionario geográfico-estadístico-histórico*.

39. Conversation with Justa Llamazares, 17 September 1980.

40. Conversation with Don Gregorio Boixo, 16 May 1981. I thank Don Gregorio for his invaluable help in understanding the growth of cattle raising in the Curueño-Porma area and other changes which have taken place in the local rural economy.

41. Conversation with Justa Llamazares, 17 September 1980.

42. Taped interview with Láutico Robles, 12 March 1981.

Chapter 2
The Village House

1. Joseph Townsend, *A Journey through Spain*, p. 374.
2. Carlos Flores, *Arquitectura popular española*, p. 81.

3. In some villages in Palencia, for example, when people wish to modernize their houses, which in adobe areas universally means constructing a façade of brick rather than daub, they leave the old mud wall intact and simply cover it with another wall made of bricks and cement, in order thereby to maintain the adaptive features of the traditional house while giving it a modern appearance (M. Inmaculada Jiménez Arques, "Las casas de barro en Tierra de Campos," p. 5). The same is true for León.

4. For an interesting analysis of the evolution of the structure of the rural house in another part of central León, see Casildo Ferreras Chasco, "La Aldea del Puente," pp. 687-690.

5. See Cuestionario del Ateneo, Museo Nacional de Etnología, for a description of this custom in Riaño and other villages of northern León around the year 1901 (response II-D-b).

6. A note on the entry of the television into the village. The first set in Santa María arrived in 1965 and was brought by the owners of the village *cantina*. The second set was brought soon after by the village priest, who allowed all the children to come watch it at his house every night. He acted as censor, I was told, sending the younger ones home if a show or movie of uncertain morals came on the air. Then the television arrived for the village Teleclub. The Teleclubs are a national phenomenon and arose as part of a government effort to bring televisions, in other words, civilization, to the villages of the nation. The other houses have gradually acquired their sets since 1970 and now no house is without one.

Chapter 3.
An Archaeology of the House

1. In rural Galicia people are known by the names of their houses—for instance, "Pepe de Airexa" or "Antonio de Souto," where Airexa and Souto are the names of the houses, not the last names of Pepe and Antonio (Carmelo Lisón Tolosana, "La casa en Galicia," pp. 152-153). For Cataluña, see John H. Elliott, *The Revolt of the Catalans*, p. 31.

In most of Galicia the "philosophy of the house" consists of the view that the house is an indivisible and enduring monolith, which must be kept whole through the practice of impartible inheritance, though there are parts where partible inheritance is practiced (for the regional variations see Carmelo Lisón Tolosana, "The Ethics of Inheritance"). A similar philosophy is held by the Vaqueiros of western Asturias (María Cátedra Tomás, "Vacas y vaqueiros," pp. 37-48). Conversely, with respect to the province of León, where the predominant rule is division, in the areas of El Bierzo and Laciana bordering on Galicia impartible inheritance was practiced at the turn of the century, according to the Ateneo questionnaire of 1901-1902.

Of course, we do well to steer clear of facile dichotomies between partible and impartible inheritance. As H. J. Habbakuk pointed out years ago, "A farm divided among many heirs, one of whom bought out the interests of the rest, might for many intents and purposes look like a farm left to a single heir, but burdened with compensation for his younger brothers and sisters" ("Family Structure and Economic Change in Nineteenth-Century Europe," p. 4). What is important is to see what effects these systems have on family structure, household composition, relations between parents and children, and on general patterns of social, economic, and cultural life. This has been the aim of much of the work done in recent years on the history of the family. See, for example, in what is a very extensive literature, the collection of papers in *Family and Inheritance* edited by Jack Goody, Joan Thirsk, and E. P. Thompson; Rosamund Jane Faith, "Peasant Families and Inheritance Customs in Medieval England"; Lutz K. Berkner, "The Stem Family and the Developmental Cycle of the Peasant Family"; Natalie Zemon Davis, "Ghosts, Kin, and Progeny"; and the recent review article by Lawrence Stone, "Family History."

2. Equal inheritance is also found in the provinces of Soria (Freeman, *Neighbors*, pp. 67-71), Salamanca (Brandes, *Migration*, pp. 120-123), Zaragoza (Lisón Tolosana, *Belmonte*, pp. 161-164), and Valencia (Mira, *Vivir y hacer historia*). These accounts focus on the division of the landed property or on property generally, but do not go into detail about the division of the actual physical house.

3. Document in personal archive of B. Llamazares, dated 25 November 1950.

4. AHPL, Protocolos, leg. 639 (Antonio Sandoval, León, 1704), f. 71.

5. AHPL, Protocolos, leg. 1336 (Pedro González Osorio, Vegas del Condado, 1784-1788), f. 29.

6. Ibid., f. 30.

7. Ibid., f. 58.

8. Ibid., f. 56.

9. Cuestionario del Ateneo, Museo Nacional de Etnología, response III-A-b-2 for Sahagún.

10. Ibid., response II-B-b for Sahagún.

11. Document in personal archive of S. Mirantes, dated 28 December 1860.

12. Document in personal archive of S. Mirantes, dated 7 June 1863.

Chapter 4
The Idiom of Equal Inheritance

1. Lisón Tolosana, *Belmonte*, p. 164.

2. Harry L. Levy, "Property Distribution by Lot," p. 43.

3. In Chapter 15 I will discuss at greater length such topics as the attitude of rural people toward historical documents, the keeping of records, and the power of the written word.

4. Inbentario o cuerpo de bienes [de Mateo Ferreras], 12 March 1886, p. 19, personal archive of S. Mirantes.

5. Ibid.

6. Levy, "Property Distribution by Lot," p. 45.

7. Hijuela de Nicolasa Ferreras, 23 March 1887, personal archive of S. Mirantes.

8. Cuerpo de vienes [de Toribio Mirantes], September 1891, p. 15, personal archive of S. Mirantes.

9. Inbentario de Mateo Ferreras, p. 25, personal archive of S. Mirantes.

10. The complex subjects of wood and woods receive detailed treatment in Part Four on the web of use-rights.

11. Cuenta, partija y dibision de vienes [de León Villapadierna], 8 March 1888, p. 58, personal archive of T. Sánchez.

12. Inbentario de Mateo Ferreras, p. 35, personal archive of S. Mirantes.

13. Ibid., p. 27.

14. Hijuela paterna de Toribio Mirantes, 20 December 1854–5 May 1859, p. 6, personal archive of S. Mirantes.

15. Inventario de León Villapadierna, p. 40, personal archive of T. Sánchez.

16. Inventario de Ignacia Rodriguez, personal archive.

17. On the concept of "metaphorical extension," as I am using it here,

see the important work of James W. Fernandez, "The Mission of Metaphor in Expressive Culture" and "Syllogisms of Association."

18. Document in personal archive of B. Llamazares, undated (1951).

19. Inventario de León Villapadierna, personal archive of T. Sánchez.

20. Hijuela materna de Toribio Mirantes, 31 January 1860, p. 7, personal archive of S. Mirantes.

21. Hijuela materna de Saturnino Rodríguez, 14 February 1895, p. 6, personal archive of L. Mirantes.

22. Hijuela materna de Magdalena de Castro, 9 December 1824–15 April 1826, p. 11, personal archive of M. Rivero.

23. Hijuela materna de Toribio Mirantes, p. 7, personal archive of S. Mirantes.

24. Inventario de Mateo Ferreras and Hijuela de Nicolasa Ferreras, personal archive of S. Mirantes.

25. Hijuelas maternas de Saturnino, Quintín y Amancia Rodríguez, 14 February 1895, personal archive of L. Mirantes.

26. Inventario y cuerpo de vienes [de Martín Mirantes], 1 June 1909, personal archive of L. Mirantes.

Chapter 5
Parents and Children

1. Homans, *English Villagers*, p. 155.

2. Ibid.

3. Marcel Mauss, *The Gift*, p. 1.

4. Ibid., p. 70.

5. Freeman, *Neighbors*, pp. 72-73.

6. Hijuela de María Rodríguez, 3 December 1889, personal archive of M. Rivero.

7. Acuerdo, 20 March 1953, p. 1, personal archive of Apolonia Robles. Note that, despite the accuracy with which the quantities to be given each year are specified, they are in fact the conventional metric equivalents of traditional measures: 2 *cargas* each of wheat and rye, 1 *carga* each of barley and oats, 1 *hemina* each of beans and chick peas.

For an interesting comment on contracts made between the generations in stem family households in eighteenth-century Austria, see Berkner, "The Stem Family," pp. 401-402.

8. Libro de difuntos (1665-1822), 4 January 1749, Santa María del Monte parish archive.

9. Manda que dejo Froylana Diez a su hija Balentina por sus asistencias, 25 December 1917, personal archive of M. Rivero.

10. AHPL, Protocolos, leg. 660 (Antonio Sandoval, León, 1725), f. 347.

11. Libro de difuntos, 11 January 1750, Santa María del Monte parish archive.

12. Testamento de Micaela Juárez, 6 February 1830, personal archive of T. Sánchez.

13. Hijuela paterna de Torivio Mirantes, p. 9, personal archive of S. Mirantes.

Chapter 6
Setting up House

1. This was a common pattern in many parts of rural Spain. See, for example, Freeman, *Neighbors*, pp. 75-77, and Lisón Tolosana, "La casa en Galicia," pp. 142-143. For an example from northeast Portugal, see Brian Juan O'Neill, "*Roda* and *Torna* in North-East Portugal," p. 3.

2. Taped interview with Maximina Sánchez, 1981.

3. Cuestionario del Ateneo, Museo Nacional de Etnología, response II-D-i for Roderos, Virgen del Camino, Laguna de Negrillos, and Villablino.

4. Taped interview with Maximina Sanchez, 1981. Millán Urdiales quotes the saying, "The *amedias* are never good" ("*Las amedias nunca son buenas*"), in *El habla de Villacidayo*, p. 219.

5. Libro de tazmía de Barrillos, 1779-1834, Barrillos parish archive.

6. "Carta dotal que damos nosotros Martin Mirantes y Vitoria Llamazares a nuestro hijo Luis Mirantes al contraer matrimo[nio] con Domitila a cuenta del que primero falle," undated, personal archive of L. Mirantes.

7. "Carta de Dote o Dotal que dieron Juaquin Aller y Leonor Gonzalez Vezinos de barrillos a su ija Juaquina Aller y se entrego a su Marido Cayetano Llamazares," undated, personal archive of J. Llamazares.

8. Hijuela paterna de Isidro Mirantes, 8 June 1858, personal archive of S. Mirantes.

9. This is a fact worth noting, for it introduces a new element into traditional family structure, one which is the product of modern social

and economic changes: namely, that young men of a farming background have little opportunity for marriage. Few young women want to stay in the countryside, let alone come to the countryside from the city. They prefer marrying men with factory jobs to marrying farmers. So in every village today one finds a class of men ranging from twenty to forty-five years of age who missed their chance to marry. They are still regarded as belonging to the category of *mozos*—unmarried men—which appears comical since they are too old to be real *"mozos."*

10. Emmanuel Le Roy Ladurie, "Family Structures and Inheritance Customs in Sixteenth-Century France," p. 58.

11. Libro de difuntos, 5 March 1827 (citing a joint testament of 27 May 1824), Santa María del Monte parish archive.

12. AHPL, Protocolos, leg. 639, f. 462.

13. Ibid., f. 470.

14. Libro de difuntos, 7 October 1753, Santa María del Monte parish archive.

15. A similar version of this verse can be found in Prisciliano Cordero de Castillo, "La familia rural leonesa," p. 93.

16. Inventario de Concepción Llamazares, 24 April 1954, p. 5, personal archive of B. Llamazares.

17. Cuestionario del Ateneo, Museo Nacional de Etnología, response II-E-a-1 for Roderos, Laguna de Negrillos, and León.

18. This is pointed out in the work of Dillard, "Women in Reconquest Castile," and Teofilo Ruiz, "Notas para el estudio de la mujer."

19. AHPL, Protocolos, leg. 1336, f. 136.

20. Ibid., f. 119.

21. Libro de difuntos, 1 August 1718, Santa María del Monte parish archive.

22. Ibid., 8 August 1745.

23. Taped interview with Leonardo Mirantes, 29 September 1980.

24. Cuestionario del Ateneo, Museo Nacional de Etnología, response II-A-c. Of the sixteen responses from the province of León, only four indicated that it would not hamper the woman's chances to marry: the one from the capital (which indicates that the woman would no doubt find "some individual of few scruples from her *pueblo*" who would marry her) and those from Bembibre, Villafranca, and the Bierzo region generally. The last three responses are all from the Bierzo region, which borders on Galicia, and they reflect the Galician attitude toward the loss of virginity: "Such a loss is not difficult to make up if the woman 'has

a few *cachos*,' that is, some wealth in real estate ..." (Bembibre). The responses from all other areas of León, and even that from Congosto within the Bierzo region, indicate a quite different attitude, as exemplified by the report from Rabanal del Camino: "Its loss constitutes a great difficulty for getting married and to do so it would have to be with a man who is poor or badly off."

25. Taped interview with Apolonia Robles, 10 July 1981.

Chapter 7
The Concejo as an Assembly

1. On the general transformation from the *concejo abierto* tradition of early medieval times to the oligarchic *consejos, cabildos*, and *regimientos*, see García de Valdeavellano, *Curso*, pp. 547-548. See Teofilo Ruiz, "The Transformation of the Castilian Municipalities," for the example of medieval Burgos, and Lisón Tolosana, *Belmonte*, pp. 207 and 251, for an ethnographic account of an oligarchic town council in Aragon. On the persistence of the *concejo* in the villages of northern Spain, see García de Valdeavellano, *Curso*, p. 549; Antonio Domínguez Ortiz, *La sociedad española*, p. 344; and Concepción de Castro, *La Revolución Liberal*, p. 38. On the community assembly in the old European rural world, see I. Chiva, *Rural Communities*, p. 19, and Jerome Blum, "The European Village Community," pp. 175 and 177, and "The Internal Structure and Polity of the European Village Community," pp. 552-555.

2. Ordenanzas, Santa María del Monte, 1776, chapter 3. For a complete transcription of these ordinances, with a commentary, see Ruth Behar, "La vida social y cultural de un pueblo leonés." See Blum, "The Internal Structure," p. 555 for a similar case of disorderly community meetings in nineteenth-century Russian villages; this phenomenon seems also to have been fairly widespread in rural France, Germany, and Austria.

3. M. Araceli Guerra García and José M. Fernández del Pozo, "Las constituciones democráticas de tres pueblos," p. 54.

4. Elías López Morán, *Derecho consuetudinario*, pp. 267-268.

5. Ibid., p. 268. No date is given for the ordinances of Villamanín, but it seems likely that they date from the eighteenth century.

6. There are, nevertheless, problems of interpretation in using this or any other local historical source. In chapter 15 I discuss in more detail the meaning of historical documents for the people who produced them.

7. Libro de cuentas, Castro, 1583, "Sobre los juramentos."

8. Ibid. During the Franco era it likewise became customary to fine persons who swore, a ruling that was strictly enforced by the parish priest, according to several of my informants.

9. Ibid., "Sobre las juntas en las tabernas y concejos."

10. Libro de cuentas, Castro, visita, 1726.

11. Libro de cuentas, Villasinta, visita, 1740.

12. Ordenanzas, Santa María del Monte, 1776, chapter 3. The role of such officers of the *concejo* as the *regidores* and the *pesquiseros* will be discussed in detail in the next chapter.

13. Florentino Agustín Díez Gonález, *La noble tierra de Ordás*, pp. 105-106. No date is provided for the ordinances, but the style of writing seems similar to that of other late seventeenth- and mid-eighteenth-century ordinances I have seen.

14. Juan Antonio Posse, "Historia biográfica" (1916), p. 265.

15. Taped interview with Leonardo Mirantes, 29 September 1980.

16. Posse, "Historia biográfica" (1916), p. 267.

17. Díez González, *Ordás*, pp. 26-27.

18. The quote is from Thompson, "The Grid of Inheritance," p. 337. I am much indebted to Thompson's paper for the development of my own argument concerning the "web of use-rights" in the Leonese context, which is discussed in detail in Part Four.

19. Vicente Flórez de Quiñones, *Contribución al estudio del régimen local*, pp. 151-152.

20. López Morán, *Derecho consuetudinario*, p. 70. These ordinances date from 1748.

21. Ibid. The date for the ordinances of Villanueva del Pontedo is not mentioned in the text. Again, they appear to be from the eighteenth century.

22. Ibid., p. 71. These ordinances date from 1774.

23. Flórez de Quiñones, *Contribución*, p. 151. The date is not given for these ordinances, but they too seem to be from the eighteenth century.

24. Ordenanzas, Santa María del Monte, 1776, chapter 19.

25. López Morán, *Derecho consuetudinario*, p. 70.

26. Ibid., p. 171.

27. Flórez de Quiñones, *Contribución*, p. 153.

28. Ordenanzas, Santa María del Monte, 1776, chapter 19.

29. Actas de concejo, 18 January 1874, Santovenia del Monte.

30. Actas de concejo, 27 December 1855, Valdefresno.

31. López Morán cites the cases of Cármenes and Canseco where

native sons did not pay to become *vecinos*. See López Morán, *Derecho consuetudinario*, pp. 70-71. On the idea of the repast as a gift see p. 72.

32. See Freeman, *Neighbors*, pp. 90-98, for a detailed discussion of other rites of commensality associated with the *concejo*, or the *común*, as it is called in Soria, which constitute what she terms a "mass-feast-meeting complex." In her discussion Freeman appropriately cites Robertson Smith: "Those who sit at meat together are united for all social effects; those who do not eat together are aliens to one another, without fellowship in religion and without reciprocal social duties" (ibid., p. 98).

33. Ordenanzas, Santa María del Monte, 1776, chapter 19. For the 1798 census, see Cadenas y Vicent, *Padrones de hidalgos*, pp. 66-67. On the question of how village citizenship was acquired in various countries, see Blum, "The Internal Structure," pp. 549-552.

34. How the *concejo* paid the lawyers' fees is not documented, but I imagine it was done by the method of *repartimiento*, according to which each *vecino* would have paid according to his abilities.

35. Untitled document 1701, Santa María del Monte, p. 1.

36. Ibid., p. 3.

37. Ibid., p. 5.

38. Ibid., p. 7.

39. Ibid., p. 13.

40. Ibid.

41. Ibid., p. 14.

42. Ibid.

43. An excellent detailed analysis of the circulation of blessed bread in a Basque community is found in Sandra Ott, *The Circle of Mountains*. I follow Ott in translating the custom of *la caridad* as "blessed bread." I discuss the custom in a little more detail later on in the context of the rotation of herding responsibilities.

44. See Bloch, *French Rural History*, pp. 186-189; Angel García Sanz, "Bienes y derechos comunales," pp. 99, 108 and passim; David E. Vassberg, "The *Tierras Baldías*," p. 401, and "The Sale of *Tierras Baldías*," pp. 633 and passim. I will treat this question at greater length in my discussion of the web of use-rights.

45. Libro de bautizados, 1779-1851, Santa María del Monte parish archive.

46. Madoz, *Diccionario*, s.v. Santa María del Monte.

47. "Foro del lugar de Santa Maria del Monte en favor del estado de Toral y casa de Guzman," 1701, p. 2.

48. Untitled document, 1698, Santa María del Monte, p. 3.

Chapter 8
The Concejo as a Polity

1. López Morán, *Derecho consuetudinario*, p. 46.

2. Ibid., p. 47.

3. Díez González, *Ordás*, p. 79. Flórez de Quiñones also cites examples of *regidores* chosen by turn in Robledo and Villapodambre. See Flórez de Quiñones, *Contribución*, pp. 164-166. The concept of the *vecera* is discussed in greater detail in chapter 11 on the common herds.

4. López Morán, *Derecho consuetudinario*, p. 48.

5. Ordenanzas, Santa María del Monte, 1776, chapter 5. Other common offices were those of *teniente* or assistant to the *regidor*, in villages where there was only one, and *estimadores* or *tasadores*, whose task it was to assess the value of lands and other properties for the *concejo*.

6. Taped interview with Leonardo Mirantes, 29 September 1980. Today the office is circulated by turn, being given each year to the oldest *vecino* who has not yet been *mayordomo*, as has also been the case in such nearby villages as Barrio de Nuestra Señora and Valdefresno.

7. Flórez de Quiñones, *Contribución*, p. 164.

8. Taped interview with Leonardo Mirantes, 29 September 1980.

9. Ordenanzas, Santa María del Monte, 1776, chapter 5.

10. Flórez de Quiñones, *Contribución*, p. 166. This ordinance dates from 1716.

11. Blum's succinct description of the role of the headman in old village Europe provides the general comparative background for the points I am making here on the much smaller scale of rural León. See Blum, "The Internal Structure," pp. 556-562; in particular see p. 560 where he cites a wonderful passage from Ladislas Reymont's novel, *The Peasants*, in which a well-off peasant explains why he would rather not be headman.

12. Flórez de Quiñones, *Contribución*, p. 168.

13. Díez González, *Ordás*, p. 81.

14. See Flórez de Quiñones, *Contribución*, p. 174. The *fiel* was sometimes paid for carrying out his office, especially in more recent times. In the nearby villages of Santovenia del Monte the *fiel de fechos* was paid 13 1/2 *reales* by the village for a year's labor. Actas del concejo, 14 January 1869, Santovenia del Monte.

15. Ordenanzas, Santa María del Monte, 1776, chapter 4.

16. Flórez de Quiñones, *Contribución*, p. 170.

17. Díez González, *Ordás*, p. 84.

18. Document dated 21 February 1964, Barrio de Nuestra Señora *concejo* archive.

19. See Joaquín Costa y Martínez, *Colectivismo agrario en España*; Costa et al., *Derecho consuetudinario y economía popular en España*; and discussion to follow on the web of use-rights.

20. These figures are taken from Concepción de Castro's analysis of Sebastián Miñano's geographical dictionary, published in 1829; altogether, 35 percent of the Spanish population lived in towns or villages of fewer than 1,000 inhabitants (*La Revolución Liberal*, pp. 25-26). The municipal law of 1877 required that all municipalities have a population greater than 2,000, though as late as 1910 only 2,191 of Spain's 9,261 municipalities fulfilled this requirement (Flórez de Quiñones, *Contribución*, pp. 17-21).

21. Elías López Morán, "León," p. 271.

22. López Morán, *Derecho consuetudinario*, p. 56.

Chapter 9
The Concejo as a Moral Presence

1. Here I call the reader's attention to the profound discussion of the *pueblo*'s failure as a society in Lisón Tolosana, *Belmonte*, pp. 250-257. Lisón Tolosana points out the various similarities that exist between the *pueblo* and the greek *polis*, but finds that there is "an essential juridical difference" between these two forms of polity: "The former has not been so powerful a generating center of juridical sensibility, a productive force of socialization. In this sense the pueblo has not really been a pueblo, that is, a society. . . . In the last four centuries individuality and particularism have prevailed over the forces of socialization and authority" (p. 257). The "anarchic character" of Spaniards has often been noticed by foreign and native observers alike, and today in the midst of democracy one still hears comments rather like that of the Civil Guard in Julian Pitt-Rivers's classic Andalusian study: "the Spaniard requires authority if he is to achieve anything" (*The People of the Sierra*, p. 156). This is the background against which I have elaborated the concept of "enforced solidarity." Yet I hasten to point out that the Leonese tradition of the *concejo* as an open assembly did allow for much of the juridical sensibility and socialization that Lisón Tolosana found lacking in the larger, oligarchic towns of Aragon.

2. Ordenanzas, Santa María del Monte, 1776, "Acuerdo."

3. The recording of *concejo* acts seems to have become widespread in the latter half of the nineteenth century not just in León but in other areas of Spain as well. Freeman remarks in a footnote that the council of the village she studied in Soria "had an unusual bent for recording its own acts" in this period (*Neighbors*, p. 44). In chapter 15 I will discuss the historical and cultural reasons for this flowering of recorded council acts.

4. Document dated 31 December 1936, Barrio de Nuestra Señora *concejo* archive. For further discussion of the ideology of the small and medium-sized peasantry in the nationalist zone of Old Castile, see Ronald Fraser, *Blood of Spain*, pp. 281-285.

5. Guerra García and Fernández del Pozo, "Las constituciones,"p. 54.

6. Díez González, *Ordás,*, p. 83.

7. López Morán, *Derecho consuetudinario*, p. 262.

8. Ibid., p. 261.

9. Ibid., p. 262.

10. Actas de concejo, 23 November 1879, Santa María del Monte.

11. Actas de concejo, 14 January 1869, Santovenia del Monte. Disentailment and the new centralized administration represented by the *Boletín* will be discussed in chapter 12 on the common lands and in chapter 14 on the state and the commons.

12. Actas de concejo, 7 August 1885, Villamayor.

13. Actas de concejo, 28 November 1883, Santa María del Monte.

14. Document dated 31 December 1936, Barrio de Nuestra Señora *concejo* archive.

15. For an account of communal prestations of labor in Old Castile, known as *cenderas*, see Freeman, *Neighbors*, pp. 37, 56-57, and 122. In Asturias this form of communal prestation is known as *sextaferia*. See James W. Fernandez, "The Call to the Commons," for an insightful analysis of the decline and recent resurgence of this form of prestation in rural Asturias.

16. López Morán, *Derecho consuetudinario*, pp. 169-170.

17. See García de Valdeavellano, *Curso*, p. 252, for the *facendera* as forced labor on the roads and bridges of seigneurial domains in medieval Spain. Noel Salomon, *La vida rural castellana*, pp. 192-193, mentions *corvea*, *serna*, and *facendera* as being the words used in different parts of New Castile to refer to corvée labor in the late sixteenth century, by which time this seigneurial obligation was in "a very advanced stage of decomposition." For the expropriation of communal labor by ecclesias-

tical and seigneurial lords, and by the state, in Asturias see Fernandez, "The Call to the Commons," p. 22.

In central León corvée labor was known as *serna*, as for instance in Santovenia del Monte where in 1165 the villagers owed one day of *serna* a month to the monastery of San Isidoro, in return for which the monastery was to give the villagers a meal of wheat bread and wine (Justiniano Rodríguez, *Los fueros del Reino de León*, 2: 98). The *sernas* seem to have disappeared in this region early on. For resistance by villagers to *sernas* in twelfth- and thirteenth-century León and Castile see Reyna Pastor, *Resistencias y luchas campesinas*, pp. 221-230.

18. Ordenanzas, Santa María del Monte, 1776, chapter 24.

19. In nearby Villamayor, for example, an annual *hacendera* is also held on Carnival. The village in Soria where Freeman did her research also holds a *cendera* on Shrove Tuesday. See Freeman, *Neighbors*, pp. 37 and 56-57. The juxtaposition of *hacenderas* (work) and Carnival (play) is curious, but by no means baffling; as we shall see, the *hacenderas* also have their festive, bacchic aspects.

20. Flórez de Quiñones, *Contribución*, p. 191.

21. Díez González, *Ordás*, p. 113.

22. Ibid., pp. 85-86.

23. Flórez de Quiñones, *Contribución*, p. 192.

24. Castigos de concejo, 1 February 1966, Santa María del Monte.

25. Ibid.

26. Castigos de concejo, 14 July 1957, Santa María del Monte. It should be noted that firewood was also brought to the schoolteachers and the priest by *hacendera* until just a few years ago.

27. Actas de concejo, 5 October 1899, Santa María del Monte.

28. Ibid.

29. Actas de concejo, 23 November 1879, Santa María del Monte.

30. ". . . no se azmitira ningun chicillo." Actas de concejo, 28 November 1883, Santa María del Monte.

31. Actas de concejo, 8 March 1878, Santovenia del Monte.

32. Actas de concejo, 4 March 1885, Ambasaguas.

33. López Morán, a native of the mountain village of Canseco, could recall at the turn of the century the role of the *mayordomos de las ánimas* as auctioneers of the bread offered to the souls. See López Morán, *Derecho consuetudinario*, p. 274.

34. Actas de concejo, 18 March 1872, Ambasaguas.

35. Actas de concejo, 31 December 1868, Villamayor.

36. Ordenanzas, Santa María del Monte, 1776, chapter 21.

37. Actas de concejo, 26 July 1885, Santa María del Monte.

38. Actas de concejo, 5 October 1899, Santa María del Monte.

39. Actas de concejo, 22 March 1874, Ambasaguas.

40. Actas de concejo, 6 January 1916, Santa María del Monte; document dated 31 December 1936, Barrio de Nuestra Señora.

41. Document dated 21 February 1964, Barrio de Nuestra Señora.

42. Actas de concejo, 9 March 1890, Santa María del Monte.

43. Actas de concejo, 6 January 1916, Santa María del Monte.

44. Castigos de concejo, 1970, Santa María del Monte.

45. Castigos de concejo, 1954, Santa María del Monte.

46. Libro de bautizados, 1929-present, Santa María del Monte parish archive.

47. Taped interview with Leonardo Mirantes, 29 September 1980.

48. Ibid. In the present day, the wake is held in this fashion only if the house of the deceased requests it. Even when it is not requested, however, the wake is attended by one villager from almost every house, as is the funeral.

49. The involvement of the community in the death of any of its members is not unique to León. Freeman documents a similar pattern for communities in Soria, where village burial societies enforce participation (*Neighbors*, pp. 41-42 and 104). Interestingly, the patterns of funerary ritual are somewhat different in the Basque country, where it is primarily kin and first or close neighbor relations that are activated at death. See William A. Douglass, *Death in Murélaga* and, more recently, Ott, *The Circle of Mountains*, pp. 117-130.

50. Taped interview with Leonardo Mirantes, 29 September 1980.

51. Conversation with Felicísimo Llamazares, 12 May 1981.

52. Ordenanzas, Santa María del Monte, 1776, chapter 27. For a detailed analysis of the meaning vows had in local communities (and more generally for the question of how religion is localized) in the sixteenth century and later, I refer the reader to the excellent recent study by Christian, *Local Religion*, pp. 23-66 and passim.

53. On the litanies see Christian, *Local Religion*, pp.115-118. As Christian notes, "the concentration of processions and vows into this two-week period indicates its cultural importance in the agricultural cycle. It was a time of great danger to the vines from worms, which attacked the first buds, as well as from late frosts, hailstorms, and drought" (pp. 116-117). Indeed, to this day, when the litanies are conducted the priest blesses the land with the cross used in village processions, a candle, and

holy water, uttering what must be described as magical incantations that fields and fruits be preserved, fire and tempests not strike.

54. Posse notes that in Llánaves the litanies were paid for by the *concejo*. See Posse, "Historia biográfica" (1916), p. 266. In the vicinity of Santa María, I found similar evidence for the villages of Villamayor, Castro, Barrio, Ambasaguas, and Santovenia del Monte. The observance of the litanies as village-based springtime processions was widespread, however, in León and Old Castile and also, as Christian points out, in New Castile.

55. Flórez de Quiñones, *Contribución*, pp. 280-281. The village of San Román de la Vega had made vows to Saint Toribio and Saint Barbara.

56. Actas de concejo, 5 October 1899, Santa María del Monte.

57. Castigos de concejo, 1966, Santa María del Monte.

58. Document dated 21 February 1964, Barrio de Nuestra Señora.

59. Christian, *Local Religion*, p. 167.

60. Libro de cuentas, Castro, visita, 1734.

61. Actas de concejo, 9 August 1874, Santa María del Monte. See Flórez de Quiñones, *Contribución*, p. 201 on *bagaje* in the villages of northwestern León.

62. Actas de concejo, 12 June 1877, Ambasaguas.

63. Document dated 31 December 1936, Barrio de Nuestra Señora.

64. Actas de concejo, 10 December 1856, Villamayor.

65. Document dated 21 February 1964, Barrio de Nuesta Señora.

Chapter 10
The Web of Use-Rights

1. Some sources are Homans, *English Villagers*; Joan Thirsk, "The Common Fields"; Warren O. Ault, "Open-Field Husbandry and the Village Community"; Donald N. McCloskey, "The Persistence of English Common Fields"; and Richard C. Hoffman, "Medieval Origins of the Common Fields" on England; I. Chiva, "Social Organization" on Corsica; and Robert McC. Netting, "Of Men and Meadows" and "What Alpine Peasants Have in Common" on the Swiss Alps. For a general perspective on the role of communal property in European village communities see Jerome Blum, "The European Village Community" and "The Internal Structure." The classic statement on the subject was made by Bloch, *French Rural History*, pp. 167-189 and 198-234. In Spain the importance of communal property and village forms of social organi-

zation was first recognized and analyzed systematically by Costa (see below, n. 2). The tradition of juridical analysis is carried on in the well-documented works of Alejandro Nieto, *Ordenación* and *Bienes comunales*. For an account based on local ordinances and council acts, see Luis Redonet y López Dóriga, *Policía rural en España*.

The subject has lately become a major focus of historical research. See the work of Salomon, *La vida rural castellana*; Mira, *Vivir y hacer historia*; Vassberg, "The *Tierras Baldías*"; García Sanz, "Bienes y derechos comunales"; Pastor, *Resistencias*; Manuel Cuadrado Iglesias, *Aprovechamiento en común*; and José M. Mangas Navas, *El régimen comunal agrario* for historical perspectives on communal property in Spain. Anthropological accounts can be found in Michael Kenney, *A Spanish Tapestry*, pp. 14-21; M. R. Redclift, "The Future of Agriculture"; Douglass, *Echalar and Murélaga*, pp. 71-84; Brandes, *Migration*, pp. 87-102; Freeman, *Neighbors*; Fernandez, "The Call to the Commons"; and Ruth Behar, "The Web of Use-Rights" and "Supervivencias de tierras concejiles y derechos colectivos en la epoca contemporánea."

The sources on León, which follow in the tradition of Costa, include López Morán, *Derecho consuetudinario*; Flórez de Quiñones, *Contribución* and "Comunidad o servidumbre de pastos"; Díez González, *Ordás*; Luis Redonet y López Dóriga, "Policía rural en España: León"; José Luis Martín Galindo, *Artículos geográficos*, "El colectivismo agrario de Llánaves," "Paisajes leoneses," and "Arcaísmo y modernidad"; and Valentín Cabero Diéguez, *Espacio agrario*. On the nearby province of Asturias, see Benjamín García Alvarez, *Concejos y parroquias de Asturias*. William A. Christian, *Religiosidad popular*, provides a set of village ordinances for Tudanca (Santander). Also interesting for purposes of comparison are Angel Cabo Alonso, "El colectivismo agrario en Tierra de Sayugo" on Zamora, and Antonio López Gómez, "Valdelaguna" on Burgos.

2. See Costa, *Colectivismo agrario* and Costa et al., *Derecho consuetudinario*. Costa's writings set the tone for all later work on the subject, which often followed him in using the notion of *colectivismo agrario*, and sometimes the term itself. For an interesting discussion of Costa's work, see Fernandez, "The Call to the Commons," pp. 9-11 and 55, n. 12. Although Costa was not alone among Spanish jurists who wrote on the history of communal property toward the turn of the century (see Rafael Altamira y Crevea, *Historia de la propiedad comunal*, for example), his account is by far the most ethnographic.

3. See, for example, Henry Sumner Maine, *Ancient Law*; Lewis H. Morgan, *Ancient Society*; Emile de Laveleye, *Primitive Property*; and Fred-

erick Engels, *The Origin of the Family*. For a well-documented account of the late nineteenth-century European debate on the origins of property, see Paolo Grossi, *An Alternative to Private Property*. Grossi devotes the second part of his book to the repercussions of this debate on Italian juridical thought. The debate, as he shows, led to a new appreciation for collective forms of landholding and, subsequently, to the gathering of data from the various Italian provinces attesting to the vitality and historical continuity of this "landholding situation that was outside the official Romanistic tradition and alternative to it" (p. 124). A similar kind of work could certainly be written about Spain.

4. Pre-Roman, Roman, and Visigothic origins of communal institutions have been suggested at different times. All seem to have played some part in the development of communal forms of landholding in the Iberian peninsula. In an interesting note on the question, Noel Salomon remarks upon the curious lacuna in the literature on the subject, which never makes reference to the possible influence of Islamic traditions on the formation of these communal practices (*La vida rural castellana*, pp. 123-124, n. 18). It is clear, however, that whatever their origin, if indeed it can be found, these practices, as Vassberg notes, were strengthened in the period of the Reconquest by the legal sanctions given to them by the Castilian monarchs ("The *Tierras Baldías*," p. 384).

5. David E. Vassberg, "Peasant Communalism and Anti-Communal Tendencies in Early Modern Castile," p. 487.

6. Grossi, *Alternative*, p. 6.

7. Ibid., p. 24.

8. See, in particular, Albert Soboul, "The French Rural Community"; Chiva, "Social Organization"; Freeman, *Neighbors*; Blum, "The European Village Community" and "The Internal Structure"; and Netting, "Alpine Peasants." As Chiva says with respect to Corsica: "Absolute individual property is certainly ancient, but there is reason to believe . . . that until the end of the 17th century it was of little importance and limited in general to gardens, orchards, and vineyards." He cites the example of an act of sale of an enclosed garden in 1602, over which "the buyer acquired for himself and his descendents . . . this enclosure with the rights of it to . . . have, hold, rent for cash, for fixed quantities in kind, to give a life interest in, to increase, enlarge, sell, make a gift of, to exchange, and to dispose of it just as with other property belonging to him." As Chiva astutely observes, "this redundant definition of the rights of property . . . bears witness of an institution so rare at the time

that it was of necessity described and guaranteed in all its aspects and for all possible uses" ("Social Organization," p. 103). I would add, for the Spanish context at least, that the institution was not rare so much as still ill-defined and encumbered by various communal "servitudes" that limited its free exercise; thus the need to define redundantly. See discussion to follow.

9. On the notion of "embedded" economies see Karl Polanyi, "Aristotle Discovers the Economy" and "Economy as Instituted Process"; and George Dalton, "Primitive, Archaic, and Modern Economies."

10. Thompson, "The Grid of Inheritance," p. 328.

11. Ibid., p. 337.

12. Bloch, *French Rural History*, p. 181.

13. In some places these *foros* persisted into the present century, long after these and other feudal dues were formally abolished by a decree of the Cortes in 1811. The jurist and historian Flórez de Quiñones, who has written extensively on Leonese customary law, acted in behalf of the villages of the Concejo of Villamor de Riello, in the mountains of León, to have abolished a *foro* still weighing upon the villages in 1931, which originally had consisted of a fourth of each vassal's total crop of rye (*pan del cuarto*, as the right was called). The *foro*, originally belonging to the count of Luna, had been sold in 1897 and continued to be exacted until it was extinguished in 1931 by decree of the president of the Republic, Manuel Azaña. See the recent edition of Flórez de Quiñones, *Supervivencias señoriales*. The village of the Sierra Ministra in Soria where Freeman did her anthropological research still paid "rent" on communal lands to the House of Medinaceli in 1966 (*Neighbors*, pp. 18, 39, and 167-172).

14. See Nieto, *Bienes comunales*, pp. 147-148; García de Valdeavellano, *Curso*, pp. 239-240; and Vassberg, "The *Tierras Baldías*," p. 385 and "The Sale of *Tierras Baldías*," pp. 631-632. To cite one among many examples showing the relationship between the crown and the villages on the question of the commons, here is a decree enacted by Philip IV in 1632: "que no venderemos ni enajenaremos tierras baldías, ni arboles ni el fruto de ellos, si no que quedará siempre lo uno y lo otro para que nuestros súbditos y naturales tengan uso y aprovechamiento que de las dichas tierras baldías y arboles y frutos de ellos han tenido y tienen conforme a las leyes de estos Reynos y a las ordenanzas que tuvieren y hicieren por Nos confirmadas" (cited in Nieto, *Bienes comunales*, p. 147). Despite its frequent reassurances to the contrary, the monarchy does

sanction the alienation of common land time and again (see below, n. 16).

15. Bloch, *French Rural History*, p. 183.

16. The process by which the common lands were put on the market in sixteenth-century Castile is documented by Vassberg, "The *Tierras Baldías*," "The Sale of *Tierras Baldías*," and "Peasant Communalism"; and García Sanz, "Bienes y derechos comunales." On the impoverishment of the peasantry and the formation of large landed estates in this period see Carmelo Viñas y Mey, *El problema de la tierra*, pp. 54-102; and Salomon, *La vida rural castellana*, pp. 213-258. For a discussion of the European situation see Bloch, *French Rural History*, pp. 184-189. The struggle over the commons goes back, of course, to the early Middle Ages, as we see in Pastor, *Resistencias*, pp. 56-112. But it becomes more acute beginning in the sixteenth century.

17. Bloch, *French Rural History*, p. 185.

18. E. P. Thompson, *Whigs and Hunters*, p. 18.

19. Bloch, *French Rural History*, p. 242.

20. This is but one aspect of Jovellanos's *Informe sobre la ley agraria* (1793). In general Jovellanos wished to see property released from the various "dead hands" into which it had fallen by the eighteenth century. We tend not to give this work as sympathetic a reading as we might (perhaps because of Costa's influence?), but a close examination shows that he was well aware of local conditions in the countryside. He felt that the common lands should be broken up and distributed to members of the community because these lands were being wasted in not being cultivated, and, more important, because otherwise the rich took advantage of the commons for their own benefit. As Jovellanos says, "by making the enjoyment of the *baldíos* common to all, it was natural that the rich rather than the poor would take advantage of them" (p. 165). Unlike what actually took place in the following century when disentailment was carried out, Jovellanos had proposed that modes of payment for the lands put on the market be adjusted to the local conditions of the rural classes of each region. He had also envisioned, of course, an equitable distribution of the land, and one that would give the landless or near landless access to it. On Jovellanos's *Informe*, see Herr, *The Eighteenth Century Revolution*, pp. 376-380; and Gonzalo Anes, *Economía e "ilustración,"* pp. 97-138.

21. Disentailment did not produce uniform results in the Spanish countryside. It has been argued that in Andalusia the effects of disen-

tailment were disastrous; the rural proletarian class grew to enormous proportions, class polarization was heightened, and the groundwork was laid for agrarian unrest and revolt (David Gilmore, "Land Reform and Rural Revolt," pp. 145-146). However, it also appears that in the highly stratified agrotowns of Estremadura and Andalusia the system of communal property use was already disappearing in the late eighteenth century (Herr, *The Eighteenth Century Revolution*, pp. 108-110). As Richard Herr points out, disentailment rarely produced cataclysmic changes in the local social structure and economy of Spanish towns and villages. Its effect was usually to maintain, even reinforce, the pattern already in existence. See Herr, "El significado." The evidence for León certainly confirms Herr's view.

22. Cited in Thompson, *Whigs and Hunters*, p. 241.

23. On the system of biennial rotation in León and Castile see the various works of Jesús García Fernández, "Aspectos del paisaje agrario," "Los sistemas de cultivo," and "Campos abiertos y campos cercados"; A. Heutz de Lemps, "Les terroirs," pp. 241-247; and Freeman, *Neighbors*, pp. 35-36.

24. See, for example, Thirsk, "The Common Fields"; and Hoffman, "Medieval Origins" on the early history of the common-field system in England; for a general overview see Blum, "The European Village Community," pp. 158-163. Concerning its development in León and Castile see Heutz de Lemps, "Les terroirs," pp. 241-242; and García Fernández, "Los sistemas," pp. 142-143, and "Campos," pp. 123-126.

García Fernández argues that the *dos hojas* system developed late in León and Castile, that is, not until the fifteenth and sixteenth centuries, because the population density remained low until then. With the subsequent rise in population, there was an increased demand for grazing land and so eventually the communities found themselves forced to turn to their own fallow for pasture. But a form of organization was needed. Thus the *dos hojas* system. Hoffman too relates the development of the common-field system in England to population increase ("Medieval Origins," pp. 32-33 and 41-53). As with Esther Boserup's more general treatise on demographic growth and agricultural change, *The Conditions of Agricultural Growth*, where she posits that intensification of agricultural production is brought about by increases in population density, one is left with the feeling that something crucial has been left out of the analysis, namely culture, or, if one prefers, the attitudes and mentalities that give meaning and sense to any system of economic and social relations. Not that demographic change is not important; clearly it cannot be ignored in any study of rural life. But the question is: why this adaptation and not another or, better, why this interpretation and not another?

25. Cited in García Fernández, "Los sistemas," p. 143.

26. Cited in Heutz de Lemps, "Les terroirs," p. 241, n. 1.

27. Ordenanzas, Santa María del Monte, 1776, chapter 11.

28. Homans, *English Villagers*, p. 65.

29. Ordenanzas, Santa María del Monte, 1776, chapter 11.

30. Homans, *English Villagers*, p. 65.

31. Ordenanzas, Santa María del Monte, 1776, chapter 16.

32. Actas de concejo, 26 July 1885, Santa María del Monte.

33. Ordenanzas, Santa María del Monte, 1776, chapter 9.

34. Ibid.

35. Actas de concejo, 22 July 1871, Santa María del Monte.

36. McCloskey, "The Persistence of the English Common Fields," p. 83.

37. Ordenanzas, Santa María del Monte, 1776, chapter 18.

38. Actas de concejo, 15 February 1870, Santa María del Monte.

39. Actas de concejo, 21 July 1901, Santa María del Monte.

40. Taped interview with Leonardo Mirantes, 26 January 1981.

41. Taped interview with Leonardo Mirantes, 29 September 1980.

Chapter 11
The Common Herds

1. The repertoire of Spanish terms for systems of turn-taking are testimony to their importance in the Spanish countryside. In the province of Soria various systems of turn-taking come under the term *adra*, from the Arabic for turn (see Freeman, *Neighbors*, pp. 33-34). In Burgos the same term is used to refer to general contexts of turn-taking, while the term *veceñada*, from the same root as *vecera*, refers to the common herd of goats raised for milk, which are herded by the various families in turn (see López Gómez, "Valdelaguna," p. 560). In Santander the various forms of turn-taking are known as *vecerías*, a term also widely used in León (see the "Ordenanza Concejil" of Tudanca in Christian, *Religiosidad popular*, pp. 228-230).

In her study of a French Basque commune, Sandra Ott points out the formal importance, not just for the Basques, but for European rural societies generally, of such traditional forms of reciprocity and exchange (see Ott, *The Circle of Mountains* and the review of this book by Freeman).

2. Eutimio Martino, *La montaña de Valdeburón*, p. 276. On the obligatory nature of the *vecera* in other Leonese villages, see Redonet y López Dóriga, "Policía rural: León," pp. 99-103.

3. Flórez de Quiñones, *Contribución*, pp. 244-245. These appear to be eighteenth-century ordinances. Unfortunately no date is given in the text.

4. Actas de concejo, 15 April 1873, Ambasaguas.

5. Actas de concejo, 5 March 1878, Santovenia del Monte.

6. López Morán, "León," p. 309.

7. For a fine reconstruction of the custom, see Ott, *The Circle of Mountains*, pp. 103-116. In Asturias, villagers blame the priests for the disappearance of this custom, which was viewed unfavorably by the Church (James W. Fernandez, personal communication). For a description of the blessed bread exchange in León, see Millán Urdiales, *El habla de Villacidayo*, p. 102. The custom still continues in some villages near Santa María, including Secos, Moral, and Villafruela; I was able to observe the offering of blessed bread at mass in Villafruela in 1984.

8. Actas de concejo, 1867, 1868, Villamayor.

9. Flórez de Quiñones, *Contribución*, p. 248.

10. Díez González, *Ordás*, pp. 92-93.

11. Ordenanzas, Santa María del Monte, 1776, chapter 15.

12. There is even a custom, which I observed, of "begging for the wolves" (*pedir para los lobos*): when someone has killed a wolf, he or she takes it from house to house around the village and is given eggs, sausage, potatoes, and other foods by grateful cattle-owners. See Brian Juan O'Neill, "*Roda* and *Torna*," for a description of this practice in Portugal.

13. Ordenanzas, Santa María del Monte, 1776, chapter 15.

14. Díez González, *Ordás*, p. 92.

15. Martino, *La montaña de Valdeburón*, p. 276.

16. Actas de concejo, 6 May 1944, Santa María del Monte.

17. Actas de concejo, 12 May 1847, Villamayor.

18. Actas de concejo, various acts from 1868 to 1893, Santa María del Monte. Libro de casados, 1852-1867, and Libro de difuntos, 1870-1929, Santa María del Monte parish archives.

19. Actas de concejo, 2 April 1869, Santa María del Monte. The payment Isidro de Robles and other herders received was entirely conventional. A village like Ambasaguas, which had more irrigated terrain, also provided the herder with a small amount of flax. But the pattern

of providing grain, some money, and daily sustenance was the same in other nearby villages such as Villamayor and Santovenia del Monte. On similar customary forms of payment given to the goatherd in Corsica, see Chiva, "Social Organization," pp. 109-110.

20. Actas de concejo, 24 October 1869, Santa María del Monte.

21. Actas de concejo, 24 April 1870, Santa María del Monte.

22. Ordenanzas, Santa María del Monte, 1776, chapter 14.

23. Actas de concejo, 26 July 1885, Santa María del Monte.

24. Actas de concejo, 9 March 1890, Santa María del Monte.

25. Actas de concejo, 30 January 1868, Santa María del Monte.

26. Actas de concejo, 15 August 1873, Santa María del Monte.

27. Ordenanzas, Santa María del Monte, 1776, chapter 20.

28. Martino, *La montaña de Valdeburón*, p. 277.

29. López Morán, "León," p. 300. This was a very widespread institution. See, among others, Homans, *English Villagers*, pp. 61-62, on free bull and boar in thirteenth-century English villages.

30. Actas de concejo, 2 April 1871, Villamayor.

31. Actas de concejo, 8 April 1877, Santa María del Monte.

32. Taped conversation with Sixto Mirantes, 5 June 1981.

33. Actas de concejo, 6 July 1873, Santa María del Monte.

34. Actas de concejo, 9 May 1869, Santa María del Monte.

35. Actas de concejo, 15 September 1879, Santa María del Monte.

36. On Aragon and Galicia, see Costa's contribution in Costa et al., *Derecho consuetudinario*, pp. 298-316. On the Basque country, see Miguel de Unamuno, "Vizcaya," pp. 56-63. In Soria there was a *contrata de caballería* centering on horses and mules, which there replaced cattle as the work-animals (see Freeman, *Neighbors*, p. 39).

37. Actas de concejo, 30 July 1893, Santa María del Monte.

38. See López Morán, "León," pp. 298-299.

39. Martin Galindo, "Paisajes leoneses," p. 136.

40. "... y como suele decir oy por tí y mañana por mí, además que entre muchos a poco se toca y se hace una buena obra." Flórez de Quiñones, *Contribución*, pp. 248-249.

Chapter 12
The Common Lands

1. "De ti he conocido que la igualdad es un efecto necesario de la comunidad de las tierras. ... Y pues que vives en un país en que apenas

pueden habitar los hombres, . . . no te olvides de que tu suerte está cifrada en que las tierras sigan siendo comunes, y que al punto que esta comunidad te falte, serás reducido a un desierto, en que sólo habitaran los buitres y las fieras." Posse, "Historia biográfica" (1916), pp. 272-273.

This oft-cited text found its way into the accounts of many Spanish jurists writing about the history of communal property at the turn of the century, most notably Costa's. It was Gumersindo de Azcárate, however, who discovered Posse, introducing this and other portions of his work in a short piece, cast in the idiom of his time, on "the vestiges of primitive communism." See Azcárate, "Vestigios del primitivo comunismo en España" and Costa, *Colectivismo agrario*, pp. 196-198. A more recent account of the common lands of Llánaves, written from a geographer's viewpoint, can be found in Martín Galindo, "El colectivismo agrario de Llánaves." I wish to acknowledge the kindness of Richard Herr in providing me with the reference to Posse's work, presently scattered through several volumes of *La Lectura*.

2. Posse, "Historia biográfica" (1916), pp. 272 and 264, for his description of the casting of lots for common lands. It should be noted that the meadows were, for the most part, privately owned in Llánaves. As in many mountain villages, the people primarily raised cattle and as a secondary occupation tilled the soil. The grain fields were probably few and far between, and not very productive, as Martín Galindo points out in "El colectivismo agrario de Llánaves." They seem to have been kept within the domain of the community so no house would ever lack land, however poor, in which to grow some rye for the family's daily bread.

3. Conversation with Felicísimo Llamazares, 21 May 1981.

4. Ordenanzas, Santa María del Monte, 1776, chapter 17.

5. Díez González, *Ordás*, pp. 110-111.

6. Flórez de Quiñones, *Contribución*, p. 154.

7. This has changed now that the consolidation of parcels plan (*concentración parcelaria*) has gone into effect, for the engineers failed to see the logic in everyone's wanting to have some land, however meager, in the irrigated terrain close to home. An informant told me of a conversation he had with one of the engineers involved in the plan. The engineer pointed out that if someone only has 500 meters in that zone he cannot make a plot for him there because the plots are given to people in those zones where they already have a lot of land. And my informant responded that this person needs a plot there more than someone who has 14,000

meters, as he does—"for where will he plant his few lettuces and onions?" The engineer answered, "Let him go buy them in the plaza in León."

8. Actas de concejo, 15 November 1858, Valdefresno.

9. Actas de concejo, 30 March 1869, Santovenia del Monte.

10. Other examples of arable land held in common in León and distributed in periodic repartitions can be found in López Morán, *Derecho consuetudinario*, pp. 106-133. For examples from various parts of Spain, see Costa, *Colectivismo agrario*, pp. 340-365. There are a few rare cases of communal grain fields not only held in common but also worked in common by all the *vecinos*, notably in the southwestern Leonese region of La Cabrera. Costa and other thinkers of his persuasion saw in this a clear vestige of an ancient collectivism, but there is reason to believe that such cooperation is intimately related to the ecological conditions of the area, which barely permit the cultivation of rye. For an interesting study of the area of La Cabrera, written by a geographer, see Cabero Diéguez, *Espacio agrario y economía de subsistencia*.

11. In a note, Ferreras Chasco cites the *Avance sobre la riqueza pecuaria en 1891*, which points out that "the communal woods that the villages have been able to salvage from disentailment ... 'are the mainstay and only resource of the poor agriculturalist and cattle keeper' " (*El Norte*, p. 231). I return to this topic later.

12. Actas de concejo, 8 April 1869, Santa María del Monte.

13. There were forty-eight signatures. Actas de concejo, 20 December 1880, Santa María del Monte.

14. Actas de concejo, 27 January 1887, Santa María del Monte.

15. Actas de concejo, 19 February 1890, Santa María del Monte.

16. Actas de concejo, 26 February 1891, Santa María del Monte.

17. Actas de concejo, 1 April 1894, Santa María del Monte.

18. Actas de concejo, 12 April 1908, Santa María del Monte.

19. Some sources on early medieval settlement patterns in newly resettled Spain are García de Valdeavellano, *Curso*, pp. 239-241; Mínguez Fernández, *El dominio*, pp. 67-84; and Vassberg, "The *Tierras Baldías*," pp. 383-386. Also valuable are González, "Reconquista" and Sánchez Albornoz, *Despoblación y repoblación*.

20. The subject of medieval land clearance receives masterly treatment in Bloch, *French Rural History*, pp. 5-20 and in an earlier account by P. Boissanade, *Life and Work in Medieval Europe*, pp. 226-238.

21. Bloch, *French Rural History*, p. 17.

22. On these points, which receive only summary attention here, see

Hellmuth Hopfner, "La evolución de los bosques" and Vassberg, "Peasant Communalism," pp. 480-481. Julius Klein's classic work on the Mesta is still full of valuable insights on the agricultural history of Castile. See, in particular, Klein, *The Mesta*, pp. 297-357 and his specific remarks on deforestation, pp. 306-308, 321.

23. Cited in Vassberg, "Peasant Communalism," p. 482.

24. For a local-level account of the process in Toledo, see Michael R. Weisser, *The Peasants of the Montes*, pp. 56-59; on Zamora, see Cabo Alonso, "El colectivismo agrario," pp. 607-611; on Segovia, see García Sanz, "Bienes y derechos comunales," p. 117. Of general interest are the remarks of Mangas Navas, *El régimen comunal agrario*, pp. 238-242. The most extensive examination of the question is that by Vassberg, "Peasant Communalism," pp. 479-487.

25. On the sale of common lands sanctioned by the crown in the kingdom of Castile during the sixteenth century, see Salomon, *La vida rural*, pp. 143-144, Vassberg, "The Sale of *Tierras Baldías*," and García Sanz, "Bienes y derechos comunales," pp. 111-127. Vassberg's geographical analysis of the sales shows that the revenues were highest in what were then the wealthiest parts of Castile: Andalusia, the cereal plains of Zamora and Valladolid, and the central provinces of Toledo, Madrid, and Guadalajara. The lowest of all revenues came from León ("The Sale of *Tierras Baldías*," pp. 646-647).

26. García Sanz, "Bienes y derechos," p. 118.

27. Vassberg, "Peasant Communalism," pp. 484, 487, 478.

28. In an early paper Gilmore describes the historical processes leading to peasant unrest in an Andalusian agro-town (see Gilmore, "Land Reform and Rural Revolt"). A subtle and original account of "the roots of rural rebellion in Spain" can be found in Weisser, *The Peasants of the Montes*. On the political circumstances surrounding rural revolt in the years preceding the Civil War, see Edward Malefakis, *Agrarian Reform and Peasant Revolution in Spain*.

While most scholars have focused on the question of peasant revolts, I have been forced by the nature of things in rural León to consider the opposite question—why peasant revolts did not occur there at a time when they were occurring in other parts of Spain, such as Andalusia and Estremadura. My discussion of the role of the common lands in Santa María in the last hundred years can be read as an attempt to answer this question.

29. Of course, land clearances had been carried out before, probably

during earlier cycles of population growth and land hunger. In the case of Santa María, a memory of past land clearances is preserved in the names of various sets of fields now in private hands—Las Bozas, El Rocín, Las Suertes—all of which are already found in the Catastro de Ensenada, the major village land survey undertaken by royal decree in 1752. In a linguistic study of the speech (*habla*) of another village in central León, José Millán Urdiales notes that these toponyms, versions of which recur in his study, all have the same meaning of "cleared lands," but each dates from a different historical period (*El habla de Villacidayo*, p. 428; see also Mínguez Fernández, *El dominio*, p. 46, on cycles of land clearances in León). Their original meaning has been lost (except in the case of *suerte*, which is a more recent term), and they are now treated as proper place-names; yet, looked at historically, they are documents of sorts, in which successive clearings of woodland carried out in the past can be read.

30. Here I have in mind the main argument of James C. Scott's interesting book on peasant rebellions in Burma and Vietnam: that the "subsistence ethic" is at the heart of many social and economic arrangements in rural societies (*The Moral Economy of the Peasant*, pp. 1-34 and passim).

31. Taped interview with Leonardo Mirantes, 29 September 1980.

32. Taped interview with Sixto Mirantes, 22 March 1981.

33. Taped interview with Leonardo Mirantes, 29 September 1980.

34. Taped interview with Sixto Mirantes, 22 March 1981.

35. I borrow here the conception of the peasantry as a "class of survivors" from John Berger, *Pig Earth*, pp. 196-213.

Chapter 13
The Common Woods

1. As Ferreras Chasco notes, in the years 1950-1956 there were many requests from villages throughout central León for permission to clear land, which are preserved in the state forestry office, ICONA, of León. "This plethora of clearances," he observes, "coincides with the last years of demographic growth and with the period just before the massive rural migration" (*El Norte*, p. 313).

2. Actas de concejo, 4 March 1880, Santa María del Monte.

3. Actas de concejo, 9 March 1919, Santa María del Monte.

4. Actas de concejo, 30 October 1879, Santa María del Monte.

5. Actas de concejo, 18 February 1890, Santa María del Monte.

6. Actas de concejo, 27 September 1936, Santa María del Monte.

7. Taped interview with Láutico Robles, 12 March 1981.

8. Taped interview with Leonardo Mirantes, 29 September 1980.

9. Actas de concejo, 23 November 1879, Santa María del Monte.

10. Actas de concejo, 15 February 1870, Santa María del Monte.

11. Actas de concejo, 26 July 1885, Santa María del Monte.

12. Actas de concejo, 3 November 1870, Santa María del Monte.

13. Actas de concejo, 19 February 1887, Ambasaguas.

14. This decree is printed, in a slightly different version from those conserved in the *concejo* archives of Santa María and Villamayor, in the *Novísima recopilación de las leyes de España*, book 7, title 24, law 2; it is discussed by Mangas Navas in relation to the *concejos* of Castile (*El régimen comunal agrario*, pp. 203-206). The deforestation of Castile by this period is well documented; Salomon speaks of "the Spain of the sixteenth century in which wood and firewood were lacking" (*La vida rural*, p. 193).

15. Hordenanzas del lugar de Villamayor . . . sobre la guarda y conservación de los montes . . . , 1599.

16. The trees and bushes listed as growing in the *monte* of Villamayor are "robles y espinos y crespa y haylagas y estepa y sauze y escobas y hiagazos, tomillos y otros arboles." Ibid.

17. Hordenanças fechas por el Concexo y beçinos del lugar de Santa Maria del monte sobre la guarda y conservazion del monte . . . , 1588.

Chapter 14
The State and the Commons

1. Gilmore follows Hobsbawm in claiming "a demonstrable causal connection between the *desamortización* and the subsequent rural ferment in Andalusia" ("Land Reform," p. 142). A similar point of view is argued by Francisco Simón Segura, "La desamortización de 1855." Weisser in *The People of the Montes*, on the other hand, has used a detailed local study to show that rural revolt in Spain has roots reaching back far beyond the nineteenth-century disentailment, while Herr argues that disentailment merely reinforced preexisting trends ("La vente de propriétés de mainmorte en Espagne," and "El significado de la desamor-

tización"). For a detailed history of "the political setting of disentailment in Spain," see Francisco Tomás y Valiente, *El marco político de la desamortización*; for an evenhanded legal history of the effects of disentailment on the fact and the concept of communal property, see Nieto, *Bienes comunales*; for a rather different view of disentailment—that of a Leonese monastery whose properties were being disentailed—see José María Fernández Catón, *San Marcos de León*.

2. Nieto, *Bienes comunales*, p. 219.

3. Copies of two documents relating to the request are conserved in the *concejo* archive of Santa María: the petition itself, and a survey of the areas to be exempted from sale. It is interesting that, at the time of the request, the village was still paying *foros* (perpetual leaseholds) on two major tracts of the common lands in question: for the wastes and pastures of Trigalejos, 30.25 *pesetas* annually to the city of León, and for the *monte* of San Pelayo, thirty-two *fanegas* of rye each year to the countess of Peñaranda de Bracamonte. The petition explicitly states that, even granted the exemption, the village is to continue paying these *foros*.

4. AHPL, Desamortización, Propios 8842 (Villafeliz, 1875). Whether these lands were finally auctioned off is not clear from the records, as so often happens; it is gaps such as these that make research on disentailment very frustrating at times, particularly when village records are nonexistent.

5. AHPL, Desamortización, Propios 8849 (Villasinta, 1875).

6. AHPL, Desamortización, Propios 8850 (Villasinta, 1875). This property was purchased by a *vecino* of the village.

7. AHPL, Desamortización, Propios 8845 (Villaseca, 1875). This meadow is bought by a *vecino* who later cedes it to the village, reserving a share for himself. The same thing happens with another terrain that had been cleared by the *vecinos* and with another meadowland; see Propios 8844 (Villaseca, 1875).

Many other cases of interaction between the state bureaucracy and the villages could be cited. Examples of refusing an exemption from sale on account of recent land clearances can be found in Propios 8930 and 8933 (Gallegos, 1876), 8931 (Santa Colomba, 1876), 8844 (Villanueva del Condado, 1877), and 9328 (Villafeliz, 1877). The state decides that village lands are alienable in spite of *foros* that weigh upon them in several cases, such as Propios 8840 (Paradilla, 1875, a *foro* of fifty-six *fanegas* of grain), 8846 (Villasinta, 1875, a proportional share in the villagewide *foro* of forty-six *fanegas* of grain, and 9284 (Alija, 1896, seventy-two *fanegas* of wheat and barley). In some cases the lands being disentailed are former parts of common woodlands already exempted from sale, but have since been ruled too far from the woodlands, as in Propios 9282 (Valdefresno, 1896) and 9286 (Garrafe, 1896). In others the *alcalde pedáneo* of the affected village writes a petition for exemption that the state bureaucracy rejects because the *pedáneos* "lack the legal capacity" (*carecen de personalidad*) to communicate with the state, a job that from 1889 on is reserved for the municipal *alcaldes*—see Propios 9223 (Vegas, 1892), 9328 (Santibañez, 1896), 9285 (Villamayor, 1896), and 9286 (Garrafe, 1896). In one case the buyer himself asks for a retroactive exemption on the grounds that, first, he has bid five times the value of the parcel, and second, that the village considers the land he has bought indispensable for its common use; perhaps he was being pressured by his fellow villagers. See Propios 9044 (Barrio de Nuestra Señora, 1888). It seems that his request was denied.

8. See Alonso Rodríguez-Rivas, "Prólogo." The section of the original *Catálogo de los montes ... de utilidad pública* (1901) which refers to the province of León has been reprinted, along with a list of the *montes* of *libre disposición*, in *Catálogo de los montes de utilidad pública ... de León* (1964).

9. Nieto, *Bienes comunales*, p. 230.

10. Actas de concejo, 29 October 1899, Santa María del Monte.

11. Actas de concejo, 8 May 1907, Santovenia del Monte.

12. AHPL, Desamortización, Clero 1850, 3038, 3106, and 5897.

13. Taped interview with Leonardo Mirantes, 29 September 1980. This informant remembered the purchase of the *mayorazgo*'s lands in Santa María by his grandfather and two other *vecinos*.

14. Apeos de las eredades que pertenecen a la Fabrica de la Yglessia Parrochial del Lugar de Santa María del Monte, 1716, Santa Maria del Monte parish archive.

15. Apeos de la parroquia de Santovenia del Monte, 1784, AHDL, Fondo parroquial ms. 454; Apeos generales ... de Villamayor, 1765, AHN, Clero 2737; Apeos generales ... de Vegas, 1746, AHN, Clero 2732.

16. Actas de concejo, 21 February 1871, Santa María del Monte.

17. Actas de concejo, 19 October 1874, Santa María del Monte.

18. Actas de concejo, 9 February 1875, Santa María del Monte. It was not uncommon for the *vecinos* of villages, in León at least, to pool their

resources and repurchase their own disentailed common lands from the state; see López Morán, *Derecho consuetudinario*, p. 139.

19. Escritura de enagenación de un foro, 14 November 1896, Santa María del Monte *concejo* archive. The *foro* that the village had contracted with the city of León for the use of the pasture and wastes of Trigalejos in 1698 was still in effect in the 1920s, as can be seen from scattered receipts in the *concejo* archive, though the amount of the *foro* had been raised from 66 *reales* to 121 *reales* annually in 1804. What happened to this *foro* is not remembered, perhaps because by the 1920s 121 *reales* (or 30.25 *pesetas*) was already less than the annual licenses fees and taxes the *concejo* was paying for its lands.

Another stretch of woodland, Valdelorio, which the *concejo* had been renting from the marquise of Valverde for 140 *reales* a year in 1753, was bought by five or six villagers from "a Lady, or a marquise, or a *foro* that there had been" (*de una señora, de una marquesa, o de un foro que había*) as Leonardo remembered being told. From the people he mentions as buying it—grandfathers and great-grandfathers of present villagers— this must have happened around the middle of the nineteenth century. Although they had planned to buy on behalf of the village, many *vecinos* did not welcome the expenditure involved and the purchasers ended up keeping it in their own names. Since that time many parcels of Valdelorio have been sold to *vecinos* of nearby villages, which lack woods of their own. Taped interview with Leonardo Mirantes, 29 September 1980.

20. Taped interview with Sixto Mirantes, 22 March 1981.

21. Ibid.

22. See Alonso Rodríguez-Rivas, "Prólogo," for a brief history of the *Catálogo*.

23. Taped interview with Leonardo Mirantes, 29 September 1980.

24. One significant example of the state's assumption of control is that of the *dos hojas* system described above. Since 1836 this system has not been binding on villagers, by national law, and the fallow or stubble of the fields has been considered not part of the common patrimony but the "inalienable property of their respective owners"; see García Fernández, "Aspectos del paisaje agrario," p. 36, on this point. In the present the owners of the sheep that graze on the fallow pay a certain amount fixed by law to the municipal seat, which then divides the money received among the owners of the fields.

I know of no work that attempts to show the links between the formation of oppressive state structures and the drawing up of the laws

of disentailment, which occurred almost simultaneously in many countries in the mid-1850s. The chronology, though, strongly suggests such
links, and it also suggests that studies of dissentailment not only at the
local but also at the "world system" level would be fruitful: Spain's Ley
Madoz of 1855 is followed in 1856 by Mexico's almost identical Ley
Lerdo; the unification of Italy in 1860 is soon followed by disentailment
acts.

Chapter 15
The Presence of the Past

1. AHPL, Protocolos, leg. 660 (Antonio Sandoval, León, 1725), ff. 332-
342.
Tombstones in rural parishes of León were frequently endowed in
the eighteenth century. In nearby parish churches I found one, sometimes
two, such memorial stones preserved. Undoubtedly they represent, in
the permanence of stone, the most prosperous and well-connected families of a past era, for these memorials, besides being costly, had to be
approved by an important member of the church hierarchy. The Salas
Celis memorial stone, for example, gained the approval of the vicar
general of the Cathedral of León. One reason permission was required
for the donation of a tombstone was that it involved the cession of a
piece of the church floor to a given family, which otherwise would be
recycled as burial space among all the families of the village.
2. Miguel's mother, Paula de Celis, had died in 1700, followed by his
father, Domingo de Salas, in 1707. Miguel had two surviving brothers.
One, Domingo, married into another village and dropped out of the
historical record of Santa María. The other, Juan de Salas Celis, had
nine children, of whom four survived, including only one son, Manuel,
who followed in his uncle's footsteps by becoming a priest. As a result,
after two generations the name of Salas Celis had died out in Santa
María. Libro de bautizados, 1665-1779, Libro de difuntos, 1665-1822,
Santa María del Monte parish archive.
3. The tombstone is inscribed with the words: "Aqui Yacen Dom[ing]o
de Salas y Paula de Celis Su Muger Bezinos que Fueron de este Lugar.
Doto esta sepultura Dn. Miguel de Salas Zelis cura de Trovajo del
Cerezedo Su Hijo para Si y los Descendientes por Linea Recta de Juan

de Salas Zelis su Herm[an]o. Paga 6 R[eale]s cada a[ñ]o, esc[ritur]a a[n]te
S[a]ndoval Es[criba]no en Leon Año De 1725."

4. In Santa María the last person to be buried in the church was the
infant Bernardo Castro Rodríguez on 20 January 1833. Libro de difuntos,
1823-1851, Santa María del Monte parish archive.

Contemporary villagers understand that people were buried around
the church, where bones have also been found, or in a plot next to it,
as was the case before the cemetery was built, but many find it difficult
to believe that people might have been buried in the actual body of the
church.

5. John H. Elliott, *Imperial Spain*, p. 170.

6. Jean Vilar, "Gloire ou raison garder?"

7. On the geographic survey of Phillip II, see Carmelo Viñas y Mey,
"Las relaciones de Felipe II y su publicación." The responses to the
questionnaire, which are extant for New Castile, have been transcribed
and published by Viñas y Mey and Ramón Paz, *Relaciones histórico-
geográfico-estadísticas*. Two important studies based on the responses to
the royal questionnaire are Salomon, *La vida rural* and Christian, *Local
Religion*.

8. Legends of buried treasure are widespread in northern Spain, where
the treasures are usually attributed to the time of the Moors. See, for
instance, Matías Díez Alonso, *Mitos y leyendas*, pp. 29-35.

9. In the first volume of his catalogue of the documents in the diocesan
archive of León, José María Fernández Catón cites a record of a 1217
pact between the monastery of San Claudio in León (also Benedictine)
and Roderico Guterriz, who is given usufruct rights over lands belonging
to the monastery in exchange for milling whatever wheat the monastery
of San Pelayo del Monte might need; and with the promise that if he
enters the order of Saint Benedict in San Claudio he will give these lands
over to San Pelayo, otherwise leaving them to the latter monastery at
his death. See Fernández Catón, *Catálogo del Archivo Histórico Diocesano*,
pp. 230-232. From a fifteenth-century copy of a thirteenth-century *Becerro
de presentaciones de curatos y beneficios* we learn that Santa María (as well
as nearby Gallegos) fell under the ecclesiastical domain of San Pelayo
del Monte. This document is transcribed and analyzed by Fernández
Flórez, "El 'Becerro de Presentaciones.'" A document from 1179 concerning the donation of lands to the monastery of San Isidoro in León
mentions, together with Santa María del Monte and other nearby villages,
San Pelayo del Monte; thus there might also have been a village by that

name, but it may be that the document is referring simply to the terminus
of the monastery (San Isidoro archive, Documento real, no. 325).

10. This much we can surmise from an undated note found among
the documents of the monastery of San Claudio which states that "around
the 1470s [Gonzalo de Guzmán] traded with San Claudio for the property
of San Pelayo del Monte, although the deed of the exchange is missing"
(Fernández Catón, *Catálogo*, p. 263). In later records the *monte* of San
Pelayo appears as the domain of the marquises of Toral, descendents of
Gonzalo de Guzmán. We also know from a number of sources that
Santa María owed the *tercia*, that is, the third part of its tithes of grain,
to the monastery of San Claudio (see, for instance, AHN, Clero, libro
5516); this right was most likely a holdover from the original ecclesiastical
jurisdiction of the monastery of San Pelayo.

11. AHM, Libro de cuentas de León, various years (for instance, 1648,
when Trigalejos is rented out for 1,000 *maravedís* or 2 2/3 *ducados*);
untitled document, Santa María del Monte, 1698; untitled document,
Villamayor, 1698 (copy dated 1701).

12. Note that in central León, where all villages are small, the word
despoblado does not have the alternative meaning of "very small settlements" which Freeman found in documents for Soria (*Neighbors*, p. 84).

13. In the documents of the Archivo Histórico Diocesano of León we
find twenty *vecinos* living in Moral as late as 1597, but when the next
general survey of the diocese is taken in 1734 it is already a *despoblado*
and the parish has been moved to the nearby village of Villafruela
(AHDL, Fondo general, ma. 32). Moral reappears in a survey of land
ownership undertaken in 1865 as a *barrio* of Villafruela, with fourteen
property-owners (Amillaramiento, 1865, Vegas del Condado muncipal
archive). By 1910 it had a population of 133, and by 1950 it had grown
to 231. It is still officially classified as a *barrio* (Fray Orencio Llamazares,
Vegas del Condado, pp. 5-6).

14. Taped interview with Francisca Rodríguez, 30 June 1981, Secos
de Porma. Díez Alonso has collected the same legend from the Leonese
mountain village of Piedrashecha, in reference to a depopulated village
called Santas Martas (*Mitos y leyendas*, pp. 159-160). Such legends deserve
a fuller study along the lines of Jean-Claude Schmitt's analysis of a
French medieval legend and rite that persisted until the nineteenth
century, and in some of its features until the present (*The Holy
Greyhound*).

15. AGS, Expedientes de Hacienda, leg. 114.

16. AGS, Expedientes de Hacienda, leg. 112. In the village of Barrillos a search turned up the stick from the year before, but none previous to that could be found. Ibid., leg. 113.

17. See, for example, Max Weber, *On Law in Economy and Society*, p. 66 and Bloch, *French Rural History*, p. 183.

18. Bloch, *Feudal Society*, p. 115. Bloch's entire discussion on customary law and its relation to literacy and to a sense of history in the early Middle Ages is extremely interesting. Law in this period rested entirely on custom and tradition, while custom in turn relied solely on memory; a claim to possession of a piece of land was justifiable above all by long usage, whereas written titles, if there were any, "were hardly ever produced save to assist memory" (ibid.; see pp. 113-116).

19. In Spain, these codifications were piecemeal and they never led, as in France, to an attempt to "enrich customary law so that it might become a common law for the whole country" (René Filhol, "The Codification of Customary Law in France," p. 270). I thank Javier Gil for this reference. Altogether the codification of custom in Spain has not received the attention it deserves.

Great energy and administrative skill had gone, for example, into the gathering of information about economic and social life in every town and village of Spain in the late sixteenth century with the famous questionnaire of Phillip II, and again in the eighteenth century with the Catastro de Ensenada. Yet these remarkable quantities of data were never put to the general use for which they had been intended. The Catastro was a massive property survey of all of Spain, undertaken with the intent of replacing the bewildering complexity of taxes which the state collected from it subjects with a single, simplified tax, the *única contribución*. The survey was completed, detailed provincial summaries were compiled, but the *única contribución* never became law.

20. See Jack Goody's "Introduction" to *Literacy in Traditional Societies*. I have also drawn inspiration from Goody's more recent work on literacy, *The Domestication of the Savage Mind*, as well as from Le Roy Ladurie's discussion of "the paths of Scripture" (*The Peasants of Languedoc*, pp. 149-171) and from Natalie Zemon Davis's fascinating account of the introduction of printing and its interpretation and use by "the people" in sixteenth-century France (*Society and Culture*, pp. 189-226). Also interesting in this context is Ginzburg's study of the cosmos of a sixteenth-century Italian miller and his relationship to books (*The Cheese and the Worms*).

21. Flórez de Quiñones, *Contribución*, p. 146.

22. López Morán, "León," p. 276.

23. Flórez de Quiñones, *Contribución*, p. 147.

24. López Morán, *Derecho consuetudinario*, p. 38.

25. AHDL, Fondo general, ms. 64.

26. "Escuela de primeras letras dotada con 200 reales, á que asisten 20 niños de ambos sexos." Madoz, *Diccionario*, s.v. Santa María del Monte. Other villages in the area with primary schools cited by Madoz included Vegas del Condado with twenty-four children, Villalboñe with twenty, Villavente with twenty, Ambasaguas with twelve children and a "wretched endowment" of 180 *reales* a year for its teacher, Gallegos with twelve children, Devesa with fourteen, Castro with ten, Santa Colomba with thirty, Barrillos with twenty, Barrio with twenty, Valdefresno and Tendal with a joint school, Riosequino, Robledo, Roderos, Ruiforco, Villanueva del Arbol, Villaquilambre, Valdesogo de Abajo, all with unspecified numbers of students, and San Feliz de Torío, which enjoyed not only a primary school but an endowed chair of Latin (*cátedra de latinidad*) which was free of tuition to all children of the Torío valley. The latter school was the only one in the area, outside of the three in the city of León, mentioned in the Catastro of 1752.

27. The figures for Vegas are: 620 men could read and write, 67 could read but not write, 250 were illiterate, and another 125 were under five years of age; 162 women could read and write, 147 could read but not write, 735 were illiterate, and another 128 were under five. In the city of León 23 percent of males and 59 percent of females over five were illiterate, and in the province as a whole the figures were 36 percent of males and 83 percent of females (*Censo*, 1863).

28. See the papers edited by Eric Hobsbawm and Terence Ranger in *The Invention of Tradition*.

Epilogue

1. Berger, *Pig Earth,*, p. 210 and Juliet Du Boulay, *Portrait of a Greek Mountain Village*, p. 37.

Afterword

1. For more detailed self-reflection, see Ruth Behar, "Death and Memory: From Santa María del Monte to Miami Beach," *Cultural Anthropology* 6(3):346–384 (1991).

2. For a sensitive account of why women in the academy often feel unable to fully express what they know, see Peggy McIntosh, "Feeling Like a Fraud: Part Two," The Stone Center, Works in Progress, no. 37 (Wellesley, Mass.: Wellesley College, 1989).

3. Gary McDonough, review in *Ethnohistory* 37:71–73 (Winter 1990).

4. See, for example, Jean Briggs, *Never in Anger: Portrait of an Eskimo Family* (Cambridge, Mass.: Harvard University Press, 1970); Lila Abu-Lughod, "Fieldwork of a Dutiful Daughter," in Soraya Altorki and Camillia Fawzi El-Solh, eds., *Arab Women in the Field: Studying Your Own Society* (New York: Syracuse University Press, 1988); Dorinne Kondo, "Dissolution and Reconstitution of Self: Implications for Anthropological Epistemology," *Cultural Anthropology* 1(1):74–88 (1986).

5. William Douglass, review in *Peasant Studies* 14(2):119–130 (1987).

6. See James Clifford, "On Ethnographic Allegory," in James Clifford and George E. Marcus, eds., *Writing Culture: The Poetics and Politics of Ethnography* (Berkeley: University of California Press, 1986) and Renato Rosaldo, "Imperialist Nostalgia," in *Culture and Truth: The Remaking of Social Analysis* (Boston: Beacon Press, 1989).

7. James Clifford, "Of Other Peoples: Beyond the 'Salvage' Paradigm," in Hal Foster, ed., *Discussions in Contemporary Culture* (Seattle: Bay Press, 1987): 122.

8. William Roseberry, "Political Economy," *Annual Review of Anthropology* 17:161–185 (1988). Roseberry states, "Behar's book ... holds an important place within a broadly conceived anthropological political economy" (p. 175).

9. Richard Herr, review in *Agricultural History* 62:108–109 (1988). Other historians also noted that the work evoked a strong sense of the past as present but that it was not exactly history; for example, see the review by Peter Sahlins in *Journal of Social History* 21(2):388–390 (1987).

10. Josep Llobera, review in *Bulletin of Hispanic Studies* 65(3):313–314 (July 1988).

11. Recently, Lila Abu-Lughod has called for "ethnographies of the particular" that would be based on stories about "particular individuals in time and place." She suggests that such storytelling in anthropology

would unsettle the typifying features of the culture concept and provide a way of writing "about lives so as to constitute others as less 'other.'" See Lila Abu-Lughod, "Writing Against Culture," forthcoming in Richard Fox, ed., *Recapturing Anthropology*, School of American Research Seminar Series (Seattle: University of Washington Press). For an example of a work that focuses on life stories in the Iberian context, see Sally Cole, *Women of the Praia: Work and Lives in a Portuguese Coastal Community* (Princeton: Princeton University Press, 1991).

12. My essay on "Death and Memory" relies almost exclusively on conversational narratives. Also see my essay, "Rage and Redemption: Reading the Life Story of a Mexican Marketing Woman," *Feminist Studies* 16(1):223–258 (1990). My book on a Mexican woman's life story will be published by Beacon Press in 1992. I have begun to experiment with the use of the personal voice in unexpected genres, such as in my piece, "The Body in the Woman, the Story in the Woman: A Book Review and Personal Essay," *Michigan Quarterly Review*, special issue on "The Female Body," 29(4):694–738 (1990).

13. With the publication of *Writing Culture* and its call for ethnographers to pay closer attention to how, and for whom, they write, the possibility of doing experimental writing has been legitimated in new ways that should make the burden of authorship less heavy for women. On the other hand, the exclusion of feminist anthropologists in *Writing Culture* on the grounds that they have not contributed to textual innovation is sobering. The implication is that it is still risky for a woman to engage in experimental ethnography, especially with a strong feminist focus, until she has earned professional status. For further discussion of these issues, see Deborah Gordon, "Writing Culture, Writing Feminism," and Kamala Visweswaran, "Defining Feminist Ethnography," in *Inscriptions* Nos. 3/4, pp. 7–44 (1988); Lila Abu-Lughod, "Can There Be A Feminist Ethnography?" *Women and Performance* 5(1):7–27 (1988).

14. Josep Llobera, *Bulletin of Hispanic Studies* review, 314.

15. Ruth Behar, "The Struggle for the Church: Popular Anticlericalism and Religiosity in Post-Franco Spain," in Ellen Badone, ed., *Religious Orthodoxy and Popular Faith in European Society* (Princeton: Princeton University Press, 1990). The essay, "Death and Memory," which is a companion piece, was written shortly after, but from a more self-reflexive perspective.

16. Renato Rosaldo, *Culture and Truth*, p. 19.

17. The most pioneering and in-depth work on the study of contem-

porary Catholicism in Spain has been done by William A. Christian, Jr., *Person and God in a Spanish Valley* (Princeton: Princeton University Press, rev. edition, 1989 [1972]). More recently, a collection of ethnographic essays on Catholicism in a variety of European communities have been brought together by Ellen Badone in *Religious Orthodoxy and Popular Faith in European Society*.

18. My essay on "Death and Memory" explores more fully the ironies of my ignorance of my own religious traditions.

19. The first quote is from Davydd J. Greenwood, "The Anthropologies of Spain: A Proposal for Collaboration," *Working Paper No. 2 of the Spanish Studies Round Table*, University of Illinois at Chicago (Society for Spanish and Portuguese Historical Studies, 1989), p. 11. The second quote is from James W. Fernandez, "Consciousness and Class in Southern Spain," *American Ethnologist* 10(1):171 (1983).

20. William Christian describes a similar feeling of having participated in primitivizing his subjects in the epilogue to the new edition of his *Person and God in a Spanish Valley*. In my case, I think there were also times when village people and I reversed roles, with them questioning what they perceived as the anthropologist's primitivity. During my first summer of fieldwork, people found the long country skirts then in fashion that I wore extremely quaint and reminiscent of how their grandmothers dressed. Years later, when I returned with my ten-month-old son, Gabriel, people were shocked that I was still breastfeeding him, a practice which they said few women followed anymore past the first few weeks after birth.

21. For an excellent analysis of the politics of folklore collecting in Spain, see James Fernandez, "Folklorists as Agents of Nationalism," in Richard M. Dorson, ed., *Folklore in the Modern World* (The Hague: Mouton, 1978).

22. The citation is from Raymond Williams, *The Country and The City* (London: Oxford University Press, 1973), p. 297. I discuss Francoist ideology in greater detail in my essay on "The Struggle for the Church."

23. For an important analysis of recent social patterns in Spain, see Víctor Pérez Díaz, *El Retorno de la Sociedad Civil* (Madrid: Instituto de Estudios Económicos, 1987).

24. David Ansen, "The Man of La Mancha," *Newsweek*, December 5, 1988, 88. Almodóvar's most popular films in the United States have been "Women on the Verge of a Nervous Breakdown," and "Tie Me Up! Tie Me Down!"

25. Vito Russo, "Pedro Almodóvar on the Verge ... Man of La Mania," *Film Comment* 24:13–17 (Nov./Dec. 1988). The youthfulness, freshness, and vitality of the new Spain is a theme that runs through a gamut of articles exploring everything from the emerging Spanish fashion industry to Spanish politics. An article in *Vogue* entitled "The New Spain" carried the headline, "Heady with artistic and cultural freedom, Spain today is *the* place to be young—like its popular King and Queen—and on the move." See Barbara Rose, "The New Spain," *Vogue* 1976:348–357 (Feb. 1989); Nina Darnton, "A New Language of High Style," *Newsweek*, December 17, 1990, 58–59.

26. Marsha Kinder, "Pleasure and the New Spanish Mentality: A Conversation with Pedro Almodóvar," *Film Quarterly* 41:33–44 (Fall 1987).

27. María Antonia García de León and Teresa Maldonado, *Pedro Almodóvar, La Otra España Cañí* (Ciudad Real: Biblioteca de Autores y Temas Manchegos, 1989): 31.

Weights, Measures, and
Monetary Units

I have frequently had occasion to quote measures from the system that was in use before the official adoption of the metric system by Spain in 1871. Most of these are no longer in common use. I list them here with their generally accepted equivalents.

Linear Measure
  1 *vara* = 0.836 meters (33 inches)
  1 *legua* = 4 kilometers
Weight
  1 *arroba* = 25 *libras* = 11.5 kilos
  1 *libra* = 4 *cuarterones* = 460 grams (1.01 lbs.)
         1 *cuarterón* = 115 grams (4.05 oz.)
Liquid Measure
  1 *cántara* = 8 *azumbres* = 16.1 liters
  1 *azumbre* = 4 *cuartillos* = 2.0 liters
         1 *cuartillo* = 0.5 liters

The word *cántaro* (pitcher, jug) is often found in documents as a liquid measure; I was told that it was equal to "16 liters and 13 centiliters," that is, precisely a *cántara*, and that it was also known as the *arroba de vino*, as opposed to the *arroba de aceite* of 11.5 kilos.

I have also made frequent reference to Spanish monetary units from both the old and the new systems. These are as follows:

real. A coin, now long out of circulation, equivalent in the old regime to 34 *maravedís* and in current usage (by older people and jokingly) to a quarter of a *peseta.* Also, *real de vellón*, a *real* made of a combination of copper and silver.

maravedí. In the seventeenth to nineteenth centuries, 34 maravedís was equivalent to 1 *real.* Plural: *maravedís, maravedises,* or *maravedíes.*

cuarto. 4 *maravedís*

ducado. 11 *reales* or 375 *maravedís*

peseta. The current monetary unit of Spain, divided into 100 *cén-timos*. At the beginning of the twentieth century equivalent to one U.S. dollar, the value of the *peseta* fell rapidly in the 1940s; during the fieldwork period there were 70 to 95 *pesetas* to the dollar.

duro. The five-*peseta* coin; "five *duros*," a small amount of money, "two bits"

The old measures of dry volume and of land area deserve a special note. They form a local system, and the measures I have quoted do not necessarily correspond exactly to the measures of the same names in use elsewhere in Spain. They are still in use, as a kind of auxiliary system alongside the metric system. And these measures, as they were and are used, are almost always approximate rather than exact, and are frequently subjective as well.

The basic units used to measure both the volume of grains or beans and the area of the land in which they are sown are the *hemina* and the *carga*, though the Castilian measures, the *fanega*, the *celemín*, and much more rarely the *cuartillo*, are also used. They are interrelated as follows:

1 *carga* = 12 *heminas*
1 *fanega* = 3 *heminas*
1 *hemina* = 4 *celemines*
1 *celemín* = 4 *cuartillos*

As a dry measure, one *hemina* is said to be equivalent to 18.5 liters, or slightly more than half a bushel. As mentioned above, in practice this is only a rough equivalent. Each family has its own hand-made wooden box used to measure the *hemina* at harvest time; I measured two of these *heminas* in the possession of one family and found one to hold 17.8 liters and the other 16.5.

Nowadays the *hemina* is generally used to measure the harvest of grains in order to have an idea of the size of the harvest. Since grain is now sold by the kilo, the following standardized equivalents are used for estimation:

One *hemina* of oats = 9 kilos
barley = 11 kilos
beans = 15 kilos
chickpeas = 16 kilos
wheat or rye = 14.4 kilos

Susan Tax Freeman quotes the same equivalents, in terms of *fanegas*, for Soria.[1]

As a square measure, the *hemina* (or *hemina de sembradura*) was defined, at least through the eighteenth century, as the amount of land needed to sow one *hemina* of grain. There could be no regular equivalent in terms of square *varas*, then—unlike the Castilian *fanega* which was defined as 3,200 square *varas* or 2,237 square meters—for each piece of land varied in quality and therefore in the amount of grain needed. Moreover, different people perceived the quality of the land differently, and what to one was three *heminas* of land might to another be two or perhaps four *heminas*. From the response for Villarrubia (an estate near Sahagún owned by the abbot of that city) to question 9 of the Catastro de Ensenada questionnaire, we can make the following rough equivalences for different types of land in this period:

One *hemina de sembradura* of:		Castilian *celemines*[2]		square meters
good quality wheatland	=	2 ⅔	=	571
medium quality wheatland	=	4	=	856
good quality rye land	=	4	=	856
medium quality rye land	=	6	=	1,284
poor quality rye land	=	8	=	1,712

In the present, lands are still spoken of as measuring so many *heminas* or *fanegas*, but they are no longer measured by the amount of grain sown.[3] In general, the *carga* of land is now roughly equated with the hectare (10,000 square meters, about 2.47 acres), which gives an *hemina* of 833 square meters. Some people, however, quote the figures they were taught in school: one *hemina* of irrigated land is 628 square meters, one *hemina* of dry land is 939 square meters. Still others equate the *hemina* with an even thousand square meters.

[1] Freeman, *Neighbors*, p. 210.

[2] The *celemín* used here is based on a *fanega* of 3,675 square *varas*, rather than the usual Castilian *fanega* of 3,200 square *varas*. This response, which I consulted in the Archivo Histórico Provincial de León, was the only one I found which used both the Leonese and the Castilian measures.

[3] One man from Santa María told me, "With an *hemina* of rye you can sow an *hemina* and one *celemín* or an *hemina* and a half" of land. Another told me that "everyone sows his own way. In an *hemina* here, let's say of a thousand meters, you couldn't put an *hemina* of rye because it would come out very thick."

Glossary

✛

abad. The head of a village confraternity (lit. "abbot").

acta. An act or record of the transactions of a *concejo* meeting, written in a *libro de actas de concejo* or book of *concejo* acts. *Levantar acta*, to draw up an *acta*.

alcabala. Under the old regime, a tax on sales.

alcalde. Mayor or headman of a village, municipality or city. *Alcalde municipal*, headman of a municipality. *Alcalde de barrio, alcalde pedáneo*, name given to headman of a village forming part of a municipality after the nineteenth-century municipal reforms.

alfileres. In eighteenth-century Santa María, payment for *vecindad* owed by women upon marriage (lit. "pin money").

ánimas, las. Bread for the souls in purgatory: bread that is auctioned off after Sunday mass to pay for masses for the souls (lit. "the souls").

ante-cocina. An antechamber before the kitchen.

apañar. To gather plants and weeds by hand or with the sickle for feeding the family animals (lit. "to grasp"). *Apañador*, one who goes to *apañar*.

aparcería. Partnership, particularly in the ownership of cattle.

ayuntamiento. Municipal seat, municipal government.

bagaje. The obligation to transport beggars to a nearby village or hospice.

bago. A furlong or group of lands known by a single name and all sown (or left fallow) at the same date. In some areas *bago* is the equivalent of *hoja*, but here it is any named group of lands; a group of *bagos* makes up the *hoja*. Equivalent of Castilian *pago*, furlong, field.

baldíos. Wastes, woodland, untilled lands considered in the public domain; also, *tierras baldías*.

barrio. Neighborhood of a village or city.

bienes comunales. Communal properties: properties used freely and communally by members of the community, as opposed to *propios*; also, *bienes de aprovechamiento comunal*, properties of communal use.

bienes raíces. Real estate, landed property (lit. "rooted goods").

Boletín oficial del Estado. The official journal of the state.

cacho. A piece or chunk of something; *cachín*, a small *cacho*.

caridad, la. Blessed bread: two loaves of bread brought to mass by a different house every Sunday, this duty being circulated *a corrida*; one loaf is given to the priest, the other blessed by him to be cut up and consumed by all the congregants in a village-wide communion.

caridades. Charities: groups of lands administered by the *concejo* and used to pay for endowed masses and charity feasts for the poor; also, the mass and feast themselves. The charities in Santa María were: the Charity of March; of April or of Palm Sunday; of Saint Andrew; of Saint Pelagius.

carta puebla. In medieval Spain, a charter given to the settlers of a new town or village describing their rights and privileges.

casa. The house. *Casa de concejo*, the meeting house of the *concejo*.

Catálogo de Montes. A catalogue published in 1901 of all the woodlands in Spain considered in the public domain which were to be exempted from disentailment (*montes de utilidad pública*).

censo. Quitrent: a contract by which, under the old regime, one or more lands or houses paid an annual pension as the interest on a sum of money given to the owner. The interest was usually at a rate of 3 percent in the eighteenth century. Also, *censo al quitar*, a redeemable *censo*.

chalet. A vacation home in the country.

cocina. The kitchen. *Cocina de horno*, kitchen with a large clay oven for baking bread. *Cocina de trébede*, the old style of kitchen, with a central chimney above an open fire where food was cooked on a trivet.

compañía de vacas. The cow company, a mutual aid society in Santa María formed by the owners of cattle to insure one another for losses of their animals.

común. The village community.

concejo. The village council; an assembly of all the *vecinos* of a place, which forms its local government; also, *concejo abierto*, the open council or assembly. *Concejo y vecinos*, a legal phrase referring to the *vecinos* considered both as a body and individually. *Concejil*, that which pertains to the *concejo*.

consejo. A town council, usually closed and oligarchic as opposed to the open *concejo*.

corral. The central courtyard of a house.

corredor. An open balcony with balustrades that runs around the upper level of the *corral*.

corregidor. A magistrate in charge of a district or jurisdiction.

corrida, la. The system of turn-taking in which things are passed around all the houses of the village *a corrida*, that is, from one house to the next, moving always in a fixed order (in Santa María, to the right); a completed circle of turn-taking.

coto. Closed off: referring specifically to the temporary enclosure of the furlong (*hoja*) which is sown in a given year. The other *hoja*, which lies fallow, is *descotada*, open.

cotos boyales. Ox pastures, closed to other animals.

cotos redondos. A large landed estate, usually enclosed.

cuarto. A room. *Cuarto alto*, an upper room; *cuarto bajo*, a lower room; *cuarto de pan*, a bread room or granary.

desamortización. Disentailment: the land reform carried out in the nineteenth century in which lands belonging to noble and ecclesiastical entailed estates, and later common lands as well, were sold by the national government. Notices of sales were published weekly in the *Boletín oficial del Estado*.

despoblado. A depopulated or disappeared village (in some parts of Spain, simply a very small village).

facendera. See *hacendera*.

facera. An irrigation ditch that borders on a private land.

fiel de fechos. Village community scribe: a person authorized to perform the services of a notary public in villages without one.

forastero. Outsider, stranger: a person from another village.

foro. A perpetual leasehold; also, *foro perpetuo*.

ganancial. Property earned by husband and wife in marriage, as opposed to what each brings to the marriage by inheritance; usually used in the plural, *los gananciales*. *Gananciar* (a neologism), to earn *gananciales*.

hacendera. A communal prestation of labor, performed by all the *vecinos* jointly for matters considered to be in the community interest; also *facendera* or *cendera*. *Hacendera de carro*, one to which *vecinos* are required to bring carts; *hacendera de a cuerpo*, one to which *vecinos* bring only their persons and the necessary tools.

hidalgo. A member of the minor Spanish nobility.

hijuela. A written document listing the inheritance portion that an heir is to receive; the inheritance portion itself.

hoja. One of two furlongs or groups of fields into which all the cultivated lands of a village are divided, with the exception of gardens and meadows. Each year one *hoja* is sown while the other lies fallow; together, the two furlongs form the *dos hojas* system of crop rotation.

in solidum. A Latin legal phrase, "for the whole," collectively. In local documents it is often found in a literal translation into Spanish as *en solido* or *ensolido.*

jornalero. A day laborer, often landless, especially when used in contrast to *labrador.*

junta administrativa. An administrative committee consisting of one *presidente* (or *alcalde*) and two *vocales*, created in the nineteenth century to form the local government of villages that are not considered municipalities in their own right.

labrador, labradora. A property-owning, self-sustaining farmer; as an adjective, industrious. From *labrar*, to work, to till.

mayordomo. Steward of the village church. In the eighteenth century there were three *mayordomos* in Santa María, all of them elected officers of the *concejo*; today the office is circulated by turn.

medias, de a. "By halves": a sharecropping agreement in which one party supplies the labor needed to raise the crops, which are split in half between the owner and the laborer.

monte. Woodland. *Monte de utilidad pública*, woodland of public use, frequently belonging to villages but subject to state control and supervision, as opposed to *monte de libre disposición*, woodland of free use, over which the state exerts less control.

mozo, moza. An unmarried youth.

para siempre. For always. Lots of cleared common lands cast *para siempre* remain the private property of a *vecino*'s heirs even after his death, rather than returning to the community.

pastos. Pasture, especially common pasture.

pena. A fine or penalty.

pesquisa. Attendance or roll call which was taken at all functions that *vecinos* were required to attend (lit. "inquiry, investigation").

pesquisero. In the eighteenth century, an officer of the *concejo* whose main obligation was to collect *prendas* and fines from penalized *vecinos.*

piso. An urban flat or condominium.

portal. A covered porch or entranceway; the *portal* of the house is a sheltered space for keeping the cart and farm tools, while the *portal* of the church is a frequent informal meeting place for the *concejo* after Sunday mass.

por vida. For life. Lots of cleared common lands cast *por vida* remain in a *vecino*'s possession until his death, after which they return to the community to be redistributed.

postigo. A small door set in or alongside the large doors (*puertonas*) of a village house, used as an entrance for people and animals.

prece-casa. A local name for *ante-cocina* or antechamber before the kitchen. Apparently from *plaza de casa*, "plaza of the house."

prenda. A bond or pledge: an article of property taken from a person who has broken a rule of the *concejo*, for instance by allowing his or her cattle into another person's sown fields, in order to force him or her to pay the penalty called for. *Prendar*, to take a *prenda*.

presidente. The president of the *junta administrativa* of a village, hence, village headman; also, *alcalde*.

procurador. "Procurator," the title of the village headman in the sixteenth century.

propios. Public properties, which the community is free to give out in rent in order to raise money, as opposed to *bienes comunales* (lit. "one's own," i.e., the community's private property).

puertonas. The set of two large doors of a village house, used as an entrance for the cart and the yoked team. Augmentative of *puerta*, door.

regidor. The title of the village headman or headmen—there were often a pair of *regidores* in a village—from the eighteenth century to the municipal reforms of the 1830s. From *regir*, to govern.

repartimiento. An assessment, the characteristic way of raising needed money by taxing each according to his means. Under the old regime the city of León divided the *alcabala* it was to pay among the villages of its jurisdiction by *repartimiento*; within each village money was and often still is raised by assessing each household according to certain criteria such as the amount of land or number of cattle it possessed.

ruego. A fee paid by widows and those *vecinos* unable to work due to age or ill health to pardon them from attending *hacenderas* (lit. "entreaty, supplication"); also, *súplica*.

suerte. A lot or portion of anything that is distributed by casting lots, especially a piece of common land (lit. "luck, fate, lot"; from Latin *sors*, fate, condition, lot). *Sortear, echar suertes*, to cast lots, distribute by lot.

tapial. A solid mud wall made from a mixture of mud and gravel poured into a large mold.

tío, tía. A title of respect used before the given name of an older man or woman (lit. "uncle," "aunt").

usufructo. Usufruct, a legal right to use property not one's own; appears in a local inheritance document as *sufruto*, its fruits.

vacada. The herd of calves and untamed cattle of the village, taken to graze in the upland pastures by the *vaquero*, a guard or herdsman hired annually by the *concejo*.

vecera. A system of herding in which each house takes all the village animals of a given category to graze by turn, each family having the duty a certain number of days per month depending on the number of cows it has. The *vecera* is both the herd of animals itself and the system of turn-taking involved, and as such is sometimes used as an equivalent of the more general term *a corrida*. From *vez*, time, turn.

vecindad. Village citizenship, the quality of being a *vecino* of a place.

vecino, vecina. Village citizen, the head of a village household and a member of the *concejo*; also means neighbor.

vocales. Assistants to the *presidente*, who together with him form the *junta administrativa* of a village.

Principal Archival Sources

Local Archives

PARISH ARCHIVES

Barrillos

Libro de tazmía de Barrillos, 1779-1834

Libro de cuentas, Barrillos, 1800-1897

Canaleja

Apeo de las heredades de la Iglesia Parroquial, 1775

Castro

Libro de cuentas, 1524-1718

Libro de cuentas, 1719-1834 (Libro de quentas de los vienes de la yglesia parroquial del lugar de Castro jurisdizion de la ziudad de León siendo cura de dicho lugar el lizenziado Don Alexandro Blanco xetino este año de mill setezientos y diez y nuebe a onra y gloria de Dios nuestro señor y de la serenisima Virgen sanctissima su bendita madre Reinando Phelipe quinto amen)

Santa María del Monte

Apeos de las eredades que pertenecen a la Fabrica de la Yglessia Parrochial del Lugar de Santa María del Monte, y a su rettoria, a las caridades, y aniberssarios y cappellanias en ella Fundadas, 1716

Libro de difuntos, 1665-1822, 1823-1851, 1852-1870, 1870-1929, 1929-present

Libros de bautizados, 1665-1779, 1779-1851, 1851-1868, 1868-1916, 1916-present

Libros de casados, 1665-1851, 1852-1867, 1868-present

Parish registers (libros de felegresía), 1920, 1945, and 1956

Vegas del Condado

Apeos de las tierras, alajas, rentas, doctaciones, y primicias de la Yglesia de Begas del Condado, rectoria, derechos parroquiales, compañias, hermitorios y anibersarios, 1721

Villasinta
  Libro de cuentas, Visita of 1740

Concejo ARCHIVES

Ambasaguas
  Libro de actas de concejo, 1870-1890
Barrio de Nuestra Señora
  Document dated 31 December 1936
  Document dated 21 February 1964
Santa María del Monte
  Hordenanças fechas por el Concexo e beçinos del lugar de Santa
  Maria del monte sobre la guarda y conservazion del monte del dicho
  lugar, fechas en Virtud de la Carta y sobre Carta y provission del Rey
  nuestro Señor que ba escrita al principio deste quaderno de ordenanças,
  1588 (copy of 1773)
  Untitled document, 1698 (Foro del lugar de Santa María del Monte
  en favor de la ciudad de León)
  Foro del lugar de Santa Maria del Monte en favor del estado de
  Toral y casa de Guzman, 1701
  Untitled document, 1701 (Pleito entre Doña Francisca Díez del
  Blanco viuda de Marcelo de la Puente, vecina del lugar de Villafeliz
  jurisdicción de la ciudad de León por sí y como madre y criadora de
  sus hijos de la una parte, y los regidores, concejo y vecinos del lugar
  de Santa María del Monte de dicha jurisdición de la otra)
  Catastro del Marqués de la Ensenada, Respuestas Particulares (legos
  y eclesiasticos), 1753
  Ordenanzas de Santa Maria del Monte, año de 1776
  Petition for *excepción de venta*, 1896
  Deslinde y clasificacion de los terrenos que el pueblo de Santa María
  del Monte, Ayuntamiento de Vegas del Condado tiene solicitado la
  excepción de la venta, 1895
  Escritura de enagenación de un foro, 14 November 1896
  Libros de actas de concejo, 1867-1894, 1899-1949, 1942-1962, 1963-
  1978
  Castigos de concejo, 1952-1961, 1962-1964, 1966-1973
Santovenia del Monte
  Libro de actas de concejo, 1866-1919

Valdefresno
    Libro de actas de concejo, 1855-1858
Villamayor
    Hordenanzas del lugar de Villamayor del Balle de la Sobarriba del
    thenor de arriba jurisdicion de la ciudad de Leon hechas sobre la
    guarda y conservación de los montes que hay en termino del dicho
    lugar en virtud de la carta acordada probision real que ba puesta por
    cabeza, 1599 (copy of 1698)
    Untitled document, 1698 (agreement with Santa María over renting
    the pasture of Trigalejos; copy of 1701, sewn together with the
    preceding document)
    Libros de actas de concejo, 1847-1885, 1887-1908, 1910-1931

Municipal Archives

Archivo Histórico Municipal de León (AHM)
    Libro de cuentas de León, 1648
Vegas del Condado
    Ayuntamiento de Vegas del Condado, Amillaramiento individual
    de la riqueza inmueble, cultivo y ganaderia del mismo, año de 1865

Provincial Archives

Archivo Histórico Diocesano de León (AHDL)
    Fondo general, libros de visita: manuscripts 32 (1734), 37 (1738-1739),
    68 (1778), 73 (1785-1787), 79 (1790), 83 (1797-1798), and Arreglo
    parroquial del año 1854
    Fondo general, manuscript 64 (Ordenanzas del Concejo de Bernesga
    de Arriba, 1547)
    Fondo general, manuscript 14259 (Capellania Santa Maria del Monte
    1818, Vacante por muerte de Dn. Manuel de Salas, Pro. su ultimo
    posehedor)
    Uncatalogued, Relaciones de vecinos, almas y cosechas de la diocesis
    de León, dadas por los respectivos párrocos a peticion del Ilmo. Sr.
    Cuadrillero, para dar cumplimiento a las ordenes del Ministro de
    Gracia y Justicia y del Consejo, 1797, 2 vols.

Fondo parroquial, manuscript 454 (Apeos de la parroquia de Santovenia del Monte, 1784)

Archivo Histórico Provincial de León (AHPL)

Protocolos, legajos 639 (Antonio Sandoval, León, 1704), 660 (Antonio Sandoval, León, 1725), and 1336 (Pedro González Osorio, Vegas del Condado, 1784-1788)

Desamortización, Clero, 1850, 3038, 3106, 5897

Desamortización, Propios, 8840, 8842, 8844, 8845, 8846, 8849, 8850, 8930, 8931, 8933, 9044, 9223, 9282, 9283, 9284, 9285, 9286, 9328

Marqués de la Ensenada, legajo 1392 (Respuestas generales for Villarrubia, junto a Sahagún. For other data from the Catastro de Esnsenada, see AGS and AHN, below)

Archivo de San Isidoro de León

Documento real, no. 325 (Doña Oro Miguel dona a San Isidoro cuantiosas heredades en Villa Ezit, Villalboñe, Solanilla, Represa, San Pelayo del Monte, Santa María y Sandrinos, 1179)

National Archives

Archivo General de Simancas (AGS)

Expendientes de Hacienda (1597), legajos 112, 113, 114, 115

Dirección General de Rentas (DGR), 1ª Remesa, libros 329, 330, 331, 332, 337, 361, 363, 365, 653 (Respuestas generales to the Catastro de Ensenada for eighty-five villages of central León)

Archivo Histórico Nacional (AHN)

Sección Clero, libros 2732 (Apeos generales de Vegas del Condado, 1746), 2737 (Apeos generales de Villamayor, 1765), and 5516 (Apeos generales de Santa María del Monte, 1766)

Sección Hacienda, provincial summaries for León of the Catastro de Ensenada, libros 7455 and 7460 (Lo que producen en dinero los alquileres de casas, renta de oficios y empleos enagenados de la Real Corona, juros, molinos de todos usos, y diezmos, con distinción de pueblos), 7456 (Lo que importa el lucro al año de los cambistas, comerciantes, mercaderos, cirujanos, boticarios, arrieros, etc., por pueblos), 7457 (Número de individuos que deben pagar lo personal, por oficios y pueblos), and 7458 and 7462 (Número de ganados, por especies y pueblos)

Archivo de la Real Chancillería de Valladolid

Protocolos, legajo 146, expediente 7 (these are the *padrones de hidalguía* for the jurisdiction of León partially transcribed by Cadenas y Vicent [1963], who unfortunately has omitted to transcribe anything relating to the *pecheros* of the area)

Museo Nacional de Etnología

Cuestionario del Ateneo, 1901-1902, responses for the province of León (Información promovida por la Sección de Ciencias Morales y Políticas del Ateneo de Madrid, en el campo de las costumbres populares y en los tres hechos más característicos de la vida: el nacimiento, el matrimonio y la muerte)

Real Academia de la Historia (RAH)

Censo de Aranda (1769)

Censo de Floridablanca (1787)

Personal Archives

Thanks to the kindness of several families in Santa María del Monte I was given access to accounts, property inventories, and inheritance records, dating from 1824 to the present.

Printed Sources

There are various ordinances and council acts from the seventeenth to the nineteenth century printed in the works of Leonese scholars, particularly López Morán, *Derecho consuetudinario* and *León*; Flórez de Quiñones, *Contribución*; and Díez González, *Ordás*. It is a pity that the various materials they cite have not been collected and printed in their entirety.

Bibliography

✠

Aceves, Joseph. *Social Change in a Spanish Village*. Cambridge: Schenkman, 1971.

————, and William Douglass. *The Changing Faces of Rural Spain*. Cambridge: Schenkman, 1976.

Alonso Rodríguez-Rivas, Daniel. "Prólogo." In *Catálogo de los montes de utilidad pública . . . de León*. León: Imprenta Rubín, 1964.

Altamira y Crevea, Rafael. *Historia de la propiedad comunal* (1890). Madrid: Instituto de Estudios de Administración Local, 1981.

Anes, Gonzalo. *Economía e "ilustración" en la España del siglo XVIII*. Barcelona: Editorial Ariel, 1969.

————. *Las crisis agrarias en la España moderna*. Madrid: Taurus Ediciones, 1970.

Ault, Warren O. "Open-Field Husbandry and the Village Community: A Study of Agrarian By-Laws in Medieval England." *Transactions of the American Philosophical Society*, n.s. 55 (1965): pt. 7.

Azcárate, Gumersindo de. "Vestigios del primitivo comunismo en España." *Boletín de la Institución Libre de Enseñanza* 7 (31 Aug. 1883): 247-248.

Barrett, Richard. *Benabarre: The Modernization of a Spanish Village*. New York: Holt, Rinehart and Winston, 1974.

Behar, Ruth. "The Presence of the Past: A Historical Ethnography of a Leonese Village." Ph.D. dissertation, Princeton University, 1983.

————. "The Web of Use-Rights: Forms and Conceptions of Communal Property among Leonese *Labradores*." *Anthropological Quarterly* 57 (1984): 71-82.

————. "La vida social y cultural de un pueblo leonés en el siglo XVIII a la luz de sus ordenanzas municipales." In *León y su historia*, 5: 567-613. León: CSIC, 1984.

————. "Supervivencia de tierras concejiles y derechos colectivos en la época contemporánea: El caso de los pueblos de Tierras de León."

In *El pasado histórico de Castilla y León*, vol. 3, *Edad contemporánea*. Burgos: Junta de Castilla y León, 1983.

Bennassar, Bartolomé. *The Spanish Character: Attitudes and Mentalities from the Sixteenth Century to the Nineteenth Century*. Berkeley: University of California Press, 1979.

Berger, John. *Pig Earth*. New York: Pantheon Books, 1979.

Berkner, Lutz K. "The Stem Family and the Developmental Cycle of the Peasant Household: An Eighteenth-Century Austrian Example." *American Historical Review* 77 (1972): 398-418.

Bloch, Marc. *The Historian's Craft*. New York: Random House, 1953.

———. *Feudal Society*. Chicago: University of Chicago Press, 1961.

———. *French Rural History: An Essay on Its Basic Characteristics* (1931). Berkeley: University of California Press, 1966.

Bloch, Maurice. "The Past and the Present in the Present." *Man*, n.s. 12 (1977): 278-292.

Blum, Jerome. "The European Village Community: Origins and Functions." *Agricultural History* 45 (1971): 157-178.

———. "The Internal Structure and Polity of the European Village Community from the Fifteenth to the Nineteenth Century." *Journal of Modern History* 43 (1971): 541-576.

Boissonade, P. *Life and Work in Medieval Europe: The Evolution of Medieval Economy from the Fifth to the Fifteenth Century* (1927). New York: Harper & Row, 1964.

Boserup, Esther. *The Conditions of Agricultural Growth: The Economics of Agrarian Change under Population Pressure*. Chicago: University of Chicago Press, 1965.

Brandes, Stanley H. *Migration, Kinship and Community: Tradition and Transition in a Spanish Village*. New York: Academic Press, 1975.

Braudel, Fernand. "History and the Social Sciences" (1958). In *Economy and Society in Early Modern Europe: Essays from "Annales,"* edited by Peter Burke. New York: Harper & Row, 1972.

———. *Capitalism and Material Life, 1400-1800*. New York: Harper & Row, 1973.

———. *The Mediterranean and the Mediterranean World in the Age of Philip II* (1949). New York: Harper & Row, 1976.

Cabero Diéguez, Valentín. *Espacio agrario y economía de subsistencia en las montañas galaico-leonesas: La Cabrera*. León: CSIC, 1980.

Cabo Alonso, Angel. "El colectivismo agrario en Tierra de Sayago." *Estudios geográficos* 17 (1956): 593-658.

Cadenas y Vicent, Vicente de. *Padrones de hidalgos de los arrabales de León y lugares de su jurisdicción, año 1798.* Madrid: Hidalguía (CSIC), 1963.

Castro, Concepción de. *La Revolución Liberal y los municipios españoles.* Madrid: Alianza Editorial, 1979.

Catálogo de los montes de utilidad pública y relación de los de libre disposición de la provincia de León. León: Imprenta Rubín, 1964.

Catálogo de los montes y demás terrenos forestales exceptuados de la desamortización por razones de utilidad pública. Madrid, 1901.

Cátedra Tomás, María. "Vacas y vaqueiros: modos de vida en las brañas asturianas." In *Vaqueiros y pescadores: dos modos de vida*, by María Cátedra Tomás and Ricardo Sanmartín Arce. Madrid: Akal Editor, 1979.

Censo de la población de España, según el recuento verificado en 25 de diciembre de 1860 por la Junta General de Estadística. Madrid: Imprenta Nacional, 1863.

Chambers, J. D., and G. E. Mingay. *The Agricultural Revolution, 1750-1880.* New York: Schocken Books, 1966.

Chiva, I. "Rural Communities: Problems, Methods and Types of Research." *UNESCO: Reports and Papers in the Social Sciences*, no. 10 (1958).

———. "Social Organization, Traditional Economy and Customary Law in Corsica: Outline of a Plan of Analysis." In *Mediterranean Countrymen: Essays in the Social Anthropology of the Mediterranean*, edited by J. Pitt-Rivers. Paris: Mouton, 1963.

Christian, William A., Jr. *Person and God in a Spanish Valley.* New York: Seminar Press, 1972.

———. *Religiosidad popular, estudio antropológico en un valle español.* Madrid: Editorial Tecnos, 1978.

———. *Local Religion in Sixteenth-Century Spain.* Princeton: Princeton University Press, 1981.

Cohn, Bernard S. "Anthropology and History: Towards a Rapprochement." *Journal of Interdisciplinary History* 12 (1981): 227-252.

Cordero del Castillo, Prisciliano. "La familia rural leonesa (un sistema llamado a desaparecer)." *Tierras de León* 32-33 (1978): 88-103.

Costa y Martínez, Joaquín. *Colectivismo agrario en España.* Madrid: Biblioteca Costa, 1898.

——— et al. *Derecho consuetudinario y economía popular de España.* 2 vols. Barcelona: Manuel Soler, 1902.

Cuadrado Iglesias, Manuel. *Aprovechamiento en común de pastos y leñas*. Madrid: Servicio de Publicaciones Agrarias, 1980.

Dalton, George. "Primitive, Archaic, and Modern Economies: Karl Polanyi's Contribution to Economic Anthropology and Comparative Economy." In *Economic Anthropology and Development: Essays on Tribal and Peasant Economies*. New York: Basic Books, 1971.

Davis, John. *The People of the Mediterranean: An Essay in Comparative Social Anthropology*. London: Routledge & Kegan Paul, 1977.

Davis, Natalie Zemon. *Society and Culture in Early Modern France*. Stanford: Stanford University Press, 1975.

———. "Ghosts, Kin, and Progeny: Some Features of Family Life in Early Modern France." *Daedalus* 102(2)(1977): 87-114.

———. "Anthropology and History: The Possibilities of the Past." *Journal of Interdisciplinary History* 12(1981): 267-275.

Díez Alonso, Matías. *Mitos y leyendas de la Tierra Leonesa*. León: Gráficas León, 1982.

Díez González, Florentino Agustín. *Laciana: memoria de su antiguo y patriarcal concejo*. Madrid: Publicaciones de Instituto de Estudios de Administración Local, 1946.

———. *La noble tierra de Ordás: monografía histórica y concejil*. Madrid: Publicaciones del Instituto de Estudios de Administración Local, 1950.

Dillard, Heath. "Women in Reconquest Castile: The *Fueros* of Sepúlveda and Cuenca." In *Women in Medieval Society*, edited by Susan Mosher Stuard. Philadelphia: University of Pennsylvania Press, 1976.

Domínguez Ortiz, Antonio. *La sociedad española en el siglo XVIII*. Madrid: CSIC, 1955.

———. *Sociedad y Estado en el siglo XVIII español*. Barcelona: Editorial Ariel, 1976.

Douglass, William A. *Death in Murélaga*. Seattle: University of Washington Press, 1969.

———. *Echalar and Murélaga: Opportunity and Rural Exodus in Two Spanish Basque Villages*. London: C. Hurt, 1975.

Driessen, Henk. "Anthropologists in Andalusia: The Use of Comparison and History." *Man*, n.s. 16(1981): 451-462.

Du Boulay, Juliet. *Portrait of a Greek Mountain Village*. Oxford: Clarendon Press, 1974.

Duby, Georges. *Rural Economy and Country Life in the Medieval West*. London: Edward Arnold, 1968.

Elliott, John H. *The Revolt of the Catalans: A Study in the Decline of Spain (1598-1640)*. Cambridge: Cambridge University Press, 1963.

———. *Imperial Spain, 1469-1716*. New York: Penguin Books, 1970.

Engels, Frederick. *The Origin of the Family, Private Property, and the State* (1884). New York: International Publishers, 1972.

Evans-Pritchard, E. E. "Anthropology and History" (1961). In *Essays in Social Anthropology*. Glencoe: Free Press, 1963.

Fabian, Johannes. *Time and the Other: How Anthropology Makes Its Object*. New York: Columbia University Press, 1983.

Faith, Rosamund Jane. "Peasant Families and Inheritance Customs in Medieval England." *The Agricultural History Review* 14 (1966): 77-95.

Feeley-Harnik, Gillian. "The Political Economy of Death: Communication and Change in Malagasy Colonial History." *American Ethnologist* 11 (1984): 1-19.

Fernandez, James W. "The Mission of Metaphor in Expressive Culture." *Current Anthropology* 15 (1974): 119-145.

———. "Syllogisms of Association: Some Modern Extensions of Asturian Deepsong." In *Folklore in the Modern World*, edited by Richard Dorson. The Hague: Mouton, 1979.

———. "The Call to the Commons." Paper presented at the Oxford Conference on Forms of Reciprocity and Cooperation in Rural Europe, St. Anthony's College, 8-11 September 1981.

———. *Bwiti: An Ethnography of the Religious Imagination in Africa*. Princeton: Princeton University Press, 1982.

———. "Consciousness and Class in Southern Spain." *American Ethnologist* 10 (1983): 165-173.

Fernández Catón, José María. *San Marcos de León: un siglo de historia, 1835-1961*. León: Archivo Histórico Diocesano, 1961.

———. *Catálogo del Archivo Histórico Diocesano*. Vol. 1. León: CSIC, 1978.

Fernández Flórez, José Antonio. "El 'Becerro de Presentaciones,' códice 13 del Archivo de la Catedral de León: un parroquial leonés de los siglos XIII-XV." In *León y su historia*, 5: 265-565. León: CSIC, 1984.

Ferreras Chasco, Casildo. "La Aldea del Puente, estudio geográfico de una localidad leonesa de la ribera alta del Esla." *Estudios geográficos* 32 (1971): 673-750.

———. *El Norte de la Meseta Leonesa: estudio geográfico de un espacio rural*. León: CSIC, 1981.

Filhol, René. "The Codification of Customary Law in France in the Fifteenth and Sixteenth Centuries." In *Government in Reformation Europe, 1520-1560*, edited by J. Cohn. London: Macmillan, 1971.

Flores, Carlos. *Arquitectura popular española*. Vol. 3. Madrid: Aguilar, 1974.

Flórez de Quiñones y Tomé, Vicente. *Contribución al estudio del régimen local y de la economía popular de España: los pueblos agregados a un término municipal en la historia, en la legislación vigente y en el derecho consuetudinario leonés*. León: Imprenta Católica, 1924.

―――. "Comunidad o servidumbre de pastos." *Revista de derecho privado* 20 (1933): 161-179.

―――. *Supervivencias señoriales en el siglo XX*. León: CSIC, 1980.

Fraser, Ronald. *Blood of Spain: An Oral History of the Spanish Civil War*. New York: Pantheon Books, 1979.

Freeman, Susan Tax. *Neighbors: The Social Contract in a Castilian Hamlet*. Chicago: University of Chicago Press, 1970.

―――. "Introduction" to "Studies in Rural European Social Organization." *American Anthropologist* 75 (1973): 743-750.

―――. *The Pasiegos*. Chicago: University of Chicago Press, 1979.

―――. Review of Sandra Ott's *The Circle of Mountains*. *American Ethnologist* 9 (1982): 596-597.

García Alvarez, Benjamín. *Concejos de parroquias de Asturias (especial referencia a las de Aller) y ordenanzas que regulan su organización y régimen*. Pola de Lena: Gráficas Lena, 1963.

García Fernández, Jesús. "Aspectos del paisaje agrario de Castilla la Vieja." Valladolid: Cátedra de Geografía, Facultad de Filosofía y Letras, 1963. Typescript.

―――. "Los sistemas de cultivo de Castilla la Vieja." In *Aportación española al XX Congreso Geográfico Internacional (Reino Unido, julio-agosto 1964)*. Zaragoza: CSIC, 1964.

―――. "Campos abiertos y campos cercados en Castilla la Vieja." In *Homenaje al Excmo. Sr. D. Amando Melón y Ruiz de Gordejuela*. Zaragoza: CSIC, 1966.

García Sanz, Angel. *Desarrollo y crisis del Antiguo Régimen en Castilla la Vieja: economía y sociedad en tierras de Segovia 1500-1814*. Madrid: Akal Editor, 1977.

―――. "Bienes y derechos comunales y el proceso de su privatización en Castilla durante los siglos XVI y XVII: el caso de tierras de Segovia." *Hispania* 144 (1980): 94-127.

García de Valdeavellano y Arcemís, Luis. *Curso de historia de las instituciones españoles, de los orígenes al final de la Edad Media*. Madrid: Revista de Occidente, 1977.

Gavira, J. "Las relaciones históricas-geográficas de Felipe II (a propósito de una publicación reciente)." *Estudios geográficos* 11 (1950): 551-557.

Geertz, Clifford. *Negara: The Theater-State in Nineteenth-Century Bali*. Princeton: Princeton University Press, 1980.

Gerhard, Dietrich. *Old Europe: A Study of Continuity, 1000-1800*. New York: Academic Press, 1981.

Gilmore, David. "Land Reform and Rural Revolt in Nineteenth-Century Andalusia (Spain)." *Peasant Studies* 6 (1977): 142-146.

———. *The People of the Plain: Class and Community in Lower Andalusia*. New York: Columbia University Press, 1980.

———. "Anthropology of the Mediterranean Area." *Annual Review of Anthropology* 11 (1982): 175-205.

Ginzburg, Carlo. "Anthropology and History: A Comment." *Journal of Interdisciplinary History* 12 (1981): 277-278.

———. *The Cheese and the Worms: The Cosmos of a Sixteenth-Century Miller*. New York: Penguin Books, 1982.

González, J. "Reconquista y repoblación de Castilla, León, Extremadura y Andalucía (siglos XI a XIII)." In *La reconquista española y la repoblación del país*. Zaragoza: CSIC, 1951.

Goody, Jack. "Introduction." In *Literacy in Traditional Societies*, edited by Jack Goody. Cambridge: Cambridge University Press, 1968.

———. "Inheritance, Property, and Women: Some Comparative Considerations." In *Family and Inheritance: Rural Society in Western Europe, 1200-1800*, edited by J. Goody, J. Thirsk, and E. P. Thompson. Cambridge: Cambridge University Press, 1976.

———. *The Domestication of the Savage Mind*. Cambridge: Cambridge University Press, 1978.

———, Joan Thirsk, and E. P. Thompson, eds. *Family and Inheritance: Rural Society in Western Europe, 1200-1800*. Cambridge: Cambridge University Press, 1976.

Goubert, Pierre. "Local History." In *Historical Studies Today*, edited by Felix Gilbert and Stephen R. Graubard. New York: Norton, 1972.

Greenwood, Davydd. *Unrewarding Wealth: The Commercialization and Collapse of Agriculture in a Spanish Basque Town*. Cambridge: Cambridge University Press, 1976.

Grossi, Paolo. *An Alternative to Private Property: Collective Property in the Juridical Consciousness of the Nineteenth Century*. Chicago: University of Chicago Press, 1981.

Guerra García, M. Araceli, and José M. Fernández del Pozo. "Las constituciones democráticas de tres pueblos de la ribera del Orbigo." *Tierras de León* 32-33 (1978): 49-55.

Habbakuk, H. J. "Family Structure and Economic Change in Nineteenth-Century Europe." *The Journal of Economic History* 15 (1955): 1-12.

Harding, Susan Friend. *Remaking Ibieca: Rural Life in Aragon under Franco*. Chapel Hill: University of North Carolina Press, 1984.

Hartley, Dorothy. *Lost Country Life*. New York: Pantheon Books, 1979.

Hélias, Pierre-Jakez. *The Horse of Pride: Life in a Breton Village*. New Haven: Yale University Press, 1978.

Hémardinquer, Jean-Jacques. "The Family Pig of the Ancien Régime: Myth or Fact?" In *Food and Drink in History: Selections from the "Annales,"* edited by Robert Forster and Orest Ranum. Baltimore: Johns Hopkins University Press, 1979.

Herr, Richard. *The Eighteenth Century Revolution in Spain*. Princeton: Princeton University Press, 1958.

———. "La vente des propriétés de mainmorte en Espagne, 1798-1808." *Annales: économies, sociétés, civilisations* 29 (1974): 215-228.

———. "El significado de la desamortización en España." *Moneda y crédito* 131 (1974): 55-94.

Herzfeld, Michael. "The Horns of the Mediterraneanist Dilemma." *American Ethnologist* 11 (1984): 439-454.

Heutz de Lemps, A. "Les terroirs en vieille Castile et Lèon: un type de structure agraire." *Annales: économies, sociétés, civilisations* 17 (1962): 239-251.

Hobsbawm, Eric, and Terence Ranger, eds. *The Invention of Tradition*. Cambridge: Cambridge University Press, 1983.

Hoffman, Richard C. "Medieval Origins of the Common Fields." In *European Peasants and Their Markets: Essays in Agrarian Economic History*, edited by William N. Parker and Eric L. Jones. Princeton: Princeton University Press, 1975.

Homans, George Casper. *English Villagers of the Thirteenth Century* (1941). New York: W. W. Norton, 1975.

Hopfner, Hellmuth. "La evolución de los bosques en Castilla la Vieja." *Estudios geográficos* 15 (1954): 415-425.

Hoskins, W. G. *Fieldwork in Local History*. London: Faber and Faber, 1967.

Jiménez Arques, M. Inmaculada. "Las casas de barro en Tierra de Campos." *Narria, estudios de artes y costumbres populares* 14 (1979): 3-6.

Jovellanos, Gaspar Melchor de. *Informe de la Sociedad Económica de Madrid al Real y Supremo Consejo de Castilla en el expediente de Ley Agraria* (1793). Edited by José Lage. Madrid: Ediciones Cátedra, 1979.

Kenney, Michael. *A Spanish Tapestry: Town and Country in Castile*. Bloomington: Indiana University Press, 1962.

Kiernan, V. G. "Private Property in History." In *Family and Inheritance: Rural Society in Western Europe, 1200-1800*, edited by J. Goody, J. Thirsk, and E. P. Thompson. Cambridge: Cambridge University Press, 1976.

Klein, Julius. *The Mesta: A Study in Spanish Economic History, 1273-1836*. Cambridge: Harvard University Press, 1920.

Kroeber, A. L. *An Anthropologist Looks at History*. Edited by Theodora Kroeber. Berkeley: University of California Press, 1963.

Laveleye, Emile de. *Primitive Property*. London: Macmillan, 1878.

Le Roy Ladurie, Emmanuel. *The Peasants of Languedoc*. Urbana: University of Illinois Press, 1974.

―――. "Family Structures and Inheritance Customs in Sixteenth-Century France." In *Family and Inheritance: Rural Society in Western Europe, 1200-1800*, edited by J. Goody, J. Thirsk, and E. P. Thompson. Cambridge: Cambridge University Press, 1976.

―――. "Recent Historical 'Discoveries.'" *Daedalus* 106(4) (1977): 141-155.

―――. *Montaillou*. New York: Random House, 1979.

Leuilliot, Paul. "A Manifesto: The Defense and Illustration of Local History." In *Rural Society in France: Selections from the "Annales,"* edited by Robert Forster and Orest Ranum. Baltimore: Johns Hopkins University Press, 1977.

Levy, Harry L. "Property Distribution by Lot in Present-Day Greece." *Transactions of the American Philological Association* 87 (1956): 42-46.

Lewis, I. M. "Introduction." In *History and Social Anthropology*, edited by I. M. Lewis. London: Tavistock, 1968.

Lisón Tolosana, Carmelo. *Belmonte de los Caballeros: Anthropology and*

History in an Aragonese Community (1966). Princeton: Princeton University Press, 1983.

———. "Una gran encuesta de 1901-1902: notas para la historia de la antropología social en España." In *Antropología social en España*. Madrid: Siglo Veintiuno Editores, 1971.

———. "The Ethics of Inheritance." In *Mediterranean Family Structures*, edited by J. G. Peristiany. Cambridge: Cambridge University Press, 1976.

———. "La casa en Galicia." In *Ensayos de antropología social*. Madrid: Editorial Ayuso, 1978.

Llamazares, Fray Orencio. *Vegas del Condado, villa y parroquia (León): datos, sugerencias e interrogantes*. Madrid, 1980.

López Gómez, Antonio. "Valdelaguna: colectivismo agrario en las montañas burgalesas." *Estudios geográficos* 15 (1954): 551-567.

López Morán, Elías. *Derecho consuetudinario y economía popular de la provincia de León*. Madrid: Imprenta de Asilo de Huérfanos del Sagrado Corazón de Jesús, 1900.

———. "León." In *Derecho consuetudinario y economía popular de España*, by Joaquín Costa et al. Barcelona: Manuel Soler, 1902.

Macfarlane, Alan. "History, Anthropology and the Study of Communities." *Social History* 1 (1977): 631-652.

Madoz, Pascual. *Diccionario geográfico-estadístico-histórico de España y sus posesiones de ultramar*. Madrid, 1845-1850.

Maine, Henry Sumner. *Ancient Law: Its Connection with the Early History of Society, and Its Relations to Modern Ideas* (1861). New York: Dutton, 1960.

Malefakis, Edward. *Agrarian Reform and Peasant Revolution in Spain: Origins of the Civil War*. New Haven: Yale University Press, 1970.

Mangas Navas, José M. *El régimen comunal agrario de los concejos de Castilla*. Madrid: Servicio de Publicaciones Agrarias, 1981.

Martín Galindo, José Luis. "El colectivismo agrario de Llánaves y las herencias étnicas en la formación del medio geográfico." *Archivos Leoneses* 6 (1952): 83-93.

———. "Paisajes leoneses: La Montaña." *Archivos Leoneses* 18 (1955): 133-138.

———. "Arcaísmo y modernidad en la explotación agraria de Valdeburón (León)." *Estudios geográficos* 22 (1961): 167-222.

———. *Artículos geográficos sobre la provincia de León*. Valladolid: Editorial Miñón, n.d.

Martino, Eutimio. *La montaña de Valdeburón (biografía de una región leonesa)*. Madrid: Publicaciones de la Universidad Pontificia Comillas, 1980.

Mauss, Marcel. *The Gift: Forms and Functions of Exchange in Archaic Society* (1925). New York: Norton, 1967.

Mayer, Arno J. *The Persistence of the Old Regime: Europe to the Great War*. New York: Pantheon, 1981.

McCloskey, Donald N. "The Persistence of English Common Fields." In *European Peasants and Their Markets: Essays in Agrarian Economic History*, edited by William N. Parker and Eric L. Jones. Princeton: Princeton University Press, 1975.

McGuire, Randall, and Robert McC. Netting. "Leveling Peasants? The Maintenance of Equality in a Swiss Alpine Community." *American Ethnologist* 9 (1982): 269-290.

Millán Urdiales, José. *El habla de Villacidayo (León)*. Anejos del Boletín 13. Madrid: Real Academia Española, 1966.

Mínguez Fernández, José María. *El dominio del monasterio de Sahagún en el siglo X: paisajes agrarios, producción y expansión económica*. Salamanca: Ediciones Universidad de Salamanca, 1980.

Ministerio de Agricultura, Instituto Nacional de Investigaciones Agrarias. *Mapas provinciales de suelos: León*. 2 vols. Madrid: Departamento Nacional de Ecología, 1973.

Mintz, Jerome. *The Anarchists of Casas Viejas*. Chicago: University of Chicago Press, 1982.

Mira, Joan F. *Vivir y hacer historia: estudios desde la antropología social*. Barcelona: Ediciones Península, 1980.

Morgan, Lewis H. *Ancient Society*. New York: Henry Holt, 1877.

Muir, Richard. *The English Village*. New York: Thames and Hudson, 1980.

Netting, Robert McC. "Of Men and Meadows: Strategies of Alpine Land Use." *Anthropological Quarterly* 5 (1972): 132-144.

———. "What Alpine Peasants Have in Common: Observations on Communal Tenure in a Swiss Village." *Human Ecology* 4 (1976): 135-146.

Nieto, Alejandro. *Ordenación de pastos, hierbas y rastrojeras*. 2 vols. Valladolid: Junta Provincial de Fomento Pecuario de Valladolid, 1959.

———. *Bienes comunales*. Madrid: Editorial Revista de Derecho Privado, 1964.

Novísima recopilación de las leyes de España. 5 vols. Madrid, 1805-1829.

O'Neill, Brian Juan. "*Roda* and *Torna* in North-East Portugal." Paper presented at the Oxford Conference on Forms of Reciprocity and Cooperation in Rural Europe, St. Anthony's College, 8-11 September 1981.

Ott, Sandra. *The Circle of Mountains: A Basque Shepherding Community*. Oxford: Clarendon Press, 1981.

Pastor, Reyna. *Resistencias y luchas campesinas en la época del crecimiento y consolidación de la formación feudal: Castilla y León, siglos X-XIII*. Madrid: Siglo Veintiuno Editores, 1980.

Peel, J.D.Y. "Making History: The Past in the Ijesha Present." *Man*, n.s. 19 (1984): 111-132.

Pérez Moreda, Vicente. *Las crisis de mortalidad en la España interior (siglos XVI-XIX)*. Madrid: Siglo Veintiuno Editores, 1980.

Pesez, Jean-Marie, and Emmanuel Le Roy Ladurie. "The Deserted Villages of France: An Overview." In *Rural Society in France: Selections from the "Annales,"* edited by Robert Forster and Orest Ranum. Baltimore: Johns Hopkins University Press, 1977.

Pitt-Rivers, Julian. *The People of the Sierra*. Chicago: University of Chicago Press, 1954.

———. "Introduction." In *Mediterranean Countrymen: Essays in the Social Anthropology of the Mediterranean*, edited by J. Pitt-Rivers. Paris: Mouton, 1963.

Polanyi, Karl. "Aristotle Discovers the Economy." In *Trade and Market in the Early Empires*, edited by K. Polanyi, Conrad M. Arensberg, and Harry Pearson. Glencoe: The Free Press, 1957.

———. "Economy as Instituted Process." In *Trade and Market in the Early Empires*, edited by Polanyi, Arensberg, and Pearson. Glencoe: The Free Press, 1957.

Posse, Juan Antonio. "Historia biográfica, o historia de la vida y hechos de don Juan Antonio Posse, escrita por el mismo hasta el año 1834." *La lectura* 1(1916)-1(1918).

Price, Richard. *First-Time: The Historical Vision of an Afro-American People*. Baltimore: Johns Hopkins Uniqersity Press, 1983.

Redclift, M. R. "The Future of Agriculture in a Spanish Pyrenean Village and the Decline of Communal Institutions." *Ethnology* 12 (1973): 193-202.

Redfield, Robert. *The Little Community and Peasant Society and Culture*. Chicago: University of Chicago Press, 1967.

Redonet y López Dóriga, Luis. *Policía rural en España*. 2 vols. Madrid: Sucesores de M. Minuesa de los Ríos, 1916 and 1928.

―――. "Policía rural en España: León." *Archivos leoneses* 9 (1955): 81-108.

Roberts, Michael. "Sickles and Scythes: Women's Work and Men's Work at Harvest Time." *History Workshop* 7 (1979): 3-28.

Rodríguez, Justiniano. *Los fueros del Reino de León*. 2 vols. León: Ediciones Leonesas, 1981.

Rosaldo, Renato. *Ilongot Headhunting, 1883-1974: A Study in Society and History*. Stanford: Stanford University Press, 1980.

Ruiz, Teofilo. "The Transformation of the Castilian Municipalities: The Case of Burgos 1248-1350." *Past and Present* 77 (1977): 3-32.

―――. "Expansión y crisis: la repercusión de la conquista de Sevilla en la sociedad castellana, 1248-1350." In *Sociedad y poder real en Castilla*. Barcelona: Editorial Ariel, 1981.

―――. "Notas para el estudio de la mujer en el área del Burgos medieval." In *El pasado histórico de Castilla y León*, vol. 1, *Edad media*. Burgos: Junta de Castilla y León, 1983.

Sahlins, Marshall. *Historical Metaphors and Mythical Realities: Structure in the Early History of the Sandwich Islands Kingdom*. Ann Arbor: University of Michigan Press, 1981.

Salomon, Frank. "Shamanism and Politics in Late-Colonial Ecuador." *American Ethnologist* 10 (1983): 413-428.

Salomon, Noel. *Recherches sur le thème paysan dans la "comedia" au temps de Lope de Vega*. Bordeaux: Institut d'Etudes Ibériques et Ibéro-Américaines de l'Université de Bordeaux, 1965.

―――. *La vida rural castellana en tiempos de Felipe II* (1964). Barcelona: Editorial Planeta, 1973.

Sánchez Albornoz, Claudio. *Despoblación y repoblación del valle del Duero*. Buenos Aires: Instituto de Historia de España, 1966.

Sargent, Frederic O. "The Persistence of Communal Tenure in French Agriculture." *Agricultural History* 32 (1958): 100-108.

Schmitt, Jean-Claude. *The Holy Greyhound: Guinefort, Healer of Children Since the Thirteenth Century*. Cambridge: Cambridge University Press, 1983.

Schneider, Jane. "Peacocks and Penguins: The Political Economy of European Cloth and Colors." *American Ethnologist* 5 (1978): 413-447.

Scott, James C. *The Moral Economy of the Peasant: Rebellion and Subsistence in Southeast Asia.* New Haven: Yale University Press, 1976.

Serrán Pagán, Ginés. "La fábula de Alcala y la realidad histórica en Grazalema: Replanteamiento del primer estudio de Antropología Social en España." *Reis* 9 (1980): 81-115.

Silverman, Sydel. "On the Uses of History in Anthropology: The *Palio* of Siena." *American Ethnologist* 6 (1979): 413-436.

Simón Segura, Francisco. "La desamortización de 1855." *Economía financiera española* 19-20 (1967): 80-126.

Slicher van Bath, B. H. *The Agrarian History of Western Europe, A.D. 500-1850.* London: Edward Arnold, 1963.

Smith, T. Lynn. "Fragmentation of Agricultural Land in Spain." *Rural Sociology* 24 (1959): 140-149.

Soboul, Albert. "The French Rural Community in the Eighteenth and Nineteenth Centuries." *Past and Present* 10 (1956): 78-95.

———. "Persistence of 'Feudalism' in the Rural Society of Nineteenth-Century France." In *Rural Society in France: Selections from the "Annales,"* edited by Robert Forster and Orest Ranum. Baltimore: John Hopkins University Press, 1977.

Stone, Lawrence. "Family History: Past Achievements and Future Trends." *Journal of Interdisciplinary History* 12 (1981): 51-87.

———. *The Past and the Present.* Boston: Routledge and Kegan Paul, 1981.

Thirsk, Joan. "The Common Fields." *Past and Present* 29 (1964): 3-25.

Thomas, Keith. "History and Anthropology." *Past and Present* 24 (1963): 3-24.

———. "The Tools and the Job." *The Times Literary Supplement,* 7 April 1966: 275-276.

Thompson, E. P. "Anthropology and the Discipline of Historical Context." *Midland History* 1 (1975): 41-55.

———. *Whigs and Hunters: The Origin of the Black Act.* New York: Pantheon, 1975.

———. "The Grid of Inheritance: A Comment." In *Family and Inheritance: Rural Society in Western Europe, 1200-1800,* edited by J. Goody, J. Thirsk, and E. P. Thompson. Cambridge: Cambridge University Press, 1976.

Tomás y Valiente, Francisco. *El marco político de la desamortización en España.* Barcelona: Editorial Ariel, 1971.

Townsend, Joseph. *A Journey through Spain in the Years 1786 and 1787*. London: C. Dilly, 1792.

Unamuno, Miguel de. "Vizcaya." In *Derecho consuetudinario y economía popular de España*, by Joaquín Costa et al. Barcelona: Manuel Soler, 1902.

Vassberg, David E. "The *Tierras Baldías*: Community Property and Public Lands in 16th Century Castile." *Agricultural History* 48 (1974): 383-401.

———. "The Sale of *Tierras Baldías* in Sixteenth-Century Castile." *Journal of Modern History* 47 (1975): 629-654.

———. "Peasant Communalism and Anti-Communal Tendencies in Early Modern Castile." *The Journal of Peasant Studies* 7 (1980): 477-491.

Vilar, Jean. "Gloire ou raison garder? La peur statistique dans l'Espagne classique." *Iberica* 3 (1981): 257-271.

Viñas y Mey, Carmelo. *El problema de la tierra en la España de los siglos XVI-XVII*. Madrid: CSIC, 1941.

———. "Las relaciones de Felipe II y su publicación." *Estudios geográficos* 12 (1951): 131-136.

———, and Ramón Paz. *Relaciones histórico-geográfico-estadísticas de los pueblos de España hechas por iniciativa de Felipe II*. 3 vols. Madrid: CSIC, 1971.

Weber, Max. "Capitalism and Rural Society in Germany" (1906). In *From Max Weber: Essays in Sociology*, edited by H. H. Gerth and C. Wright Mills. New York: Oxford University Press, 1958.

———. *On Law in Economy and Society*. Edited by Max Rheinstein. New York: Clarion Press, 1967.

Weisser, Michael R. *The Peasants of the Montes: The Roots of Rural Rebellion in Spain*. Chicago: University of Chicago Press, 1976.

Wolf, Eric. *Europe and the People without History*. Berkeley: University of California Press, 1982.

Index